London

DOCKLANDS

BY

ELIZABETH WILLIAMSON

AND

NIKOLAUS PEVSNER

WITH

MALCOLM TUCKER

THE BUILDINGS OF ENGLAND

PENGUIN BOOKS

PENGUIN BOOKS
Published by the Penguin Group
27 Wrights Lane, London W8 5TZ, England
for
THE BUILDINGS BOOKS TRUST

Viking Penguin, a division of Penguin Books USA Inc.,
375 Hudson Street, New York, New York 10014, USA
Penguin Books Australia Ltd, Ringwood, Victoria, Australia
Penguin Books Canada Ltd, 10 Alcorn Avenue, Toronto, Ontario, Canada M4V 3B2
Penguin Books (NZ) Ltd, 182–190 Wairau Road, Auckland 10, New Zealand

Penguin Books Ltd, Registered Offices: Harmondsworth, Middlesex, England

First published 1998

ISBN 0 14 071096 5

Typeset at Cambridge Photosetting Services, Cambridge
Made and printed in Great Britain
by Butler & Tanner, Frome and London
Set in 9/10pt Monotype Plantin

TO M.S.H.

CONTENTS

LIST OF TEXT FIGURES AND MAPS

PHOTOGRAPHIC ACKNOWLEDGEMENTS

We are grateful to the following for permission to reproduce photographs:

CZWG: 61, 82, 85 (photo Jo Reid and John Peck), 63 (photo Jordi Sarra)
English Heritage Picture Library: 45
Jeremy Dixon (photo Jo Reid and John Peck): 78
John McAslan & Partners (photo Peter Cook/View): 70, 79
Newham Council: 27
Richard Rogers Partnership (photo Peter Cook/View): 58
Shepheard Epstein & Hunter: 84
Michael Squire & Partners (photo Richard Cheatle): 64
Wickham & Associates (photo Desmond Lavery): 62

All other photographs are reproduced by kind permission of the RCHME (Crown copyright)

Every effort has been made to contact or trace all copyright holders. The publishers will be glad to make good any errors or omissions brought to our attention in future editions.

The photographs are indexed in the indexes of artists, and streets and buildings, and references to them are given by numbers in the margin of the text.

ABBREVIATIONS AND
LISTS OF OFFICIALS

GLC	Greater London Council (1965–86)
LCC	London County Council (1888–1965)
LDDC	London Docklands Development Corporation (1981–98)
PLA	Port of London Authority
RCHME	Royal Commission on the Historical Monuments of England
UDA	Urban Development Area

LONDON DOCKLANDS DEVELOPMENT CORPORATION, 1981–98

Chairmen

1981–4	Sir Nigel Broackes
1984–8	Sir Christopher Benson
1988–92	Sir David Hardy
1992–8	Sir Michael Pickard

Chief Executives

1981–7	Reginald Ward
1987–8	Edward Oliver (Acting CE)
1988	Major General Jeremy Rougier
1988	Eugene Bannon (Acting CE)
1988–90	Michael Honey
1990–1	Sir David Hardy (Acting CE)
1991–7	Eric Sorensen
1997–8	Neil Spence and Roger Squire

PLANNING COMMITTEE

Chairmen

1981–4	Sir Hugh Wilson
1984–8	Sir Andrew Derbyshire
1988–92	Sir John Garlick
1992–3	Ronald Spinney
1993–	William Jack

Senior Planning and Design Officers

1981–5	Edward Hollamby (Chief Architect and Planner)
	Dru Vesty (Principal Planner)
	Peter Dean (Principal Architect/Planner)
	Charles Attwood (Principal Architect from 1982)
	Peter Wright (Principal Landscape Architect)

1985–91   Chris Farrow (Area Director, Surrey Docks)
Howard Sheppard (Area Director, Wapping and
  Limehouse – including the Isle of Dogs from 1989)
Dru Vesty (Area Director, Royal Docks)
Mike Wilson (Area Director, the Isle of Dogs –
  until 1989)
Charles Attwood (Principal Architect until 1988)
Barry Shaw (Head of Urban Design from 1988)
Peter Wright (Principal Landscape Architect)

1991–   Howard Sheppard (Director, City Design and
  Planning)
Jeff Hennessey (City Design and Planning Manager)
Michael Scott (Development Control Manager)
David Simpson (Development Planning Manager)

FOREWORD AND ACKNOWLEDGEMENTS

London: Docklands *is a new departure for the* Buildings of England, *the first paperback companion to the six hardback volumes which will cover the whole of Greater London. The slimmer companions are intended as convenient guides to key London subjects and areas. The content of this book will be incorporated in the planned volume dealing with a larger area of East London:* London 5: East and Docklands.

The book deals with a part of London that has changed beyond all recognition over the last fifteen years. The area it covers was previously described in the three earlier Buildings of England *volumes – Sir Nikolaus Pevsner's* London 2 except the Cities of London and Westminster *and* Essex, *and* London 2: South *by Bridget Cherry and Nikolaus Pevsner – but only fragments of those accounts are relevant today. In 1981, narrow slices of the London Boroughs of Tower Hamlets, Newham and Southwark, dominated by the defunct docks and decaying riverside, were put under the planning jurisdiction of an Urban Development Corporation (the London Docklands Development Corporation), with responsibilities for regeneration (see Introduction p. 19). The special status of these areas, known collectively as London Docklands, has between 1981 and 1998 given rise to the dramatic developments in architecture and planning described in this volume. Although Docklands is quite small, stretching ten miles along the river (its extent is shown on the endpaper maps), it encompasses a unique variety of buildings, ranging from merchants' houses and C18 churches to C19 and C20 dock structures and the Postmodern office city of Canary Wharf.*

The areas within Docklands are quite distinct, each retaining its own character despite post-1981 redevelopment. Following Buildings of England *tradition, they are described in a gazetteer, here arranged alphabetically in two sections, according to whether they lie N or S of the river. The name of the London borough to which they belong comes after each title, e.g. North Woolwich, London Borough of Newham. The gazetteer is preceded by an introduction that discusses a wide range of themes particular to Docklands and helps put the buildings in their London-wide context.*

London: Docklands *would not have been published without the generous support of the London Docklands Development Corporation, nor would this volume have been possible without the wholehearted cooperation of the Royal Commission on the Historical Monuments of England, who provided most of the photographs and, through the Survey of London, many of the text illustrations.*

From the London Docklands Development Corporation, I have to thank particularly Eric Sorenson, who as Chief Executive saw the merits of this project, and Howard Sheppard, the Director of City Design and Planning, who has been an enthusiastic supporter throughout, giving time, information and expertise in a most generous and friendly way. I must also thank Vicki Blyth, Head of Media and Public Relations, Andrew Dick, former Conservation Officer, and all their staff.

Special thanks are due to many members of the Royal Commission on the Historical Monuments of England: to John Greenacombe, the general editor of the Survey of London who gave access to much of their material and arranged for us to use illustrations; to Peter Guillery of the London Threatened Buildings Section who was instrumental in arranging for Derek Kendall to take the photographs that so greatly enhance the book; and to June Warrington, who made sure communications between the RCHME *and* The Buildings of England *ran smoothly.*

There have been many contributors. Chief among them has been Malcolm Tucker, whose extensive knowledge of the docks, the river and the docks' buildings and engineering structures, has enriched the book immeasurably. Also very important was the help given by Geoff Brandwood, who not only wrote about the churches of Newham, but also gave me the benefit of his expert opinion on many other church visits. Roger Bowdler wrote the sections on churchyards, and he and his colleagues, Susie Barson and Chris Miele, kindly allowed me to mine information from research reports prepared by English Heritage. Also generous with information and advice have been Howard Bloch of Newham, Tom Ridge of Limehouse, Donald Findlay of the Council for the Care of Churches, Zoe Mair, conservation officer of the London Borough of Southwark, Nicholas Long of the Twentieth Century Society, John Schofield of the Museum of London Archaeology Survey, Stephen Humphrey of Southwark's John Harvard Library, the staff of the Tower Hamlets Local History Collection and Bob Aspinall of the Museum in Docklands' library and archive. Hamish Pollock patiently drove me round the whole of Docklands and proffered excellent advice from his standpoint as an architect. I have also benefited from enjoyable discussions with Piers Gough, James Thomas, Michael Barraclough, Rae Hoffenberg and with Ben Kochin of Docklands Forum.

Almost all the factual details about modern buildings have kindly been provided either by the LDDC or by the many architects and designers involved in the regeneration of Docklands. Mention of an architectural practice does not always imply that it was responsible for the design in detail, for in many design-and-build schemes, the final stages have been the responsibility of the developer or builder. Many owners, custodians and clergy were helpful in showing me their buildings or answering questions; I must thank particularly the Rev. Helge Pettersson at the Norwegian church, Rotherhithe and Father Jones at St Peter, Wapping. Any opinions are, of course, mine.

The production of the book was the work of several hands and minds. Reg and Marjorie Piggott drew the map of Docklands in 1980, and Alan Fagan the informative area maps and the plan of St Mary Graces, Wapping. These, together with all the other illustrations, were managed in a masterly way by Alison McKittrick. Georgie Widdrington was the overall designer and Leslie Straw the inset designer. Tye Blackshaw made the research as straightforward as possible by her efficient preparation and Sue Machin followed up many queries in a tenacious fashion. Stephany Ungless scrupulously edited the manuscript and guided it through every stage. My colleague Bridget Cherry gave me invaluable advice from her vast store of knowledge about London and great encouragement at all times.

Major Dates in the History of the Docks 1600–1921

1600	Foundation of the East India Company
1696–9	Howland Great Wet Dock (Rotherhithe) built
1799–1806	West India Docks (London's first secure docks) built on the Isle of Dogs
1801–5	London Docks (Wapping) begun with construction of the Western Dock
1803–6	East India Docks (Blackwall) built
1803–10	Commercial Road laid out
1804–7	Surrey Docks (Rotherhithe) development begun
1812	Limehouse Basin (Regent's Canal Dock) begun
1824–8	London Docks Eastern Dock (Wapping) built
1825–9	St Katharine Docks (Wapping) built
1832	London Docks Shadwell (Old) Basin built
1836–40	London & Blackwall Railway built to connect the City and East India Docks
1850–1	Poplar Dock (London's first railway dock) converted from a timber pond
1850–5	(Royal) Victoria Dock built on Plaistow Marshes
1854–8	London Docks Shadwell New Basin built
1863–9	Millwall Docks (Isle of Dogs) built
1875–80	Royal Albert Dock constructed E of (Royal) Victoria Dock
1886	Tilbury Dock (Essex) opened
1912–21	King George V Dock, last of the Royal Docks, built

Dock Closures and Regeneration 1965–98

1965	East India Docks closed
1966–70	Fred Olsen Terminal built in West India and Millwall Docks
1968–9	Seven container berths built at Tilbury, Essex
1968	London, St Katharine and Surrey Docks, Poplar Dock and Limehouse Basin, all closed
1969	Greater London Development Plan (no mention of dock closure)
1970	PLA commission development plan for London Docks
1971	Private development of St Katharine Docks begun
	Government commissioned report from Travers Morgan
1972	National Dock Strike
1974	Labour government elected
	Docklands Joint Committee formed by GLC and London Boroughs
1976	Docklands Joint Committee published Strategic Plan
1979	Conservative government elected
1980	West India and Millwall Docks closed
1981	Royal Victoria and Royal Albert Docks closed
	London Docklands Development Corporation established
1982	Enterprise Zone established on the Isle of Dogs
1985	Royal Docks Development Framework published
1986	News International moved to Wapping
1987	Docklands Light Railway and City Airport opened
	Daily Telegraph and *Guardian* moved to Enterprise Zone
	Canary Wharf contract signed between Olympia & York and LDDC
	Stock Market crashed
1989	Design Museum and London Arena opened
	Extension to Jubilee Line announced
	Kentish Property Group plc (Kentish Homes) into receivership
1991	Docklands Light Railway extended to Bank in the City of London
1992	Olympia & York, developers of Canary Wharf, into administration
	Enterprise Zone special conditions ended
	Royal Docks Development Framework updated
1994	DLR extension to Beckton opened
1995	First area (Bermondsey) returned to local authority control
1996	New consortium (IPC) took over development of Canary Wharf
	Beckton returned to Newham Borough Council
1997	Wapping, Limehouse and Isle of Dogs returned to Tower Hamlets
1998	Jubilee Line to be opened
	Royal Docks to be returned to Newham Borough Council
	LDDC to be disbanded

INTRODUCTION

During the last thirty years docks throughout the world have declined and closed. The reasons for decline are universal – mechanization, containerization, relocation of port facilities and the growth of air transport being the most influential. The picture is not all gloom: closure has offered the opportunity for redevelopment. Waterfronts previously cut off or polluted have been rediscovered and transformed into unrivalled settings for leisure, business, housing, culture and recreation: it was perhaps Utzon's conception for the Sydney Opera House that first showed in 1957 how thrilling the combination of water and daring new architecture could be. North America and Britain have generally led the way, though Australia, Continental Europe, Asia, and particularly Japan, which in 1996 had sixty-three developments on redundant port land, have had to tackle the same problems. London Docklands outstrips all these developments in size and ambition. The London Docklands Development Corporation was entrusted in 1981 with planning jurisdiction over $8\frac{1}{2}$ square miles of disused docks, derelict industrial land and decaying riverside and given the task by central government of regenerating the area, involving the improvement of the infrastructure and the creation of new jobs and homes. By mid 1997 jobs had increased by 44,800 to 72,000; estimated housing stock by 21,615 to 35,665.

This volume is concerned with the architectural record of Docklands. Nowhere in London since the 1960s has there been such a huge amount of new building in such a short time: the new buildings present a Postmodern snapshot, including all the stylistic strands, innovations and clichés of the last seventeen years. They also show that unfettered enterprise does not necessarily unleash good buildings: some of the worst buildings have gone up within the former Enterprise Zone on the Isle of Dogs, some of the best have been built under the stricter planning guidelines introduced by the LDDC since the mid 1980s. Money is not always the key that unlocks good design either: some of the best buildings, such as Heron Quays, the Millwall Docks Sailing Centre and Maconochie's Wharf housing, are the cheapest and, certainly, the huge amounts of money invested in Canary Wharf have not ensured consistent excellence. Docklands is also the place to examine late C20 attitudes to the conservation and conversion of historic buildings, and the vital contributions to the environment made by landscape design, public art, roads, bridges and even pavements. The following pages put the excellent and the odd in their historical and architectural context. They also chart the buildings of the

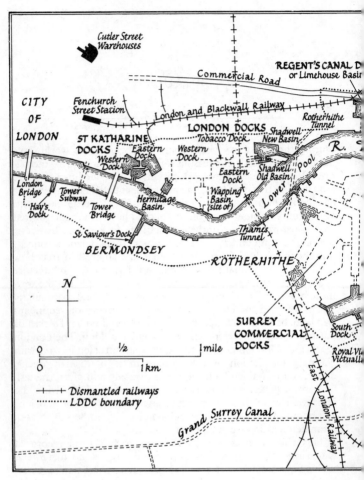

riverside settlements before and after the building of the docks. The docks transformed the riverside, both N and S of the Thames, from a string of hamlets and villages whose prosperity depended upon the river and on the cultivation of the drained marshes behind, into intensely industrial and densely developed eastern suburbs of London. Without this huge original enterprise of dock-building and development, there would be no modern Docklands.

The docks' history belongs to the story of the growth of trade on the Thames, which began in earnest with the founding of Londinium soon after A.D. 43. One of the site's advantages was that there was sufficient deep water for a port serving the continent of Europe. After the building of the first stone London Bridge, completed in 1209, the port was divided into two parts: below the bridge there was deep-water anchorage but only small craft could

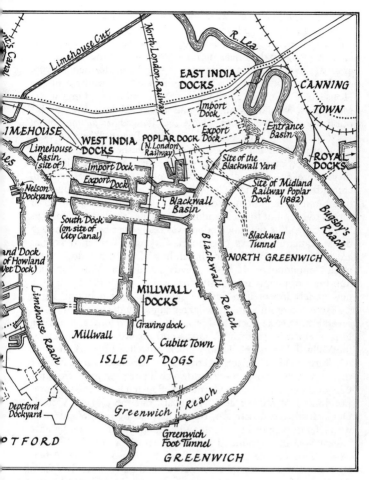

Docklands in 1980

venture upriver through its arches. The need for regulation led to the establishment of legal quays below the bridge on the N bank from 1558 to control the imports and exports of dutiable goods. All foreign goods had to be landed there. By the C18, London had 1,400 ft (430 metres) of Legal Quays, still only a third of the space available at Britain's second port, Bristol. 3,700 ft (1,100 metres) of sufferance wharves were ultimately licensed mainly on the S bank for lower value imported goods. Even so, by the late C18 the river was so jammed with ships that unloading a cargo could be delayed for weeks: by 1794 3,663 ships per annum entered the river from abroad, most of them in the short summer season. Delayed handling led to piracy and pilfering from ships and unsecured high-value goods on the quays, especially the East and West India cargoes of sugar, rum, coffee and hardwoods.

Secure trading docks were the solution to lack of space and security. Liverpool had developed the first 1710–17 and by 1795 had an extensive system. Although the City Corporation was against giving up their near-monopoly of trade via the legal quays, gradual pressure from a committee of merchants, formed in 1793, eventually took effect and in 1796 a Select Committee of the House of Commons agreed to docks in principle. One of the merchants, William Vaughan, had identified four sites in his publication *On Wet Docks, Quays and Warehouses for the Port of London...*, 1793 – St Katharine by the Tower, Wapping, and the more distant Isle of Dogs and Rotherhithe (the last two on undeveloped marshland which was cheaper to acquire). By 1830 there were docks in all four places plus another at Blackwall created by the East India Company in 1803–6 from the Brunswick fitting-out dock. The new docks were enclosed by high walls or moats to keep out thieves, and had lock gates to allow unloadings at any time. The first dock boom was really over by 1815, though the St Katharine Docks, close to the City, were built in 1825–9 as an attempt to capitalize on the ending of the other dock companies' monopolies. It was a greedy speculation, that displaced hundreds of people from a site that was to prove too small for a new generation of iron-built vessels. The second boom began *c.* 1850 to accommodate these larger ships. By the end of the C19, several more large docks had proved worth developing, including Poplar Dock, the (Royal) Victoria and the Royal Albert Docks, the Millwall Docks and Tilbury Dock, as well as huge additions to the Surrey Docks in Rotherhithe. They depended on rail rather than road transport of goods, and so could be sited miles from the City and dug out of cheap farmland. Poplar Dock of 1850–1 was London's first railway dock (for coal), but the (Royal) Victoria Dock, further downstream, begun in 1850 by railway entrepreneurs, far outstripped it in scale. When it opened in 1855 it had the largest area of impounded water (94 acres) of any dock in the world. This and the later docks of the Royals group (Royal Albert 1875–80; King George V 1912–21), several miles downriver from the City, offered miles of berths. These and the Millwall Docks, built s of the West India Docks in 1863–9, dealt not so much in high-value goods as in bulky imports from Europe and the growing Empire, such as foodstuffs and meat (in the Royals), timber (at Millwall) and grain. The Royal Docks were the last docks to close in 1981. The story of the docks is told in more detail on pp. 27–32.

The decline and closure of all the docks and of the riverside wharves and warehouses forms an essential prelude to the story of their redevelopment and regeneration, recounted in a later part of the Introduction.

THE RIVERSIDE UP TO 1800

The Roman and medieval riverside

The PREHISTORIC Thames valley was wide and shallow, bordered with marshes and mud flats amidst which small islands and beaches of flood-plain gravel stood slightly higher and formed refuges and convenient landfalls. Such terrain was hospitable to Neolithic and early Bronze Age settlers, who certainly exploited the land round Bermondsey (3000–2000 B.C.), where signs of agriculture have been found together with remains of a timber causeway, perhaps built across the marsh *c.* 1500 B.C. to what became known as Beormond's ea (Bermondsey).

The lowest crossing point on the Thames forms the w boundary of the present-day Docklands s of the river. It was here that the ROMANS probably built the first London Bridge, to link the N and s parts of their new city, founded soon after the Roman invasion in A.D. 43. As early as the A.D. 60s, there were important buildings in the s part, which grew up along the road to Richborough and Dover and was later to become the Saxon settlement of Southwark, just w of Docklands (*see London 2: South*). Further E along the river, however, only slight traces of building, dating from the C2 to C3, have been found in Bermondsey at Cotton's Wharf and Chamberlain's Wharf. On the N bank, Roman roads ran from Londinium (now beneath the City of London) due N and NE, avoiding the marshy riverside, which had probably already been partly drained for agriculture. The only building excavated, at Shadwell where there was a gravel beach, was connected with river traffic which grew in importance from *c.* A.D. 150. The Shadwell watchtower, probably accompanied by barracks, was built in the mid to late C3 as part of a crackdown on piracy.

Of all the MEDIEVAL SETTLEMENTS along the river outside the City of London, most important was Southwark, linked to the City of London by a successor to the Roman bridge from *c.* 1000. The areas E of Southwark, Bermondsey and Rotherhithe also became substantial settlements, though nothing medieval is visible now. Bermondsey had a Cluniac abbey, founded 1089 (its remains lay just s of Docklands), and a parish church, as well as St Olave by the river near London Bridge of which nothing remains. Large C14 and C15 'inns' and palaces, built by the clerical dignitaries of south-eastern England and by important landowners such as Sir John Fastolf, stood between the road to Greenwich and north Kent and the Thames, just as similar palaces lined the N bank along the Strand w of the City. Edward II built The Rosary palace in Bermondsey in 1323 (remains of the precinct wall have been found in Abbot's Lane), and, just to the E in Rotherhithe, Edward III enlarged a moated manor house as a royal residence, the remains of which have been laid out for the public to study.

Most of the N bank of the Thames E of the City was embanked from an early date, probably from Roman times, though the last stretch between Wapping and Shadwell was not drained until the early C16. The riverside hamlets of Wapping, Shadwell and Ratcliffe, all Anglo-Saxon by name, lay within the parish of St Dunstan Stepney and, before the rise of marine activities from about the mid C14, were mentioned only for their tidal mills and for fishing. The industrialization of the area began as primitive facilities were

created along the shore for the building, repair and victualling of
ships trading with the Port of London, but, although there was
activity at Blackwall by the late C15, the Isle of Dogs and the shore
E of Blackwall remained almost deserted, except for a short-lived
chapel on the Isle of Dogs and the hamlet of Hammarsh, close to
what is now North Woolwich. Another industrial enterprise
developed E of Ratcliffe in the C14 where the lime-oasts that gave
Limehouse its name began burning lime, imported from Essex
and Kent into Ratcliffe for use in the London building trade. As
might be expected, no built evidence survives from these industrial communities.

The only MEDIEVAL BUILDINGS of consequence on the N
bank belonged to the religious foundations which lay close to the
City walls. By the river the Royal Foundation of St Katharine,
begun in 1147 by Queen Matilda, administered a hospital, had
its own dock, and enjoyed privileges as a Royal Peculiar that
attracted a settlement of the poor and outlawed. To its N lay the
p.   Abbey of St Mary Graces, the last Cistercian foundation before
210 the Dissolution, established in 1349 by Edward III. The Hospital,
its settlement and the remains of St Mary Graces (by then a Royal
Victualling Yard) were swept away in the early C19, the Hospital
for St Katharine Docks, the abbey for the Royal Mint. The most
important architectural loss was the church of St Katharine,
rebuilt from the mid C14 and attributed by Harvey, on account of
the royal connections, to the royal mason *William Ramsay*. The
elaborate stalls may also have come from royal workshops for they
were apparently similar to those made just previously for St
Stephen's Chapel, Westminster: benches from the St Katharine
stalls survive at the present Royal Foundation of St Katharine in
Ratcliffe. St Mary Graces, though a C14 royal foundation intended
as an E counterpart to Westminster, was always underendowed. Its
buildings seem to have been of little interest beyond the unortho-
dox layout, unique among Cistercian houses, which is still partly
traceable beneath the converted Mint.

Riverside hamlets and villages 1500–1800

The SIXTEENTH, SEVENTEENTH and EIGHTEENTH CENTURIES
saw the growth of shipping and shipbuilding all along the N and S
banks of the river, a rise in population in the riverside hamlets, the
building of churches, chapels-of-ease, schools and merchants' and
shipbuilders' houses, and the development of the hinterland with
market gardens, orchards and ropewalks. In the C16 Ratcliffe
became a victualling and launching point for merchant-venturer
expeditions and voyages of discovery, and a new high street was
laid out along the newly drained shore at Wapping. Particularly
important was the growth in power and influence of the East India
Company after its foundation in 1600. The company established
itself on the river on both sides of the Isle of Dogs peninsula, in
the marshy depression known as Limehouse Hole where it repaired
ships, and at Blackwall where it established a shipyard for its large
vessels. Among the C17 developments on the less congested S

bank was the trading wharf, established in 1651 by Alexander Hay just S of London Bridge. It survived for 300 years, and was one of the long line of wharves and warehouses that gradually spread E to Rotherhithe. At Rotherhithe, where shipbuilding was already well established, the largest dock to date – the Great Howland p. Wet Dock – was built in 1696–9 for ship repair. Contemporary 272 prints show dock, windbreak planting and dockmaster's house laid out like a Baroque house and garden.

Nothing remains from the C16 except the long, narrow riverside sites of a few inns, such as the Town of Ramsgate and Prospect of Whitby in Wapping, but from the late C17 and early C18 there are still enough buildings to show that at least some riverside inhabitants shared in London-wide architectural fashions.

CHURCHES AND CHAPELS-OF-EASE were first built in the C17 to serve the growing population on the N side of the river, where overcrowding in the City stimulated an eastward spread of people and buildings, especially after the Great Fire in 1666. Churches were built at Wapping in 1615–17, at Shadwell, where a new parish was established in 1656, and at Poplar, where the East India Company began their own almshouse and provided a proprietary p. chapel for the people of Poplar and Blackwall in 1652–4. Poplar 172 chapel (later St Matthias) survives as a rare representative of an 6 early type of Protestant church, its central-planning devised p. specifically for reformed worship. Like its immediate predecessor, 166 the Broadway Chapel, Westminster (demolished), it hid a fairly austere classical interior inside a conservative Gothic envelope. The only notable item of C17 furnishing to survive is the early C17 pulpit from the church of St Katharine by the Tower, now at the modern Foundation in Ratcliffe. Unusual amongst C17 woodwork, it is carved with bold reliefs of buildings, said to be views of the ancient Hospital but apparently more exotic.

The most magnificent EIGHTEENTH-CENTURY CHURCHES were built E of the City under the New Churches Act, passed in 1711 in response to this demand for parish churches to serve the burgeoning communities. Of fifty new churches planned, only about twelve were built to designs by architects associated with the Office of Works but these included St George-in-the-East for 8 Wapping, and St Anne for Limehouse. They were built between 7,9 1714 and 1730 to designs by *Nicholas Hawksmoor* and stand far above all other Docklands churches in size, lavishness of materials and architectural quality. Both show Hawksmoor's idiosyncratic manipulation of the Baroque style, St George-in-the-East being particularly original and powerful. Their plans reflect the theo- pp. logical interest in the rites and buildings of the Early Christian 144, church which underlay the re-assessment of the Anglican church 203 after the Restoration. Hawksmoor envisaged precincts of sacred buildings round the churches to recall the 'Manner of Building the Church as it was in ye fourth century...', but these plans were abandoned in favour of large churchyards, a requirement of the Church Commissioners who rejected intra-mural burial. Indeed, the handsome high crypts beneath both churches were intended by Hawksmoor for schools rather than coffins. *John James's* replacement of the medieval St Mary Rotherhithe was also started in 1714–15. Though only a modest brick box, it was not finished until 1748 and not fully furnished until the later C18 (*see* below). The medieval St Olave, Bermondsey, and the C17 St John's chapel, Wapping, were also replaced in the mid C18: St Olave in 1738–9 by the Palladian *Flitcroft*, St John in 1756 probably by *Joel Johnson*, in brick with an unusual, still-Baroque tower.

The FURNISHINGS of St George-in-the-East, St Anne, Limehouse and St John, Wapping have been destroyed, but at St Mary Rotherhithe handsome fittings still give some idea of the prosperity and maritime professions of the village's mid-C18 inhabitants. The reredos is delicately carved by *Joseph Wade*, King's Carver in His Majesty's Yard at Deptford and Woolwich, †1743, who is commemorated in an equally fine wall-monument. N of the river at Wapping, Poplar and Limehouse, the best monuments are in the churchyards: these also chart a maritime and industrial class rather than an aristocratic one. Especially prominent is the large early C18 pyramid at St Anne, Limehouse, curious because now dissociated from its plinth, but in fact similar to the Raine monument at St George-in-the-East and of a not uncommon early C18 type.

The next wave of church building followed the opening of the docks, the consequent growth in population and the rise in rates made available by the dock companies. The establishment of the brand new parish of All Saints Poplar and the building of its
14 church, designed by *Charles Hollis* in 1820, were supported by dock companies: the East India Company's chaplain became All
13 Saints' first rector. St Paul, Shadwell, a rebuilding by *J. Walters* of the C17 parish church, was also begun in 1820. Though both churches are fashionably Greek, their towers are still composed in the accretive manner used in the Cities of London and Westminster by Wren, Gibbs and Dance. They were followed in the 1830s by two additional parish churches, St James Ratcliffe by *Lapidge* and Holy Trinity, Rotherhithe, by *Kempthorne*, both in the thin Gothic of the date and both demolished after 1945.

SCHOOLS AND HOUSES also give clues to C17, C18 and early C19 life in the riverside hamlets. Peter Hills School, Rotherhithe, which now occupies a narrow house of *c.*1700, was founded as early as 1613. Wapping has two schools: the parish school, founded *c.*1695 and rebuilt together with St John's church in
11 1756–60, is plainly classical, but the earlier charitable Raine's school, built in 1719 by a wealthy local man, has an elaborate façade, all in brick with the sort of quirky details used by London interpreters of the Baroque. The main late C17–early C18 domestic survival is the row of speculatively built plain brick two- to three-
10 bay houses in Narrow Street, Limehouse: old photographs show rows similar to those in Narrow Street in the main streets of other hamlets. Unfortunately the most elaborate speculation – a new quarter for Shadwell, with market, church and houses, planned and built by Thomas Neale between 1630 and 1650 – was swept away in the C19. Slightly later (1730s) and on a grander scale is
12 Nelson House, Rotherhithe, the only surviving example of an C18

shipbuilder's house, designed to link with street and shipyard and to command a view of the river. The style is still an entertaining Baroque, not unlike that of Raine's school. The only other substantial C18 house is late C18 (1795–6) and was built on his premises at Ratcliffe by the sugar merchant, Matthew Whiting. *Thomas Leverton*, who worked in Bedford Square, Bloomsbury, and was an associate of Whiting, may have been involved in its very plain Neoclassical exterior. Inside, though, there is remarkable and incomparable painted decoration in two rooms, landscapes probably done in the early C19.

The only other Georgian houses belong to fragments of PLANNED RESIDENTIAL DEVELOPMENTS round the churches. Newell Street dates from just after the completion of St Anne, Limehouse; Newby Place and Mountague Place were laid out

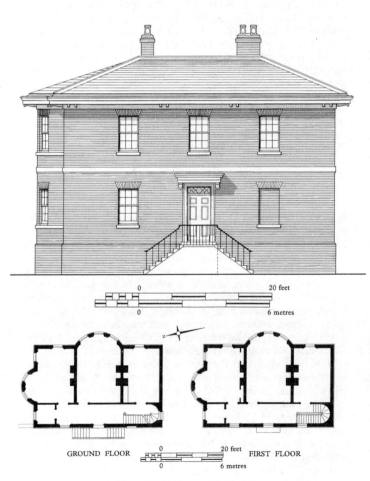

0   20 feet

0   6 metres

GROUND FLOOR   0   20 feet   FIRST FLOOR

0   6 metres

No. 1 Coldharbour, Isle House.
Elevation and plan, 1986

round All Saints, Poplar, just before and just after it was built,
p. together with Hollis's handsome, Neoclassical All Saints Rectory.
165 The East India Company Almshouses in Poplar, rebuilt by the
p. Company Surveyor, *Henry Holland*, in 1801–2, made an impressive
172 Neoclassical composition on Poplar High Street, but the chaplain's
house, originally the centrepiece, is the only part to survive.

Otherwise the houses of the early C19 belong to the develop-
15 ment of the docks. There are DOCK OFFICIALS' HOUSES over-
p. looking the entrances to the London Docks, St Katharine Docks
27 and the West India Docks. They are all roughly contemporary
with the construction of the docks and share a restrained
Neoclassical style with many London houses of the early to mid
C19. Their distinguishing characteristic is the use of full-height
bows on one or two façades, to overlook the river, and to monitor
the dock entrance. Those that flank the former entrance to the
16 London Docks at Wapping Pier Head are the terminal blocks of
substantial terraces designed by *D. A. Alexander* in 1811–13 to
make a fine gateway to the docks. The original customs buildings
at the former NW entrances to the London Docks and the West
India Docks follow a similar formula. And on a modest scale and
without bows are the cottages in Garford Street, built for the constables of the West India Docks.

INDUSTRIAL DEVELOPMENTS
FROM 1800 TO THE C20

BY MALCOLM TUCKER

Docks and wharves from 1800

It was on the Isle of Dogs that construction commenced of the
first and finest of the new docks, the West India. The London
Docks, in the market gardens behind Wapping, were hard on
its heels. Initially, the privately financed Dock Companies were
protected by twenty-one-year monopolies in certain classes of
goods, which were stored under customs bond in their huge new
warehouses, vaults and sheds – the West India included coffee,
sugar, mahogany and rum, the London Docks tobacco, wine and
spirits. The East India Company, with long-held monopolies in
eastern goods including spices and tea, created their own docks at
Blackwall, but maintained their existing warehouses in the City.
The various docks in the Surrey marshes behind Rotherhithe
developed major trades in grain and softwoods. A second era of
dock building began *c.* 1850 in an age dominated by new tech-
nologies and freedom of trade. The size and form of ocean-going
ships had previously been limited by their timber construction,
and the early docks were sized accordingly. Wrought-iron hulls
and steam power were at first applied to small packet boats and
tugs, but longer ships were appearing by the 1840s, while paddle
steamers needed greater width. Foreseeing further growth, the
huge (Royal) Victoria Dock of 1850–5 therefore had an entrance
lock almost twice as long and wide as previously seen in London.

Iron and concrete made its construction economical and hydraulic power eased its operation, matters discussed in the following section. It was railway access that unlocked the distant marshland of West Ham for this cheap and speculative promotion.

The (Royal) Victoria Dock started a trade war which culminated in its amalgamation with the London and St Katharine Docks in 1864–5. The 1860s saw new docks at Millwall and extensions in the Surreys, followed by an economic depression. Not until 1880 was the long-awaited E extension of the (Royal) Victoria Dock opened and named the Royal Albert Dock. It was efficiently laid out for transfer direct to rail and its engineering was up to date. But it provoked the East and West India Dock Company to open a similar dock for still larger ships, fifteen miles further down river at Tilbury, in 1886. Such cut-throat over-investment put a brake on further improvements on the N bank until the Port of London Authority was created in 1909, although the rebuilt Greenland Dock was opened on the Surrey side in 1904.

While the dock companies struggled financially, the later C19 was a boom time for riverside wharves. Between 1842 and 1853 Parliament removed customs duties from most imported goods and all exports, freed the corn trade of import restrictions and simplified the duty-free storage of the remaining dutiable goods. Large warehouses were constructed on the waterfront, starting among the existing wharves near London Bridge but spreading E to displace other activities, as at Metropolitan and Crane Wharves, Wapping. Goods were at first brought by lighters from the docks, then after 1900, jetties were increasingly built to allow ships to berth. Goods ranged from grain and spices to dairy produce and tallow, while the dockside warehousing maintained a hold on wool, tobacco, sugar and spirits. Grain was handled in bulk, from 1864–5 at Canada Wharf, Rotherhithe, also at the Millwall and Surrey Docks.

Engineering

WHARF WALLS were built out on to the foreshore so that lighters might moor against them at high water. As the tide ebbed, they would settle comfortably into the mud, or on to a beach that had been levelled behind sheetpiling (campshedding), while continuing to load or unload their cargoes. Wharf walls of timber were widely used until the early C19, consisting of king piles held back by wooden or later wrought-iron horizontal ties. Walling beams between them supported timber sheeting. Similar constructions were used in dry docks and the laying-up basins such as the Howland Dock (1696) or the Brunswick Dock (1790) and the early C19 trading docks on the Surrey side. The riverside walls are now mostly of brick.

Heavy brickwork was required for the tall QUAY WALLS of the early C19 docks on the N bank. The West India Docks were the model for others and their engineer *William Jessop* introduced elegantly curved walls, leaning gently backwards (they earned the nickname banana walls from a propensity to slip if a dock is hastily drained). Jessop also introduced LOCK CHAMBERS with substantial inverted-arch bottoms, among which the disused western entrance to the City Canal (West India South Dock) of 1805 remains intact.

The excavations for the docks were remarkable, three quarters of a million cubic yards of soil being dug from the West India Import Dock in little more than a year. Steam engines drained the ground, mixed mortar for the brickwork and, in the London Docks, hauled waggon loads of spoil up inclined planes. Large cofferdams were erected for building the locks.

Most docks were built with separate ENTRANCE BASINS (tidal basins) which served as reservoirs to fill the entrance locks and were replenished at high tide. The water level at the quays was held constant by communicating locks which separated the docks from the basins. This system continued in use until the PLA provided impounding stations with powerful pumps in the early C20. The St Katharine Docks, with their restricted space, used a pumping engine from the start. The layout, and the fine brickwork and masonry of quay walls and locks, can be studied in *John Rennie*'s Western Dock at the London Docks.

To cross the locks, double-leaf SWING BRIDGES were introduced at West India in 1802 and the first of cast iron were devised by *Rennie* at the London Docks in 1804. The only early bridge surviving is the unusual retracting footbridge of 1829 *ex situ* at the St Katharine Docks; the next earliest, the wrought-iron swing footbridge of 1855 formerly at the South Dock, is now at the Norway Dock Passage in the Surrey Commercial Docks.

Around the early enclosed docks, very high brick BOUNDARY WALLS were built, either as a part of the warehouses themselves as at the West India Import Dock (which had an outer moat), or else freestanding, often on their own wooden-piled foundations. There are preserved sections at the London Docks and East India Docks. The grand gateways were deliberately constricting and are therefore ill-represented in survival; preservation has produced some incongruities, as at Leamouth Road, Blackwall.

As the C19 progressed and works became larger, NEW CONSTRUCTION TECHNIQUES improved the economics. For the steamboat quay at Brunswick Wharf, Blackwall, in 1832–4, *James Walker* used cast-iron piles and sheeting, anchored by iron rods and backed with lime concrete, a development of the traditional timber walls. *George Bidder* repeated the principle for the huge Victoria Dock of 1850–5. His 80 ft (24 metre) wide entrance lock, with wrought-iron lock gates, set a new standard. Lacking robustness, the cast-iron structures have now gone.

MASS CONCRETE using Portland cement was incorporated in quay walls from then onwards, at first behind protective facings of brickwork. *J. M. Rendel*'s quay wall at Shadwell New Basin, 1854–8 (the London Docks' tactical response to the Victoria Dock), had piers of concrete and relieving arches below the water line, saving on brickwork while improving the balance of the wall. The Royal Albert Dock, 1875–80, used walls with a mechanically efficient stepped back and a projecting toe. By then concrete had improved sufficiently to be left exposed on the face. The Royal Albert also used steam-powered excavators for the first time.

Changes may be observed in the LAYOUT of quays. The early enclosed docks sorted their cargoes on broad quays, to which sheds were added for shelter. The St Katharine Docks' cramped 22 quays were tucked under the warehouses. The advantage there of hoisting directly from ship into warehouse applied only to cargoes so destined. Some riverside wharves adopted the principle (e.g. Butler's Wharf, Bermondsey, and Metropolitan Wharf, Wapping). 21 The Victoria Dock had finger jetties, supporting small warehouses, to maximize the length of quayside within the plan area. These were cramped, and turntables had to be used for access by railway wagons; they also restricted the lengths of ships. They were abolished in the 1930s rebuilding. The Royal Albert Dock returned to long quays on which cranes and railways wagons could readily travel, backed by transit sheds for the sorting of cargoes. They set the pattern for the King George V Dock and later improvements up to the 1960s. The principal C20 development was to build reinforced-concrete jetties forward of the old quay walls so that dock bottoms could be deepened and modern vertical-sided ships could berth comfortably.

The cranes, capstans, swing bridges and lock gates of the early docks were entirely manually powered. HYDRAULIC POWER, the use of high-pressure water pumped through mains to drive mechanical equipment, swept through the London docks in the early 1850s, as soon as the weight-loaded accumulator had been invented. Accumulator towers to hold this pressure-regulating device may be seen in several places, notably the Regent's Canal Dock (Limehouse Basin) and Poplar Docks, while hydraulic pumping station buildings remain at Wapping, Rotherhithe, East 28, India Dock and Tower Bridge. While the dock companies had 29 their independent systems, the London Hydraulic Power Company provided hydraulic mains under the streets from 1883, to the great benefit of riverside wharves (*see* Wapping Wall). Hydraulic wall-cranes lingered in older warehouses until the early 1970s and are occasionally preserved, as at Hope (Sufferance) Wharf, Rotherhithe. The winch of distinctive appearance, called a jigger, was the basis of most of the hydraulic machinery.

Hydraulic power worked the large, wrought-iron plate-girder BRIDGES that spanned the new, wide dock passages. Only one remains, across the Royal Albert Dock at Manor Way, but their substructures are displayed at Connaught Road, and at the Russia Dock Passage in the Surreys. The Surrey Docks have a variety of other preserved bridges, and the hydraulic equipment which operated the magnificent Greenland entrance lock of 1904 is instructively displayed, as is the huge hydraulic jigger which worked the gates at the old Millwall Dock entrance in Westferry Road.

Specialized technology developed for BULK GRAIN HANDLING. Ventilated silos were built at Canada Wharf, Rotherhithe, from 1864, but the Millwall Docks came to dominate the trade through the ingenious devices developed by *F. E. Duckham*, their engineer, including moveable quay cranes from 1873 and pneumatic elevators from 1892. Two huge floor granaries, of bins fed by bucket elevators, were erected there, with nine floors in 1883 and eleven floors in 1903, the largest structures in the docks until replaced by the grain terminal at Tilbury in 1969. ELECTRICITY was used for lighting at the Royal Albert Dock in 1880 but its use for power awaited the C20. The prominent landmarks of the C20 which remain are the preserved quay cranes in the West India, Millwall, Poplar and Victoria Docks, the rolling bascule bridges in the London and Surrey Docks and the pneumatic grain elevators in the Victoria Dock.

Warehouses

Warehouses dominated the upriver docks and the riverside from the City down to Rotherhithe and Limehouse until the late 1960s, symbolizing London's trading wealth. They stored mainly imported goods and commodities of a seasonal character. Security against theft and fire were primary considerations, balanced against economy and convenience. The London Building Act of 1774 extended to much of the present Docklands the rules already existing in the City for external walls and party-walls of brick, carried up as parapets above roof level. By the later C19 older weatherboarded and wood-partitioned buildings had gone, through redevelopment or fire (as at Irongate Wharf by St Katharine Docks in 1847). The dock companies were exempted but were keen on fire security because of the value of the goods stored. The sizes of compartments between the fire walls in their warehouses were much larger than permitted elsewhere, but danger was mitigated by strict management regimes. In the Surrey (Commercial) Docks granaries were erected in timber from 1821 through to the 1870s without ill effect.

The early dock warehouses set the pattern of construction for the rest of the C19. INTERIORS almost invariably had floors of timber, keeping down costs and loads on foundations, but cast-iron columns were introduced for their load-bearing capacity, first retrospectively in 1810 in the London Docks South Stacks and in 1814 in the surviving West India No. 2 Warehouse. *Daniel Alexander*'s New Tobacco Warehouse of 1811–14 in the London Docks is particularly innovative in its use of iron, while tri-branched heads are seen at No. 112 Wapping High Street. Cruciform-section columns were preferred in London throughout the C19, but granaries in Bermondsey continued with traditional timber stanchions. The late C18 Grice's Granary in Rotherhithe has wooden knee braces from local shipbreaking yards. Timber beams trussed or flitched with wrought iron were used in the mid C19, e.g. the London Docks. The London and St Katharine Docks had magnificent groin-vaulted CELLARS, still seen at Tobacco Dock and beneath the so-called Ivory House. FOUNDATIONS in the marshlands might use timber piles, causing problems where the ground water has fallen and exposed the footings to rot.

The ROOFS of the earliest large warehouses remaining, at Free

18
pp.
200
–1

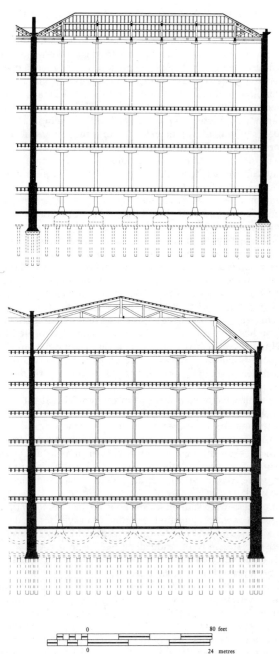

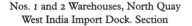

Nos. 1 and 2 Warehouses, North Quay
West India Import Dock. Section

Trade Wharf, Ratcliffe (1795), and the Dickens Inn at St Katharine Docks, have queenpost trusses steeply pitched for common tiles. Welsh slate roofs and shallow pitches soon became the norm, although the exceptionally long roof trusses at West India No. 2 Warehouse (1802) supported upper slopes of copper. Trusses of over 50 ft (15 metre) span were once common – some remain in the Pennington Street sheds in the London Docks (1811–13). Iron hanger rods reduced the weight of such roofs in the mid C19, as in K warehouse, Victoria Dock (1859) and St Anne, Limehouse (1850–1). In granaries, lofts extended into the roofs, which might be constructed of long-span trusses propped by stanchions, as at Warehouse WII in Shad Thames and No. 29 Bermondsey Wall. An alternative logic of flat-topped roofs is seen around St Saviour's Dock.

Economics and constructional logic did not always run hand-in-hand. To circumvent the Building Act stipulations on compartmentation, the warehouses at Hay's Wharf (1856–7) had floors alternately of timber and brick jack-arches, a questionable practice. They were partly destroyed in the Tooley Street fire. Concrete-pugged floors were also used there. Large warehouses in Wapping in the 1860s and 1870s (e.g. Metropolitan Wharf) brick-arched their lower floors in a consistent manner. 'I' warehouse, now Ivory House, of 1858–60 in the St Katharine Docks adopted wholeheartedly incombustible, so-called fireproof construction of brick-arches on wrought-iron beams, as newly advocated by Sir William Fairbairn. It is wholly untypical of London warehouses. The same architect, *Aitchison*, used an early and very prominent plate girder in the now demolished 'H' warehouse of 1852. Fire protection at affordable cost was eventually achieved with concrete floors, at first using filler joists as in the now gutted extension of Hay's Wharf (1887).

REINFORCED CONCRETE brought a revolution. It was used by the PLA from 1912 when regulations still hampered its use outside the docks. Although widely applied in the Royal Docks (*see* Transit Sheds, below) only the shed of 1914–17 within the new Billingsgate Market at West India Docks remains of their warehouse work.

Warehouses were laid out for the goods to be hoisted by powered cranes on the water side and lowered to road vehicles on the landward side. As wharves expanded and landside warehouses were added, the streets were bridged by tiers of iron GANGWAYS for goods to be wheeled across on barrows. Once widespread, they have been preserved in Shad Thames.

The major dock and wharf companies applied high standards of ARCHITECTURE to their warehouses in the C19, with formal compositions and details generally in a classical idiom. Portland stone or, later, stucco was widely used for cornices, stringcourses and other embellishments. Except in the almost blind boundary walls, windows were generally large, to light the deep interiors without the risk from oil lamps. *George Gwilt* and son at West India Docks from 1802 made the windows broader than tall, with secure cast-iron frames (often supplemented by spikes), in what became a universal style. Granaries, however, used wooden shutters in small openings. Walls were pierced by tiers of loading doors or loopholes, with robust wooden jambs and hinged platforms, accompanied by swivelling wall-cranes, the smaller ones often of elegantly forged iron.

At St Katharine Docks in 1828, *Philip Hardwick* introduced giant blind arcades and pilaster strips, motifs used less chastely and in double tiers at Hay's Wharf in the 1850s by *Snooke &* 23 *Stock*, and recurring until the 1920s. St Katharine Docks are best remembered for their Doric colonnades of cast iron, the model for the surviving Albert Dock in Liverpool. Old Aberdeen Wharf (1843–4) had attached columns, and Italianate modillioned cornices were used from that time. Gothic ornament was applied rarely, as at Oliver's Wharf, Wapping (1869–70); Canada Wharf, Rotherhithe (1864 and 1871) has multi-segmental and Moorish arches in polychrome brickwork. The common, segmental-headed window was expressed in contrasting colour in much late C19 work, and hardwearing bricks such as Staffordshire blues were adopted for the bull-nosed door-jambs and dados. Functional rolled-steel lintels appeared around 1900.

Reinforced-concrete framing removed the need for loadbearing walls from the 1910s. Early work was decorously concealed in simple brickwork, as at Free Trade Wharf, Ratcliffe (*c.* 1920, demolished). Gun Wharves, Wapping (*c.* 1920 onwards), retained 65 the loadbearing elements, and revived the giant arcade in artificial stone. Thereafter utilitarianism prevailed for a period, with ungainly exposed frames and large bulk. The late 1930s cold stores at Chamber's Wharf, Bermondsey, have architectural brickwork on one token façade. This may be contrasted with the expressionist horizontal banding of brick and concrete, with staggered loading doors, in cold stores off Tooley Street at Symon's Wharf (1937–9) and the river front of Hay's Wharf (as rebuilt after war damage *c.* 1945), both examples now lost.

Brief mention is needed of TRANSIT SHEDS, used in the docks to shelter goods in transit on the quays. Less secure than warehouses, they were seen as a fire risk, calling for very early IRON ROOFS from 1810 in the London Docks (details unknown) and 1813 for the Rum Sheds at West India Docks, commissioned by Rennie. Corrugated-iron roofing was developed by *Henry Palmer* at the London Docks in 1829. Transit sheds with wrought-iron roof trusses on cast-iron columns were the principal buildings of the railway-orientated Royal Albert Docks (1880).

Large open sheds with wooden roofs were used for the storage of timber, such as dominated the Surrey Docks until the wartime conflagration, fireproofing being unfeasible. The West India Mahogany Shed of 1817 by *Rennie* had early overhead travelling cranes. Improved CRANAGE and reinforced-concrete construction facilitated transit sheds of two storeys in the early PLA period, with particular efficiency of layout (incorporating long-span concrete trusses) at the King George V Dock opened in 1921. Most remarkable was 'M' shed between the South West India and Millwall Docks, as late as 1967, by *Harris & Sutherland*. It was three-storeyed for the rapid unloading of ships and incorporated pre-stressed waffle-slab floors, steel barrel-vault roofs and vehicular ramps. The huge steel-handling sheds of Express Wharf, Westferry Road (1976 and 1986), their overhead crane runways cantilevered high above the water, may be noted as a singular recent investment on the riverside. By then, as narrated elsewhere, warehousing in the docks had become a business of tall, long-span steel portal-framed sheds for mechanically stacked loads, only to be superseded by the international container, handled at berths and depots remote from the Docklands.

Industry

From today's appearances, it is hard to imagine that the riverside was highly industrial until the 1960s and later, with heavy engineering and the processing of diverse imported products.

SHIPBUILDING, with ship repairing and ship breaking, could at first be performed on any out-of-the-way corner of the foreshore. The earliest records are for naval shipbuilding, with the Royal Dockyards situated nearby in Deptford and Woolwich from *c.* 1513, while there were free shipwrights in Rotherhithe in the late C16 and others on the N bank. In 1614 the East India Company established Blackwall Yard at Poplar, which developed in private hands and was the nation's most productive shipbuilding yard in the later C18. The main facilities of the yards were slipways for new building, dry docks usually for repair and (occasionally) basins for fitting out and refitting – the earliest such wet dock, at Blackwall Yard was in use from 1661 until the mid C19. The old dry docks continued in widespread use until the late C19 in Wapping, Rotherhithe and Limehouse, with later ones in the Isle of Dogs, and remains may be seen at Nelson Dock, Rotherhithe, Orchard Dock, Blackwall, and the site of Blackwall Yard – the latter in use until the 1980s.

As shipbuilding started to move from wood to iron in the 1830s, shipyards were established in the Isle of Dogs, notably the Millwall Ironworks where there are standing buildings and part of the special slipway built in 1854 to launch the Leviathan *SS Great Eastern*. Clipper ships of composite iron and timber construction were built at Nelson Dock, Rotherhithe. Shipbuilding crashed in the late 1860s and most moved away from London. The last big shipyard, on Bow Creek, closed in 1912.

The curious Pontoon Dock (1858) at the Victoria Dock, where ships were lifted hydraulically on to floating platforms, was the first of several repair facilities within the trading docks as attractions to dock users. Dry docks can be seen at Millwall Dock (1868) and Blackwall Basin, West India (1878). There were three dry docks with major workshops in the later Royal Docks, where repairs to big ships continued until closure in 1980. The workshop for smaller repairs in the London Docks is now the John Orwell Sports Centre (q.v.). The vestiges of barge-building and repair yards at No. 110 Wapping High Street, No. 94 Narrow Street, Limehouse, and No. 135 Rotherhithe Street, and the C18 and C19 gridirons on the foreshore at Fountain Stairs, Bermondsey, are reminders that smaller vessels needed minimal facilities.

London's ENGINEERING interests spread far wider than ship-building, and there were numerous works, particularly in Millwall, making equipment such as anchor chains, screw propellers, grain elevators and swing bridges and serving also the wider construction needs of London and the Empire. Ropewalks had earlier been a common feature of the back lands, while No. 11 West India Dock Road was a sailmaker's factory. The Trinity House yard where buoys and lightships were maintained, at Orchard Place, Leamouth, has the unexpected feature of an experimental lighthouse.

The PROCESSING INDUSTRIES were major users of mechanical equipment. CORN MILLERS took early advantage of the river's large tidal range to work tidemills on marshland creeks in Wapping, Bermondsey and Rotherhithe. Windmills later gave their name to Millwall. With steam power from the mid C19, mills for flour, barley, split peas, rice and spices became particularly strong in Bermondsey, where there are mill buildings recently converted around St Saviour's Dock, and also at Rotherhithe. Smaller flour mills in Wapping and Ratcliffe declined and became warehouses at the end of the C19, when roller mills were erected in the Millwall and Royal Victoria Docks – those were in turn rebuilt on a huge scale in the C20, but closed with the docks. Biscuit making was an allied trade in Bermondsey, arising from naval victualling requirements while the principle brewhouse for the navy was adjacent to St Katharine Docks until 1792. Understandably, the brewery at Limehouse had a strong export trade. Courage's brewery at Horselydown has been interestingly converted.

Limeburning, at Limehouse in the Middle Ages, was the first of the OBNOXIOUS INDUSTRIES of down-wind E London. The first gunpowder mills recorded in England, at Rotherhithe in the mid C16, may have been of that class as certainly were the whale-blubber boilers at the Greenland Dock in the C18 while lead works in Rotherhithe and Millwall were probably the last. There was a short-lived porcelain works at Limehouse in the C18. Imported raw materials and local coal-gas by-products gave rise to numerous MANUFACTURING works in the late C19 and C20. Eastern Rotherhithe, the Isle of Dogs, Bow Creek and Silvertown had soapworks, vegetable-fat processors, tar works, oil works, paint factories, chemical works, fertilizer works, sugar refineries, sweet factories, food preservers, metals processors and telegraph-cable works. The tall brick chimneys of Millwall Lead Works, Burrell's colour works and Cumberland Oil Mills still dominated the end of the Isle of Dogs in the 1970s. Tate and Lyle's enormous sugar refineries in Silvertown, started in the 1870s, receive the raw materials directly by ship and have developed into a different class of modern industry.

There is one notable new industry in Docklands, the newspaper-printing plants which moved out of central London in the 1980s. They are reliant on bulk supplies of paper imported through a large wharf just outside the Docklands area.

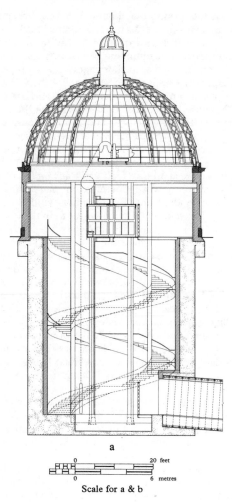

a

0   20 feet

0   6 metres

Scale for a & b

Transport

The RIVER THAMES formed a highway, conveying passengers and
goods by the power of oars, sail and, particularly, the tides. Large
'West Country' barges once carried upriver to and from Abingdon
and Newbury (and smaller craft beyond that) while sailing barges
traded to creeks and ports down the estuary and round the coast.
For passengers, the journey to Gravesend in Kent was called from
medieval times the Long Ferry. From the later 1810s, paddle
steamers plied the route to the North Kent resorts and the
Continent, and steamboat quays were built at St Katharine's
Wharf (1829) and Brunswick Wharf, Blackwall (1834). Brunswick
Wharf had elegant baggage sheds and an hotel by *Tite*, a foretaste

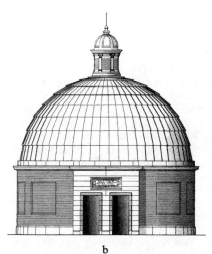

b

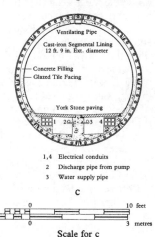

c

Scale for c

Greenwich Foot Tunnel, rotunda. Elevation and sections

of the Gallions Hotel (1881–3) for more distant voyagers from the Royal Albert Dock. The River Lee Navigation was reconstructed largely as a CANAL in 1767–70, its Limehouse Cut avoiding the long and awkward journey via Bow Creek and the Isle of Dogs. The Regent's Canal also arrived at Limehouse in 1820, providing a direct connection to the Midlands and for long the distributor of much seaborne coal and timber.

The meandering Thames and its marshes caused early MAIN ROADS to skirt the area (*see* p. 23). A Roman road which is now The Highway followed the northern river bluff to the probable Roman outport at Ratcliffe. The Commercial Road (including the West India Dock Road) of 1802–4 and its tributary East India Dock Road conveyed valuable goods from the docks up to the City, and the traffic was such that the Commercial Road stoneway was laid along it in 1828–30, with slabs of granite to reduce the wear and rolling resistance of the heavy road wagons. To the E, an iron bridge by *Rennie* spanned the River Lea in 1814 (replaced in a major road scheme of 1929–35). While London's first RAILWAY, from London Bridge to Greenwich (1833–8) narrowly avoided the Docklands, its counterpart on the N side, the London & Blackwall (earlier Commercial) Railway of 1836–40, ran past the docks to the Blackwall Wharf steamer quay. It was extended in 1865–72 down the Isle of Dogs and become a major carrier of goods, while the North London Railway (1846–52) provided an essential northward connection and built London's first railway dock, at Poplar Dock. The speculative line from Stratford to North Woolwich (1844–7) opened up a large new area for dock and

27 industrial development; its elegant Italianate terminus at North Woolwich (1854) and the tunnel under the Royal Docks (1878) are major features.

CROSSING THE THAMES was at first achieved by FERRIES. Steps and hards down to the water's edge had traditionally provided access for watermen and their passengers. The Metropolitan Board of Works established the Woolwich Free Ferry, with floating landing stages, opened in 1889 under its Act of 1885, as a balance to the freeing of toll-bridges in W London. Bridging the crowded shipping channel was achieved at Tower Bridge (1885–94).

The first THAMES TUNNEL, intended as a road crossing from Rotherhithe to Wapping, was completed for foot passengers only, and against all odds, through the ingenuity and heroic perseverance of *Sir Marc Brunel* in the years 1825–43. The East London Railway of 1865–76 by *Sir John Hawkshaw* closed a gap in the railway system by major tunnelling works either side of it. This was followed by the Blackwall Tunnel, built with the aid of compressed air and public finance in 1891–7 (Act of 1887). Tower Subway of 1869 had proved the feasibility of small-bore railway tunnels in the London Clay, but that stratum was inconveniently absent beneath the river downstream. Following the success of Blackwall Tunnel, the LCC built another road tunnel at Rotherhithe

pp. (1904–8) and foot tunnels accessed by stairs and lifts at Greenwich
38–9 (1897–1902) and Woolwich (1909–12). The Blackwall Tunnel was duplicated in 1960–7.

NEW TRANSPORT ROUTES to serve the later C20 Docklands began with the DOCKLANDS LIGHT RAILWAY, which started in a modest way in 1984–7 (using single-unit articulated cars, short platforms and 130 ft (40 metre) radius curves) reconnecting the Isle of Dogs with the City and Stratford by mainly old railway routes. Much was spent from 1987 on upgrading its capacity in response to the office boom, and the station at Canary Wharf and

52 the extension to Beckton of 1988–92 are in a different league from the original concept. Private finance has now taken on the tunnelled crossing to Greenwich and Lewisham (1996–2000). The JUBILEE LINE EXTENSION of 1992–8, crossing the Thames three times in the Docklands area, is an underground railway at considerable depth, and is remarkable for the architectural ambitions and

spaciousness of its stations and the enormous civil engineering works in often very difficult ground conditions.

LONDON CITY AIRPORT (1982–7) at the Royal Docks was entirely a private venture. The spectacular cut-and-cover tunnels of the LIMEHOUSE RELIEF ROAD (1989–93), its extension sweeping E across the Lea, the new road system at the Royal Albert Dock, and several eye-catching footbridges are among the LDDC's memorials.

1,53, 87

Services

SERVICES dating from before the later C20 have left only a few visible remains. WATER SUPPLY now comes from outside the area. Enormous improvements in river quality in the later C20 have still not returned the Thames to its condition before the C19, when it fed waterworks at London Bridge and Shadwell. The only remains of GASWORKS within the LDDC area are a gas holder and the piers of the coaling jetty of Rotherhithe Gasworks. From ELECTRICITY GENERATION there is the converted jetty of Stepney Power Station at Limehouse – the site once had a 350-ft (107 metre) high chimney. Brunswick Wharf Power Station, built 1945–52 in the style of Battersea within the drained East India Export Dock, once dominated Blackwall. HYDRAULIC POWER is the one utility to have left appreciable remains (see Engineering, above).

The THAMES BARRIER (1972–82) is the climax of the work of the GLC on the flood defences of London. It allowed the lowering of obtrusive flood walls upstream (but necessitated their raising downstream) and the dismantling of a short-lived guillotine barrier (1971–3) across Bow Creek. Less in the public mind nowadays are achievements in SEWERAGE. In place of the tidal outfall sluices and marshland drainage channels (which in the Jacob's Island area of Bermondsey became grossly polluted in the mid C19), surface and waste waters are conveyed underground to pumping stations en route to treatment works beyond the LDDC area. The system was enhanced for the new Docklands developments in the 1980s, and provided with architecturally expressive pumping station buildings at Stewart Street (Isle of Dogs), Tidal Basin Road (Royal Docks) and North Woolwich.

57, 58

BUILDING FROM 1800 TO THE LATER C20

Nineteenth-century communities

The picture of C19 communities, such as Bermondsey, Poplar, Limehouse, Shadwell and Ratcliffe, is distorted by the way in which they have been divided by the LDDC's late C20 boundary. In most of these neighbourhoods, much of the C19 industrial and domestic development occurred on then-empty sites N of the Commercial and East India Dock Roads, i.e. outside modern Docklands. Though much has been replaced in the C20, enough remains in those N parts to give an idea of their former character, with industrial premises and terraces of workers' houses. There was surprisingly little new building of houses, churches, schools and social amenities in the original riverside settlements. The majority of the population were forced by the building of the docks into multiple occupation of the remaining C17 and C18 houses, which had been abandoned by their original owners as the riverside became more industrial and less salubrious. These handsome properties soon became slums. Most notorious were Jacob's Island in Bermondsey, where a few C18 houses survived until the 1950s, and the riverside parts of Shadwell and Ratcliffe, swept away for a park in 1902.

Most HOUSING FOR WORKERS was speculatively built from the mid to late C19 in the areas where new industries were being developed. On the Isle of Dogs from *c.* 1840, several landowners exploited the land between docks and riverside wharves for unexceptional terraced housing, much of which was demolished after Second World War damage. Similar terraces were also built in the communities planted as new industrial settlements, such as Cubitt Town, begun on the Isle of Dogs by William Cubitt in 1842, and Silvertown, started in West Ham by the rubber manufacturer Abram Silver in the 1850s. The only exceptional housing belonged to the Gas Light and Coke Co.'s new township of Beckton, laid out complete with institute and chapel from 1868: the handsome Italianate terraces along Winsor Terrace are the only remains. There was by no means enough available space to house all the workers required close to their workplaces in the docks and riverside industries and many commuted quite some distance. This was especially true of the Royal Docks where workers were ferried across the river or later walked through the foot tunnel from Woolwich, or travelled from the swathes of speculative housing built N of the docks in new areas, such as Canning Town, or round the existing villages of Plaistow, Stratford, and East and West Ham. The worst houses, without proper foundations or drainage, were built in the 1870s on the marshes N of the Royal Docks at Cyprus.

It was this sort of new slum housing, as much as the tenemented older property, that provoked immediate condemnation from writers such as Dickens and inspired the building of PHILANTHROPIC HOUSING. It began in a small way in the mid C19 with improved dwellings such as those provided in Wapping by Alderman Waterlow in 1864–5, and by grimmer tenements in Bermondsey (*see London 2: South*). Early attempts by borough councils to improve living conditions were made by East Ham, which pre-First World War built cottages at North Woolwich, and tenements (since replaced) at Cyprus. The LCC built the Swan Road Estate, Rotherhithe, in 1902–3, specially for those displaced by the building of the Rotherhithe Tunnel, and housing by the Blackwall Tunnel.

CHURCHES, both High Anglican and Roman Catholic, were built to serve the poor older housing and the new industrial developments, but most have not survived the Blitz. Even the chief survivor amongst the Anglican missions, *Pownall's* muscular Gothic St Peter, Wapping, founded from St George-in-the-East in

1856 as St Peter London Docks, was badly bomb-damaged and has been extensively reconstructed. It was in any case never finished: its stop-start history reveals ambitions to build in a lavish and uplifting style and a lack of funds to carry them through. The only church comparable in its muscularity to St Peter is *S. S.* 32 *Teulon*'s St Mark, 1860–2, which asserts itself at Silvertown with Teulon's characteristic bravado. Almost as insistent is the new Gothic casing given to St Matthias, Poplar, by *W. M. Teulon* (brother of the more famous S. S. Teulon), after this proprietary chapel became a district church in 1866. Most Anglican churches built in working-class suburbs were less elaborate: Christ Church, Cubitt Town, of 1852–4 by *Frederick Johnstone*, as well as others on the Isle of Dogs since demolished (St Luke, Millwall, by *E. L. Blackburne*, 1868–70; St John, Roserton Street, by *Blomfield* 1871–2; St Peter, Garford Street, by *Ewan Christian*, 1882–4) were in a fairly simple medieval parish-church manner, though all of them acquired ritualistic furnishings from *c.* 1880: a large collection has been gathered at Christ Church, including a fine painted 33 pulpit by *Strudwick* of *c.* 1914. *Butterfield* imposed a greater ritualism of layout on the furnishings at St Mary Rotherhithe and St Paul, Shadwell, but, despite a dramatic redecoration scheme at St Mary, left their Georgian characters generally intact. The most extensive work on an C18 church was done at St Anne, Limehouse, where *Philip Hardwick* carried out a remarkably faithful rebuilding after a disastrous fire in 1850. The young *Arthur Blomfield* worked on the C18-style refitting, returning nearly forty years later as Sir Arthur to remodel the E end, again with impressive sensitivity to what was by then acknowledged as a masterpiece in the Wren tradition.

The ROMAN CATHOLICS built fairly extensively, mainly to serve the Irish who came to work in the docks. Most popular, N and S of the river, was *Francis Tasker*, protégé and friend of Cardinal Manning, who took a particular interest in the urban poor. Most of Tasker's churches were Gothic and barn-like (see his St Peter and the Guardian Angels, Rotherhithe) but St Patrick, Wapping, of 1879 is Italianate in a simple, almost rustic 31 way, unusual at a period when most non-Gothic Catholic churches were floridly Baroque: its style may have been influenced by Manning's fondness for Italy and things Italian.

Few NONCONFORMIST CHURCHES survive, though several were established from the end of the C18. A handful of quite grand churches continued the classical tradition into the C19, such as the (demolished) Congregational Trinity Chapel provided by George Green in 1841 close to his seamen's home in the East India Dock Road. The most outstanding now is *T. E. Knightley*'s St Paul 30 Presbyterian Church in England, Millwall, of 1859, small but with p. a fashionably polychrome façade on North Italian Romanesque 97 lines and a roof that incorporates laminated timber beams, probably not used before in England for such a relatively narrow span.

PUBLIC BUILDINGS are mostly of only local significance. Rotherhithe acquired a group in the 1880s that dignified the Lower Road (now all gone), and Limehouse and Poplar have

slightly earlier town halls by the local *A. & C. Harston*; the latter,
34 designed with *Hills & Fletcher* as the district board of works, is an
elaborate but unsophisticated example of High Victorian eclecticism. The inventive Domestic Free Style adopted by the LCC in
the 1890s appears here and there. The best examples are the
entrances to the Blackwall Tunnel (*see* above) and the pretty little
Poplar Coroner's Court of 1910–11 – a rare survival of a building
type formerly more familiar in London.

Metropolitan POLICE ARCHITECTURE of the turn of the C19
also appears in the Free-Style guise developed by its architects
John Butler and his son, *John Dixon Butler*. Unique to the Thames
are the river police stations, built for a force founded in 1798 to
combat piracy and pilfering from ships. The Blackwall (Isle of
35 Dogs) and Wapping stations, by father and son respectively, have
striped façades in the manner of Norman Shaw's New Scotland
Yard (where Butler senior had worked for Shaw), oriels to take in
views up and downriver, and police barge entrances beneath. *J. D.
Butler*'s land-based police station of 1904 at North Woolwich is
of the same easily recognizable manner, but the same year he rose
to Baroque drama in Tooley Street, Bermondsey, to front a combined magistrates court and police station.

SCHOOLS are mostly plain. Earliest is the early C19 parish
school in the churchyard of St Paul, Shadwell, which looks like a
late Georgian terrace. Next in date are three schools designed for
the School Board for London soon after it started in 1870.
Harbinger School, Isle of Dogs, by *R. Phené Spiers*, 1872–3, and
the well-detailed Riverside School, Bermondsey, by *M. P. Manning*,
1874, belong to the first generation of schools built before the
Queen-Anne style was generally adopted by the Board as appropriate to its non-denominational stance. Both schools continue
the Gothic style commonly used pre-1870 but represent two types
of plan: Spiers's school is a classic three-decker, generously laid
out and intended for spacious, open sites such as those available
on the Isle of Dogs; Riverside School a narrow rectangle with
ground-floor playground tailored to a densely built-up site. The
Italianate Glengall School, Isle of Dogs, was begun by the Board's
own architect *E. R. Robson* in 1874, and is vaguely Italianate. The
two grammar schools, originally charitable foundations, are predictably larger and more elaborate. George Green's Grammar
School at Poplar of 1883–4, by *Sulman*, an architect well-known
for his Congregational churches, is in an old-fashioned North
German idiom. In contrast, only ten years later at St Olave's
Grammar School, Bermondsey, *Mountford* was already moving
from an up-to-date asymmetrical Free Style towards Edwardian
Baroque grandeur, cf. his contemporary public buildings nearby
in Battersea (Wandsworth: *see London 2: South*).

The building type special to Docklands and to ports throughout
Britain is the SEAMEN'S MISSION, connected not with local
communities but with the river and docks. It provided accommodation and facilities for seamen of every nationality including
those paid or laid off, and those who had married locally or
jumped ship. The missions had a strong religious or national bias.

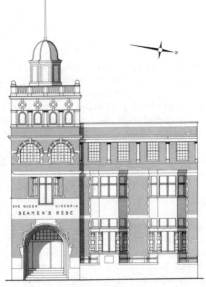

EAST ELEVATION OF SOUTH BLOCK

0   20 feet

0   6 metres

Scale for elevation

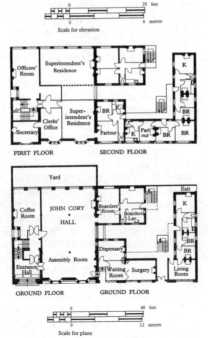

FIRST FLOOR   SECOND FLOOR

GROUND FLOOR   GROUND FLOOR

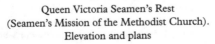

0   40 feet

0   12 metres

Scale for plans

Queen Victoria Seamen's Rest
(Seamen's Mission of the Methodist Church).
Elevation and plans

Among the first were those organized by the Rev. George Smith, a midshipman turned Baptist minister, one of the founders in 1818 of the Port of London Society for Promoting Religion among Merchant Seamen, forerunner of the British and Foreign Sailors' Society, who *c.* 1850 converted early C19 villas at Poplar and Limehouse: the Limehouse villa, used as a boys' sea-training establishment, still exists in Newell Street. A few missions were organized by individuals, such as the Congregationalist shipbuilder George Green, others by the churches of a particular nationality or denomination. Several of the missions were sited on the Commercial and East India Dock Roads, the natural route for sailors from Blackwall and the docks into the City. Most employed architectural devices to attract the passing sailor for his own good: on the East India Dock Road (Poplar) George Green's Sailors' Home of 1839–41 had a grand Greek Revival portico; the Methodist Queen Victoria Seamen's Rest (by *Gordon & Gunton*, 1901–2) an entrance tower and cupola; and the Missions to Seamen Institute by *Blomfield*, begun in 1892, a friendly, obviously English exterior. The Sailors' Palace by *Niven & Wigglesworth*, former headquarters of the British and Foreign Sailors' Society, is the most original, Art Nouveau in spirit, a welcoming gateway in form, and fluently carved with maritime symbols. Built in 1901, it was part of a major rebuilding programme by the society which swept away many earlier hostels. The missions continued on an even larger scale after the First World War with Limehouse's austere Empire Memorial Sailors' Hostel by *Daniel & Parnacott*, 1923–4, and The Flying Angel of 1934–6 by *Petch & Fernand*, crowned with a tower and a flashing beacon to distinguish it from the many other, less edifying sailors' lodging houses ranged along the Royal Victoria Dock. Inside, all the missions combined accommodation with churches or chapels, reading rooms, recreation rooms, offices and refreshment rooms.

FOREIGN CHURCHES had established communities in London as early as 1694–6, when the first Scandinavian church was built in Stepney (just beyond Docklands) by the sculptor of Danish birth, *C. G. Cibber*, for Danes and Norwegians involved in the timber trade. Carved figures from there are now in the Danish church in Regent's Park (*see London 3: North West*). When the timber trade moved chiefly to the Surrey Commercial Docks in the mid C19, most of the Scandinavian churches began to cluster round them in Rotherhithe, except for the Danish church which moved to Limehouse in 1873. The present buildings, mostly C20 replacements, still represent recognizable images of their respective countries, particularly the Norwegian church of St Olav with its tower based on that of Oslo Cathedral, and the Swedish and Danish missions, well crafted in the natural materials of 1950s and 60s Scandinavian architecture. The architects were of Scandinavian origin too: *John Seaton Dahl*, designer of St Olav in 1925–7, was the son of a Norwegian based in England; *Cyril Mardall*, architect of the Finnish church (1957–9), was born *Cyril Sjöström*; and the Swedish and the Danish churches were both designed by Scandinavians in cooperation with British architects. Scandinavians also built the

late C19 seamen's hostel close to the West India Docks and its
associated officers' house of 1902–3, in a charming amalgam by 36
Niven & Wigglesworth of late C17 English and Scandinavian
styles.

Building and rebuilding between the wars

Provision of PUBLIC HOUSING occurred mainly after the First
World War, when metropolitan and borough councils all over the
United Kingdom were required by the central government to
build homes for the families of the returning troops. Most of this
type of housing is found in the Isle of Dogs, where there was still
land available to build new estates. Remarkable in London-wide
terms is the LCC's Chapel House Estate for, though its layout is 40
of standard garden-suburb type, the elevations of its cottages and
cottage-flats are, unusually, modelled on early C19 London houses
rather than the rural types used for outer suburbs. Poplar Borough
Council's neighbouring estates, provided by a few years later, follow
the more conventional patterns.

A larger proportion of interwar public housing was built as a
result of SLUM CLEARANCE. Along Poplar High Street, in
Limehouse and in the centre of Wapping, jerry-built courts of
houses and the wrecked remains of C17 and C18 property were
swept away for flats. For the Wapping Estate of *c.* 1926 the LCC
again adapted early C19 London models, but the most distinctive
flats are those of the 1930s in the centre of Poplar. Here, the
socialist Poplar Borough Council took pride in demonstrating
what it could do for its residents, providing many large, stream- 41
lined blocks of flats, luxurious public baths designed by the 42,
Borough Architect *Harley Heckford*, and (just outside our area) a p.
new Town Hall by *Clifford Culpin*. The style chosen by the council 169
was the 1920s brick modernism of Holland.

PHILANTHROPIC HOUSING was less in evidence between the
wars, eclipsed by public housing. There are a few blocks of flats,
including those built by the Presbyterian Housing Association off
Poplar High Street (and continued after the war as part of the
Festival of Britain exhibition of architecture) and some in Millwall.
They differ from the council blocks only in detail and in general
are more conservative (the block in Millwall has delightful C18
details) and friendly in scale. In Bermondsey, the local philanthropist, Dr Alfred Salter, disappointed by the inhuman character
of tenement housing, promoted a rare private cottage scheme
designed by *Culpin & Bowers*.

Building and rebuilding 1945–68

Bombing during the Second World War devastated the docks and
much of the industry and housing round it. The Isle of Dogs, the
Royal Docks and the premises along the Thames at Silvertown
and North Woolwich were particularly badly affected. The chief
task was patching the damaged areas. Despite *The County of
London Plan* drawn up for the LCC by Forshaw and Abercrombie

in 1943, comprehensive replanning was undertaken only in Poplar where the Lansbury Estate (N of our area) was laid out as a model new community and formed the Festival of Britain Exhibition of Architecture in 1951. Forshaw and Abercrombie were especially conscious of the need to inject the claustrophobic East End with open space, both as a public amenity and to attract development. They proposed that the river from the Tower of London to Shadwell should be opened up, with a park on site of St Katharine Docks as a setting for the Tower and demolition of the riverside wall of warehouses for a treed riverside walk through Wapping. In fact only one small park was created from the churchyard of the bombed St John.

Many CHURCHES were damaged beyond repair and eventually demolished. Most of the rebuilding was on a modest scale, for example Holy Trinity, Rotherhithe, rebuilt as little more than a plain hall by *T. F. Ford* in 1959–60. Most ambitious is the new 44, Roman Catholic church in Bermondsey, designed by *Goodhart-* 46 *Rendel*, an imaginative reinterpretation of High Victorian architecture and one of the finest traditional post-war churches in London. While Most Holy Trinity represents the end of one long tradition, the excellent churches built by European architects for the seamen's missions of their respective countries (*see* above) 45 started something new. *Yorke Rosenberg & Mardall*'s Finnish mission of 1957–9 was in fact one of the first of a persistent type, in which a simple, separate bell-frame was the means of distinguishing an otherwise simple modern box as a church.

HOUSE-BUILDING began immediately after the war. Hundreds of prefabs were erected on empty PLA land N of the Royal Albert Dock and centred on Cyprus (they have now all gone). On the Isle of Dogs, flats and houses were built quickly in 1945–8 using the Orlit system, one of the many industrialized systems invented during and straight after the war to answer the shortage of housing, materials and labour. Rawalpindi House in Millwall (1947–8) was the first block of flats ever built using the system. Medium-rise slab blocks of flats in the Corbusian mould appeared straight after the war (1946–9) at the LCC's Osprey Estate, Rotherhithe, where *Yorke Rosenberg & Mardall* designed in the same spirit as Powell & Moya at Westminster Council's contemporary Churchill Gardens, Pimlico. Elsewhere, large housing schemes, usually mixed developments of high and lower blocks of flats and maisonettes combined with terraced houses, did not get underway until the late 1950s, 60s and 70s: a fairly early version can be seen in North Woolwich on East Ham Borough Council's 1960s Pier Estate. The GLC (which took over from the LCC in 1965) favoured a then more fashionable, tougher aesthetic of raw concrete and chunky forms. Several estates come out of this mould – the Samuda Estate, Cubitt Town; the Barkantine Estate, Millwall; and the Canada Estate, Rotherhithe – but the most extreme 48, expression of this harsh aesthetic is *Alison & Peter Smithson*'s pp. Robin Hood Gardens, Poplar, of 1966–72, in which the 174, Smithsons' theories of vertical urban living found a late outlet, 175 with a forbidding result.

MODERN DOCKLANDS

*The docks and river from the founding of the Port of London
Authority until the establishment of the LDDC 1909–81*

In 1900, with London increasingly threatened by competition
from the modernized parts of Antwerp, Rotterdam, Hamburg and
Amsterdam, a Royal Commission was set up to study the problem
of the surfeit of dock space, which was uneconomically dispersed
and of the wrong kind for modern shipping. The upriver London
and St Katharine Docks were served only by lighters and short-sea
shipping but their warehouses were in use for storage and display
of goods. The outcome of the Commission was the founding in
1909 of the Port of London Authority to administer the Thames
from Teddington to the sea. Any excess revenue it could collect
from shipping was to be invested in dock maintenance and
improvement. Between 1909 and 1939, the PLA enlarged some
entrances to the docks from the river, raised the level of others and
made deeper basins for the new generation of large vessels. In
1912 it also began the King George V Dock in the Royal Docks,
which was to be virtually the last dock within the existing system,
capable of taking the largest liners. The Authority rationalized the
West India and Millwall Docks with new cuttings, and constructed
new quays in the West India and Millwall and Royal Docks,
served by electric cranes. It also provided new warehouses, as well
as cold stores for meat imports, a growing trade. The fine compressor house at the Royal Albert Dock is typical of the handsome, red brick-clad but structurally innovative work of the PLA's
first decade. The attached warehouse has gone but that was
typically concrete-framed, as is the *Hennebique*-system transit shed
in the West India Docks, now used as the New Billingsgate
Market. Grain-handling was also mechanized from *c.* 1870, with
pneumatic grain elevators after 1890; one of them has been re-
erected at the Royal Victoria Dock, where only the most majestic
of four huge interwar and post-war flour mills still bears witness to
the scale of the grain-import and flour-milling trade.

New facilities were still being built along the river between the
wars. The Hay's Wharf Co. built innovative headquarters at
Bermondsey, designed by *Goodhart-Rendel*, in 1929. The Butler's 39
Wharf Co. built new warehouses, and further along the river in
Bermondsey two massive cold stores went up at Chamber's Wharf.
There was similar modernization in Wapping, at Gun Wharves
where the last parts were built in the 1930s, and at Metropolitan
Wharf. Further on in Ratcliffe, Free Trade Wharf was restructured
and extended using concrete. Activity continued post-war, when
bombed warehouses, such as those at Hay's Dock, were rebuilt.
Out at Newham, in Silvertown and North Woolwich, industry
developed on an even bigger scale despite extensive bomb damage, though the only post-war architecture of note is one of Tate
& Lyle's office buildings of 1946, still completely pre-war in style.

Though the Second World War had a devastating effect on the
docks – the Surreys and the Millwall Docks especially – they

swung back into action afterwards with increasingly mechanized handling methods. The first was the use of pallets and fork-lift trucks, introduced to the docks by the Americans during the war, followed by unit-loads. Such methods, and later on the de-casualization of the dock labour force, sowed the seeds for the decline of the docks in the LDDC area. They reduced the need for dockers and created the necessity for larger types of ware-houses where pallets and unit-loads could be stacked high. Even the great vaults of the London Docks became redundant after 1959, when wine began to be stored in tanks rather than casks. The main rebuilding activity was concentrated at the West India and Millwall Docks. The new warehouses built from 1959 were mostly huge sheds, many with structurally innovative tubular-steel frames designed by PLA engineers, all for fork lifts and mobile cranes. They rivalled the largest in the world, yet all except the very largest (designed in 1969 for the Olsen Line and now incor-porated in the London Arena) have gone. The Olsen Line was also responsible for the most memorable (but now demolished) dock building, offices and passenger terminal of 1966–9 designed by *Norman Foster* with engineer *Tony Hunt*, which formed one of the earliest and most widely publicized ventures into British High-Tech. Now the most prominent relics of this post-war period, re-employed as evocative landscape features, are the huge quay cranes made by *Stothert & Pitt*.

Containerization set the seal on the decline of London's docks and of many older docks throughout the world. It also affected the riverside where, at Bermondsey, Rotherhithe, Wapping and Limehouse, warehouses were gradually deserted, demolished, or taken over by squatters and artists (for their redevelopment *see* pp. 58–60). Small containers had been used from the late C19 in a minor way but they came into their own in the 1960s and 70s with international standardization on a large module. There were no deep berths for the huge container ships nor quays for handling and stacking. Container transport relied on roads not rail and none of the roads in Docklands then had the capacity for fleets of container lorries; nor was there space to marshal them. Tilbury, downriver in Essex, was expanded as a container port in the 1960s (following the Rochdale committee's report on British ports in 1963). Britain's first container port opened there in 1968, and by 1972 it was second only in Europe to Rotterdam, handling many times the capacity of the old docks. The downriver wharves con-tinued to flourish; in 1992 the Port of London remained Britain's biggest port and ranked eighth in Europe. The old docks started closing in 1965, when the already partly infilled East India Docks closed, quickly followed in 1968–70 by the St Katharine Docks, the London Docks, and the Surreys. The West India Docks and the Royal Docks continued with traditional traffic, but this declined rapidly. The PLA streamlined labour (the number of registered dockers was halved between 1969 and 1973) and sold property to make a profit, and attempted to find new uses for what remained. Two new schemes were tried in the West India Docks in the late 1970s: the conversion of the former workshops into industrial units supplemented by an industrial estate and the reuse of an early C20 warehouse into the New Billingsgate Fish Market. When the LDDC took over the docks in 1981 (*see* below) they continued this scale of development with *Terry Farrell & Partners'* transformation of a post-war warehouse into the stylish Limehouse Studios. The two PLA buildings survive; the TV studios were superseded by Canary Wharf four years after they were finished.

The planning of Docklands 1967–98

To the compilers of the 1971 edition of the Oxford English Dictionary 'dockland' or 'docklands' was an unrecognized term, though within a year the word, traced back to 1904, was sufficiently current to be included in the 1972 supplement. Adopted, originally by journalists, as a convenient way of referring to the districts round the docks whose common way of life was threatened by the closure or predicted closure of the docks, it soon became a universal part of planning and, later, marketing jargon.

Until the late 1960s, the docks had been a distinctive but integral part of the Port of London and of the industrial East End. The older docks closest to the City of London were introverted pockets of activity, hidden by high walls and unvisited except by those who worked or traded there; the later docks in Millwall and out in Newham were isolated by virtue of geography. It was the closure of the docks that made their physical importance public. The boroughs – Greenwich, Lewisham, Southwark and Tower Hamlets – in which they were situated and for which they had been so economically important suddenly found within their boundaries acres of derelict land and buildings which stretched E to the Royal Docks and S to the Royal Dockyards at Deptford, and also thousands of unemployed inhabitants occupying housing that was 80 to 90 per cent local-authority owned. Yet, although by 1970 three of the Port of London's six docks had closed, only then did the PLA and the GLC begin to see the need for a strategic plan to cope with the loss of jobs and the future of what became known as Docklands. And it was not only the docks that were problematic: all along the river in Tower Hamlets and in Southwark, industries and warehouses had been abandoned as new methods of handling goods and the change from river to road transport affected the riverside as thoroughly as the docks.

But actually developing a regeneration strategy for Docklands was a long drawn-out process, and putting any of the ideas into practice was frustrated by many different vested interests, by political struggles between the GLC, central government and the Boroughs and, most of all, by lack of money. The first plans were those drawn up by the PLA in 1970 for the future of the docks themselves. These were followed by a government-commissioned feasibility study, published in 1973, in which the engineers, Travers Morgan, made no fewer than eight alternative proposals of which that for a 'water city for the 21st century' probably had most long-term influence. In 1974 the Docklands Joint Committee, composed of representatives of the GLC and the boroughs, was set up to control planning, but it was not until 1976 that their Strategic Plan was published, with ideas for providing new employment, new public housing and amenities, and for opening up the dock areas and riverside with green spaces. By then most of the London Docks and the Surreys had been filled in with the intention of building-over, the former by the PLA who saw the land, near the City, as ripe for commercial exploitation, the latter by the Borough of Southwark. From 1976 the strategic plan was implemented patchily in Wapping and in the former Surrey Docks in Rotherhithe, under detailed local plans drawn up by Tower Hamlets and Southwark respectively.

It was the Conservative government, who came into power in 1979 along with a Conservative GLC, that revived an idea, first mooted in 1973 by the planner Barrie Sheldon: he had suggested that a development corporation should be set up to control the land that the PLA was eager to sell. The government's establishment of an Urban Development Corporation was a deliberate move to seize control from the boroughs by granting money directly to inner city regeneration rather than through local government. The LDDC was officially formed in 1981 under the Local Government and Planning Act of 1980, though the first Chief Executive, the irrepressible Reg Ward, was at the helm from 1980. Docklands was the first of two UDCs, the other being in Liverpool. What distinguished the LDDC was its size ($8\frac{1}{2}$ sq. m.), which far exceeded any subsequent British UDCs and even any similar organizations in the United States of America, where the concept had originated. Eventually the LDDC managed to acquire 1,756 acres of development land (plus 417 acres of water) through vesting orders and compulsory purchase from the major, and really very few, landholders – British Gas (Beckton), PLA (docks), British Rail (docks and railway land), CEGB and local authorities: these in 1981 had owned 80 per cent of the land within Docklands.

The new boundary followed fairly closely that scribed by Travers Morgan, leaving out Deptford (LB Lewisham) and Woolwich (LB Greenwich) but including for the first time the s bank between London and Tower Bridges and Beckton, where Newham had already begun draining and redeveloping derelict PLA land N of the Royal Albert Dock, as well as land destined in 1910 for a further dock which was never made. In addition part of a Beckton gasworks site further E became available. The boundary was drawn tightly round the older docks and the immediately adjacent derelict industrial land, cutting through historic parishes such as St Anne Limehouse, All Saints Poplar and St Mary Bermondsey along the line of major roads and railways.

As a UDC, with financial resources, development control and land-acquisition powers granted by government, the LDDC's brief was 'to secure permanent regeneration of the docklands area'. It was to do this by improving Docklands' image through programmes of physical works which created confidence; by bringing roads and transport networks up to the standards of the rest of London; and by bringing about improvements in the choice and quality of housing, employment and training. It was intended that the financial resources should be used as a lever rather than to fulfill all these aims directly and, at times, the LDDC seemed to be more an estate agent than anything else. True to its initial ideals, in the first few years the LDDC laid down few planning or design rules. Development Frameworks were published identifying development opportunities for each area. These were as much marketing brochures as design guidelines but were also used to consult on proposals locally and feed into the formal plan-making process being carried out by the Boroughs. In the late 1980s, a major reappraisal of aims took place. It was decided to give more emphasis to social regeneration (a Community Services department was set up and planning-gain deals encouraged). In 1994 the LDDC started to return its 'city districts' to local authority control, starting with Bermondsey, continuing in 1995 with Beckton, 1997 with Wapping, Limehouse, Surrey Docks and the Isle of Dogs and 1998 with the Royal Docks. On divesting it provided each area with a framework for regeneration, to be incorporated in the borough's own statutory planning document. By mid 1997 the population had increased from 39,400 to 81,231, jobs from 27,200 to 72,000, and businesses from 1,000 to 2,450. 21,615 new dwellings and 2.3 million square metres of new commercial buildings had been completed.

When the docks began to close in the late 1960s, there were no models for regeneration on Docklands' immense scale. Even as late as 1981, few developments involved existing industry and old settlements, or historic buildings together with great artificial stretches of water. The pioneers were mainly North American and on a small scale, for example the mixed redevelopment by a development corporation of Baltimore Inner Harbor from 1964, and the mid-1970s waterfront revival in Pittsburgh, where C19 houses and railway buildings were reused. Olympia & York, who proved so important within the Enterprise Zone, were really the only developers pre-Canary Wharf to take on cheap but derelict industrial land and exploit its advantages commercially, as they did in 1980–3 at Queen's Quay Terminal, Toronto, and, on a huge and successful scale at New York's riverfront Battery Park, where Pelli built the World Financial Center for them from 1982. Other comparable schemes are later, for instance SOM's Boston Harbor redevelopment, slightly earlier (1985–7) than Canary Wharf but similar in its heavy classicism. There are now dockland schemes throughout Europe; the largest and most successful in terms of infrastructure at Barcelona where the Old Port accommodated the 1988 Olympic Games. All over Britain docks, quaysides, canals and warehouses have been transformed since the mid 1980s, including Liverpool's Albert Dock, Newcastle's Quayside and the docks at Bristol and Gloucester, though even the biggest enterprise, the regeneration of Cardiff Bay begun in 1991, involves an area only 2 miles ($3\frac{1}{4}$ km) square.

In all these schemes water is exploited as an asset – a visual asset, a recreational asset and, because of these, also a marketing asset. Perhaps the LDDC's most important move was to rediscover

the exceptional value of Dockland's vast expanses of water. As a
result expensive infilling of the docks immediately came to an end
in 1981, and some docks were even reopened and new waterways
created.

Infrastructure

One of the LDDC's chief tasks was to provide the INFRASTRUC-
TURE on which development depended. This includes not only
the vital works, such as the provision of public transport and the
planning of networks of roads and pedestrian and cycle ways, but
also the remedial work designed to make the area attractive to
potential developers. The former has been criticized as too little,
too late or too expensive or all three, but the latter has been
almost universally praised.

In the first category comes PUBLIC TRANSPORT. The Docklands
Light Railway was conceived in the early stages of the LDDC as
a cheap alternative to the extension of the Jubilee Line through
Docklands to Thamesmead, a plan which had been shelved in
1980. It opened from Tower Gateway to the tip of the Isle of Dogs
in 1987. It was extended W to Bank in 1991 and E to Beckton in
1994. The first sections use existing viaduct or new ugly raised
track and the stations are perfunctory. The Beckton branch shares
the glamour of the new generation of stations in major cities as far
apart as Hong Kong and Bilbao, and has a series of elegant stations
assembled from a recognizable kit of parts designed by *ABK*. The
54 interchange between West India Quay and Poplar stations looks
arresting by night and day and, like the other stations, is as transparent as possible to improve security. Modelled on light railways
in America (e.g. Fort Lauderdale), it quickly outgrew its customers
after the scale of development on the Isle of Dogs tripled with the
arrival of Olympia & York at Canary Wharf. It was Olympia &
York who demanded the extension of the DLR to Bank as a condition of their development. The Jubilee Line Extension also
belongs to the new generation of railways: the stations have been
designed under strong direction from the commissioning architect, *Roland Paoletti*, by leading designers with a penchant for
technology. They are all adapted for their sites: *Sir Norman Foster
& Partners'* Canary Wharf bubbles are designed to be seen from
above and to be discreet at ground level. Conversely, *Troughton
McAslan's* Canning Town station dramatically advertises a major
transport interchange.

ROADS have been a subject of great debate and most hotly
debated has been the Limehouse Link, which goes under Limehouse
on its way on to the Isle of Dogs and out to the Royal Docks by
56 taking a very expensive route beneath the Limehouse Basin. Its
importance for *The Buildings of England* rests in the gigantic
portals, Postmodern versions of, say, 1930s cinema façades, which
loom huge in the urban scene. There is nothing else so boldly
architectural in British road engineering of the 1980s.

Whereas new arterial roads have made a brutal impact, the new
pedestrian BRIDGES commissioned by the LDDC to complete

the river walk and span the docks are subtle pieces of engineering, dramatic in their structural form and effective as works of art. The new interest in expressive bridges was probably inspired by the work of the Spanish engineer, *Calatrava*. Although Calatrava's design for the East London River Crossing was rejected in the 1980s, bridge design has been enthusiastically developed by younger architects and engineers skilled in High-Tech architecture, such as *Lifschutz Davidson* (at the Royal Victoria Dock), *Chris Wilkinson* with *Jan Bobrowski* and *Future Systems* with *Anthony Hunt Associates* 1, 53, (both at the West India Docks), *YRM/Anthony Hunt & Associates* 87 (at Limehouse) and *Nicholas Lacey* with *Whitby & Bird* (at St Saviour's Dock, Bermondsey).

A purely practical preparation of potential sites has been land drainage. Here again, a necessity has been turned into an architectural advantage by the employment of architects to design the superstructures of PUMPING STATIONS. The contrast between the 1970s pumping station at Gallions Roundabout in the Royal Docks and those commissioned by the LDDC is striking. *John* 57 *Outram*'s primitive temple is a wonderful surprise in a back street on the Isle of Dogs; *Richard Rogers Partnership*'s colourful cylinders 58 make a sculptural incident in the open spaces of the Royal Docks.

Landscape and Public Art

Much of the other infrastructure is coincidental with LANDSCAP-ING, which gives neighbourhoods their distinctive characters, ties each one together physically and visually, and gives quality and permanence to the docks themselves. The style is quite conservative, though the range of landscape architects employed has been wide: there is none of the romantic cultivated dereliction popular in Germany where substantial ruins and relics are interwoven in natural landscapes intended as permanent reminders of the industrial past, neither is there any North American Postmodern jokiness with overscaled or brightly coloured features to symbolize or entertain.

Much of the virtue is in the detail, the careful treatment where water and land meet, both along the river and round the docks, as in the paving and street furniture of the Royal Docks, for example round the W Warehouse, or in the draw docks on the Isle of Dogs. Once the decision had been made to retain the water in the docks, the landscape architects orchestrated remaining buildings, cranes 5 and new hard landscaping into impressive compositions, especially round the Royal Docks. In the Surrey and the London Docks what remains of the docks has been rediscovered (often at great expense) and incorporated in the landscape as ecological park and townscape, respectively, thereby turning areas fast losing discernable character into something unique. At Beckton a district park has been used to unite a disparate and undistinguished collection of suburban developments.

One problem – that of giving Londoners access to their river – has recurred over many decades, especially since the riverside was so densely built up with warehouses, wharves and industry in the

C19. The largest riverside park was made in 1902 in place of the slums of Shadwell and Ratcliffe, but after that there was only the small Lyle Park made in 1924 by the borough of West Ham at Silvertown. In 1944, Abercrombie made suggestions about access in his *Greater London Plan*, and in 1976 *Shepheard Epstein & Hunter* endeavoured to provide pockets of public space in their masterplan for Wapping. A 180 m. long Thames path, not always closely following the river, has been established along most of the river's length between Kemble, Glos, and the the Thames Barrier. In Docklands, despite the LDDC's efforts to keep a path open by agreement with private developers and even to continue it over intervening docks and inlets by means of excellent new bridges (*see* Infrastructure above), in many places the right of way is now blocked and public access barred. This is especially frustrating for pedestrians, cyclists and those in search of a view along densely built-up stretches of riverside such as Wapping and Limehouse. Much of the river path is broad and elegant: in Wapping at the Carron and Continental Wharf and by Shadwell Basin where it swells into a circular viewing deck; on the Isle of Dogs at Burrell's and Maconochie's Wharves, whose embankments have been beautifully paved (by *Livingston McIntosh Associates*); and in Newham where the most ambitious landscape scheme of all, a park to link the Royal Docks with the river and Thames Barrier, has been begun in 1997. The Thames Barrier Park (Silvertown) by *Groupe Signes* with *Patel & Taylor* is very different in character from back-to-nature ecological parks created in the Surrey Docks and on the Leamouth peninsula, and instead has the strongly layered geometry and symbolism of form of its Parisian counterparts, especially Groupe Signes' Parc Citroën and Tschumi's Parc de la Villette.

68   Only one outstanding landscape has been commissioned by a private developer: *Hanna Olins*'s setting for the architecture of Canary Wharf is as formal and as Beaux-Arts inspired as the buildings, and like them impresses not by originality but by the quality of the materials and the street furniture, designed by *SOM*, and the art integrated as railings, ventilation shafts and fountains.

PUBLIC ART has also been a major contribution of the LDDC, both directly and by persuading developers to provide it. The LDDC's work can be seen on a huge scale providing drama or focus on roundabouts in the East India Docks and Newham, see *Allen Jones*'s Aerobic figure on the Leamouth Roundabout, or in the landscape, as in Rotherhithe where *Philip Bews*'s Deal Porters are silhouetted against Canada Dock. Sculpture is used in conjunction with water in West India Dock (by *William Pye* and *Wendy Taylor*) and to punctuate pedestrian routes (at Butler's Wharf in Southwark). It can be as popular and excellent as *Brian*
55 *Yale*'s screen at Prince Regent Station in the Royal Docks, or as sophisticated as *Richard Wentworth*'s Globe near Westferry Circus.
59 The best figurative work is also on the Isle of Dogs, where *André Wallace*'s enigmatic couples row through Harbour Exchange at the mercy of the Wind of Change.

Conservation and reuse of historic buildings 1968–97

CONSERVATION of what remained of the docks and riverside industry was not something high on the agenda in the 1970s. The dock and riverside warehouses, granaries and mills, as well as the dock basins and their associated structures, seemed then to have outgrown their use and be the barrier to redevelopment. Second World War bombing had already destroyed or damaged a large number of warehouses original to the docks, including most of those along the North Quay of the West India Docks and the E half of the St Katharine Docks. The warehouses that remained tended to be smoke-grimed, shabby and patched, several of the best receiving unsuitable modern windows. Nevertheless, several important groups of warehouses survived the closure of docks, including *D. A. Alexander*'s magnificent North Stacks and South Stacks and Pennington Street sheds in the London Docks and some of Hardwick's warehouses round St Katharine Docks, only to be demolished for redevelopment in the 1970s. Unfortunately, though authors such as John Pudney were recording what survived just before it vanished and a London Docklands History Survey was founded in 1979 with support from, among others, the GLC and the Museum of London, a special statutory Listing of dockland buildings in 1982 came too late to protect many important buildings.

There were proposals too during the 1970s for several riverside sites as their warehouses closed, though little was done until the 1980s. One of the most comprehensive redevelopments was on the S bank between London Bridge and Tower Bridge, where a single property company demolished most of the warehouses and saved only a token few. There were other extensive losses at Free Trade Wharf, Ratcliffe, threatened with redevelopment in 1977 by the City of London Polytechnic. In the end, the oldest group of warehouses was retained in the midst of a massive residential development.

Many sites offered the potential for interesting MIXED DEVEL-OPMENT, with converted warehouses and industrial buildings interwoven with new build. The first development of this kind and surprisingly early for its date was St Katharine Docks, where the GLC's brief on selling the dock to Taylor Woodrow specified a mix of offices, council and private flats, with a hotel and leisure facilities. Hardwick's remaining warehouses were unnecessarily sacrificed for some terrible architecture, but the mix of uses was provided and works well. Similar mixed development might have come into gradual life within the West India Docks (*see* the previous and next section). The model of this type of redevelopment, perhaps for the whole country, has been the remodelling of what was mainly Courage Brewery and Butler's Wharf property E of 21 Tower Bridge in Bermondsey. Here two developers, the Jacob's Island Co. and Conran Roche, worked side by side during the early 1980s, exploiting the attractions of the warehouses with clever and sensitive conversion, and filling the gaps with exciting Modern and Postmodern buildings. Some architecturally less important

warehouses have been quite dramatically transformed, for example
the post-1945 warehouse converted by *Conran Roche* into the white
66 geometry of the Design Museum, no doubt under the influence of
Farrell's Limehouse Studios (dem.) q.v., in the West India Docks.
Conran Roche tried to repeat the successful formula N of the river
in Wapping at New Crane Wharf in the late 1980s but work was
halted early by the recession. The recipe of flats and offices com-
23 bined with shops has been used in a more limited way at Hay's
17, Galleria, Bermondsey, and at Free Trade Wharf, Ratcliffe. The
67 rehabilitation of one of the most historically important industrial
26, complexes in Docklands, Burrell's Wharf at the tip of the Isle of
83 Dogs, began as a mixed development with flats, health club and
offices, but was completed as housing from 1992 after the original
developers, Kentish Homes, went into receivership. The main
lines of this imaginative scheme survive: well-converted and
reconstructed buildings of what began in 1836 as an iron and shipbuilding works, combined with monumental new blocks of flats
by *Jestico & Whiles*.

The majority of the conversions of warehouses, granaries and
mills has been for RESIDENTIAL USE. The trend began in the
1960s with the colonization of some of the empty riverside and
dock warehouses by artists, who seized upon them as studios but
who also frequently turned them into unofficial homes as well. A
little colony of artists, craftsmen and actors established themselves
in Rotherhithe village, where from 1974 the Industrial Buildings
Preservation Trust turned Hope (Sufferance) Wharf into work-
spaces and *Nicholas Lacey* made a flat over workshops at Thames
Tunnel Wharf. Where artists go (Francis Bacon had lived in
Limehouse and caroused on the Isle of Dogs during the 1950s),
the more conventional follow, as in New York where the factories
of SoHo were turned post-war into studios and then into fashionable 'lofts'. The tide has now turned so far that in London companies have specialized since the recession of *c.* 1990 in converting
redundant industrial and even office buildings directly into 'loft'
4 apartments. But that is to leap ahead. Oliver's Wharf, Wapping,
was perhaps the first warehouse in Docklands to be converted to
flats for sale in 1970-2 by a young architectural practice, *Goddard
& Manton*. Though change of use was possible here because the
warehouse lay immediately adjacent to existing residential property
on Wapping Pier Head, in general conversion from industrial use
to residential property was frustrated by zoning policies which
sought to retain industrial areas in industrial use. For instance,
another 1970s scheme, the remodelling of a row of warehouses in
Narrow Street, Limehouse, by the designer Rae Hoffenberg, was
delayed for years. It was not until the LDDC took planning
control in 1981 that changes of use became generally acceptable,
facilitating the mixed developments described above and, latterly,
a plethora of flats.

Pre-war warehouses, granaries and mills present several problems
for those converting them: deep plans, small fixed windows and
solid timber loading doors make it difficult to provide enough
light and access, while, in some warehouses, exceptionally low

storey-heights necessitate radical internal reconstruction. *Hunt Thompson Associates* in their pre-LDDC period conversion (1980–3) of Thames Tunnel Mills, Rotherhithe, overcame some 2 difficulties by creating a glass-roofed lightwell or atrium lined with balconies to individual flats. In the largest buildings, such as the Globe Wharf (Rotherhithe) conversion projected in 1996 by *PRP Architects*, more than one atrium or internal courtyard is necessary. Such atriums, though hidden from the street, can have a dramatic effect on the silhouette: at *Terry Farrell & Partners'* Miller's Wharf (Wapping) of the mid 1980s, blue-painted steelwork and glass bursts through the roof. Exteriors have sometimes been heavily remodelled to provide light, access and more accommodation, as at Vogan's Mill, Bermondsey, where *Michael Squire* 64 *Associates* made a crisp modern insertion, including a tower, between C19 blocks. In other attempts to increase accommodation, rooflines have been spoilt with clumsy additional storeys, most obviously on the S bank at Hay's Galleria and Butler's Wharf, Bermondsey. The row of successful small-scale conversions, started in 1976 by *Rae Hoffenberg* with *Berman & Guedes* in Narrow Street, Limehouse, combines frankly modern insertions with the imaginative but conservative treatment of new upper storeys. In some of the most successful conversions, fixed small-paned windows of timber or cast-iron have been replaced by similar but opening versions, e.g. at Miller's Wharf and *PRP's* Prusom's Island, Wapping. In loading bays, doors have generally been replaced by long windows, and the hinged loading platforms retained or reproduced, sometimes to form balconies. The retention of other external features, such as hoists and wall-cranes (e.g. at Butler's Wharf) has been sporadic.

Radical reconstruction has been the order of the day in most changes to domestic use. Only occasionally, as at New Concordia 1 Wharf, has much of the structure been retained: often, as at Butler's 3,21 Wharf, an entirely new concrete shell or at least floors have been built inside, with structural elements, such as timber beams and cast-iron columns, redeployed to give a marketable warehouse feel. The *Gwilts'* West India Dock warehouses have perhaps 19 proved the most intractable, due to sensitivity to their historic importance (they are Grade-I Listed), their huge scale and floor areas, and in the case of No. 2 Warehouse their very shallow floor-to-ceiling heights. Conservatively restored in 1984–5 by *Feilden & Mawson*, they are in 1997 subject to a proposal to create a mixed development including 'loft' spaces on the upper floors. They will also provide a home for the long-awaited Museum of Docklands. Whether such huge buildings are suitable for domestic use is a vexed question. They seem to suggest a dramatic and romantic treatment and a public use, as can be seen in the 1860s warehouses of the Old Port of Marseilles, converted in the 1990s. A rare example of this romantic style can be found in Limehouse, where Sun Wharf was transformed into a theatrical home for the film director David Lean by *Scott, Brownrigg & Turner* in 1983–5. One of the most unattractive aspects of most warehouse conversions has been the provision of carparking.

Now, too often warehouses present to the street gaping vehicle entrances and glimpses of cars within a basement or ground floor entirely devoted to secure parking.

Fortunately some warehouses and industrial buildings have been converted for public or commercial use and so are still acces-
24 sible. The Wapping sports centre created in 1977–80 by *Shepheard Epstein & Hunter* from part of the Western Dock of London Docks, bounded by an original dock wall, was pioneering. Also within the former Western Dock is one the most remarkable build-
18 ings to have been saved: *Alexander*'s former Tobacco Warehouse
pp. was the only survivor of the range of warehouses that stood along
200 the N quay. The model for its conversion was the GLC's transfor-
⁻¹ mation of Covent Garden Market into a shopping centre *c.* 1980, but Tobacco Dock still stands empty, waiting for a tourist tide to flow E from St Katharine Docks or for regular shoppers from an
25 enlarged and transformed residential area. In the Royal Victoria Dock the fine W Warehouse has been given an imaginative set-ting, and the massive K-R warehouses are intended to be public spaces in connection with the exhibition centre planned for this side of the dock. In the Royal Albert Dock the compressor house of a PLA former cold store has been restored as a visitor's centre for the adjacent business park. Functioning dock structures have been carefully conserved or at least mothballed, particularly the quay walls, cranes, locks and bridges, some in a working con-dition, others, such as hydraulic pumping and impounding stations, for new uses. Two structures have special educational value: one the accumulator tower of the 1860s pumping station at Limehouse Basin, where occasionally visitors can climb up inside the tower to inspect the works and get a fine view; and the remains of the huge slipway next to Burrell's Wharf, Isle of Dogs, from which the *SS Great Eastern* was launched in 1859. There are also open-air displays of hydraulic equipment, e.g. at the Surrey Docks (for which and much else, credit is due to Edward Sargent, the LDDC's first conservation officer).

Other conservation projects have significance for the local com-munities. Among churches, much rebuilding was done to repair bomb-damage in the 1940s and 50s, conservatively at St Peter,
14 Wapping, and more drastically at All Saints, Poplar, where the interior was entirely reconstructed. Regeneration since 1981 has involved a large number of projects, some funded or assisted by the LDDC, some in part privately developed or funded. The
8 LDDC has sponsored improvements to St George-in-the-East,
7,13 St Anne, Limehouse, and St Paul, Shadwell, which all attract
30 notice along one of the main routes into Docklands. St Paul Presbyterian Church in England, long out of use as a church, has been exceptionally well restored as The Space arts centre, and
6 St Matthias, Poplar, as a community centre. Both charity schools
11 in Wapping have been restored, Raine's School by the GLC *c.* 1985, St John's School as houses by *Dransfield Design*, 1994–5. In fact most non-industrial historic buildings have been saved by private developers through conversion to houses or blocks of flats which range in size from the small Church Institute next to St

Anne, Limehouse, to the massive former seamen's mission (now 37 The Mission) on the East India Dock Road. In many cases, LDDC intervention has rescued buildings, such as the K–R warehouse in the Royal Docks, that had lain empty and abandoned for years.

New commercial development 1967–97

Commercial and industrial redevelopment was meant to be the lynchpin of regeneration. In fact it started very slowly and took until the mid 1980s, following the aggressive outward-marketing policies of the LDDC, to gather any pace. Canary Wharf, now 51 the most potent image of Docklands for the whole world, was not even begun until 1987.

All the efforts of the boroughs, the GLC and the PLA to stimulate commercial activity throughout the 1970s brought very few results. The most successful venture was the regeneration of St Katharine Docks by Taylor Woodrow from 1969, which benefited from its position on the fringes of the City. Though the N part of the infilled London Docks was set aside for industry, only the newspaper magnate Rupert Murdoch seized the advantage of cheap industrial land close to the City, and set up his new technology on a site away from Fleet Street in the so-called Fortress Wapping in 1976. In Rotherhithe, where Southwark Borough had infilled the Surrey Docks with the aim of attracting new industry, an unsuccessful scheme was launched to start an American-style trade mart as the focus of further development. The PLA had a modicum of success in re-using its redundant property within the West India Docks (see p. 50 above).

The LDDC did not start by attracting investment on the scale of Canary Wharf. The initial development model was the conventional New Town, the sort of thing already tried, though on a greenfield site, by the GLC at Thamesmead (Greenwich) in the 1960s. The small industrial estates of starter units, cheaply built for rent, in Poplar, Newham and along Millharbour on the Isle of Dogs show the original scale. They slotted into existing suburban settings rather than set the tone for a completely new environment. The much-loved Heron Quays by *Nicholas Lacey, Jobst &* 51 *Hyett*, 1981–9, was a model that many thought Docklands should pursue, that of a small-scale mixed-development closely related to the water. Efforts were concentrated on the Isle of Dogs, where the problems of attracting industry and reviving local communities seemed as intractable in 1987 as they do in the Royal Docks ten years later. But the establishment there of the Enterprise Zone in 1982, modelled on an idea for experimental freedom from planning, published by Paul Barker, Peter Hall and Cedric Price in the *New Soc.*, 1969, gingered up development so successfully that a new generation of larger buildings was spawned.

Then, in 1986, the Big Bang occurred: this deregulation of the trading of stock and shares meant that most dealing could be done from offices via computer, rather than face-to-face: just in advance of it, there was an explosion in demand for office buildings large enough for the huge dealing floors suddenly necessary. The Americans saw that Docklands had what the City of London lacked – space – and Canary Wharf was born in 1985.

51–3, 68– 71 CANARY WHARF, on site by 1987, changed the face of Docklands for several reasons. It decisively shifted the focus of Docklands from light industry to the burgeoning financial sector, creating a need to attract highly skilled white-collar workers from outside the area and initially relegating most local people to support jobs. In turn this contributed to the demand for new housing of a more luxurious type than low-cost family houses. Perhaps most importantly it brought dramatic changes to the infrastructure: the developers were so important to the government and the LDDC that they could demand, and get, the extension of the Jubilee Line. Above all, the new development provided the landmark by which Canary Wharf and the whole of Docklands is recognized and marketed.

Architecturally Canary Wharf had a huge impact on London. Broadgate, the City of London development begun, like the proposals for Canary Wharf, in 1985, by the developers Rosehaugh Stanhope, can be claimed as a rival in introducing to Britain the American pattern of commercial development, in which the developer provides the public realm and its works of art, often at the expense of controlling access. But the first phase of Broadgate (1985–91) was relatively intimate and sensitive. Canary Wharf introduced the British to the speed and efficiency of American fast-track construction on a huge scale, and to the size, eclecticism and luxury of North American Postmodern commercial architec- 69, 71 ture and landscape. It includes work by the famous *Skidmore Owings & Merrill*, by the Chinese-American *I. M. Pei* and by the Argentinian-American *Cesar Pelli*, who designed the single gleaming skyscraper, an inescapable reminder of Canary Wharf all over London. This tower set its own records: it was the first skyscraper in Britain and at 800 ft (244 metres) the tallest in Europe when completed in 1991. Olympia & York changed expectations not only in Docklands but also in the City of London, especially at the second phase of the Broadgate development (1990–2) and on the *Daily Telegraph* site in Fleet Street (1988–91), where *SOM* and *Kohn Pederson Fox* were also employed. Pelli's tower stimulated competition from the City of London, leading to *Sir Norman Foster*'s proposal for a 1,076 ft (328 metre) rival tower in 1996. The latest post-recession, post-Olympia & York phases of Canary Wharf promise to be more global and yet more diverse in character, with so-called signature buildings commissioned from architectural stars such as *Sir Norman Foster* and the French *Philippe Starck*. The same trend is evident in every major city worldwide, including the City of London (for all this City activity *see London 1: The City of London*).

There is no office building on the scale of Canary Wharf in the rest of Docklands – indeed when it was conceived in 1985 Canary 59 Wharf was the largest development in Europe. Harbour Exchange, begun in the Enterprise Zone in 1986, and Thomas More Square, Wapping, 1988–90, close to the City, both show the influence of North American office development but nothing of its lavishness.

And neither are there any exciting small office developments fitted amongst the buildings in Wapping or Limehouse, except for No. 2 Pennington Street, close to Fortress Wapping, which dis- 73 plays layers of Postmodern clichés, some of them (like the wavy glass wall) invented by the architect *Rick Mather* himself for other buildings. Nor are there any interesting retail ventures, except for the conservation projects at Hay's Galleria and Tobacco Dock, already mentioned. The demands of the new generation of financial traders for information technology has stimulated a new building type, the telecommunications centre, a blank-faced box that houses more equipment than people. Both the *Richard Rogers* 75 *Partnership*'s for Reuters and *YRM* for KDD have managed to turn this unpromising type into two of the best and most dramatic buildings in Docklands. They stand at Blackwall alongside former *Financial Times* printing works that *Nicholas Grimshaw & Partners* 72 built in the spirit of the most famous printing works of the C20, the transparent boxes designed by Sir Owen Williams for the *Daily Express*. Many newspapers followed Rupert Murdoch's 1970s lead in relocating from Fleet Street: their huge printing works are without exception blots on the landscape.

Housing and public amenities 1967–97

In the 1970s the building of new HOUSING was restricted to small-scale schemes of public and social housing, which, in reaction to the huge post-war estates, was designed on a friendly scale, with pedestrian routes and private gardens. On the Isle of Dogs, Tower Hamlets Borough Council had just completed the large council projects begun after the war. The council and a number of housing associations took advantage of the failing industries and cheap land prices along the riverside of Cubitt Town, Isle of Dogs, to build social housing, including a particularly good scheme of 1979–83 by *Levitt Bernstein* for Circle 33. *Shepheard Epstein & Hunter*'s housing for Tower Hamlets in Wapping, built over the London Eastern Dock, is singularly well laid-out. One private house-builder, Michael Barraclough, with architects *Stout* 49 *& Litchfield*, also took advantage of this depressed period to instigate the building of a group of houses for himself and other like-minded people. He was able to acquire a site with a view of Greenwich Hospital, as well as timbers, slates and other handsome materials from warehouses in the process of being demolished.

The advent of the Conservative government in 1979 and its instrument the LDDC in 1981 brought a change in policy from publicly financed to private housing. In 1981, 80 to 90 per cent of housing within Docklands was in public ownership: in 1997 the proportion (43 per cent in owner occupation) was closer to the Great London average. The operation of the market soon took effect. Riverside sites, especially near the City in Wapping and Bermondsey, became desirable for warehouse conversions and new speculative housing. In Rotherhithe and on the Isle of Dogs, further away from the City and from good public transport, volume house-builders began to build lower-cost flats and houses.

INDIVIDUAL DEVELOPERS have strongly influenced the types of housing built. One of the most enlightened was Roy Sandhu who commissioned *Ian Ritchie Architects* to design a small, urbane scheme on a derelict site in Limehouse. Among larger developers, most innovative was Kentish Homes, after Keith and Kay Preston took over in 1985. They concentrated on East London, picking young, adventurous architects' practices – *CZWG* at Cascades and *Jestico & Whiles* at Burrell's Wharf – and using American methods of fast-track construction and pre-completion marketing. Unfortunately the firm crashed in the recession, leaving Burrell's Wharf incomplete. Of the volume house-builders, Regalian were among the first to employ named architects for initial designs, beginning with *Holder Mathias Alcock* at Free Trade Wharf, and most recently (1997) using *Chassay Architects* at Premier Place on the Isle of Dogs. Other developers have also realized the marketing value of architect-designed homes, especially to overseas buyers. Ballymore commissioned *CZWG c.* 1996 to design two theatrical schemes, Dundee Wharf and Millennium Wharf, which, with Cascades, will belong to a succession of dramatic landmarks along the Thames close to Canary Wharf. *Lifschutz Davidson*, who refitted the nearby Oxo Tower, have provided the design for a butterfly-roofed tower on a prominent Berkeley Homes site near the Design Museum in Bermondsey. Overseas developers have employed architects of their own nationalities to initiate schemes – the well-respected *Kjaer & Richter* for the Danish ISLEF at Greenland Dock and Lawrence Wharf, Rotherhithe; and *ED Architects* for the Dutch VOM at London Yard, Isle of Dogs.

NEW HOUSING on cleared sites close to the docks includes a handful of well-designed schemes from the mid 1980s. Three were widely published: Shadwell Basin housing by *MacCormac Jamieson Prichard & Wright*; and, on the Isle of Dogs, Compass Point by *Jeremy Dixon* with *BDP* and Cascades by *CZWG*. All are Postmodern in spirit but distinct in their interpretations. The first two conform closely to the manner and principles used by MacCormac and by Dixon elsewhere, creating a strong sense of place and drawing on historical, and especially London, precedent. Cascades, like CZWG's contemporary Circle and China Wharf in Bermondsey, is more obviously Postmodern – playful with geometry, symbols (see the mast motifs on the Circle, the boat-balcony at China Wharf), and colour. Cascades has proved to be the most influential of the three within Docklands, establishing a taste for landmark blocks that read dramatically in the wide watery landscape and for luxury flats. Ironically, the wedge-like Cascades, with its stepped fall of balconies and conservatories and its polychromy, seems to have been inspired by that archetype of social housing, Tom Collins House on Ralph Erskine's Byker Wall, Newcastle upon Tyne, completed in 1981.

A handful of other schemes from the second half of the 1980s stand out from the mass of housing. Four different groups in Greenland Dock show four distinctive approaches: *Richard Reid*'s Edwardian-influenced housing, grouped to make an impact across the expanse of water; *Price & Cullen*'s artfully massed but fussy

Swedish Quays; *Kjaer & Richter*'s Greenland Passage, which makes a monumental gateway to the dock; and *Shepheard Epstein & Hunter*'s The Lakes, the only scheme in Docklands except for 84 Heron Quays (*see* above) to fully integrate water and buildings. On the Isle of Dogs, *Alan Turner & Associates*' Cumberland Mills 81 is notable for its ingenious planning, *Michael Squire Associates*' The Anchorage for its stylish elevations. Most unusual of all is Maconochie's Wharf, a self-build scheme of unusual sophistication, 50 for which the house designs were provided by *Stout & Litchfield*.

Many of the schemes described above were done under 'design and build' contracts, in which the architect provides the design but the project is managed by the house-builder who has control over any changes. This often proved detrimental to the quality of construction and detailing, resulting in embarrassment for the architects and distress to lovers of architecture. In general, even the most exciting exteriors conceal dull plans and small and boxy rooms. The developers that use external styling as a lure, usually play safe, and even tasteless, inside. Many developments, starting in the 1980s with, for example, the Circle and Burrell's Wharf, include central amenities such as health clubs and swimming pools and, of course, carparking. Following the recession, such things have become commonplace in London, but it was probably Docklands that stimulated the revival of the luxury flat.

Among more average speculative developments of the 1980s, two themes predominate: the warehouse as a model for flats; and the narrow-fronted, gabled brick house of Dutch or Scandinavian origin, obviously chosen because of its canalside associations. The latter appears in its most attractive manifestation along the Thames as part of *Jeremy Dixon*'s Compass Point; along the canal in the former Western Dock of the London Docks by *Boyer Design* 76 *Group*; in Arts and Crafts fashion at *Richard Reid*'s Finland Quay, Greenland Dock; and, most insistently in the Dutch development, London Yard, Isle of Dogs. The warehouse theme is ubiquitous and seems to be the last refuge of the unimaginative. It is best where the relationship with the original is loose, as at *PRP*'s Towerside or, also in Wapping, at *Goddard Manton*'s President's Quay. There is a distinctly Postmodern trend evident, for example in *BUJ*'s Timber Wharves village on the Isle of Dogs and in Beckton N of Tollgate Road, and that is the organization of standard spec 86 housing into monumental compositions, under the influence of architects such as Rob Krier. In Beckton, the inspiration seems to be a selection of standard London housing types – the mansion block, the paired villa, the terraced cottage – but these are organized in axial avenues, crescents and gardens, emphasized by obelisks and columns, layouts that at least give some urbanity and form to an otherwise amorphous suburb.

The recession brought house-building in Docklands to a standstill by 1990. It soon began again *c.* 1992, encouraged by the fall in land prices, the reviving taste for inner-city living and by overseas investment. Dundee Wharf, Limehouse, for instance, aims at a much more affluent market than earlier blocks, and includes some huge flats attractive to overseas buyers used to buying by cubic foot or metre. The glut of office space has been turned to advantage: office blocks, such as Baltic Quay, Greenland Dock, never occupied as offices, have been turned into apartments and land half-developed with offices, such as Meridian Gate, Marsh Wall, Isle of Dogs, filled with blocks of flats. Planned developments, such as West India Quay opposite Canary Wharf, are heavily biased towards housing, and the last available sites in Docklands are being snapped up, not by office-builders, but by companies such as Barratt's, Wimpey and Berkeley Homes. *Barratt* have dominated a long stretch of the riverside in Rotherhithe since 1990. Their approach is distinctive: quasi-historical elevations screen standard flats. The ersatz Regency of Sovereign View and the fake Edwardian of Prince's Riverside must, in due course, become period-pieces of speculative style, on a par with the most grandiose examples of by-pass variegated.

The predominance of housing throughout Docklands, unleavened by shops, offices and amusements, threatens to turn the area into a huge residential suburb – a densely built-up one, in places grittily urban in appearance, but nevertheless a dormitory for the affluent rather than the vital part of London envisaged by architects and planners. Perhaps growth will be organic and the demand for shops, restaurants, libraries and theatres will eventually make an impact on these quiet acres of housing. Or may be it will be the acres of park for recreation and water for sport that will prove the main attraction, just as in Milton Keynes and the other third generation New Towns.

New SOCIAL HOUSING has been almost squeezed out by the market, though from the mid 1980s the LDDC funded many rehabilitation schemes, such as energy-efficient improvements to the Barleymow estate, Limehouse, as part of their more socially and environmentally aware policies. In Newham there are three notable schemes. The earliest one (1981–3) by *Neylan & Ungless* in Savage Gardens, Beckton, gave a sense of place to what was then desolate derelict land. Winsor Park, Beckton, provided under a special agreement of 1987 between Newham and the LDDC, is a big estate unified by means of a strong design by *Chris Wilkinson Architects*. Britannia Village in Silvertown, intended in the plans for the Royal Docks to be part of an 'urban village', that is a self-contained community within the city, has in execution become a better-than-average housing estate with a small component of more adventurously designed social housing and amenities.

The community has benefited from the LDDC's intervention in many small ways. City Farms in all the boroughs, started before the LDDC was formed, have been given appropriately rustic new buildings, specially designed gardens and works of art: all are worth visiting. Similarly informal but effective in their settings are the sailing centre by *Kit Allsopp Architects* on the Millwall Docks and the Limehouse Club for local activities by *Michael Squire & Partners*. Only one conventional public building has been built by the LDDC within Docklands but that is exceptionally good: the Isle of Dogs Neighbourhood Centre, originally designed in 1988 by *Chassay Architects* to house the Tower Hamlet's Isle of Dogs

Neighbourhood Council (since disbanded). It makes a strong contribution to the townscape at the crucial junction of Marsh Wall and the main Manchester Road. Schools of the 1980s and 90s are subdued and domestic-looking (see the group by Newham Borough Council in Beckton). Most appealing of that generation is Arnhem Wharf School on the Isle of Dogs by *PTP Architects*, but much more interesting are the earlier schools by the *GLC Architect's Department*, for example, the Cyril Jackson School, Limehouse (*c.* 1973), an early example of the low-key, friendly type; Hermitage School, Wapping, that proclaims itself as confidently as a c19 Board school; and the George Green School on the Isle of Dogs, Brutalist but carefully tailored to a sensitive site close to an important view of Greenwich Hospital. Supermarkets, though commercial, seem to have become one of the most important late c20 public amenities: best is Savacentre at Beckton by *Aukett Associates*, 1992–3, which represents a new generation of supermarkets that have at last shaken off the image of barn or temple to don a more appropriate High-Tech guise.

After the LDDC, 1998–2000

The last area of Docklands to be handed back to local authority control in 1998 will be the Royal Docks, the largest, emptiest and most intractable part of the whole regeneration programme. Olympia & York's view, formulated in the 1980s, was that because of its isolation the Royal Docks should become a great suburban recreation area, focused on watersports, parks and housing. Despite the establishment of a small business park close to Beckton, that seems to be the way development is tending. The buildings and open spaces, including a regatta centre by *Ian Ritchie Architects*, a park by *Groupes Signes* with *Patel & Taylor* and a university campus planned by *Edward Cullinan Architects*, have already been begun and should distinctly improve the environment for Londoners and those in the neighbouring, sub-rural parts of Essex and Kent. But much depends on what route and form is chosen for the East London River (now Thames Gateway) Crossing, a long-delayed decision outside LDDC and local control. One day, the crossing will link the Royal Docks to the rest of Britain and the whole of Europe.

From the beginning, the LDDC intended that the areas under its control should be fully integrated back into the boroughs from which they were carved, but two forces – the opening of the Jubilee Line in 1998 and the influence and aftermath of the Millennium Experience, close by at North Greenwich in the year 2000 – will no doubt powerfully affect the future relationship of Docklands with the rest of London. Until the mid c20, the east ends of almost all British cities were doomed by the prevailing west wind to be the recipients and transmitters of air-borne filth, a disadvantage that doomed east-end developments aiming at political, commercial and social cachet. In this ostensibly cleaner post-industrial age and with better communications perhaps East London, both N and S of the river, will at last throw off its traditional grimy, isolated and subservient image and forge a new identity. And let us hope that this new identity will eventually be, both socially and architecturally, inclusive and varied rather than exclusive and monolithic.

FURTHER READING

Books on London's docks have concentrated on history rather than buildings. The best, most readable survey and one that deals with both history and buildings, is still that by John Pudney. His *London's Docks* (1975) has additional value in the snapshot it gives of the docks at a point when many had just closed and others were threatened. But the most indispensable modern work on the development of Docklands is now the Survey of London, *Poplar, Blackwall and the Isle of Dogs: The Parish of All Saints*, XLIII, XLIV (1994). These two volumes, in the recent tradition of the Survey of London, give an exhaustive architectural and historical picture of this limited but vital area from the medieval period to the present day. They are particularly good on the impact of the construction of the docks and the building of modern Docklands on the Isle of Dogs, but also include much new material on C20 public housing in Poplar and numerous illustrations of buildings now gone. For those primarily interested in Docklands post 1981, the Survey has produced a well-illustrated paperback, *Docklands in the Making: The Redevelopment of the Isle of Dogs, 1981–95* by Alan Cox (1995), which uses the material on this period from the larger volume. The best architectural guide to the buildings of Docklands so far is Stephanie Williams, *Docklands*, a Phaidon Architectural Guide, 2nd ed. 1993, which has perceptive analyses of the main buildings (mostly the modern ones) in a very lively style. Also useful as guides to the modern buildings are K. Ellison and V. Thornton, *A Guide to London's Contemporary Architecture*, 1993, and S. Hardingham, *London, a Guide to Recent Architecture*, 2nd ed. 1994. Two special volumes of *Architectural Design* put Docklands architecture in its London and global context: *Post-Modern Triumphs in London*, ed. C. Jencks, (1991) and *World Cities: London*, ed. K. Powell (1993). Books and articles about the redevelopment of docklands worldwide are so far disappointing: we still await the definitive work. For individual buildings of the last two decades, there are articles in a wide range of international periodicals: the best way to find these is through the printed periodical index of the British Architectural Library.

There are also several books and articles on the planning processes that formed modern Docklands, notably S. Brownill, *Developing London's Docklands: another great planning disaster?* (1990), and M. Hebbert, One 'Planning Disaster' after Another: London Docklands 1970–1992, *London Journal*, 17, ii (1992). As their titles imply, these authors have a gloomy view of what has happened but include much useful information otherwise only available in official reports, such as the Docklands Joint Committee, *Strategic Plan*, 1976. The Docklands Forum, a pressure group that carries on the work of the Docklands Joint Committee, has produced many booklets, mostly on social issues, that also counterbalance the officially marketed image of Docklands.

Though there are many older books about the Port of London (many of them are listed in the GLC Historic Buildings Division, *Docklands History Survey: a guide to research* (1984)), there are only a limited number of late C20 publications useful for information about dock structures and buildings. Among these are the proceedings of a conference held by the RCHME in 1995, entitled *The Thames Gateway: Recording Historic Buildings and Landscapes on the Thames Estuary* (see especially E. Sargent on the development of the Royal Docks); and T. Smith, 'Hydraulic Power in the Port of London', *Industrial Archaeology Review*, XIV, i (1991). Also, E. Sargent, 'The Planning and Early Buildings of the West India Docks', *The Mariner's Mirror*, 77 ii (1991). An essential study of the early docks' construction is A.W. Skempton, 'Engineering in the Port of London, 1789–1808, and 1808–1833', *Trans. of the Newcomen Soc.*, 50 and 53 (1979 and 1982), while for C20 works *see* I. Greeves, *London Docks 1800–1980: a civil engineering history* (1980). The essays by M. Tucker on warehouses, P. Calvocoressi on lost buildings, and I. Greeves on the work of the dock engineer are useful items in the rather uneven *Dockland: an illustrated history of life and work in east London*, ed S.K. Al Naib and R.J.M. Carr (1986). The *Proceedings of the Institution of Civil Engineers* and *PLA Monthly* have also charted many dock developments, both contemporaneously and in retrospect. R. Douglas Brown, *The Port of London* (1978), gives the most comprehensive account of the development and decline of the docks.

On the pre-docks development of the area, the most informative general books are D. Perring, *Roman London* (1991), K.G.T. McDonnell, *Medieval London Suburbs* (1978), the invaluable *Encyclopaedia of London*, ed. B.Weinreb and C.Hibbert (2nd ed. 1992), periodicals such as the *London Journal, Transactions of the London & Middlesex Archaeological Society* and the *London Archaeologist* and the reports of the Museum of London Archaeological Survey (MOLAS). Recommended publications on particular areas are C. Jamieson, *The History of the Royal Hospital of St Katharine by the Tower of London* (1952); S. Humphrey, *The Story of Rotherhithe* (1997); and an article on Shadwell in the *London Journal. . .* Best on churches are B.F.L. Clarke, *The Parish Churches of London* (1966) and K. Downes, *Hawksmoor* (2nd ed. 1979).

Those interested in carrying research further will need to use *The Bibliography of Printed Works on London History to 1939*, edited by Heather Creaton (1994); the Department of National Heritage's *Lists of Buildings of Historic and Architectural Interest;* and the well-catalogued resources of the Borough of Tower Hamlets' Local History Collection, the Borough of Southwark's John Harvard Library and the archive of material, formerly owned by the Port of London Authority and now in the care of the Museum of London.

DOCKLANDS:
NORTH OF THE THAMES

Docklands north of the river stretches for ten miles along the Thames
from the City of London, through the southernmost part of the
London Borough of Tower Hamlets, and to the E edge of the
London Borough of Newham. It encompasses the earliest docks,
built in the early C19 on the Isle of Dogs and in Wapping, and the
most recent (opened in 1921) in more distant Newham. Docklands'
N boundary is an invention of 1973, when Travers Morgan produced
their government-commissioned report on the future of the docks:
it was designed to define the area of dying docks, riverside and
associated industrial land most in need of regeneration, and in
doing so it cut this area off from the rest of East London. For most
of its length the boundary follows the A13 but W of the Isle of
Dogs dips down through Tower Hamlets along The Highway
and East Smithfield W to the Tower of London, cutting right
through established entities such as Limehouse and Shadwell.
Even in Newham, the boundary defines only the formerly derelict
land N of the Royal Docks, excluding Canning Town which grew
up in part to house workers at the (Royal) Victoria Dock.

Though the London Borough of TOWER HAMLETS dates only
from 1965, when the metropolitan boroughs of Bethnal Green,
Poplar and Stepney were amalgamated, the name Tower Hamlets
was used as early as the C16 for the string of medieval hamlets due
E of the Tower of London. Strype listed twenty-one hamlets in
1720 but only five – Shadwell, Ratcliffe, Limehouse, Poplar and
Blackwall, all fronting the Thames – come within Docklands.
Until the C17, when the first new parishes were formed and new
churches and chapels built in response to an influx of population
from the overcrowded City, they all lay within the parish of St
Dunstan, Stepney. Small slipways and wharves existed along the
river from the C15 for the building, repair and victualling of ships
trading with the Port of London, but the C16 and C17 saw immense
growth in shipping and shipbuilding: Ratcliffe became a launching
point for merchant-venturer voyages and voyages of discovery,
and the East India Company, chartered in 1600, began to build
and repair their ships at Blackwall and Limehouse Hole. The tiny
medieval settlements, hemmed between river and marshland and
dependent on milling, agriculture and fishing, became in the C17
and C18 distinctive villages with maritime and other industries.
They acquired grand churches, such as St George-in-the-East,
Wapping, and St Anne, Limehouse, the smart houses of shipbuilders,
tradesmen and speculators, and charitable institutions: traces of this
prosperity can still be seen in Limehouse, Wapping and Ratcliffe.

But the transforming moment in the history of these hamlets was the opening of London's first enclosed, secure docks. First were the West India Docks established in Poplar on the then almost deserted Isle of Dogs (1799–1806), but these were quickly followed by the London Dock in Wapping (1800–5), the East India Docks at Blackwall (1803–6), and St Katharine Docks, again in Wapping (1825–9). Finally, in 1863–9, the Millwall Docks were excavated out of the still-empty centre of the Isle of Dogs. Though most of the docks were carved out of virgin land, the existing inhabitants of Wapping were displaced or crowded into the surviving property which quickly degenerated. New routes and railways, many specially built to serve the docks, propelled the whole area into becoming an intensely industrial suburb of outer London. The Limehouse Cut, built to the River Lea (1767–70), the Commercial Road, which linked the West India Docks with the City (1806), and the London and Blackwall Railway (1836–40) all encouraged or brought industry. All along the river, wharves were developed with a wide variety of industries, all of which required river transport for bulky raw materials or finished goods. Warehouses, on a huge scale from the mid C19, took much of the trade that by 1800 had overwhelmed the quays and river within the Pool of London. Most of the hamlets burst their riverside bounds and spread into new neighbourhoods of speculative houses N of the Commercial and East India Dock Roads (and so N of modern Docklands), while in the Isle of Dogs a ring of speculative housing was squeezed in between docks and river. New churches, schools and libraries were built to serve the old and the new communities.

The docks and riverside industry continued to flourish after the First World War, especially in the West India and Millwall Docks which were heavily remodelled to take larger ships. The associated settlements changed radically as slums were cleared away. Clearance had begun well before that war, when the riverside part of Shadwell was totally obliterated for a new park, but after the war the centres of Limehouse, Poplar and Wapping were also transformed by the replacement of old property with new tenements.

The next dramatic change was brought about by the intensive and intensively destructive bombing in the Second World War. The Isle of Dogs, with its extensive docks, was most severely affected and C19 housing here gave way almost entirely to post-war estates. Despite the post-war rejuvenation of the West India and Millwall Docks, trade in all the docks within Tower Hamlets became increasingly uneconomic, as it was overtaken by changes in handling methods (*see* below). The East India Docks were the first to close in 1967, followed by the London Docks and St Katharine Docks, both of which had been used chiefly for warehousing for many years. The West India and Millwall Docks stayed open longer. Trade along the riverside was similarly affected and industry, especially on the Isle of Dogs, was gradually killed off by poor communications: many warehouses and wharves were occupied only by scrap-merchants, haulage contractors and very small-scale light industry. A few adventurous souls colonized warehouses and the surviving C18 houses, and some even began to build new houses or to restore warehouses (Michael Barraclough in the Isle of Dogs, Rae Hoffenberg in Limehouse), but generally the surviving communities lived amongst dereliction, romantic only in retrospect, with very few jobs left to support them and very few attempts, after 1970, to improve their housing.

The full story of the regeneration of Docklands from the mid 1970s is described in the Introduction (p. 49), but as far as Docklands N of the river is concerned it was in Wapping, where both the London Docks and the St Katharine Docks had closed, that the first attempts at improvement were made – at St Katharine Docks by the GLC and in the rest of Wapping by the Borough of Tower Hamlets. Their approaches – and the results – were very different, one being commercially-, the other community-based. The work of restoration and renewal was continued from 1981 in Wapping and Limehouse by the London Docklands Development Corporation (LDDC), with one important change: reliance on the market has meant that speculative housing has come to dominate in these areas so conveniently near the City. The role of riverside Wapping especially has changed from that of an introverted working-class community into a partly gentrified residential suburb of the City. The remodelling of the Isle of Dogs and Blackwall (qq.v.) has wrought far more dramatic changes. Canary Wharf, the centrepiece of the West India Docks, has become the new heart of Docklands N of the river, with commercial development on a scale and with a visual impact intended to rival the City of London. It has its own suburb on the rest of the Isle of Dogs, where private housing has replaced riverside industry.

NEWHAM is on the very fringes of London. Here the atmosphere is of the flat, open Essex countryside to which East Ham and West Ham, the main constituents of the present borough, belonged until 1965. But what distinguish this part of Newham from the neighbouring industrial suburbs of Barking and Dagenham to the E are the Royal Docks (q.v.), basins on a magnificent scale dug out of the marsh between 1850 and 1921. A hive of activity for only just over a hundred years, they have lain idle and eerily quiet since they closed in 1980. Newham's riverside, unlike Wapping or Limehouse, is not gentrified, nor is it packed with new private housing as on the Isle of Dogs: it remains heavily industrial, devoted to food processing and chemicals. After the Royal Docks closed, the LDDC took planning control of the riverside, docks and the partly developed partly derelict industrial land to their N, an area which stretches S from the Barking Road (A13) to the river, and from Bow Creek E to Royal Docks Road.

Historically, the area was divided between West Ham, East Ham and North Woolwich, which was a detached part of Kent until 1889 when it became part of London, administered from Woolwich. The historic Essex parishes of West and East Ham were divided by a line that runs N from W of North Woolwich, at the point where, before the C19, Ham Creek met the river. West Ham and East Ham were (originally) hamlets standing on raised ground in the N of the present borough. The area that falls within modern Docklands lay s of them below high-tide level and was used only for pasture. The whole area was opened up by the construction in 1812–14 of the New Road (now Barking Road), an extension of the Commercial Road turnpike, which formed the route to the fishing port of Barking (on Barking Creek) from Central London, but little happened until the mid C19, when a simultaneous combination of events dramatically changed the whole area into one of heavy industry and docks.

The first stimulus to change was the extension of the railways across the area after 1839, linking East Anglia to London via Stratford, and London to the Thames and its s bank via North Woolwich and its ferry. The railways made it possible to build docks this distant from the City of London. From 1850 the dock promoters took advantage of the many acres of cheap marshland already on the railway network, which could provide at relatively low construction costs the huge docks that were needed for the new generation of iron steamships.

Then, in 1844, the Metropolitan Building Act proscribed noxious industries within the metropolitan area. West Ham and East Ham lay beyond the metropolis in Essex, so, from c. 1850, their undeveloped riverside proved a magnet for many dangerous and insalubrious trades, ranging from indiarubber manufacture to carcass rendering. Slightly later, huge gasworks and sewage works colonized the marshes next to Barking Creek. Several townships grew up to serve the new industries, the main one being Canning Town (outside the Docklands area), begun in the 1840s for the workers in the Thames Ironworks on Bow Creek. On the riverside, Silvertown grew up round Silver's indiarubber works, and Beckton was planted by the Gas Light and Coke Co. North Woolwich developed round the ferry, the railway and local telegraph cable works. Dickens in 1857 criticized both Silvertown and Beckton for their 'new streets of houses without drains, roads, gas or pavement', fortunately mostly replaced later in the century by more civilized conditions.

Most of the housing between the docks and river, heavily bombed in 1940, was replaced in the 1960s. On the empty farmland N of the Royal Albert Dock, reserved for dock expansion, hundreds of prefabs were built after the war. Until the 1960s the docks' immediate environs were alive with traffic and people, as goods were transported by road and rail from the sheds, cold stores and warehouses within the docks, and sailors and dockers came and went from seamen's lodging houses and dockers' pubs. Many of the activities associated with the Port of London were centred there after the First World War, for example the Anglican Missions to Seamen which moved here from Poplar in the 1930s. The riverside was equally busy.

Then, in the 1960s a number of factors caused the swift decline of the docks and of some of the heavy industry. Closure of the docks was first predicted in the early 1970s and planning for redevelopment began, first by the local authority and then by the

Docklands Joint Committee (*see* Royal Docks). Some developments, such as the replacement of many of the prefabs at Cyprus
by council housing, came to fruition but there have been many
grandiose and abortive schemes, ranging from a huge American-
style arena on the N side of the Royal Victoria Dock to a massive
domed shopping and leisure centre, just one part of a masterplan
of 1988 by (*Sir*) *Richard Rogers* for the Royal Albert Dock. The
LDDC, during its relatively brief reign as planning authority
(1981–98), managed to establish an infrastructure of roads,
bridges and the DLR extension, and quayside landscaping, a
district park and a substantial area of social housing, as well as the
conservation of the few remaining dock buildings and structures.
A so-called urban village has been started at Silvertown and a
business park NE of the Connaught Crossing: an exhibition centre
and a university campus have been planned. Most successful
has been the encouragement of water sports, which dates back to
the 1970s before the docks closed and which has led to the building of an Olympic rowing course and regatta centre in the Royal
Albert Dock. Beckton was returned to Newham's jurisdiction in
1995. From 1998 English Partnerships, working with Newham,
will carry redevelopment forward: the scale of the task, made
especially difficult by the isolation of the area, is daunting.

BECKTON
London Borough of Newham

Beckton, though mostly post-war and suburban, owes its
existence to the Gas Light and Coke Co. which in 1868 bought
540 acres of land for new works to serve much of Metropolitan
area N of the Thames. Opened in 1870, they became the largest in
Europe, at their peak serving $4\frac{1}{2}$ million customers. The site,
fronting the Thames and Barking Creek, was chosen to facilitate
the import of coal from NE England: the company had riverside
piers, its own steam colliers, and its own railway with 42 m. of
track. It also established communications between its works and
the rest of West Ham, building a private road (now Winsor
Terrace and Tollgate Road) on an axis with the gasworks' gate
and a railway line from Custom House which they leased to the
GER.

The township, named Beckton after the then Governor of the
Company, Simon Adams Beck, was laid out along the company
road W of the main gates. It consisted of two rows of houses, a
church, a chapel and an institute; only the S row of houses
survived the Blitz. The gasworks was built on the marshes E of
the township (i.e. E of the Docklands boundary). Beyond them to
the E, and at the same period, a sewage works was established at
the terminus of the Metropolitan Board of Works' Northern Outfall
Sewer (1859–64) which served the whole of North London. The
gasworks and the Royal Albert Dock, which opened in 1880,
employed a huge number of people, many of whom travelled from
well beyond the immediate neighbourhood.

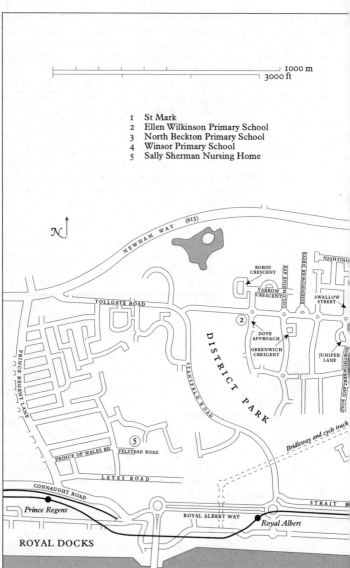

1   St Mark
2   Ellen Wilkinson Primary School
3   North Beckton Primary School
4   Winsor Primary School
5   Sally Sherman Nursing Home

    Most of the workers came from Canning Town and surround-
ing districts (now beyond Docklands). Only one pocket of housing
was built on the marshes to the s in the late 1870s and early 1880s.
New Beckton, known as Cyprus after the colonization of that
country in 1878, never progressed further than a few streets of
houses, pubs and shops, built without drainage and soon in poor

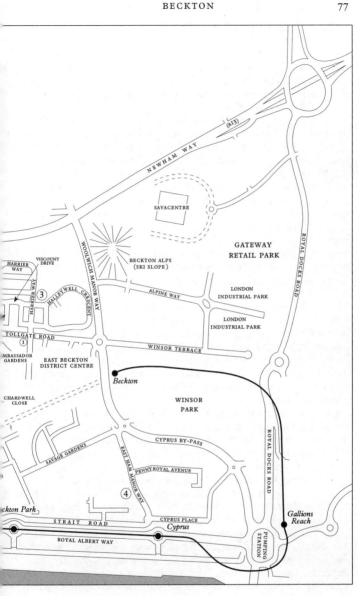

Beckton

condition. Projecting to its w into the surrounding fields, better but equally isolated housing was provided in 1903 by East Ham Borough Council along an embryo park and named Savage Gardens. The rest of the marshy farmland between the Albert Dock and Beckton was reserved for dock expansion until the 1960s.

The 1960s were a turning point in the development of the area. Coal gas manufacture ceased in 1969 and natural gas was gradually introduced, freeing industrial land N of old Beckton. Nothing much was done until the 1970s when the Docklands Joint Committee was established. Its London Docklands Strategic Plan proposed new housing and industry at Beckton, and a population increase from 6,500 (1971) to 28,000.

The Beckton District Plan, devised by Newham, was published in 1976. The blueprint was that of a post-war New Town like Harlow, with a low-density mix (70–1,000 persons p.a.) of parkland, housing and light industry to be developed by a combination of private and public investors. The settlement was to have been focused on a district centre built along the spine road, with an industrial estate on the redundant acres of the Gas Co.'s tar distillery, and a mixture of open space and low-density housing to replace decayed housing and prefabs to the S. Some work was begun before the LDDC was created in 1981. The land was drained properly, derelict land cleared for the industrial estate, council housing built at Cyprus and private housing at West Beckton, historically the E fringe of Canning Town.

The Corporation completed the implemention of the broad lines of the plan before Beckton was returned to local authority control in 1995, but with notable differences largely determined by the play of market forces rather than social need. Of the large amount of housing built, most is private, though there is a greater proportion of new social housing than in the rest of Docklands. The district centre in 1997 comprises a supermarket, a group of church, library and community hall and a health centre, more like a suburban than a town centre. The commercial heart is a supermarket and retail park on the NE edge. The roads have been improved, the DLR extended to East Beckton, and the last of the 68 acres of derelict land N of Tollgate Road cleared. The piles of waste materials from the purification of gas, augmented by spoil from the basement of the new British Library at St Pancras, were used to create the conical hill and dry ski-slope known as Beckton Alps, now the highest point in this part of Newham. The LDDC's main success has been the welding of this fragmented area into a cohesive whole by the interweaving of the district park. The decentralizing tendency seen even in established towns has here been enshrined in the planning, the model, as with the earlier Milton Keynes, being the low-rise, low-density, car-dependent but very green North American conurbation rather than the English early C20 Garden City model of the original District Plan.

CHURCHES AND PUBLIC BUILDINGS

St Mark, Tollgate Road and Kingsford Way. 1989 by *APEC Architects* of Birmingham. An interdenominational church and community centre for Beckton's post-1980 housing developments. Large, sweeping roofs at different levels and windows in long bands to the main road. The golden brick of the walls is repeated inside, with an extensive amount of timbering and top-lighting, which creates a warm attractive interior. The church lies E of a central corridor; offices above make for a low 'nave' but the liturgical centre swells upwards and is brightly lit. W of the corridor is a large sports hall; elsewhere are a shop, refreshment bar, meeting rooms etc. At the back a local LIBRARY and COMMUNITY BUILDING, opened 1997 as part of East Beckton's District Centre, which at that time centred on an ASDA supermarket.

PRIMARY SCHOOLS. By the *London Borough of Newham*, 1980s. All of the same type with wide-spreading wings at the front, low-pitched roofs and colourful details: ELLEN WILKINSON, Dove Approach; NORTH BECKTON, Halleywell Crescent; WINSOR, East Ham Manor Way.

SALLY SHERMAN NURSING HOME (former Albert Dock Hospital), Felsted Road. The earliest buildings of 1887–90 stood nearer the dock. They were superseded by a pavilion hospital in 1937. Only the main block survives as the nursing home. Neo-Georgian on the cheap with a pedimented centre-piece and second floor in a prominent tiled mansard.

OTHER MAJOR DEVELOPMENTS

LONDON INDUSTRIAL PARK, Woolwich Manor Way. Begun in 1979 on a small scale by *Fewster & Partners*. It lies on the former gasworks land N of Winsor Terrace. Entrance by Beckton Alps. On Alpine Way, the former LADKARN WORKSHOPS, designed by *Nicholas Grimshaw and Partners* in 1984–5 for haulage contractors and built originally at the West India Docks; it was moved here to make room for Olympia & York's Canary Wharf in 1986. Distinctive silver steel-clad shed, with a mezzanine of offices, supported from six red masts to free the internal floor area and, in its original situation, to minimize piling. To the W later industrial sheds imitate the exposed trusses in a much cruder way.

GATEWAY RETAIL PARK extends this development NE to the A13. Planned and landscaped by *Aukett Associates* whose B&Q STORE, 1995–6, in Claps Gate Lane is one of the best of the retail sheds. SAVACENTRE, *Aukett Associates*' sleek steel-framed white-clad shed of 1992–3, makes an effective statement on Newham Way at the NE gateway to Beckton. Predominant is the elegant, curved aerofoil roof sailing out on angled struts to make a shady canopy all round. In front, the usual sea of carpark, generously landscaped but particularly large and intimidating.

DISTRICT PARK. Created by the LDDC from the fields and derelict industrial land left between the old settlements and the new developments. The overall effect is informal and semi-rural, though there are strong links, such as the cycle track, between the communities. – AMENITY BUILDING South Beckton District Park. Designed by *Carr, Goldsmith & Fallek*, to read clearly in this flat landscape. – Near the E end of the main

bridleway and cycle track, three sculptures by *Brian Yale* set
tellingly in the landscape: HORSES in stainless steel appear to
walk elegantly through a paved paddock, enclosed by a SCREEN
of stylized trees; futher W a kinetic group of BIRDS poised on
branching pole. – DOCKLANDS EQUESTRIAN CENTRE, E of
Woolwich Manor Way, is an indoor arena and barn for twenty
horses. 1994–5 by *Aukett Associates*, architects of the adjoining
Savacentre (*see* above). Appropriately simple and rustic in
blockwork, timber and metal roofing. This and the adjacent
Beckton Alps are part of a fringe of recreational land which
continues the District Park along the A13.

PUMPING STATION, Gallions Roundabout. Built 1975–8 by
Mason, Pittendrigh & Partners, consulting engineers. To drain
the surface water from Beckton marshes before redevelopment
with housing and industry. An innovative layout within a
reinforced-concrete diaphragm wall, set in the Thanet sand,
which was temporarily dewatered. Brick-clad steel superstructure with a distinctive precast pleated roof and a travelling
crane spanning the diameter.

EAST LONDON RIVER (Thames Gateway) CROSSING. Since the
1940s there have been proposals for a road crossing between
Beckton and Thamesmead (Woolwich) in the vicinity of Gallions
Reach, to complete a link between the M11 and the A2. These
crystalized in the early 1990s in the ELRIC scheme, which
secured planning approval but ultimately did not proceed due
to environmental concerns associated with the connection to
the A2 S of the river. In 1997 ELRIC was superseded by plans
for a package of new river crossings: a third road crossing at
Blackwall; a rail tunnel to Woolwich; and a new multi-modal
crossing at Gallions Reach called Thames Gateway Bridge.
These changes were provoked mainly by objections to the road
being cut through the ancient Oxleas Wood, SE of Woolwich,
resulting in a public enquiry, 1985–6, and the re-routing of the
Channel tunnel railway to Stratford. One casualty of the scheme
was a dramatic design for a cable-stayed bridge by *Santiago
Calatrava*, rejected as too extravagant.

HOUSING

There is no high-rise in Beckton. Almost everything, except on
the W fringe in West Beckton, dates from after 1970, that is after
towers and slabs generally went out of favour. The only C19 relic,
except the terraces along Prince Regent Lane, is Winsor Terrace,
an exceptionally dignified example of C19 workers' housing. The
local authority's housing of the late 1970s is in the quiet neo-
vernacular style of that period, rather sombre in colour and packed
into high-density schemes, leaving much open space all around.
The homes built from the mid 1980s are more varied, ranging
from the twee and nostalgic to the crisp and colourful. Some of
the best schemes have quite cleverly adapted types of Victorian
and Edwardian London housing. The best place to see the contrasting approaches is along Tollgate Road.

East Beckton

Winsor Terrace, the original street of Beckton named after Friedrich Winzer, founder of the Gas Light and Coke Company in 1812, is preserved as the main axis of East Beckton. The District Centre (*see* above) lies just W of it on Tollgate Road. This is close to Beckton DLR station where the tour might well begin.

WINSOR TERRACE ends E at the gates of the former gasworks. Along the S side, handsome terraces of two-storey red brick houses of the 1870s, with three-storey, shallow-gabled houses for senior staff at the ends of each row. The style is slightly Italianate with round-arched doorways and fretted bargeboards; mostly well preserved. The N rows were demolished after war damage.

WINSOR PARK estate, 1987–95, was built on former gasworks land to the S. The plan by *Chris Wilkinson Architects* echoes the arrangement of Winsor Terrace. Here taller blocks of flats flank two-storey terraces with small front gardens lining conventional streets. A restricted Postmodern vocabulary appears in different combinations and colours – yellow and grey striped brick, dark-red brick with yellow stripes. The end blocks have gridded canted bay windows. Neat street furniture and metal fencing. Bradymead, the central street, has shops and ends E at a very minimal social centre. Winsor Park provided the first built of 1,500 social housing units planned for the Royal Docks as part of the social compact made by the LDDC and Newham in 1987.

North Beckton

TOLLGATE ROAD, Beckton's main spine, links a number of post-1981 housing schemes. Off the N side a number of schemes, some social housing and some speculative, designed with consistent palettes and vocabularies. Though many are crude in detail, they display quite interesting Postmodern variations on historicist themes. The layouts are generally more engaging than the houses. The taste of Aldo Rossi, the Kriers and other Neo-Rationalists for the axial and monumental becomes rather caricatured from time to time, but most of the schemes seriously attempt urbanity in this amorphous outer suburb, establishing a strong link with the spine road and a definite barrier between the centre of Beckton and the inhospitable A13. Straight streets and avenues are varied with crescents, squares and courts.

On the N SIDE, E to W: HALLEYWELL CRESCENT, built for the Southern Housing Group, completed 1994, is one of the most cramped and basic groups. Neo-Victorian style with prominent timber dormers. Mixed-height terraces round very tight little mixer-courts off the crescent that makes a single loop. Minimal landscaping.

In the garden square bounded by AMBASSADOR GARDENS and 86 CONCORDE DRIVE one of the most successful schemes by *Form Design Group*, 1987. On the main road, big four-storey blocks set close together form the gateway into a long garden square of what look very like Edwardian mansion flats. Square two-storey bays topped by balconies serving a third storey. On the ground floor dark-buff brick with red stripes, above buff only. Off-the-peg details quite cleverly used. The flavour is, distantly, of Lutyens at Hampstead Garden Suburb. Lower cottages, to the w in BRACKEN CLOSE by *Adamson Associates*, 1993, have severely plain, Soanian door surrounds.

NIGHTINGALE WAY, NW of Ambassador Gardens, is lined with three-storey semi-detached houses in early C19 London style with pedimental gable to each pair (a type revived by architects such as Colquhoun & Miller in Hackney and Milton Keynes). Rudimentary pediments within the gables and over the doors. At the w end the houses are built in a forthright combination of bright-red brick with cast-stone quoins and a patterning of cast-stone blocks. The front walls curve in neatly to take trees planted in circles of paviours. The white panel-clad bays and gables make an otherwise satisfying scheme look unnecessarily shoddy. A similar design, by *Newham Borough Council*, 1984, continues down the E side of EISENHOWER DRIVE. Here pairs of taller houses are joined with big recessed arches and a single pedimental gable; they look quite dramatic, rather in the manner of the eccentric C19 architects Roumieu & Gough. More drama towards Tollgate Road where they stand back behind a green accented with an obelisk. Medium-size houses in this scheme have big lunettes on the second floor, e.g. in BERYL AVENUE.

Housing breaks down at this end of Tollgate Road into a selection of much smaller less cohesive schemes. COLUMBINE AVENUE and YARROW CRESCENT have three-storey, much simplified Neo-Georgian houses by *Ronald Toone International*, 1985, that look best in the crescent. Oddest is ROBIN CRESCENT, a tiny paved drive with Neo-Victorian houses behind quaint palings, all on a disturbing toy-like scale: by *Hough August Partnership*, 1985. There is more of this archness s of Tollgate Road.

On the s SIDE of Tollgate Road, there is a great mixture of small speculative schemes, mostly of no distinction. The roads here are cramped and formless, veering to the picturesque, the houses mostly tiny. Most picture-book is GREENWICH CRESCENT by *George F. Johnson Associates*, 1984, Regency-style cottages with central chimneys round a square green, a layout devised, like that round Mavis Walk to the w, by *Neylan & Ungless* in 1983. Off JUNIPER LANE, miniature Essex-style cottages along miniature winding paths: by *Stanley Bragg Partnership*, 1984. Less derivative and better quality though slightly old-fashioned for 1982, the robust neo-vernacular off Northumberland Road in CHARDWELL CLOSE by *John Reynolds Associates*.

South Beckton

SAVAGE GARDENS has its origin in the long, isolated row of tenements built by East Ham in 1903 to improve the lot of local workers who otherwise inhabited jerry-built houses on the undrained marshes. The present housing is all post-1981. First to be built along here in 1981, when the whole area was still derelict and inhospitable, was the inward-looking housing group for vulnerable residents at the E end, designed by *Neylan & Ungless* for two housing associations in 1981. Furthest E STAPLES HOUSE, for the elderly, with big white-clad gables, then a deep horseshoe-shaped court, followed by a would-be stable court. The flavour is comfortably domestic, English Arts and Crafts meets Frank Lloyd Wright, especially in the Wright-inspired common room of the horseshoe block, which has hollyhock glass murals by *Bill Ungless*. Another glass mural in Staples House, its flats arranged along internal streets and round courts. The scheme was meant to extend to nine court-yards along the whole of Savage Gardens, but the rest of the street has been built up from 1981 with Beckton's first LDDC-period private housing. Several small groups all on garden suburb lines. Savage Gardens faces the remodelled park of *c.* 1903, now part of the District Park (q.v.) and with the appearance of an informal village green.

Cyprus

The C19 hamlet has gone: in its place Newham Borough council housing begun in the late 1970s. Off STRAIT ROAD along the S side of the park, dark-brown brick terraces with monopitches and diagonal boarding. To the E of East Ham Manor Way, timber-framed terraced houses and flats with projecting bays gridded in brown and cream off PENNYROYAL AVENUE and CYPRUS PLACE. This Radburn-type layout, with a planted pedestrian path between the two rows of closes, replaced the cottages of central Cyprus. The FERNDALE pub is the only Victorian survival.

West Beckton

West Beckton is really the E fringe of Canning Town (*see London 5: East*) and so has a mix of C19 terraces and interwar and post-war council housing centred on Prince Regent Lane, which originated in the early C19 as the road from Plaistow to the ferry to Charlton (Greenwich). Housing has been extended W to form an irregular fringe round the W edge of the district park.

BLACKWALL AND THE EAST INDIA DOCKS
London Borough of Tower Hamlets

The old settlement of Blackwall is no longer identifiable; the remains of the decayed houses were swept away for the Blackwall Tunnel in 1893. The original hamlet clustered round Blackwall Stairs just beyond the bend of the river E of the Isle of Dogs and W of the River Lea, and developed around what was in the C17 and C18 the biggest shipbuilding concern on the Thames. But the district was known as Blackwall from the C14; John Norden (1593) said it took its name from 'the blackeness or darkeness' of the wall which embanked the Thames here. The houses, the first early C17 for workmen at the yard, followed the narrow causeway from Poplar High Street. This continued s to Coldharbour, which still remains (*see* The Isle of Dogs Perambulation 4).

Ship repairing began in what was to become the BLACKWALL YARD probably in the late C15 (in 1514 a dock was specially dug for the repair of the *Mary Rose*) and only ceased in 1987. There is now nothing to be seen except an early C19 graving dock close to 75 Reuter's (*see* p. 90 below). The area was a victualling point and a place where passengers disembarked for the overland route into London. In 1614–52 the East India Company established the Blackwall Yard, which expanded hugely from 1652 to 1718 under Sir Henry Johnson and his son, who built the first small wet dock in 1661. The owner William Perry II added his 8-acre Brunswick Dock in 1789–90. This in turn became the Export Dock of the East India Docks (*see* pp. 85–7 below). The n part of the yard was cut off by the London and Blackwall Railway in the 1830s and sold. The remainder was partitioned in 1843. The w part became a Midland railway collier dock in 1877 but the e part was worked, until it closed in 1987, by R. & H. Green, at first alone and then as part of larger companies.

In 1803–6 the East India Company built the EAST INDIA DOCKS at Blackwall to provide secure facilities and deep moorings for their large ships on the stretch of the river they had used since the company's formation in 1600. They were the third set of wet docks after the West India Docks and the London Docks. No warehousing was required at first (the company had just built magnificent secure warehouses in Cutler Street (*see* London 1: The City of London) and cargoes were taken to them in lighters via the Lower Pool, or after 1806 along the specially built Commercial Road, or from 1840 via the new railway. Warehouses were built post-1838 to serve general trading after the end of the company's monopoly and its merger with the West India Dock Company.

The docks finally closed in 1967 and were infilled. What little remains is described below. The remains have been incorporated into the LDDC's sweeping restructuring of the area with new transport links out to the Royal Docks (q.v.) and beyond. The buildings that stand monumentally within this still-industrial landscape are the products of the LDDC's Enterprise Zone (*see* The Isle of Dogs Introduction pp. 94–5) which encompassed the area of the East India Docks.

To the e of Blackwall lies LEAMOUTH. Before the Lower Lea Crossing was built, the only access to the odd L-shaped peninsula of land within the bends of the Leamouth was by the Leamouth Road, which ran between dock walls, parts of which survive. Industrial from the late C18, the peninsula is now dominated by a vegetable oil refinery. The long narrow peninsula on the opposite bank has been transformed by the LDDC into an Ecological Park (1996).

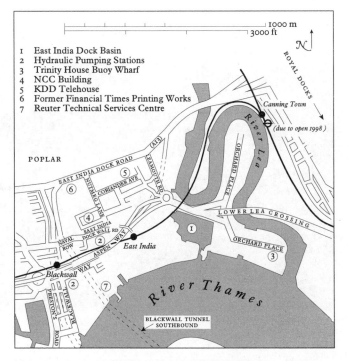

1 East India Dock Basin
2 Hydraulic Pumping Stations
3 Trinity House Buoy Wharf
4 NCC Building
5 KDD Telehouse
6 Former Financial Times Printing Works
7 Reuter Technical Services Centre

Blackwall and the East India Docks

MAJOR SITES AND BUILDINGS

The area formerly occupied by the Blackwall Yard and East India Docks is not easy to perambulate, though it can be done starting from Blackwall DLR station amid inhospitable surroundings, much of them still undeveloped in 1997. The new buildings sit like sculptural objects in the landscape and make a powerful group as seen from the DLR. They are so spread out and scaled to road travel that they are listed individually here after the historic sites, themselves described from w to E.

Historic Sites

EAST INDIA DOCKS. Only the Entrance Basin, irregular on the w side reflecting the entrances to the two vanished docks, and a tiny w fragment of the Import Dock, naturalized as a pond, survive. The Export Dock was bombed, then filled in for the Brunswick Wharf Power Station (1947–56, architects *Farmer and Dark*; demolished 1988–9). The Import Dock was pumped dry in 1943 for the building of wartime Mulberry Harbours, but was not filled in until after the docks closed in 1967.

The docks built in 1803–6 for the East India Company by *John Rennie* and *Ralph Walker*, joint engineers, were about half the size of the West India Docks and comprised the 8-acre

Export Dock and Entrance Basin, adapted from Blackwall Yard's c18 Brunswick Dock, and a 12¼-acre Import Dock. The brick quay walls were similar to those at the West India and London Docks but were founded on clay and prone to slip.

The ENTRANCE BASIN LOCK is of 1897, a new cut s of the existing passage made by *H. E. & F. A. James*; gates by *Thames Iron Works Co.*, gate machinery by *Sir W. G. Armstrong Whitworth & Co.* Of the MAIN GATE on East India Dock Road, only a replica of the giant inscription plaque, placed near the Blackwall Tunnel N approach. The big triumphal arch by *Ralph Walker*, 1805–7, was replicated in *Hennebique* ferro-concrete in 1913–14 after road widening, and demolished in 1958 for the tunnel approach. Along Leamouth Road, stretches of the original Import Dock WALL, 20 ft (6 metres) with battered buttresses, and one of the three simple arched openings flanked by niches. Some of the s wall, especially the rounded corner overlooking Naval Row, belongs to an 1833–4 realignment. Also in Leamouth Road but rebuilt in 1993 by the LDDC on a slightly different site, the former entrance GATEWAY to the East India Company's group of Pepper Warehouses, sited just outside the secure area because designed for bulky goods of small value not worth importing to Cutler Street: bombed in the Second World War, site cleared 1983. The gateway is of 1807–21 by *S. P. Cockerell*, early Egyptian revival; Portland stone pylons with caducei, originally in *Coade* stone but now carved in Portland. Timber gates and, above, a timber 'portcullis' to strengthen

View of the East India Docks, by W. Daniell, 1808

them when lowered (reconstruction of 1993). To the w visible from Aspen Way but reached from East India Dock Wall Road, the Italianate former HYDRAULIC PUMPING STATION, 1857, probably by the dock company engineer *Henry Martin*; extended 1877–8 to power new lock gates, probably by *A. Manning*, then engineer, with a w engine room in matching style. Machinery (by *William Armstrong & Co.*) replaced by electrically powered machinery 1925. Accumulator tower with blind arcading, oculi and pyramidal cap.

LONDON AND BLACKWALL RAILWAY, originally the Commercial Railway. Built 1836–40 to connect the East India Docks with the City. Nothing to be seen of this except, at Blackwall Way and Preston's Road, two cast-iron BRIDGES with slate panelled parapets and the handsome VIADUCT through Limehouse (q.v.). *Sir John Rennie* planned the alignment; he was succeeded in 1836 by *Sir William Cubitt*, in turn replaced in 1838 by *G. P. Bidder* and *George & Robert Stephenson*, who devised the original system of cable haulage by stationary engine (less noise and fewer dangerous sparks in this densely built-up area).The impressive Italianate terminus and hotel by *William Tite*, the company's architect, 1839–40, stood on Brunswick Wharf until the power station was built in 1947. Passengers sailed thence to Thames-side resorts and the Continent.

Former HYDRAULIC PUMPING STATION, Duthie Street and Blackwall Way. Squeezed into this unpropitious corner, it is almost the only relic of the area redeveloped in the 1880s by the

Midland Railway Company with branch lines to serve a new coal dock at Blackwall Yard. Of 1881–2 by *John Underwood*, Midland Railway engineer, in the characteristic house style, see the brick corbelling and cast-iron tracery of the squat accumulator tower.

BLACKWALL TUNNEL. The NORTHBOUND TUNNEL, by (*Sir*) *Alexander Binnie* of the LCC, 1891–7, is 4,410 ft (1,344 metres) long excluding the approach cuttings. 3,115 ft (949½ metres) were driven through mixed water-bearing strata using a Greathead shield and compressed air; it was the first time that these techniques had been combined, representing a major advance in sub-aqueous soft-ground tunnelling. A temporary sealing layer of clay was laid on the river bed. The lining, of cast-iron segments filled with concrete, is faced with white glazed bricks. The pattern was followed for the LCC's other tunnels at Greenwich, Rotherhithe, and Woolwich. The internal diameter is 24 ft (7⅓ metres), with a carriageway only 16 ft (just under 5 metres) wide, and sharp bends. Astride the S approach, the SOUTHERN TUNNEL HOUSE, of red sandstone, an ambitious building with steep pavilion roofs and angle turrets of characteristic Art Nouveau outline. Pretty and progressive. By *Thomas Blashill*, architect to the LCC. The SOUTHBOUND TUNNEL (1960–7) is by the *GLC Directorate of Highways and Transportation*, the 2,870 ft (875 metres) bored section by *Mott, Hay & Anderson*. Internal diameter 27 ft (8¼ metres): driven under compressed air with the ground consolidated by grouting from two pilot tunnels. The shell-concrete ventilation stacks, of eyecatching aerodynamic shape, are by the *GLC Department of Architecture and Civic Design*, project architect *Terry Farrell*. Seen most effectively from the DLR.

TRINITY HOUSE BUOY WHARF, Orchard Place, Leamouth, on the SE point of the peninsula. Trinity House had a buoy store from the 1760s. The CHAIN AND BUOY STORE and EXPERIMENTAL LIGHTHOUSE of 1864–6 by (*Sir*) *James Douglass*, Engineer-in-Chief, survive; possibly to be refurbished as an exhibition space. The store is a brick shed. A railway track for moving buoys originally ran right through it. Integral to the E the polygonal brick lighthouse tower with a lantern by engineers *Campbell, Johnstone & Co.*: thick diamond panes by *Chance Bros*. It superseded the original experimental lantern, put up in 1854 on a storehouse but moved to the W gable of the buoy store where it stood until the 1920s. Faraday, the Company's scientific adviser, used it for lighting trials which led to the first installation in 1858 of electric lighting in an operational lighthouse (the South Foreland, Dover). Faraday's experimental chamber within the store has gone. The river wall of 1803–4, heightened 1881, also survives here.

Twentieth-century buildings

NCC BUILDING, Nutmeg Lane. A Swedish commercial development designed by a Swede, *Sten Samuelson*, with *Beaton Thomas*

Partnership, 1989–92. The complex has been built round a series of water features created by the LDDC. The SW edge of the site is bounded by the wall of the Import Dock, determining the quadrant form. Pompous Postmodern, with expensive cladding materials and much reflective glass. The main axis a deep court with a canal, trees and footbridges, flanked by arcades. The canal turns N between further blocks of up to ten storeys. – Within the bleak courts, lavish use of SCULPTURE, commissioned by the developers and Art for Offices. Renaissance by *Maurice Blik*, symbolizing the building and regeneration of the docks. Expressionist bronze figures, the strong male reaching up to capture an elusive female form. – Meridian Metaphor by *David Jacobson*. A landscape assemblage, which uses granite blocks salvaged from the East India Dock pier to create a meeting place with ritualistic overtones. – Shadow Play by *David King*, a strong piece in painted steel: cut-outs of dockers at work help to compose a form representing the original triumphal arch entrance to the docks; a cut-out tree grows from it and a bronze figure dances on top. – Domino Players in bronze by *Kim Bennett*; very literal. – The series of bronze PLAQUES on different local themes were produced by children from six local schools.

KDD TELEHOUSE, Coriander Avenue. Designed by *YRM*, 1988–90, to house not people but high-tech telecommunications equipment which services the City of London. Silvery-grey boxes suspended from a taller, slimmer, darker grey service core. A grid of cladding and narrow horizontal window strips is co-ordinated with a metal maintenance grid-cum-brises-soleil with a decorative quality; it is hung from trusses projecting from the core.

Former FINANCIAL TIMES PRINTING WORKS, 240 East India 72 Dock Road, NW of Blackwall station. 1988 by *Nicholas Grimshaw & Partners*; sadly abandoned by the FT in 1995 in favour of the aesthetically inferior West Ferry Printers (*see* The Isle of Dogs Perambulation 3). This high-tech box with an innovative structure, when in use, adds drama to its surroundings by night and day. The N façade lights up from within to show the printing process, in the manner of Sir Owen Williams's works of the 1930s for the *Daily Express* in London, Manchester and Glasgow. The S façade is a mirror image except for the bold aluminium-clad staircase towers that serve the three floors of offices on this side; print shop and offices are divided by a spine of plant. Apart from the towers, the main articulation is the metal fins that project along each wall and support the network of steel braces on to which the glazing is bolted, so that inside, the glass walls are absolutely flush.

REUTER TECHNICAL SERVICES CENTRE, Blackwall Way, off 75 Preston's Road on the site of the Blackwall Yard. 1989 by the *Richard Rogers Partnership*, a neo-industrial partner to the oil refinery close by. This building is similar in purpose and form to the Telehouse, but much more dramatic. Blank cladding to machinery, glazing to office floors, massive green rooftop plant.

As usual with Rogers, services are expressed boldly on the out-side. Against the background of the river, there is unexpected poetry in the contrast between the dark bulk of the main block and the transparent service towers, walkways and low restaurant pavilion.

The main building was built astride the site of the Blackwall Yard's upper graving dock of 1878. The earlier GRAVING DOCK survives close to it, refurbished 1991–2 and cut back to its original length by *Richard Rogers Partnership*. Rebuilt and lengthened before 1850 in brick and stone with the stepped bottom faced with ashlar granite blocks. Present caisson gate probably *c.* 1950. It was the yard's fourth dry dock, probably built between 1779 and 1799, i.e. one of the earliest remaining on the Thames. Accessible by a public walkway.

SCULPTURE. Two major pieces as landmarks at strategic points in the LDDC's new Blackwall landscape. On the Leamouth Roundabout, the huge silhouetted, painted metal figures of Aerobic, by *Allen Jones*, 1993. – As the gateway to East India Dock Basin from Orchard Place, the austere and architectural SALOME GATES by *Sir Anthony Caro*, 1996.

THE ISLE OF DOGS
London Borough of Tower Hamlets

Until 1800 when construction of the West India Docks began, the Isle of Dogs was a lonely windswept peninsula, lying below high-tide level and bounded on the N by the highway through Limehouse and Poplar and on the E by Blackwall Causeway. The contrast with the busy settlements of Rotherhithe and Deptford SW across the Thames, and the grandeur of Greenwich Hospital almost due S, could hardly have been greater. Wren noted that no view of his hospital was better than that from the S tip of the Isle of Dogs. That view (from Island Gardens) is still preserved but otherwise all has changed dramatically.

In the Middle Ages, the Isle of Dogs was known as Stepney Marsh and came within Stepney parish. In the middle of the marsh a hamlet called Pomfret had fields, a windmill, manor house and chapel, first built in the later C12 by William of Pontefract. For a short period from 1448, when 500 acres were drained by the Bishop of London, to 1529, when the embank-ment burst, the land was used for grazing. By the 1520s, the peninsula was known as the 'Isle of Dogs', probably in reference to its unattractive aspects rather than to the dog kennels which Stow claimed Henry VIII kept here for hunting when at Greenwich. Though the marsh was thoroughly drained in the C17 and grazing resumed, the Isle kept a melancholy reputation. Windmills were built along the W flood bank, known from the late C18 as the Mill Wall. The first mill appeared towards the N end *c.* 1679 and by the 1740s there were twelve, chiefly of postmill type and run by millers from the S bank at Rotherhithe. At that date, there was inland only one farmhouse, Chapel House, perhaps developed from the medieval chapel, another house by the ferry to Greenwich, and a white-lead factory on the river close to Limehouse. A mast house was built at the sw inlet known as Drunken Dock *c.* 1766 and, by the time the docks opened in 1806, there was a scattering of industries along the river, including the Millwall Foundry.

The building of West India Docks (*see* below) transformed the N of the peninsula and development in a small way followed their opening. But it was the building of the E and W roads to the Greenwich ferry in 1812–15 (now East Ferry and Westferry Roads) that encouraged development over the rest, at that time divided between a number of landowners but two-thirds owned by William Mellish, one of the promoters of the West India Docks. Industry was quickly established along the W bank of the peninsula. The large sw sites were taken by shipbuilders, such as Sir William Fairbairn (*see* Burrell's Wharf), but shipyards thrived only until the late 1860s when economic depression took hold. The other smaller sites were constantly changing as new proprietors introduced new industries and amalgamated wharves. The E side was developed more comprehensively by William Cubitt from 1842, on land bought from Mellish's daughter. He masterminded the embankment of the river, leasing the wharves, laying out the roads and encouraging speculative builders (*see* Cubitt Town); subsequently the same process of change and amalgamation occurred along the river here. The centre of the peninsula remained completely empty until the Millwall Docks and its wharves, chiefly for grain and timber, took a huge slice out of it in the 1860s. By the end of the C19 the range of industries was immense, from milling flour and oilseed and baking, to the iron and maritime trades and wharfage. Chemicals and engineering became especially important, but these declined after the Second World War. At the same time the successful industries relocated to new industrial estates, leaving mainly a rump of warehouses, depots and scrapyards, ill-favoured by communications once road became more important than river.

Houses, inhabited almost entirely by dockers and industrial workers, crept over the farmland only slowly and included both average London terraces and mean rows of off-street cottages built by speculators. By 1854 this polluted but respectable district, almost as isolated as it had been a century before, had a population of 5,000 at a density of about 10 per house. By 1901 there were 21,000 people, but even this local population did not supply sufficient workers for the docks and industries and many commuted from adjacent communities. The last empty greenfield site was built over by the municipal Chapel House estate, as late as the 1920s. This was the first council scheme. By 1970 almost all the housing on the Isle of Dogs was council-built, the result of massive clearances in the 1930s and restitution post-1945. The wartime destruction on the Isle of Dogs was massive, as enemy planes targeted the docks. A fair amount of the interwar housing stock in Millwall survived, but large pockets needed rebuilding and almost all of Cubitt Town was replaced during the 1950s

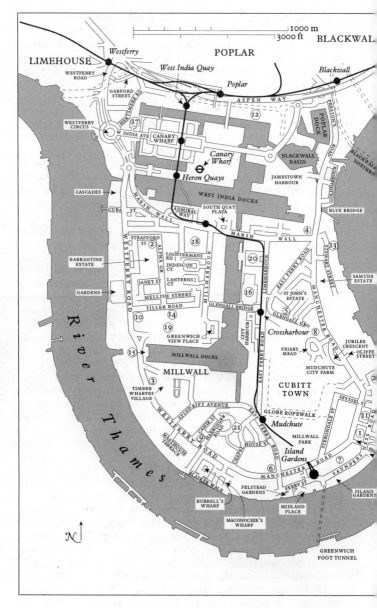

and 60s. Of the half-dozen C19 churches, only two survive. For
the docks themselves *see* pp. 101–8.

The pattern today is odd and almost entirely the result of the
LDDC's intervention following the closure of the docks in 1980
(*see* below). Round the docks is a commercial area comparable to

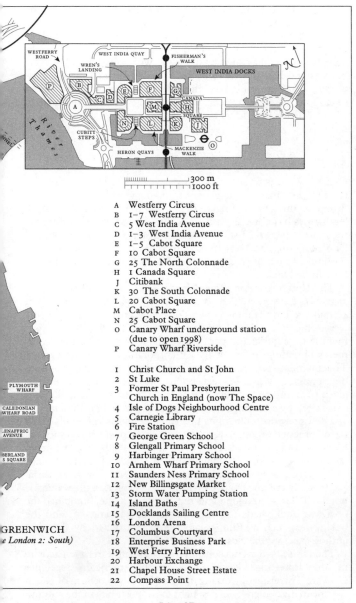

A Westferry Circus
B 1–7 Westferry Circus
C 5 West India Avenue
D 1–3 West India Avenue
E 1–5 Cabot Square
F 10 Cabot Square
G 25 The North Colonnade
H 1 Canada Square
J Citibank
K 30 The South Colonnade
L 20 Cabot Square
M Cabot Place
N 25 Cabot Square
O Canary Wharf underground station
   (due to open 1998)
P Canary Wharf Riverside

1 Christ Church and St John
2 St Luke
3 Former St Paul Presbyterian
   Church in England (now The Space)
4 Isle of Dogs Neighbourhood Centre
5 Carnegie Library
6 Fire Station
7 George Green School
8 Glengall Primary School
9 Harbinger Primary School
10 Arnhem Wharf Primary School
11 Saunders Ness Primary School
12 New Billingsgate Market
13 Storm Water Pumping Station
14 Island Baths
15 Docklands Sailing Centre
16 London Arena
17 Columbus Courtyard
18 Enterprise Business Park
19 West Ferry Printers
20 Harbour Exchange
21 Chapel House Street Estate
22 Compass Point

Isle of Dogs

many that mushroomed during the 1980s, distinguished only by the wonderful setting of water and quayside, by the few carefully preserved relics of the docks and by the mini-Manhattan of Canary Wharf. In a loop round this are the council estates, originally compressed between docks and heavy industry but now hemmed in by commercial glitz on one side and on the other by the private housing. Like its industrial predecessors, much of this housing turns its back on the established community and its face towards the now-picturesque and salubrious Thames. In very few cases has any relationship with surrounding streets been established and views of the river and access to it are spasmodic. Most appealing to the inland residents is the broad swathe of park that stretches across Cubitt Town to the edge of Millwall Dock and, at its best, recaptures a ghost of the pre-c19 farmland.

The Enterprise Zone, 1982–92, and its Aftermath

Canary Wharf is what the majority of visitors to Docklands come to see. The chance to experience this nugget of North America dropped into one of England's most important c19 industrial landscapes has obvious attractions. But Canary Wharf is only the most prominent part of the so-called Enterprise Zone, a band of land bordering the West India and Millwall Docks and covering the infilled area of the East India Docks (*see* Blackwall and the East India Docks).

The Enterprise Zone was designated in 1982 with the aim of attracting new enterprises to the Isle of Dogs by the granting of certain tax and planning concessions. The financial inducements were, chiefly, freedom from local rates until 1992; no development land tax; and 100 per cent capital allowance for new commercial buildings to be set against corporation and income taxes. The planning procedure was simplified so that any proposed development, with a few exceptions, was deemed to have been given planning permission, unless, because it was a specially sensitive site, it was exempt from the general planning provision.

The Enterprise Zone in its first three years spawned only small developments of units for new or small businesses, such as Skylines and Indescon Court, or simple sheds like Milltech. These, grouped round Millharbour in a wide-open treed landscape, gave Docklands the look of any other New Town industrial estate. Only the imaginative Heron Quays exploited the waterside potential. These developments did not stand alone, but joined the post-war dock sheds (*see* Introduction pp. 36 and 50) and the businesses, such as Billingsgate Market, attracted by the local authority before the closure of the docks.

Then in 1985–6 events conspired to stimulate a frenzy of activity in the Enterprise Zone. The North American developer G. Ware Travelstead, working on behalf of a consortium of North American investment banks, sought the opportunity in the autumn of 1985 to acquire a huge acreage on the favourable Enterprise Zone terms, having failed in his quest to find a suitable site for one of the banks, Crédit Suisse First Boston, within the City of London. Other North American companies, such as Fluor Daniel, made moves to establish themselves in the Enterprise Zone, but it was the development of Canary Wharf (*see* Perambulation 2a) that raised confidence in Docklands. This, combined with changes to

the national tax rules concerning industrial buildings and deregulation of trading in stocks and shares (the 'Big Bang') during 1986,
led to a boom in office building. By December 1986 nearly
1½ million sq. ft (457,000 sq. metres) of office space had been built
on the Isle of Dogs, mostly speculative and mostly within the
Enterprise Zone, while earlier industrial premises were turned into
office space. In 1987, with no development yet in place, Olympia
& York, Canadian developers with vast experience of development
within North America, took over Canary Wharf: their fast-track
methods led to completion of phase one in 1991, i.e. within three
years from the start of building.

But by then there were clear signs that bust would soon follow
boom. Even in 1988, the over-provision of office space was evident.
Docklands was already in competition with the City of London,
which had relaxed its planning controls in 1985 to allow development on hitherto unexploited sites. In addition, planning codes
dealing with the uses of buildings within the City had also been
changed so that Docklands no longer had an advantage in this
respect either. In 1990, affected by the world-wide property slump
and rise in interest rates, the price of office space dropped: there
was then as much available to rent as had been planned or built
altogether by 1986. In 1992, Olympia & York, Canary Wharf's developers, went into administration, just as the special conditions of the
Enterprise Zone ended. From 1990 until 1995 very little new building was done at all, and projects such as the intensive, high-rise
redevelopment of Heron Quays were put on hold. But in 1995 the
demand for inner-city residential property, particularly from overseas
investors, began to pick up and property developers, ever resource-
ful, began to convert some office buildings into housing and to
build new homes rather than offices. Since then the recession has
eased and the demand for commercial premises has also increased.
The scene in the former Enterprise Zone in 1997 is again one of
activity, though less frenetic than before, with work proceeding on
Canary Wharf under the IPC consortium of developers that
includes Paul Reichmann, formerly the leading figure in Olympia
& York. The demand for residential property is reflected in the
proposed conversion of the long-empty West India Dock ware- 19
houses into flats, as well as a museum, hotel and shopping outlets.

For the buildings of the Enterprise Zone *see* Perambulations 1,
2 and 3.

CHURCHES

CHRIST CHURCH AND ST JOHN, Manchester Road, corner
Glenaffric Avenue. 1852–4 by *Frederick Johnstone*, built and paid
for by *William Cubitt*. E.E. in stock brick, with Portland stone
dressings. Cruciform and aisleless. Tower in the angle of nave
and s transept; heavy broach spire. Thoroughly repaired and
given a larger vestry (N) in 1906–7 by *J. E. K. & J. P. Cutts*.
Subdivided, W, by *Levitt Bernstein Associates*, 1982–3. The
interior deserves a more dignified prelude than the poky W community rooms. The transept arms are broader than those of

nave and chancel, but all four are embraced by a prominent timber crown-post roof with arched braces intersecting at the crossing. Gold decoration in the E arm. Long chancel with chancel arch. S transept screened off making a S chapel and a room above behind the elaborate organ loft, presumably early in the early C20. The timber roof inside the tower is painted green and red with gold brattishing, remains of a 1909 baptistery created within the tower base by *Bodley & Hare*.

The High Church FURNISHINGS are more interesting than the architecture. Some of them come from the grander St John, Roserton Street, by (*Sir*) *A. W. Blomfield*, 1871–2, demolished in the 1950s: it had been much embellished with ritualistic furnishings from the late 1880s on. A few other items come from St Luke (*see* below). – MURAL PAINTING. Over the chancel arch, The Company of Heaven, by *F. A. Jackson* of Ealing to designs by *J. R. Spencer Stanhope*, 1907. – CHANCEL REDECORATION, 1954–5 devised by *Alan Lindsay*, architect *J. Morris*. Handsome red and white 'contemporary' wallpaper by *Coles*; black-line figures in three blocked E lancets after sketches by Lindsay. – PULPIT painted with Pre-Raphaelite-style panels of the Annunciation by *John Melhuish Strudwick*, *c.* 1914, a memorial to J. R. Spencer Stanhope †1908. – ALTARS. Chancel altar with neo-Quattrocento paintings. Plainer High Altar, and the altar and reredos, N transept, with Italian Primitive-style painting, both from St John. – STATIONS OF THE CROSS, *c.* 1938. Well-drawn figures on gold backgrounds by *Ian Howgate*, from St John. – ORGAN, 1911, possibly containing C17 pipework; rebuilt 1950s by *Noel Mander*. Along the organ loft, angel CANDLEHOLDERS, *ex situ*. – STAINED GLASS. N transept S. Fragment of 1902 glass from the demolished girls' institute, St Mildred's House, Westferry Road (founded 1897), moved here 1991. – SW lancet, Edward the Confessor by *A. K. Nicholson*, *c.* 1920. – MEMORIAL, S porch. Frances, wife of Thos. Murray Gladstone †1863. Cast-iron tablet with good heraldry.

VICARAGE to N. 1858, also built by *Cubitt*. Plain gabled brick.

ST LUKE, Strafford Street, Millwall. The coarse E.E. church with spire by *E. L. Blackburne*, 1868–70, was bombed, then demolished in 1960. It was strongly Anglo-Catholic with lavish furnishings, some of which were removed to Christ Church (*see* above). To replace it a chapel with 'stained-glass windows was added to the parish rooms built 1883 and extended 1912 by *W. G. St J. Cogswell*. The Gothic VICARAGE of 1873 by *Hooper & Lewis* remains.

Former ST PAUL PRESBYTERIAN CHURCH IN ENGLAND (now THE SPACE), Westferry Road. 1859 by *T. E. Knightley*. Built to serve the Scottish workers who flocked to work for Millwall shipbuilders in the 1850s. Saved from dereliction and fitted out discreetly as a performance space-cum-film theatre 1993–6 by *Janet Collings* and *Bevis Claxton* of *Claxton d'Auvergne Collings*. (For the successor to this church *see* Perambulation 4: Island House, Roserton Street.) Italian Romanesque front, a mini-

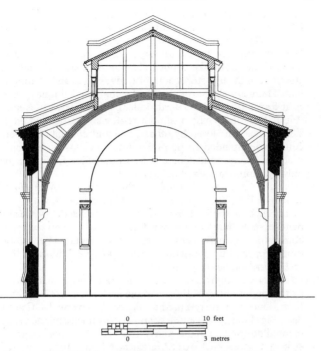

Former St Paul Presbyterian Church in England (now The Space).
Section

ature, polychrome interpretation of the w front of Pisa Cathedral, with three tiers of stone arcading and red, yellow and dark-blue brick. The clerestory is clad with fishscale slates. Big NW door left over from a former use in a crane-maintenance shop.Vestry and classrooms (now bar etc.) behind, with Venetian window: 1906 by *T. Phillips Figgis*. Art Nouveau-style railings and over-throw, 1993–6.

The plan is not basilican, as it appears outside, but a single clerestory-lit space with small sanctuary of 1906. Open timber roof with three semicircular ribs of laminated timber below the clerestory carrying an upper truss. Known as a monitor roof and unusual in church building at this date; laminated ribs were more commonly used then for large spans in textile mills and public buildings (e.g. Leeds Town Hall, 1853–8). Later wrought-iron tie rods. Windows with cast-iron tracery and Art Nouveau-inspired GLASS engraved with the building history.

PUBLIC BUILDINGS

ISLE OF DOGS NEIGHBOURHOOD CENTRE, Jack Dash House, 74 Marsh Wall. 1988–91 by *Chassay Architects* (*Tchaik Chassay* and *Malcolm Last*). One of the few post-1980 public buildings in Docklands. Though modest in size, it has great presence on its prominent corner site. Commissioned by the LDDC for the Isle of Dogs Neighbourhood Council, one of the several neighbourhood councils into which the administration of Tower Hamlets was devolved until 1994. Local democracy – in the form of the drum-like council chamber – is symbolically separated from the five-storey administrative offices and community hall. There is a clear articulation of smooth and simple geometrical forms that recalls North Italian Postmodernists, such as Botta. The offices have a sinuous roof, glazed attic, and pilotis. Within the U enclosed by offices, hall and council chamber, a courtyard, intended to be public but now closed. Exhibition space in the ground floor of the drum; office foyer screened only by a long curving blue brick wall.

CARNEGIE LIBRARY, Strattondale Street. 1904–5 by *C. Harrold Norton*. A long Bath stone front of odd proportions, with the air of a French railway station. Heavy stone cornice below the attic, panelled piers marking the bay. Centrepiece with an *œil de bœuf* above the doorcase and a crowning cupola. The interior, though opened up and with an early 1960s E addition by *Welch & Lander*, still has some 1904 character.

FIRE STATION, Manchester Road and East Ferry Road. 1904–5 by the the Fire Brigade Branch of the *LCC Architects Department*. In the Queen Anne style used for fire stations by the LCC at that date. Big chimneys, a central swan-neck pediment, pilasters, pedimented dormers. N of the courtyard a row of firemen's cottages.

GEORGE GREEN SCHOOL, Manchester Road. 1972–7 by *(Sir) Roger Walter, GLC Department of Architecture and Civic Design*; job architect *R. A. Dark*. A community school on a sensitive site within view of Greenwich Hospital, built as successor to the C19 George Green School, East India Dock Road, Poplar (q.v.). It responds to the curve of the road with four storeys of concrete blocks stepping back gently, the steps broken into for entrances to the main school, day centre and social services, and a thrusting wing of sports facilities. Concrete decks and staircases step down casually at the back in a series of broad terraces towards the open ground, which stretches via Island Gardens to the river, in a manner familiar from contemporary housing. Informal teaching spaces inside, as in most 1970s GLC secondary schools. Crisp SW wing of 1996.

PRIMARY SCHOOLS. The Isle of Dogs has two early Board schools, though both are much altered. GLENGALL, Glengall Grove, in three phases by the Board's first architect, *E. R. Robson*, 1874–6, 1878, 1884–5. Two- to three-storey with Italianate towers. Further addition 1935–9, by *Albert Monk*. Reorganized as a primary school 1970–1 by the *GLC Department of Architecture and Civic Design*. – HARBINGER, Westferry Road/Harbinger Road. A rare early Board school design (1872–3) by *R. Phené Spiers*, Master of Architecture, R.A. Schools, closely following Robson's ideas for separating infants, girls and boys in a three-decker building. Gothic details on the top floor. Originally T-shaped but partly demolished and rebuilt as a U in 1906–11. Schoolkeeper's house 1909.

Post-1945: ARNHEM WHARF, Westferry Road. By *PTP Architects*, 1995. Light-hearted and inviting. Two back-to-back L-shaped blocks with two-storey timber verandas along the inner faces and a curved rear elevation. Metal roofs. Larger hall block at the far end. – SAUNDERS NESS, Saunders Ness Road. By *Howard V. Lobb*, begun after bombing in 1940, completed 1952, incorporating 1930s parts of the former Board school. Yellow and red brick with pilaster strips; a bit Swedish. – MURAL. By *W. Kempster & B. Evans*. The docks and Greenwich Observatory.

NEW BILLINGSGATE MARKET, Billingsgate Road, NE end West India Docks. A conversion in 1980–2 by *Newman Levinson & Partners* of one of the concrete-framed transit sheds built on the *Hennebique* system by the PLA from 1912 round the West India Docks. This is Shed E, completed 1917, closed 1971. Extended N with a steel-clad pavilion, its spaceframe supported by 62 ft (19 metre) high tubular steel masts projecting above the roof to echo neighbouring cranes. Red brick walls to match the warehouse walls, ochre profiled metal. It now looks very unsophisticated in its slicker surroundings and in no way a worthy heir to Sir Horace Jones's Billingsgate Market of 1874–8 (*see London 1: The City of London*).

STORM WATER PUMPING STATION, Stewart Street. By *John Outram*, 1987–8. Postmodern in its symbolism, classicism and vivid colour, inside and out, but in no way routine. This primitive classical temple still looks fresh in 1997. It is a utilitarian building imbued by the architect with layers of meaning: according to him, it is 'a temple to summer storms' in which the walls represent a blue brick river flowing between tree trunks, and the round hole of the fan which splits the gable the cave between mountain peaks through which the river issues to fall as blue bricks down the wall. In the paving of the river terrace, columns are represented by discs of red brick between which the river of paving swirls in waves of dark and light blocks. Practically, the brick chamber conceals a subterranean concrete pumping chamber, tank and control room. The columns carry ducts and the axial fan in the metal-panelled gables prevents build-up of methane. Gates painted like an Egyptian eye in a battered and curved engineering-brick wall.

ISLAND BATHS, Tiller Road. 1963–6 by *Adams, Holden & Pearson*, who designed some of the Isle of Dogs' council housing (*see* Perambulation 6). Brown brick walls, copper roof. Foyer whale MURAL by *Will Adams*, 1991.

DOCKLANDS SAILING CENTRE, Westferry Road. 1987–9 by *Kit Allsopp Architects*, who won the limited LDDC competition. Its spreading boathouse form fills the W end of the dock, and makes an effective *point-de-vue* from the other end. The roof is the governing feature, shallow-pitched and extending far on the l. to cover the entrance in a way characteristic of this architect. It is carried on exposed trusses set on concrete columns, the glazed front wall being set back; the effect is of a kind of rustic Tuscan portico.

LONDON ARENA, Limeharbour. This is the largest public hall to be developed in London since the Wembley Arena opened in 1934. Converted in 1985–9 by *Stewart K. Riddick & Partners* from a former dock building, Fred Olsen's shed No. 2 of 1969, designed by PLA architects. It gives some idea of the huge scale of the post-war dock buildings that have otherwise all disappeared. The shed survives at each end, S with offices, N as a sports hall. Centre bays reconstructed higher to seat over 12,000, and form a vast central space, within a periphery of services. For the other (demolished) Olsen buildings *see* Perambulation 3: Marsh Wall, Thames Quay.

OPEN SPACE. Between the Millwall Dock and Manchester Road, a broad expanse of landscaped open space, mainly created post-war from derelict land and relandscaped by the LDDC post-1981. Through it, the GLOBE ROPEWALK, on the site of a late C19 rope works, forms an important formal link between docks, Mudchute City Farm, park, housing and shopping centre.

MUDCHUTE CITY FARM, to its N, was created in 1977 on a landscape of low mounds formed by the earth dredged from Millwall Docks 1875–1910. The mounds were used as gun emplacements in the Second World War; the pillboxes have been adapted for livestock. FARMHOUSE on Pier Street by *Kate Heron*. STABLES by *Kit Allsopp Architects*. Landscaping and trellised entrances by the LDDC, 1985–6.

MILLWALL PARK, Stebondale Street, is an LCC park of 1919. On its E edge, the ONE O'CLOCK CLUB (recreation centre). A crisp neo-Modern Movement design by *Avanti Architects*, 1991–2, commissioned by the LDDC. N entrance under a glazed canopy that divides the simple wing of changing rooms from the main hall with its serpentine glass brick wall screening a cloakroom area. Rendered walls, warm-coloured on the N and E, cool to the S and W facing a generous garden.

ISLAND GARDENS, a small park designed 1895 by *John J. Sexby* of the LCC Parks Sub-Department. From here one has, according to Wren, the best view of Greenwich Hospital. The land was part of that acquired from Cubitt by the Commissioners of Greenwich Hospital in 1850 expressly to preserve this view free from industry. In 1856 the hospital's architect, *Philip Hardwick*, had advised on laying out what is now Saunders Ness Road, with terraced houses between it and Manchester Road and detached villas in a garden by the river. The George Green School (*see* above) is now on the site of the houses. The two villas that were built were short-lived. – RAILINGS, 1985. – To the W, the red brick ROTUNDA at the entrance to the Greenwich Foot Tunnel (*see* below).

DOCKLANDS LIGHT RAILWAY. The part of the railway S of Crossharbour uses the twenty-seven-arch brick viaduct of the Millwall Extension railway, built by the GER 1869–72. *See* also Introduction p. 54

CANARY WHARF STATION (Jubilee Line). *See* Perambulation 2a, Canary Wharf.

38–9 GREENWICH FOOT TUNNEL, Island Gardens. 1896–1902, to

plans by (*Sir*) *Alexander Binnie* (LCC Engineer). The entrance rotunda has a glass and steel dome. Staircase and lifts in the steel entrance shaft. Tunnel, 12 ft 9 ins (*c.* $3\frac{3}{4}$ metres) in external diameter, 11 ft ($3\frac{1}{3}$ metres) internal, of cast-iron rings lined with concrete and white glazed tiles.

BRIDGES. Blue Bridge (Manchester Road Lift Bridge) *see* West India Docks below; Floating Footbridge *see* Perambulation 1; South Dock Footbridge *see* Perambulation 3.

THE WEST INDIA AND MILLWALL DOCKS

The West India Docks were the first and finest of the great enclosed docks. They were built between 1799 and 1806. Millwall Dock did not follow until 1863–9: never very successful financially it was linked to the West India Docks after the PLA took over in 1909. The docks on the Isle of Dogs reached their final form in 1924–8, when the South Dock Basin was incorporated in the South Dock and all the docks, including the Millwall, were linked. The Limehouse Basin was filled in just before the Second World War. The bombing in 1940 resulted in the loss of 80 per cent of covered storage, including almost all of the magnificent Import Dock warehouses. Post-war mechanization and pallet storage brought a brief period of prosperity, but decline set in after 1968 as the new large container ships berthed at the huge container ports in Britain (Tilbury, founded in 1886, at last came into its own) and on the Continent. From 1973 most business was transferred downstream to the Royal Docks. The bulk grain trade had been transferred to Tilbury in 1969. Final closure came in 1980 with a few tenanted berths kept on into the early 1980s. The basins survive in their 1973 form, disguised by the massive presence of Canary Wharf, which was named after the pre-war banana warehouses on the SW corner of the Import Dock. The substructure overlaps the S quay of the Import Dock and the N quay of the Export Dock, almost completely filling the latter. But Canary Wharf is just one element of the Enterprise Zone (*see* p. 94) that has transformed the docks through the agency of the LDDC.

The West India Docks

The campaign to build secure, enclosed docks specially devoted to the West India trade, with its exceptionally valuable cargoes and large ships, began in 1793 with the formation of a committee of merchants, led by William Vaughan, a naval architect, and Robert Milligan, a planter. In 1793 Vaughan published an influential pamphlet proposing four possible sites – St Katharine by the Tower (Wapping), the Isle of Dogs, Rotherhithe or Wapping. Wapping became the preferred site, but in 1794 the initiative was seized by the Corporation of the City of London who feared their control over the port would be weakened. Two rival bills were submitted to Parliament in 1797, one by the West India merchants for docks at Wapping, the other by the City for docks on the Isle of Dogs. The City's scheme involved

a single T-shaped dock and a canal to the s to make a more direct link between Blackwall and the City through the Isle of Dogs. The Wapping scheme, based on that devised by *Ralph Walker*, a former captain in the West India trade and a Jamaica planter, was for two dock basins surrounded by 'fireproof' warehouses, all within a secure perimeter wall: he also proposed a canal across the Isle of Dogs and another to the docks from Blackwall. Both bills were deferred, but, through the agency of Robert Milligan and George Hibbert, a leading merchant and a City Alderman, an Isle of Dogs scheme was developed, in which the docks would be financed by the West India merchants and planters. A joint committee of merchants and City interests was formed to carry the scheme forward. The plan was drawn up in 1797 by *George Dance the younger*, as Clerk of the City Works, *John Foulds*, his assistant and a former millwright, the engineer *William Jessop*, as consultant engineer, and *Walker*, representing the merchants. The plan that received Royal Assent in 1799 was similar in form to Walker's for Wapping, though in the final, post-Royal Assent plans the basins were laid out in parallel (as they are now, *see* map on pp. 92–3) rather than side by side, with the proposed canal s of them. There were two main dock basins rather than one for, in order to permit customs clearance at the dock, the Board of Excise insisted on a separate Export Dock, with independent access from each dock to the Thames, and a secure wall and ditch to surround them both. Dance provided designs for monumental warehouses

View of the proposed West India Docks and City Canal,
by W. Daniell, 1802

along the quays, which were very influential on the finished
buildings. The land for the docks was sold on to a new joint-
stock company, the West India Dock Company, the City retaining the land for the City Canal, which it built in 1802–5.

Ralph Walker was appointed Resident Engineer and started
work on the docks alone, but, because of Walker's lack of
engineering experience, *Jessop* was appointed in 1800 as civil
engineer to oversee him, with his son, *Josias Jessop*, as assistant.
Jessop was the designer and supervisor of construction until
1804, with Walker acting as site manager until 1802 when the
Import Dock (of 30 acres and 23 ft (7 metres) impounded
depth, the largest of that period) was opened, together with the
Blackwall Basin and entrance lock. Walker and the company
architects *George Gwilt & Son* (*George the younger* was clerk of
works) were superseded by *Thomas Morris* in 1803. The Export
Dock opened in 1806, all works being complete by 1809.

In 1809–21 *John Rennie* was Engineer to the Company, followed by his sons (*Sir*) *John* and *George Rennie*, 1821–34. The
company's monopoly expired in 1823 and, with increased competition, trade declined, leading to the formation of a single
West India and East India Company in 1838. In 1829 the
company had bought the City Canal, which had been a dismal
failure. It became the South Dock, with the addition of a timber
pond by *Rennie* in 1832–3; in 1853–5 it was connected to the
Blackwall Basin by the Junction Dock (infilled 1979–80). The

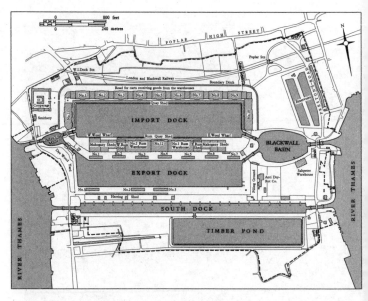

West India Docks in 1841, Plan

conduct of business at the dock was transformed after the 1850s with the arrival of the railway in 1851, and the introduction by *James Meadows Rendel* of hydraulic machinery in 1854–5. However, in 1855 the much larger Royal Victoria Dock, capable of handling steamships, opened. In response, (*Sir*) *John Hawkshaw*, then Company Engineer, remodelled the South Dock and its timber pond in 1866–70 as one larger dock. Competition increased yet again with the opening of the Royal Albert Dock in 1880, forcing the dock company into building docks further downriver at Tilbury in 1886, joining forces with the London and St Katharine Dock Co. in 1888, and enlarging the Blackwall entrance locks, 1892–1900. When the PLA was formed in 1909 the docks on the Isle of Dogs became one of its five groups of docks, known thereafter collectively as the India and Millwall Docks. The West India Docks reached their present form in the 1920s: the South Dock Basin was incorporated in the South Dock and its lock enlarged to become the main entrance; the Limehouse Basin was filled in; the original w entrance locks were blocked off; and all the docks, including the Poplar and the Millwall Docks, were linked by new cuts. The engineer was *Sir Frederick Palmer*. The Millwall entrance lock, the last on the w side, was closed by a bomb in 1940, and the Blackwall Entrance is now also closed, leaving only the South Dock Entrance in Manchester Road in use. The Canary Wharf development has now encroached over much of the surrounding Import and Export Docks.

As originally built in 1800–1, the BLACKWALL BASIN was a shared entrance basin, oval in shape to facilitate the towing in of

ships. Of the two passages, one to the Import Dock and one to
the Export Dock, only the former survives: the Export passage
was filled in 1926–8, when the docks were linked by wide central passages. When built the Blackwall Basin was the first
impounded, i.e. non-tidal, entrance dock ever built, with a
water level to match that of the docks; it had banked not walled
sides, though these were later quayed. Off it, SE, the remains of
a graving dock, made 1875–8 (*see* Perambulation 4). The
ENTRANCE LOCK, rebuilt to a larger size 1893–4, has been
dammed under a new bridge as part of the LDDC's improvements to Preston's Road (*see* Perambulation 4); the middle one
of the nearly 40 ft- (12 metres) high steel and wrought-iron
gates was removed. It was the first to use direct acting hydraulic
rams to the gates: original equipment derelict in 1997.

The SOUTH DOCK is mostly (*Sir*) *John Hawkshaw*'s work of
1866–70. At its E end, the SOUTH ENTRANCE is the only
remaining working lock in the West India and Millwall Docks.
The lock was rebuilt to serve the whole West India and Millwall
system in 1926–9: engineer *Sir Frederick Palmer*. At 995 ft
(303¼ metres) overall, with a 450 ft (137 metre) inner and a
140 ft (42⅔ metre) outer chamber; 80 ft (12 metres) wide and
35 ft (10⅔ metres) deep it is the same size as that of the Royal Albert
Dock. Walls and invert in mass concrete, dressings originally of
granite and granite concrete. Repaired 1959–60. Waterborne
steel gates. Across it, BLUE BRIDGE (Manchester Road Lift
Bridge), a single-span steel drawbridge, 1967–9 by the PLA, the
fifth bridge on the site. Part of the original LOCK CHAMBER of
1803–5, the old W entrance of the City Canal, remains by
Westferry Road: three-centred brick invert, and sides faced with
stone ashlar. For the Impounding Station *see* Perambulation 3.

The original DOCK CONSTRUCTION was designed by *Jessop*,
who had used it before at the Ringsend Docks in Dublin
(1791–6) and at Bristol. His are the quay walls of brick with a
concave section for stability and to suit ships' hulls; they are
now exposed only on the N side of the Import Dock and the S
side of the Export Dock. 6 ft (2 metres) thick with counterforts,
i.e. buttresses, behind bound to the walling by iron hoops, the
earliest known example of such reinforced brickwork. Mid-C19
granite copings replace the original gritstone. Lattice timber
fenders originally protected the walls from shipping, later
replaced by false quays. The locks (altered 1892–1902) were
spanned by innovatory double-leaf swing bridges in timber.
Hawkshaw's South Dock quay walls are of brick with a mass-
concrete core.

The Import Dock had remarkable BUILDINGS. Along the
North Quay *Gwilts*'s multi-storey warehouses formed a con- p.
102
tinuous, montonous wall half a mile long. Dance had originally
envisaged such warehouses but Walker advanced the idea for
ten of them on each main quay, starting with the North Quay
of the Import Dock which was to house sugar and rum. The
Gwilts built nine upon the North Quay in 1800–3, of up to six
storeys plus a loft in the roof space, but three were initially

built lower as capital was short. There were low link blocks
between, raised by *Rennie* in the 1820s. For description, *see*
pp. 112–13. A timber shed on cast-iron columns was built along
the whole length of the North Quay in 1818, similar to sheds
that survive in the Quadrangle (now the Cannon Workshops)
W of the docks. The South Quay was devoted to rum and
mahogany. The first warehouses, built in 1804–8 by *Morris*,
using timber construction, proved too small. Consequently,
vaults protected by sheds were built on the fields each side in
1813 and a separate shed (Rum Quay Shed) the length of the
quay (443 ft, 135 metres) for gauging. The sheds were all innovatory structures by *John Rennie*, the Rum Field Sheds having
Thomas Pearsall's patented wrought-iron roofs, comprising
what were among the first completely wrought-iron trusses in
Britain; of exceptional span (35 ft) they proved unstable and
were replaced in timber in 1815. The Rum Quay Shed was
entirely of cast iron (the roof slated) by the *Butterley Company*.
Trusses triangulated in the manner of a kingpost roof, with
shallow arch braces below, spanned between cast-iron arcades.
In 1817–18, Rennie replaced Morris's warehouses, except the
central one, by sheds with cast-iron columns and early arched
beams supporting roofs of timber, with lantern skylights (cf.
Tobacco Dock, Wapping). E and W stood Rennie's Mahogany
Sheds, 1817 (E) and 1820s (W), with timber roofs on cast-iron
columns and brick outer walls. The E one incorporated heavy
overhead travelling cranes. The W Rum Field Shed and warehouse burnt down in 1933 and were replaced in 1937 by the
Canary Wharf fruit warehouse. This, with its name boldly spelled
out, lasted until 1986–7 and survives in name as the present
commercial giant that covers its site. The rest went in 1940.

For the surviving warehouses *see* Perambulation 1: North Quay.
Also surviving at the far end of the Blackwall Basin, two dock-
masters' houses; *see* Perambulation 4.

Poplar Dock

London's first railway dock built for coal and goods export traffic.
This was converted in 1850–1 by the Birmingham Junction
(later North London) Railway Co. from a timber pond, itself
converted in 1844 from reservoirs developed by the West India
Dock Co. in 1827–8. A second, W basin was added in 1875–7 to
provide depots for other railway companies.

Much of the dock still survives, though the N end and the W
end of the W basin were infilled in 1988–9. To see what remains
it is necessary to follow Perambulation 4 down Preston's Road,
where it is protected by a wall of 1828–9, raised 1850. The dock
still has its timber WHARF-WALLING, very old-fashioned for its
date, and two *Stothert & Pitt* travelling CRANES on the W quay.
SE of the footbridge (1988) between the two basins is the
passage to the West India Docks made in 1850–1, enlarged
1898–90. On Preston's Road at the S end of the basin, the
simple, pyramid-roofed shell of a remote ACCUMULATOR

TOWER, built in 1877–8 when the 1850–1 hydraulic system was extended; there is another due W inside the curtilage of Billingsgate Market (*see* Public Buildings). The main 1870s pumping station was demolished in 1981. Nothing remains of the railway works.

The Millwall Docks

The Millwall Docks (1863–9) were conceived not for trade in the high-value bonded goods of the enclosed West India Docks, but to increase the waterfront of the Isle of Dogs for general industry, bulk trade, and for shipbuilding and repair. The idea originated with Nathaniel John Fenner, Millwall oil merchant and wharfinger who saw the advantage of non-tidal wharves, and *Robert Fairlie*, civil engineer and inventor of the double-bogie railway engine, but it became a contractors' speculation (cf. the (Royal) Victoria Dock, opened 1855). The contractors were *John Kelk* (builder of the 1862 Exhibition and the Albert Memorial) and *John Aird & Son*, who had an eye to selling on to the West India Dock Co. for amalgamation with their docks, an idea not realized until 1924. *William Wilson*'s original plan, refined by (*Sir*) *John Fowler*, was reduced in execution from an inverted T to a reversed L, as it appears now, with only one graving dock provided of the several intended (*see* Perambulation 5: Clippers Quay, Millwall). Warehouses, not part of the original conception, built from 1867 to encourage lessees, were brick single-storey sheds designed by *F. E. Duckham* to respond to the change in dock business from long-term storage to transit. Warehousing in fact proved to be the most profitable activity, though by the 1880s Millwall Docks were most famous as the centre of the European grain trade, stimulated by new grain-handling methods invented by Duckham (unloading direct to railway trucks introduced 1876 and pneumatic elevators 1892). Huge granaries stored the grain in bins: the Eastern Granary of 1883 had nine storeys, the Central Granary of 1903, twelve. In addition, timber was attracted away from the overcrowded Surrey Docks. The docks were hydraulically powered from the beginning and had travelling cranes from 1873, among the earliest in the Port of London.

Post-war reconstruction included improved quays, slightly deepened docks, and the erection of huge sheds for high-stacking by fork-lift trucks and mobile cranes. Innovative tubular-steel bow-string trusses of 1959–64 spanned up to 150 ft (45 metres), while space frames clear-spanned 200 ft (60 metres) in the Fred Olsen Terminal (1966 and 1970) which was among the largest and most advanced dock sheds in the world, with conveyor systems for palletized fruit. 'M' shed (opened 1967) in the adjoining South Dock was a sophisticated concrete structure. The redeveloped berths, among the most efficient in the world, were in demand right up to closure in 1980. All has since gone except a part of the Olsen Terminal converted for the London Arena (q.v.) and two sheds re-erected at Tilbury.

The present QUAYS are formed by 1980s hard landscaping. The original brick and concrete walls survive but, because of later rebuilding, are only exposed at the N end of the Inner Dock and on the S quay of the Outer Dock. The ENTRANCE LOCK was filled in by the LDDC in 1990 (though this process had already been started prior to the LDDC's involvement) as far as the outer gate recesses, leaving a slipway to the river, W of the Sailing Centre. S pier head landscaped, and hydraulic jigger of c. 1875 added to the middle gate machinery now mounted on display. Some early BOLLARDS survive here too. Other bollards are 'horn'- or Y-shaped patent 'Bean' bollards from the 1920s on, with the earliest round type, especially on the N and W quays.

PERAMBULATIONS

Perambulations 1–4 tour all the buildings round the West India and Millwall Docks (formerly the LDDC Enterprise Zone). Perambulations 5 and 6 investigate the older settlements of Millwall and Cubitt Town, and the buildings that have replaced riverside industry.

1. West India Docks North Quay (West India Quay)

19, The North Quay and the area just to the W now have the only
20 significant concentration of dock buildings. They should be approached, as they originally were, from the NW via West India Dock Road (Westferry DLR station), which immediately gives a taste of the docks' fortified and forbidding character. Because the road network now focuses on Canary Wharf, this route is somewhat hostile. Those for whom modern architecture is the prime interest, and who see the dock relics as only historic fragments among the more exciting later buildings of Canary Wharf (Perambulation 2), should start there and cross via the footbridge to the North Quay. At the time of writing, the warehouses, repaired by *Feilden & Mawson* 1984–5 and in the early 1990s, are on the verge of being absorbed into a new architectural composition, the extensive WEST INDIA QUAY, on part of the former Olympia & York landholding. In 1997 leisure facilities and flats, planned by *Michael Squire & Partners* for a consortium of developers, are destined to stretch all along the quay and end E in a thirty-storey tower of hotel rooms and flats. The warehouses themselves are planned to contain flats, a restaurant and shops, all by *Franklin Stafford*, and in three bays, converted by *Purcell Miller Tritton*, the Museum of the Docklands. Tucked behind them, alongside the DLR, will be a modishly modern complex of cinema and carparking.

This perambulation follows the historic route from the NW. A diversion just before the dock gate into GARFORD STREET, created in 1807 just after the docks opened, gives the first demonstration of the importance of dock security, essential because of the high value of the goods (sugar, rum and coffee) stored in the bonded warehouses. On the S side a row of DOCK

CONSTABLES' COTTAGES (Nos. 10–18) built for members of the Dock Police Force, which was formed in 1802. Designed by *John Rennie*, 1819, two pairs and one detached for the sergeant, behind small front gardens. Lower windows set in segmental-arched recesses. There was another group in Blackwall, since gone. Back E, tucked in by the dock, two Salvation Army hostels, originally the Scandinavian Seamen's Temperance Home. First built was the plain RIVERSIDE HOUSE, 1887–8, by *Richard Harris Hill*, a specialist in such institutions, followed by GRIEG 36 HOUSE for officers, 1902–3 by *Niven & Wigglesworth*, free and festive despite its awkward site. Queen Anne with Scandinavian overtones, in yellow and bright-red rubbed brick and terracotta. The end bays are blank except for arched doors and read like broad pilasters, framed with angle pilasters linked by festoons. Hipped roof with central cupola. For the W end and N side of Garford Street *see* Limehouse.

Beyond the railway viaduct, S in HERTSMERE ROAD, the Commercial (later West India Dock) Road entrance to the secure area of the docks, which was bounded by a ditch, a low railed wall just inside it, and a high inner brick perimeter of which the cliff-like N wall of the North Quay warehouses formed part. Of the outer wall (1802), two of the three GATEPIERS of 1809 survive: rusticated stone, capped with pediments and acroteria (renewed 1984). The central pier was removed in the 1950s. From 1875 it had formed the plinth for a statue of Robert Milligan, which now stands in its original position S of the Dock Office (*see* below). Just outside, the so-called DOCKMASTER'S HOUSE, built as the Excise Office, 1807–9 by *Thomas Morris*, but remodelled as a tavern in 1846 after the NE corner of the Customs Office, the twin that originally faced it, had been demolished for the London and Blackwall railway. The Italianate pub additions of 1877, dismantled in 1927–8, have been restored and Morris's clumsy Greek Doric portico replaced by a slighter Roman Doric one. Best feature is the broad bow overlooking the dock entrance (cf. the dock officials' houses in Blackwall). The garden boundary is a restored section of the OUTER DOCK WALL, mostly dismantled in 1928–9; the ditch, mainly covered in 1892, is represented by the drop to the garden.

Now for the rest of Hertsmere Road, before examining the warehouses. First on the r. the former PLA POLICE OFFICES, 1914 by *C. R. S. Kirkpatrick*, Chief Engineer, red brick with a tetrastyle Doric portico. Then a large open space, formerly the works yard. The small, circular, domed GUARD HOUSE, 1804–5 by the *Gwilts*, was one of two: this one was an armoury for the Military Guard and the dock's own regiment, the S one (dem. 1922–3) was a lock-up. They flanked the main gateway through the inner wall, dismantled 1932. Called the Hibbert Gate, it was a pedimented arch topped by a 10 ft (3 metre) *Coade* stone sculpture of a West Indiaman (*The Hibbert*); 1802–3 by the *Gwilts* who concentrated here the architectural flamboyance conspicuously absent within the docks. The archway to the stores, workshops and cooperage of 1824–5 by (*Sir*) *John Rennie* lay on an axis with the Hibbert Gate. Now the stores etc. are the CANNON WORKSHOPS, small business units created by *Charles Lawrence* and *David Wrightson* for the PLA, 1980–1, in one of the PLA's early attempts to introduce new industry after the docks closed in 1980. Single-storeyed buildings with broad-eaved roofs round a large quadrangle announced by a dignified triumphal arch of Portland stone. Brick-built E and S ranges: the offices (SE) were entered from within the arch. Stores (NE) continued round the N and W ranges: here wooden slats, later replaced by weatherboarding, originally concealed

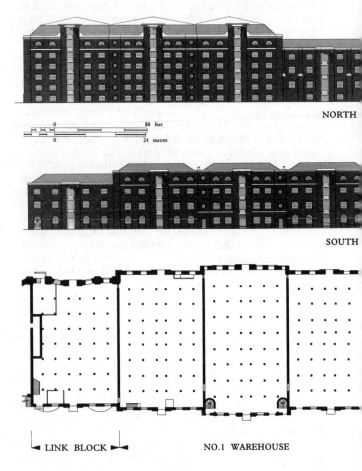

NORTH

SOUTH

LINK BLOCK   NO.1 WAREHOUSE

the slim cast-iron columns, but aluminium cladding has been set back behind some to form loggias. Centre s, the former carpenters' shop, well lit by continuous s glazing: doubled by an inner block, 1980–1. In the quadrangle, the cooperage, U-shaped, its courtyard now roofed over. Near the arch the c19 cannon, after which the group is called, and the benchmark for the docks inscribed TRINITY H.W. 1800. Of cast iron, it represents the mean high-water level of spring tides: the ground level is lower. On the E side of Hertsmere Road, stepping down E to the dock, an interloper, HERTSMERE HOUSE by *Newman Levinson & Partners*, 1987–8. Half-hearted attempts to echo the

ELEVATION

ELEVATION

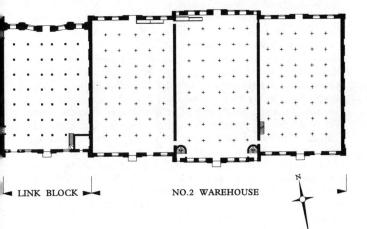

LINK BLOCK   NO.2 WAREHOUSE   N

Nos. 1 and 2 Warehouses, North Quay,
West India Import Dock. Elevations in 1827. Plan in 1987

North Quay warehouses and horrible details. In the dock in front of this, ARCHIMEDES, 1997 by *William Pye*, an artist skilled in using water as an integral element of his sculpture.

19
pp.
110–
11

pp.
102–
3

To the NE for a closer look at the WAREHOUSES from the North Quay. Only No. 1, at the W end, and No. 2, to its E, remain of the nine sugar and coffee warehouses of 1800–3 designed by the *Gwilts*, as the largest warehouses of that period in London. All the others were destroyed by bombing so now only imagination can conjure the immense wall of brick building that stretched along the North Quay of the Import Dock for over half a mile. It was originally composed of a row of six tall and three lower warehouses. The tall warehouses (Nos. 2, 3, 4, 6, 7 and 8) presented five storeys to the quay, which stood almost a storey higher than ground level, and effectively six storeys to the N by virtue of the semi-basement below quay level. They slightly preceded the lower ones, which followed when the dock company had limited capital and when the demand for sugar storage seemed well supplied. The lower warehouses (Nos. 1, 5 and 9) stood at the E and W ends and in the centre of the row and were of only one to two storeys over semi-basements. The centre one had a Baroque clock turret. Each warehouse, whether low or high, was 223 ft (68 metres) long and divided into three separate sections: the outer sections were of five bays each, the central one of seven. Between the warehouses and at each end were low link blocks of one storey plus basement. Warehouses and link blocks formed a massive perimeter wall between the docks and their outer defences (*see* above). The Gwilts' varied composition did not last long, for in 1827 *Sir John Rennie* raised the height of the three lower warehouses to that of the higher ones, cleverly adapting the composition to retain a consistent classicism and thereby concealing the evidence of the previous design.

No. 2 WAREHOUSE is still the original five storeys tall plus semi-basement and attic, in three sections separated by fire walls, each section having a central line of loading doors at front and rear standing slightly forward. At attic level these form dormers to the mansard roofs. Stock brick walls with Portland stone cornice, stringcourse and sills. Window openings wider than tall, under segmental heads: cast-iron windows (the earliest known in a warehouse), embellished with spikes on the lower floors for greater security. Circular windows light staircases within brick cylinders; lunettes above the cornice light attics (for coffee). The timber floors rested originally on oak storey-posts but these were replaced to increase load capacity by stocky cruciform cast-iron posts from the *Horseley Iron Co.*, Staffs, in 1813–18 on *John Rennie*'s suggestion. Shallow roof trusses of long spans remain in the two side sections. The flatter roof slopes were originally clad with copper and the steeper faces with slates. The 72 ft (22 metre) span timber-trussed roof in the central block was re-created in 1994–5 by *The Morton Partnership*.

No. 1 WAREHOUSE, like the other lower warehouses, was designed on the same ground plan but with two-storey central blocks flanked by single-storey sections, all on semi-basements. They were raised to four storeys plus basements by *Sir John Rennie* in 1827, in anticipation of housing East India Company goods after the ending of their monopoly. No. 1 reveals Rennie's higher storey heights, made so that the cornice lines up with that of No. 2. Its loopholes do not rise into the roof. Severely damaged by fire in 1901, the interior was replaced almost as original.

Between Nos. 1 and 2 and at the w end, four-storey blocks without attic storeys. These are the heightened LINK BLOCKS, originally one-storey-and-basement sheds built between the warehouses in front of the sections of wall that, with the warehouses, sealed the dock on this side. Raised to three storeys in 1827, their cornices also line through. Five bays wide with central loopholes and round-headed windows to the quay. The w link, a baggage warehouse, has blocked w windows and a more generous staircase. The N elevations of the warehouses are almost identical except that they are of cheaper plum brick.

Attached to the w, the LEDGER BUILDING, the *Gwilts*'s 20 Dock Office of 1803–4, remodelled as a ledger office by *Sir John Rennie*, 1827. Single storey, the rear outer walls formed by the end quadrant of the perimeter wall. Symmetrical façade with round-headed windows within relieving arches and rectangular panels over; timber Doric tetrastyle portico, date unknown. In front the bronze figure of Milligan (1810–12), bluff in everyday 19 clothes and quite unusual for *Sir Richard Westmacott* who preferred the dignity of classical dress. Vitruvian N door probably 1827. General office E, its strong-room, 1889, projecting into No. 1 warehouse. The w annexe was a fire station, remodelled 1812 as a police office; top storey perhaps 1875.

The N quayside of the IMPORT DOCK is now of the 1980s, but the dock walls are *Jessop*'s, of concave section to fit the ships' hulls. On the s side the massive raft and slabs of Canary Wharf, reached via the delicately poised deck of *Future Systems*' FLOAT- 53 ING FOOTBRIDGE, engineers *Anthony Hunt Associates*, 1994–6. As much a work of art as a practical structure that respects the dock walls. Lime-yellow tubular cross-braces straddle between pairs of pontoons like rubber shoes. The central section can be lifted hydraulically to let boats through.

The north quay continues as far as the Blackwall Basin. In 1997, the stretch between the warehouses and the DLR line awaits redevelopment (*see* above). E of the DLR line most of this area is in 1997 undeveloped, occupied only by New Billingsgate Market, one of the PLA's *Hennebique* sheds put up post-1912 (*see* Public Buildings). There is nothing else significant left here of the docks.

2. Canary Wharf

Canary Wharf, though spawned by the Enterprise Zone, is a curiosity within it – a tightly planned, axial development of formal spaces within the Enterprise Zone's *laissez-faire* confusion of buildings. The masterstroke in the planning of Canary Wharf, obvious but nevertheless successful, was the building of a single 51 skyscraper at the centre of the development to serve as a permanent advertisement for Docklands and an inescapable challenge to Canary Wharf's rival, the City of London. Most Londoners have come to admire the tower as a landmark, its monolithic simplicity subtly changing with the light and weather as it emerges gleaming from the river fog or, at night, shows a dependable winking eye. Companion towers were planned and others may yet be built – a new configuration may be more exciting or just banal – but the memory of Britain's first skyscraper, potent symbol of post-war North American financial and cultural dominance, will linger.

To unaccustomed British eyes, Canary Wharf looks extraordinary whichever way it is looked at – as a Manhattan-in-miniature framed in numerous riverside views, a floating island on its raft within the docks, a sheer gorge looming above the DLR track, or silvery alien towers above the brick buildings of Poplar High Street. The impression changes slightly closer to: from the South Quay of the South Dock, it makes a huge and glossy backdrop to the more rustic textures of Heron Quays; from North Quay, its artificiality is heightened in comparison with the straightforward brick character of the early C19 sugar warehouses.

Its history is as follows. The site is centred on the quay between the Import (N) and Export Docks (S) of the West India Docks, which closed in 1980. Canary Wharf, for fruit imports, gave its evocative name to the whole site. Redevelopment of the West India Docks started in 1982–3 with the conversion by *Terry Farrell & Partners* of one post-war warehouse into Limehouse Studios and the building of *Grimshaw*'s Ladkarn Workshops in 1984 (moved to the London Industrial Park at Beckton, *see* p. 79). Mixed-use proposals for another existing shed in 1984 were quickly superseded by the grandiose plans drawn up by the American *Skidmore, Owings & Merrill, Chicago* (project architect *Bruce Graham*), *I. M. Pei* (project architect *Henry Cobb*) and the British *Yorke Rosenberg Mardall* for a consortium of American banks, led by the American developer G. Ware Travelstead. These plans were approved in 1985. In outline they resembled what exists now – a formal layout of medium-rise blocks and skyscrapers opening on to a raised deck above a basement as deep as the dock, with several floors of carparking and services.

In 1987, the consortium collapsed when Travelstead was unable to find the funds to continue development. The Canadian company Olympia & York was approached to continue the scheme, which they did in their characteristic fashion. They were experienced in erecting good-quality buildings on cheap and unpropitious land (*see* e.g. the World Financial Center at the run-down Battery Park, New York, an office city of twenty-six buildings for 40,000 workers on the lower Manhattan waterfront). Using fast-track techniques they completed phase 1 by 1991. By then, as is described elsewhere, a world-wide property slump had set in and they were forced into administration in 1992. After much negotiation, which included a guarantee that London Underground's Jubilee Line would be extended to Canary Wharf, a loan was granted in 1993, and work on the incomplete phase 2 and phases 3 to 5, planned by *SOM* and *Koetter Kim & Associates*, was resumed under a management company in control of the remaining assets and subsequently a multinational consortium.

Olympia & York's site was slightly larger than the original 71 acres, which included 25 acres of water. Their development incorporated a related scheme on the North Quay of the Import Dock (called West India Quay), including the sugar warehouses, and another to the s, with an extension of the main deck to link with Heron Quays. The changes to the masterplan were relatively minor: they involved repositioning the tower blocks to the E end of the artificial island and making two of them lower, because of the sensitivity of the site in relation to Greenwich Park; and lowering the height of the deck by two storeys to relate it more closely to the water and to bring traffic and people in direct contact, a reaction to post-war city planning with its pedestrian and vehicle segregation. The deck was extended out over the dock each side on special piles designed to sit over the original dock walls without harming them. The developers acquired parts of the enclosed docks adjoining the wharf, enabling them to extend beyond the original wharf and combine a large number of buildings, with the huge floor areas and deep floor-plates then required for dealing rooms and modern technology, and room for traffic circulation and open space. The disadvantage of this plan is that the positioning of the blocks round the edge of the peninsula has led to a mono-cultural, self-sufficient scheme that looks inward to a narrow corridor of public open space, rather than a flexible development 68 for all types of businesses oriented to the water. Though many of the offices have magnificent views of river and dock, the quaysides are merely peripheral and overwhelmed by the great cliffs of building they skirt. When the buildings on the North Quay and Heron Quays (s) are complete, the Import and Export Docks, reduced by the surrounding scale, will become merely the watercourts envisaged by the planners. The only breath of air enters at the more spacious Westferry Circus, which opens w to a river panorama.

SOM (Chicago), as masterplanners, set guidelines for planning and architecture, a common North American strategy. These were incorporated into the agreement for the purchase of the site from the LDDC. They determined dimensions for individual buildings, heights of cornice lines and the location of arcades. They also laid down that natural stone should be used for the bases of buildings, that reflective glass cladding should be prohibited, and that special care should be taken with rooftops as these would be seen from the neighbouring towers. All the selected architectural firms but one were North American, experienced in designing commercial buildings and in supervising fast-track construction. *Cesar Pelli*, chosen to design the skyscraper, had been the architect of the World Financial Center. One firm, *Kohn Pederson Fox*, had then only recently come to prominence in the

USA. The executive architects, such as the New York *Perkins & Will*, were chosen specially because they offered the appropriate type of expertise. *Troughton McAslan*, a young British firm, were only commissioned after complaints that all the jobs were going to North Americans. The promise in 1995, when work restarted after the recession, was that more architects would be chosen as the result of competition and that prestige headquarters (the first is Citibank) would be preferred to speculative offices. The mid-1990s taste is for ever more idiosyncratic 'signature' buildings, resulting here in the commissioning of *Aldo Rossi* (†1997) and *Sir Norman Foster*.

Olympia & York's requirement for the architecture of Canary Wharf was quintessentially Postmodern in its desire for a development that looked rooted in place and time, that is, it had not only to look as if it was an established part of London but that it
71 had evolved over time. So *SOM*'s buildings hark back not only to the 1890s (old in terms of American cities) but to British architecture of different types and periods. *Kohn Pederson Fox* used, as they had done for all their buildings to that date, American architecture of the 1920s and 30s as a model (though their 1985 proposal for Travelstead's three skyscrapers had invoked the Houses of Parliament). Only *Pelli* and *Pei Cobb Freed & Partners* used modern forms and even they responded to the British climate
70 and industrial context respectively. *Troughton McAslan*'s building, though ostensibly representing the present day in Olympia & York's invented history, can be related to 1930s models such as Frank Lloyd Wright's Johnson's Wax building and Owen Williams's designs for the *Daily Express* and Boots, though here the sources have been absorbed and not just mined for superficial motifs.

68   Canary Wharf is set apart from any British development of the 1980s and 90s as much by the formal, Beaux-Art planning and the landscaping as by the architecture. The landscaping by *Hanna Olins* (consultant *Sir Roy Strong*) incorporates very high-quality street furniture by *SOM* and various pieces by artists. It is all admirably well executed and of excellent materials, but any sparks of originality there might be are very small and subservient to a conventional whole. The long North American tradition of the provision of public spaces by private developers is evident here but limited. The open spaces are small compared with the floor area of the buildings, and only three buildings, No. 1 Canada Square, No. 5 Cabot Square, and No. 7 The North Colonnade, have public foyers integrated into the overall plan (and these are now private because of security risks): there is nothing on the scale of the great winter garden designed by Pelli as part of Olympia & York's World Financial Center, New York.

2a. Canary Wharf : Cabot Square and Canada Square

CABOT SQUARE is the heart of Canary Wharf and where most people arrive, via the DLR, and receive their first close-up impres-
68 sions. First the square itself, a small room-like space, hemmed in

at all four corners by buildings alike in height but wilfully different
in style. Though the deck on which the square sits is raised quite
high above the water, there are no generous views out across the
docks. Changes of level between the raised deck and the level of
the original dock quays interrupt the view and the easy passage to
the water's edge. The central GARDEN is, after the fashion of a
London square, turned into an island by the roadway that rings it.
At each end, steps lead up between over-prominent pavilions
(carpark access) to the paved central piazza with stepped seating.
Central fountain a shallow basin with rhythmical play of jets by
the American *Richard Chaix*. At each angle four small circular
enclosures of translucent glass panels (carpark vents) by *Jeff Bell*
that light up at night; in the daytime they look insignificant. All
this is raised above a shady outer perimeter, very French in style
with a double row of pleached limes and, behind them, water-
stairs dropping down from the piazza. Seats between the trees,
unpleasantly close to the roadway; the noisy rush of water deadens
the sound of vehicles. Street furniture by *SOM*, sturdily designed.

The square has strong axes, E–W aligned on Pelli's tower and
the broad West India Avenue, N–S on the docks, but the insistent
individuality of the buildings unbalances the underlying symmetry.
The N–S axis is open to the dock between the buildings and
steps down to the broad pedestrian quays at water level. On the
N, WREN'S LANDING, the steps have scribbly metal railings by
Bruce McLean and lead to the exciting vivid yellow streak of 53
bridge across the Import Dock. The view from this quayside,
FISHERMAN'S WALK, is of the magnificent warehouses of the 19
original West India Dock (*see* Perambulation 1). On the S,
CUBITT STEPS lead down to MACKENZIE WALK, lined with
cafés and bars slotted into the base of the buildings on this side.
The view SW is of Heron Quays and Cascades, with a relaxed,
almost seaside feel that would probably be lost should Heron
Quays be redeveloped. To the SE the less attractive prospect of
South Quay and the DLR track, though the curving FOOTBRIDGE
makes a spectacular sculptural distraction (*see* Perambulation 2b).

Now for the buildings, excluding Cabot Place, the neo-1930s
striped stone entrance to the station and associated shopping
mall, which belongs to Pelli's tower (*see* below). Starting at the
entrance to West India Avenue, where the framing blocks have
stocky towers and lower wings towards the square:

Nos. 1–5 CABOT SQUARE, NW corner, by *Pei Cobb Freed &
Partners*, originally for Crédit Suisse First Boston. It is the most
straightforward and satisfying building of those round the square.
Its bluntness is refreshing when compared with the historicist
posing of its neighbours, yet it has a subtle modelling that
deserves more than a glance. Silver limestone cladding, striped
with darker grey granite beneath the sills. Regular windows
slightly canted within the openings. Undisguised plantroom
louvres make a band round the top. Geometrically it is formed
by series of interlocking octagons, the tallest eighteen-plus
storeys, only about a third as high as Pelli's tower but taller

than its eight- to ten-storey neighbours. Lower wings gradually detach themselves from the main block through variations of the octagon theme, a simplified version of the way in which complex geometrical forms unfold from the main column at Pei's much more dramatic Bank of China, Hong Kong, 1982 on. Inviting entrance: the public space of the external colonnade continues in a wedge beyond the glass screen-wall and doors, but the openness is deceptive. At one end of the foyer a silver-panelled apse ritualistically marks the division between the public and secure banking domain. Standard office floors round central services: the canted bay windows give some character to the bland spaces and draw the eye to the panoramic views. On the sixteenth floor the art collection of the Crédit Suisse, specially commissioned for a series of meeting rooms since 1993. Decoration in luxury-hotel style makes an uncomfortable setting for the modern but fairly conservative pieces, e.g. by *Tony Cragg*. Most impressive, the Wall Drawing Number 765 by *Sol LeWitt*, 1994. The bank's enlightened patronage was entirely successful in the staff restaurant, where 'Spaghetti alle Vongole Twice' by *Bruce McLean* with architect *Sophie Stourton* of *Whinney Mackay-Lewis Partnership* (1994) created a complete and joyful escape from the bland office environment, but this was heartlessly destroyed in 1997 for yet more dull office space. Gone are the delightful wall paintings and sculptures in the form of glass and coloured plaster and metal screens that articulated the space.

No. 25 CABOT SQUARE, the HQ of Morgan Stanley on the sw corner, answers No. 5 as the frame to West India Avenue. By *SOM (Chicago)*, this is the building closest in style to the firm's contemporary work in Chicago, e.g. No. 225 West Washington Street of 1984–8. Like that building, this one is based on the form and materials of late C19 steel-framed buildings by Chicago architects like Holabird & Roche or Burnham & Root. Here polished ox-blood granite and cream cast-stone imitate the red and white Chicago stone. But in deference to its context, the architects also claim to have been inspired by the 'warehouse buildings previously on the site': though the strictly rectangular forms are reminiscent of a framed red brick industrial building, the richness of the cladding makes this relationship seem very distant. Like No. 5 this has an L-shaped footprint and a stubby tower detaching itself from the main block. The tower's open top stage shields the penthouse and plant, in accordance with the planning guidelines for roofs. The building steps s from this in flat-topped stages down to the quay. Regular mullioned and transomed windows in the Chicago tradition.

71 No. 10 CABOT SQUARE, diagonally opposite (NE), is another *SOM (Chicago)* building but of different character. Here, the Chicago classicism has been infused with what the architects perceived to be English character: their aim was to capture 'the spirit, human scale and texture of the traditional buildings of London'. Hence the medley of classical details deployed in the profligate manner of the Edwardian Baroque, the ground-floor

arcades inspired by enclosed passages off Piccadilly, and the yellow brick cladding imitating London stock brick. They used the same prescription for their Bishopsgate building at Broadgate, 1987–91 (*see London 1: The City of London*). More whimsical the Sullivanish cast-stone bands of Celtic ornament, like all the superficial detail, of excellent quality. The composition is crude, on a large scale to be read from afar. Giant pediments break the skyline each side, disguising plant-rooms, that on the s atop a Chicago-style shallow canted bay. sw corner drum with an entrance porch in its base, domed with bronze gallery. In this bay and the central one s, elaborately stone-panelled foyers give access to twin service cores. No clue on the outside to the nine-storey central atrium where the same opulence prevails: three tiers of balconies ornamented by bronze grilles and a *faux* oval lantern dispensing artificial light. Most important to the passer- 69 by is the ground-floor arcade within the two lowest floors of rusticated stone: it has patterned marble flooring, hanging lanterns, and bowed shopfronts of teak and glass, all very close in style to the Bishopsgate building.

No. 25 THE NORTH COLONNADE, to the e, replaced, late in the 70 day, a block intended by SOM to match their No. 10 Cabot Square and to make with it a symmetrical group to correspond to KPF's along the s side. Though symmetry has been for-feited, a good building, well planned to relate to its surround-ings, has been gained. It was designed by the British *Troughton McAslan*, with *Adamson Associates*, North American experts in office design. It is the only block to break the street line in an interesting way and the only one that allows communication with the quayside through what in effect is a covered street link-ing the two blocks of the composition. The e block is wedge-shaped, and wedge-shaped steps sheltered by a space-frame funnel between the blocks invite the passer-by through the building. The sleek external skin of flush window and floor bands, the latter in grey polished granite, curves round the angles of the block and is threaded through on the lower floors with slim steel pilotis, which on the ground floor form The North Colonnade. The building actually meets the water on the e side, where a timber deck is sheltered by tensile canopies.

No. 30 THE NORTH COLONNADE and No. 20 CABOT SQUARE are composed as a single group along the South Dock. By *Kohn Pederson Fox*, with the architects *EPR Partnership*. KPF rose to prominence only in the early 1980s through astute marketing and designs that drew knowingly on the repertoire of North America's extravagant commercial buildings of the 1920s and 30s. This is a genuine American import, that does not attempt to fit into the invented history of Canary Wharf. The composi-tion is split into two by the track of the DLR: where it splits girders project as if the two halves have been forced apart. The inner elevations are almost featureless. Each block ends in a slow curve to the quayside. In the long view, e.g. from South Quay, the bold tripartite horizontal division of the curved elevations shows the sort of broad-brush effects for which the practice is popular. The elevations follow, in diagrammatic form, those typical of an American Beaux-Arts classical office block. They are faced in the light-reflecting, silvery cladding (here obviously expensive white, figured Vermont marble) that KPF favoured in the early 1980s. Coarse functional detailing replaces overt classical features, instead of the ornamented cast-stone panels used at No. 10 Cabot Square: the square-profile *faux* cornice and projecting metal fins flanking the window strips are both typical of 'clip-on' details seen in other KPF work. At the ends of each block, a feeble octagonal corner tower (cf. their contemporary No. 500 East Street South West, Washington), which forms an entrance porch but otherwise has no ramifications for the plans. No sign on the outside of the central five-storey atrium in each block, which starts from the third floor, or of the overheight floors intended as dealing rooms. Square open bays continue as a perfunctory ground-floor arcade along both blocks. The E block, No. 30 The North Colonnade, forms the SW corner of Canada Square.

51, No. 1 CANADA SQUARE is the proper name of Canary Wharf's 68 first tower, the showpiece of Phase 1 and the hub and landmark of the whole development. By *Cesar Pelli & Associates*. Pelli claimed this to be England's first skyscraper. To celebrate that fact he designed the simplest form possible, square in plan, pyramid topped and sheer, with a taut skin of stainless steel to reflect the English sky – a simple gleaming prism that, as Pelli sees it, has an elemental quality and responds to changes of light on the water and in the sky and to the misty English weather. Stepped recession at the angles and at the top to make the forty-six storeys seem more slender (the slight squatness results from a conflict between a height restriction imposed by flight paths from the City airport and the developers' demand for maximum floor space). When finished in 1991 the building surpassed in height all British and all but one European rivals, at over 800 ft (244 metres) high compared with the City's 618 ft (188 metres) NatWest tower, completed 1979, and Helmut Jahn's Messerturm, Frankfurt, of 1985–91 (251 metres). The tower seems to touch ground lightly, with no modulation in the even, steel walling except a band of triangular patterning above the two-storey-high flush glazing round the base. At ground level along the N and S sides, projecting steel posts make schematic colonnades. For those accustomed to the work of Foster, Rogers and Grimshaw, the use of stainless steel seems unexceptional, but in 1987 it had never been used for cladding an American skyscraper. Pelli's choice of material was an open acknowledgement of the pervasive influence of the English High-Tech style. The panels are technically a rain screen attached by aluminium framing to a curtain wall; the pyramid is a perforated cap to the cooling towers.

CABOT PLACE, attached to its W, is the solid anchor to the soaring tower. The result is a slightly uncomfortable combination of monumentality and delicacy characteristic of some of Pelli's other work (c.f. e.g. NTT Shinjuku Centre, Tokyo).

This part of the scheme was executed with *Adamson Associates* and *Frederick Gibberd Coombes & Partners*. Cabot Place faces Cabot Square and The North and South Colonnades with distinctly Postmodern façades subtly striped in red and cream sandstone and greenstone, materials which continue with polished luxury into the base of the tower as a magnificently spacious foyer with strong axes. (In 1997, alas, a private and quite separate space.) Cabot Place is split apart N–S by the DLR line and the dramatic red-painted steel and glass canopy above it. This reinterpretation of the C19 station shed, designed with *A.S.F.A. Ltd*, covers CANARY WHARF STATION. The 52 high parabolic arches could hardly make a more exciting gateway into the centre of the development. Flanking the station and linking underneath it, three levels of shopping mall (with *BDP*), mostly top-lit but uninspiring. At the W end on the first floor a public hall. All the buildings described above belong to phase 1 of the development, 1988–91.

CANADA SQUARE, incomplete in 1997, will soon be framed by the buildings of phase 3, for which two more towers were originally approved. Already rising in 1997 at the SW corner, *Sir Norman Foster & Partners'* CITIBANK, Canary Wharf's first building by one of the founding fathers of the High-Tech movement. On the S side the central 'landing', NASH PLACE, leads S from Canada Square to the CANARY WHARF JUBILEE LINE STATION on the E extension of Heron Quays (*see* Perambulation 3). Also by *Foster* and, though envisaged as the most prestigious among the string of glamorous new Jubilee Line stations (*see* Introduction p. 54), it is nevertheless a low-key solution that interferes little in the overall townscape (cf. Foster's Crescent Wing, Sainsbury Centre, University of East Anglia) but looks interestingly sculptural from the surrounding high buildings. Entrances through two glass, oval bubbles embanked in the grass slopes of Canary Wharf's main recreation space. The W one faces the water of S dock and a plaza extension of Nash Place. To the E a more minor entrance into a bus interchange.

Beyond the Eastern Access Bridge round Cartier Circle, future developments (phase 5) will be low-rise. In 1997 nothing has been begun so, for now, we must return through Cabot Place and down the E–W axis of West India Avenue straight into Westferry Circus, the second phase of the development.

2b. Canary Wharf: West India Avenue to Westferry Circus

WEST INDIA AVENUE AND WESTFERRY CIRCUS belong to the original masterplan of 1985. Westferry Circus was begun first and the W part of the NE quadrant was built very quickly in 1991–3. The rest was abandoned when Olympia & York collapsed and was only restarted in 1994. A further West India Avenue section was not begun until 1996; Canary Wharf Riverside, the SE quadrant of Westferry Circus, has just been started by a new consortium in 1997.

WEST INDIA AVENUE is planted with shady trees, a central double row of limes with a carpet of periwinkles beneath. The handsome aluminium lampstandards by *SOM*, used throughout Canary Wharf, are especially prominent here. Only the N side has been built up in 1997 (*see* below) so that on the S the road bridges land developed earlier on a much smaller scale at the proper ground level. Nudging up to the roadway is No. 1 PARK PLACE of 1985–7, eight-storey, brick-clad offices with an elaborate plan of overlapping polygons. Equally mannered elevations with arched windows between buttresses, mansards over the large polygons, lanterns over the small ones. By *Stanley Trevor* for City accountants, Littlejohn Frazer. The N side belongs with the development of Westferry Circus.

WESTFERRY CIRCUS, created in 1987–91, provides the link between the Canary Wharf deck and the rest of the Isle of Dogs. At the deck level it forms a circular garden 'square', intended to be enclosed on all but the W, where a wide promenade overlooks the river, commanding an impressive panorama. From W to E: on the N bank, Limehouse from Free Trade Wharf, Narrow Street and Dundee Wharf, and, E, the overhanging canopies of Sea Containers at Millwall; on the S bank, opposite, Rotherhithe with Nelson Dock, and Columbia and Canada Wharves. Below the promenade, gardens slope steeply down to Canary Wharf Pier. Beneath the deck a roundabout guides traffic to and from the underground services and the rest of the Isle of Dogs. On top of it, free-spirited leafy
60   entrance gates and railings by *Giuseppe Lund* enclose a circle of fairly informal planting and lawn, more English and much more spacious than Cabot Square, and, on Westferry Road as it swings away N, the landmark is GLOBE by *Richard Wentworth*, 1997.

Nos. 1–7 WESTFERRY CIRCUS and No. 5 WEST INDIA AVENUE form eight- to ten-storey interlocking buildings of the circus's NE quadrant, designed as a single scheme by *SOM* and *Koetter Kim Associates*. Massive, dull and limestone-clad; built 1991–3. Nos. 1–7 are by *SOM* (who also designed No. 11, completed 1995); Nos. 1–3 by *Robert Turner*, Nos. 4–7 by *David Childs*. No. 5 West India Avenue is by *Fred Koetter* of *Koetter Kim & Associates*, with *Perkins & Will*, in the same vein. The parts are not distinctly different; they follow the North American Neoclassical pattern of interwar office blocks, and make a plainer, more severe backdrop than the *primedonne* of Cabot Square. At the back, where the blocks face the unfishished COLUMBUS COURTYARD, a piazza opening on to the SW corner of the Import Dock, they are a bit more playful, with some curious pink-chequered details.

A slightly broader cultural mix and late 1990s taste for individual expression occur on CANARY WHARF RIVERSIDE, SE of the promenade facing the river, where the construction of flats and a hotel has just begun (1997). Designed by the American *Koetter Kim & Associates*, the British *Novo Architects*, and the French *Philippe Starck*, these more varied buildings cluster round garden squares and a river promenade by *Derek Lovejoy*.

3. Buildings round the South Dock and Millwall Docks

This perambulation starts at the N end of Marsh Wall at Heron Quays and examines the rash of buildings spawned under the special terms of the LDDC's Enterprise Zone, established 1982.

The architectural results of the free-for-all post-1985 boom predominate. Some of the first, pre-boom industrial units of the Enterprise Zone, like Heron Quays, Great Eastern Enterprise and No. 33 Millharbour, demonstrate skill and charm. Almost all the buildings that followed from 1986, at first medium-rise and then, as the demand for office space grew, high-rise, fail to show any sophistication. The monumentality inherent in early 1980s Postmodernism is their distinguishing characteristic, but they lack totally the sense of irony or delight in symbolism or ornament that one might also expect. Postmodern forms are rendered in glitzy mirror-glazing and marble veneer and, surprisingly, in sombre colours, as if to persuade potential occupiers of their seriousness. Very few of the mid-1980s buildings, most notable being Thames Quay, hold out for a form of Late Modernism. Interiors are generally strictly functional and inaccessible, public spaces, in contrast to Canary Wharf, minimal and uninviting: Harbour 59 Exchange has a pleasant courtyard, though this development, like almost all the others, makes nothing of the quayside or the most beautiful element of the surroundings, the vast expanse of water. Here, even the LDDC infrastructure, the saving grace of many of the other areas, is less in evidence and much of the area, including the South Dock, is blighted by the ugliness of the DLR's viaduct. Since the IRA bomb-blast of 1996 at South Quay, some improvements have been made, notably the supremely elegant bridge across the South Dock, and these lift the spirits considerably.

HERON QUAYS, a much-admired, even loved, mixed develop- 51 ment by *Nicholas Lacey, Jobst & Hyett*, 1981–9, is the most imaginative piece of architecture from the first phase of the LDDC. A clever variation on the usual light steel-framed industrial building, clad in vitreous enamel panels, and one of the few Docklands schemes to exploit fully the watery site. Lacey's deep-red and purple units, of up to three storeys and with a variety of roof pitches and angles, are composed like a waterside village round leafy courts and project over the Listed dock wall on to steel piers. Canary Wharf, which looms over it, has destroyed the original setting of a long narrow peninsula between the West India Export Dock and South Basin, and redevelopment has begun with the Canary Wharf tube station on the E part, where a further five stages of Lacey's scheme were originally planned. Intended for the roundabout at its entrance (W), TRAFFIC LIGHT TREE, 1997, by *Pierre Vivant*.

CASCADES, another of Docklands' most memorable landmarks, 82 stands on a fine open site bounded by the river and the remains of the entrance passage into the South Dock W of WESTFERRY ROAD, just outside the former Enterprise Zone. By *CZWG* for Kentish Homes, 1985–8. A surprising use of residential high-

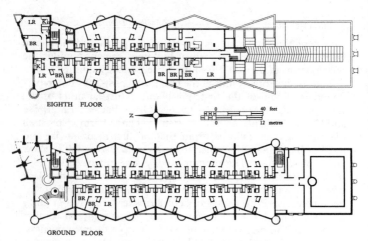

EIGHTH FLOOR

GROUND FLOOR

Cascades. Plans of ground floor and eighth floor

rise in a period that generally eschewed it and shocking when first completed, Cascades conveys a sense of fun then lacking in Docklands except in CZWG's work. Its dramatic silhouette and delightful details wear well. A narrow twenty-storey slab of concertina form, banded in yellow and blue brick. To the S the cascade of terraces and conservatories, bisected by a glazed slope of fire escape, that gives the block its name. Lots of entertaining nautical references culminating in the N prows with their
80   clever little crow's-nest balconies, sculptural in the upward view. Alongside the entrance from Westferry Road, a restrained six-storey block including shops.

The ANCHORAGE on the S half of Sufferance Wharf by *Michael Squire Associates*, 1988–90, is more serious; though it matches its taller neighbour in materials it has none of Cascades' daring. It mediates between the dock and the existing streets with a ten-storey block by the water, low blocks round a courtyard and commercial units to Westferry Road. The tall block is crisply articulated. A white rendered block appears behind an outer skin of yellow brick, forming balconies, and emerges at the top in a series of barrel-vaulted penthouses. At ground level a double-height arcade and bold blue post-and-lintel portals. Nautical portholes and metal balconies here too, the whole block with interwar echoes.

MARSH WALL leads E from the roundabout along the S side of West India Dock's South Dock. On the W side in the angle between Westferry Road and Marsh Wall, the red brick former
51   IMPOUNDING STATION, built by the PLA in 1926–8 when they dammed the W entrance to the South Dock. On the E side a sweeping view of Canary Wharf, with Heron Quays in telling contrast below it, and, in the foreground, a steel SCULPTURE (Spirit of Enterprise) by *Wendy Taylor*. Interlinked shapes based on the outline of the Isle of Dogs.

Between here and the passage between the West India and the Millwall Docks, some of the most vulgar buildings in Docklands. First No. 161, designed as the Scandinavian Trade Centre (now Price Waterhouse) by *Sten Samuelson* and *Klas Nilsson*, 1986–8. White-clad cube clasped at the angles by four inverted ziggurats of mirror-glass in a timber grid that does not align with the other rows of small square windows. Atrium originally intended as an exhibition space. Then the INTERNATIONAL HOTEL, low-grade design of similar date, its glazed corner projection to the dock topped by a railed terrace. On the S side, a better piece of urban design, as the quiet and unexceptional Nos. 30 and 40 of 1990–2 follow the curve of Marsh Wall with a tall colonnade. Set back at No. 50, a former ELECTRICITY CONVERTER STATION of 1919–20, which supplied electricity to Millwall Docks. The usual good-quality, slightly classical PLA work; now offices. Just beyond, a circular plaza, featuring a SCULPTURE by *Eilis O'Connel* (Vowel of Earth Dreaming of its Roots), 1997.

WATERSIDE, grouped by the dock along Admiral Way, incorporates a variety of different blocks, their varying sizes charting the progress of the Enterprise Zone from low-rise to medium-rise and then to high-rise, from boom to bust, and from the 1980s speculation in offices to that of the 1990s in homes. Along the quay low, domestic-style office apartments by *Richard Hemingway*, 1985–6, represent the first phase, the medium-rise speculative BEAUFORT COURT and QUAY HOUSE, 1987–8 by *Newman Levinson & Partners*, the second. The third, the nineteen-storey, pyramid-roofed former EURO TRADE CENTRE by *Whittam Cox Ellis Clayton Partnership* 1988–92, was built just as the demand for offices dried up due to the recession. It stands empty despite the demand for residential rather than office space which began to take hold in about 1995.

SOUTH QUAY PLAZA surrounds South Quay station and opens to the dock. The particularly glum concrete-framed, blue glass-clad blocks with pedimental gables, designed by *Richard Seifert & Partners*, 1986–9, were badly damaged by an IRA bomb in 1996. The tallest block is, in 1997, being reclad with a lighter touch by *Rolfe Judd*, who are providing new retail units. *Swanke Hayden Connell* are refitting the entrance and all common areas for another of the three blocks, and the third is to have a new entrance by *Whinney Mackay-Lewis*. The plaza will also be much more imaginatively treated in a scheme by the LDDC, which includes the magnificent sculptural steel S of a cable-stayed FOOTBRIDGE by *Chris Wilkinson Architects* with *Jan Bobrowski*, engineer, 1994–7. The S is composed of a fixed half and a movable part, each with its own dramatically inclined mast and cables. The bridge now spans from here to Heron Quays, but is designed so that it can be reused in two halves, with the swing-opening half rotated to a new position on an axis with the Canary Wharf tower, and the fixed half moved to a new position elsewhere.

MILLHARBOUR is the street that runs S from just opposite South Quay and follows the W side of Millwall Inner Dock. It is lined by some of the earliest industrial buildings of the Enterprise Zone, small scale and set in the leafy landscape of a conventional industrial estate, known as the ENTERPRISE BUSINESS PARK when it was begun in 1983. First w and also along LIGHTERMAN'S ROAD, two-storey pavilions by *Newman Levinson & Partners*, 1983–5. Their faceted walls of buff-coated panels are fixed to brightly coloured frames; also brightly coloured oriels. Phase 2, 1985–7, was used by the *Guardian* as its printing works. Red and grey cladding, exposed roof trusses and tensile supports. Mast-like tower. At the start of the E side of Millharbour, GREAT EASTERN ENTERPRISE by *D. J. Curtis & Associates*, 1984–9 to initial designs by *Howell Killick & Partridge*. Crisply designed and laid-out units. The unifying element is the apparently continuous glass curtain walling, gridded in bright green; it wraps round the squat drums that punctuate the façades. Further down, w, INDESCON COURT (w) by *Richard Seifert & Partners*, 1982–3, steel-framed with neat white-metal cladding, mirror glass, and bright-blue glazing bars; and LANTERNS COURT, 1983–4, brick-clad units, based on a pre-existing industrial building but with echoes of a stable yard. Best of all is No. 33, built 1983–7 as offices, workshop and storage for Advanced Textile Products. Here *Nicholas Lacey Jobst & Hyett* have made the most of a simple shed with intricately patterned silver and red cladding, which conceals three levels inside. Red and silver planting in harmony. Last and simpler, the silver metal MILLTECH shed by *John Brunton Partnership*, 1984.

GREENWICH VIEW closes the S end of Millharbour. It is an extensive speculative development overlooking Millwall Inner Dock, which began with the five low-rise E blocks (1985–8) by *Richard Seifert & Partners* for Indescon. Mirror-glazed with sliced-off round towers, they have none of the modesty of the earlier Indescon Court. These were followed by the desperately overweening City Reach (1988–9), comprising City Reach One and West Tower, two tall tinted-glass office slabs linked by a lower gabled atrium at the angle of the dock, and the white, would-be modern movement Pointe North (1988–90) projecting into the water on a rhomboid platform. Among these blocks, salvaged cranes. All of this is most easily seen from the E side of Millwall Dock.

WEST FERRY PRINTERS lies to the W of City Reach, with the main entrance from Westferry Road. Designed as the *Daily Telegraph* printing works by *Watkins Gray Wilkinson Associates*, 1984–6. Extension 1988–9 for printing *Express* newspapers and from 1995 also the *Financial Times*, in retreat from their far superior building in Blackwall (*see* below). In form a massive press hall, spanned by huge trussed steel girders, surrounded by multi-storey offices. A glass-roofed 'street' links a smaller, lower section.

Back N a little to where Pepper Street crosses the dock to the E side as Glengall Bridge. Along here separating the houses of North Millwall (Tiller Road and Mellish Street, *see* Perambulation 4) from the industry of Millharbour is a wall, to some an unfortunate reminder of the walls that once shut residents out from the West India Docks. There is only one narrow gateway through it on an axis with Glengall Bridge.

GLENGALL BRIDGE begins on this side with an arcaded quadrant of offices. The concept of a narrow pedestrian bridge lined with shops, flats and offices is a good one, though this is a bridge purely in planning terms since only the narrow central section span is clear of the water: the rest is built out on jetties. The architecture, by *Richard Seifert & Partners*, 1987–91, for a consortium of developers, is dismal. Brownish-red brick elevations with green-tinted windows throughout. Along the main route, Pepper Street, rows of shops shelter behind concrete arcades, based on, say, St Katharine Docks. The w end of the street is latest (1989–91). Opening off it oversized office blocks round gloomy, uninviting courts with underground parking. The central Dutch-style double drawbridge is flanked by asymmetrical groups of small apartments that can be used for offices or flats, an early exploitation of the Enterprise Zone terms allowing flexible use. The groups are composed with layers of balconies and pitched roofs to make a reasonably picturesque view in the long view from N and S. The E stretch has on the N side the London Arena (*see* Public Buildings) and another square of offices, Lanark Square.

The CITY HARBOUR development, by *BDP* and *Holford Associates*, 1987–90, opens s off Lanark Square, and overlooks the E side of the Millwall Inner Dock from Selsdon Way. In two parts: to the E, The Terrace, a yellow brick block of various heights, with greenhouse excrescences on top; to the w, two sleeker blocks (Woodchester House and Northern and Shell Tower, formerly Merchant House) round Waterman's Square, six to nine storeys, grey panel-clad. Most distinctive the prominent projecting rails all round the roofline, very reminiscent of those used by Sir Owen Williams on his Southwark Sainsbury factory of 1935. Another office block and a twenty-storey hotel were originally planned to complete the square, but in 1997 flats are under construction instead. From here an excellent view of the low-rise housing all along the s side of the Millwall Dock (*see* Perambulation 5), and of the Sailing Centre spreading across the E end (*see* Public Buildings).

LIMEHARBOUR is the N continuation of East Ferry Road from Crossharbour station: it forms the boundary between the Enterprise Zone and Cubitt Town (*see* Perambulation 6). Its course is shadowed on the w by the DLR line; on the E, a number of unremarkable small office blocks ending N in SKYLINES office village, 1984–6, which belongs in date and type to the small industrial units in Millharbour. Planned when the huge spreading dock sheds of the Fred Olsen Line lay to the w and N, it asserted itself by the angular sail-like prisms of the individual blocks and the bright colours. By *Hutchinson Partners, Libby & Co.*, extended in a similar way by *Sidney Kaye Firmin*, 1988–9.

HARBOUR EXCHANGE commandeers the NW corner of Limeharbour with Marsh Wall, replacing Fred Olsen's No. 2 shed (the London Arena to the S incorporates No. 2) and the famous Fred Olsen Centre, 1966–9, which contributed to establishing the reputation of *Norman Foster* as a master of High-Tech. His intervention at Olsen's was especially important for its early use of mirror glass, specially made in Pittsburgh, for the walling of the office and amenity block slotted between two of the transit sheds.

A complex development, 1986–90, which involved four architectural firms, several developers and a masterplan by *Sheppard Robson*, but with a straightforward commercial result. Outwardly a curved multi-storey wall of blue reflective glass following the line of the DLR. The blocks that comprise it, by *Sheppard Robson* (Nos. 3–5) and *Frederick Gibberd Coombes & Partners* (the rest) face inwards towards the well-landscaped Exchange Square, with its raised planting, overflowing basins and still pools, and SCULPTURE, Wind of Change by *André Wallace*, 1989–90, for the developers, Charter Group. Two pairs of mysterious bronze figures in tiny boats; in each pair a woman reclines languorously on a beached boat, while a hunched man drifts with long, upraised oars. The row of very sculptural cranes, by *Stothert & Pitt*, 1960s, though original to the dock, seems marooned, barred from the water by an ill-conceived moored paddle-steamer of a building, Harbour Island, resting on piles over the dock (of which the developers had bought part). By *Haverstock Associates*, timber-framed and, surprisingly, part of the original concept.

THAMES QUAY lies to the N, on the N side of Marsh Wall. This is perhaps the best building along Marsh Wall, probably because it was designed in 1985 by *YRM* as a company headquarters, something rare in the Enterprise Zone. Though intended for the American petrochemical company Fluor Daniel as its European offices, it was finally built speculatively in 1987–9. Crisply anonymous and, despite being specially tailored for its site by the passage between the West India and the Millwall Docks, somewhat cavalier about the charms of the waterside setting. Three grey-clad blocks, linked in a generous L-shape, step down towards the dock in broad terraces allowing maximum daylight within; between them glass slopes, roofing lightwells. Service towers break up the horizontality.

THE MANSION (No. 197 Marsh Wall) is a pretentious Postmodern block by *Richard Seifert Ltd*, 1988–9. Diagrammatic framing of polished and plain granite bears little relation to the real structure it conceals. As so often in the Enterprise Zone, a decent building, such as Thames Quay, is let down by its neighbours. Further on there is similar frivolity at MERIDIAN GATE, 1987–90 by *SSC Consultants*, with a third phase (housing) of 1997. It continues behind a much better building, the INNOVATION CENTRE (No. 225), 1989–92 by *Feilden & Mawson*, its silvery metal cladding of high quality, its details restrained and thoughtful. Two parallel sheds, containing small high-tech research and development suites, are linked by a top-lit atrium. Marsh Wall ends with the bold public statement of *Tchaik Chassay*'s Isle of Dogs Neighbourhood Centre (*see* 74 Public Buildings).

4. The Blackwall Basin and Coldharbour

From the E end of Marsh Wall, MANCHESTER ROAD and its con-tinuation, Preston's Road, give access to the E side of the West India Docks (q.v.). The Blue Bridge spans the operational entrance to the South Dock. Further N, off the W side of Preston's Road, lie the Blackwall Basin and Poplar Dock. Lovegrove Walk crosses what was the Blackwall Basin Graving Dock of 1875–6; it projects SE from the Basin. Now surrounded by the unexceptional Wates housing that composes JAMESTOWN HARBOUR, begun 1982 by *Whittam, Cox, Ellis & Clayton*. In the graving dock, LEAP, *c.* 1982, by *Franta Belsky*, a sculptor whose work was popular in the post-war New Towns: eight stylized dolphins spouting water.

PRESTON'S ROAD crosses the entrance lock to the Blackwall Basin via a 1980s bridge. On the N side, the very handsome BRIDGE HOUSE, 1819–20 by *John Rennie* for the West India Dock Company's Principal Dockmaster or Superintendent. Like a Thames-side villa, its pyramidal roof with flues gathered into an arched, almost Baroque chimneystack. Ground floor raised over a basement with originally blind windows. Bows each end face docks and river; Greek Doric distyle in antis portico. C19 external alterations reversed by *Whittam, Cox, Ellis & Clayton*, who radically changed the interior for flats, 1987.

COLDHARBOUR forms a narrow backwater parallel with the E side of Preston's Road. This is the one place on the Isle of Dogs that still has a close-packed riverside character. It originated in the causeway from Blackwall (q.v.), probably developed from the pathway along the top of the 'Blackwall'. There were build-ings along here by the second decade of the C17, but no houses now date from before the early C19, when it had become isolated by the building of the docks. At the N end, in the vicinity of Bridge House, ISLE HOUSE (No. 1), another dockmaster's 15 residence, this one 1825–6 by (*Sir*) *John Rennie*. Similar but p. simpler with an unusual plan presumably to command dock 27 entrance and river, i.e. on the raised ground floor three rooms along the river-front with bows to the N and the centre room. The entrance hall runs parallel with the street, staircase at the E end. Restored by *Carole A. Gannon* of the *Welling Partnership*, 1995–6. No. 3, NELSON HOUSE, very narrow, is an amalgama-tion *c.* 1820 of two houses by Samuel Granger, coal merchant and lighterman, who added tall arches round the windows, and two (timber-framed) bows to the river above a veranda. The front doorcase had part-fluted Doric columns in antis (stolen 1990). Nos. 5–7, perhaps also 1820s, minimal. Then Nos. 9–13, CROWN WHARF, in 1971 an isolated effort by *Bernard Lamb* to upgrade the neighbourhood. A tall white-boarded terrace, ground floors open as carports, rooftop terraces with belvedere penthouses and severe river fronts that fit well with the early C19 neighbours. No. 15, 1843–5, plain, comes before the former BLACKWALL RIVER POLICE STATION (Nos. 19–19a), 1893–4 by *John Butler*, Metropolitan Police Architect. Very similar to the Wapping station but simpler. Barge entrance below a banded brick and stone façade with a single gable and two small triangular oriels. Converted to flats with two houses in the yard by *Rothermel Cooke*, 1981–2. At the S end, THE GUN (No. 27), which may incorporate old fabric (there has been a pub here since the 1710s). Oldest part the N end, single storey to street, extended 1875 by *F. Frederick Holsworth*. Round the corner Nos. 29–51, 1889–90, stand on the E end of the South Dock Pierhead.

POPLAR DOCK (*see* West India and Millwall Docks above) lies W of Preston's Road. Its N end is dominated by the road engineering that links Canary Wharf to points N, E and W. SCULPTURE is used to punctuate the confusing surroundings. On Cartier Circle, VOLTE FACE by *Alex MacGregor & Richard Clark*, 1994. At the dock's NE corner, FIGUREHEAD by *Anna Bissett*, 1997.

5. Millwall from near Island Gardens station NW to Marsh Wall

The W side of the Isle of Dogs was embanked by the C17. Development with industry along the river and housing just inland was well established by the time the Millwall Dock was built in 1864–8. The N part was the first to be developed, from 1807, the year after the West India Dock opened. The first streets, just S of what became the South Dock of the West India Dock, were those now named Cuba and Manila Streets. Westferry Road followed in 1812–15, which immediately stimulated the industrial development, already established in a minor way, all along the riverside. S and SE of the first streets, house building on the Byng and Mellish estates as far E as Alpha Grove and slightly W on Tooke family land (Tooke Town) did not get under way until the late 1840s and then proceeded sporadically with a mixture of good-quality and inferior dwellings. A few very ordinary bay-windowed houses in Mellish Street remain but the rest, in bad repair before the Second World War, have been replaced with council flats. C19 houses and then-new flats went in the bombing of 1940, together with the Anglican church, St Luke.

The S part of Millwall was built up along the riverside by the 1860s with shipyards and a variety of industries, almost all replaced by post-1981 housing schemes. There was also a pocket of cottages (since demolished) built mid-century for workers in the shipbuilding industry, including Scots who had flocked to work on the *Great Eastern* (*see* Burrell's Wharf). Of this settlement the most distinctive survival is the Presbyterian church of St Paul on Westferry Road. The R. C. St Edmund, one of *Tasker*'s cheap East End churches, 1873–4, has gone. Almost nothing remains of before 1914 on this S part of the Mellish estate, except a few mid-

C19 houses in Westferry Road and, from the early C20, part of Harbinger Road and Cahir Street and an LCC fire station (Public Buildings, p. 98). The mission church of St Cuthbert (by *J. E. K. & J. P. Cutts*, 1897), also on Westferry Road, was bombed and demolished. The southernmost part between Millwall Dock and Westferry Road remained undeveloped until the pioneering and exceptionally good local authority Chapel House estate was built after the First World War.

The perambulation starts at the s tip of the Isle of Dogs and goes from the East Ferry Road junction w via Westferry Road to Millwall Dock, first along the riverside where some of the best housing on the Isle of Dogs is encountered immediately.

MACONOCHIE'S WHARF, off Westferry Road at Maconochie's 50 Road, is rare in Docklands as a self-build scheme for local people, initiated by Jill Palios and Dr Michael Barraclough, a philanthropist in the mould of Bermondsey's Dr Salter. The architects *Stout & Litchfield* (chiefly *Roy Stout*) had previously built a group including Dr Barraclough's own house (*see* Perambulation 6). This scheme was built in three phases, 1985–90, and continued the cottage tradition of early garden suburbs: like Stout & Litchfield's previous work for Dr Barraclough, these houses are picturesque but forceful. Many of the early self-builders, who formed the Great Eastern Self-Build Housing Association, were involved in the building trade so the construction is traditional, unlike for instance the special self-build systems developed by Walter Segal. Simple terraces step from two to three storeys under catslides and gables, each house slightly varied to suit the builder. Bay windows with slated roofs or sturdy cross-braced timber balconies are well-composed within restful areas of plain walling. Taller houses to the river. The first houses (E) are of white calcium-silicate brick, the later ones (W, 1987–90) of yellow brick because they abut the street and, on the riverside, Burrell's Wharf. The landscaping, with interesting textures and good street furniture designed by *Livingston McIntosh Associates*, continues on to BLASKER WALK, the riverside promenade that links this housing to Burrell's Wharf and beyond (E) to MASTHOUSE TERRACE. This has cheerful housing association flats and houses by *Alan J. Smith Partnership*, 1990–2, on the site of a famous mast house of *c*. 1766, closed 1861.

BURRELL'S WHARF combines industrial relics of great historical 26 interest with modern flats. Begun in 1987, it was one of Kentish Homes' imaginative projects (cf. Cascades), though after they went bankrupt in 1989 it was completed by other developers. The architects were *Jestico & Whiles*, who converted some of the surviving structures and designed new blocks of flats with an industrial toughness. Their monumental CHART HOUSE 83 and DECK HOUSE frame the site. Concrete-panel clad with an ochre tint, they have massive details such as the broad torus round the base. The roof line builds up from six to nine storeys plus a penthouse.

The INDUSTRIAL BUILDINGS represent all three main occupa-
tions of the site, beginning with its laying-out in 1836–7 as the
Millwall Ironworks by (Sir) William Fairbairn, pioneer of structural ironwork, whose main works were in Manchester. By the
river lay a shipyard; to the N of Westferry Road heavy process
works of 1860, e.g. rolling mills. By 1848 the works were owned
by John Scott Russell and his partners, who launched from the
adjoining Napier Yard the *Great Eastern*, I. K. Brunel's gigantic
steamship built in 1854–9 to carry 4,000 passengers on the busy
India route. The venture bankrupted Scott Russell and from
c. 1859, C. J. Mare & Co. took the site, until in 1888 it was bought
by Burrell & Co., colour, paint, and varnish manufacturers.

The CHIMNEY, with its arcaded octagonal base, dates from
Fairbairn's time, and was designed to draw smoke though
underground ducts from furnaces throughout the site. At the
centre, Scott Russell's Italianate PLATE HOUSE, built 1853–4
by *W. Cubitt & Co.*, now converted to flats and a sports
club. Yellow brick trimmed with black terracotta rope moulding.
s water tower and staircase topped by a rebuilt bell-turret.
Wide-span roof with an unusual truss structure of timber and
iron, designed so that the floor of what was presumably a laying-out loft is hung from it. Below the attic-level loft was a void
the height of three floors: here was the mould shop, for pattern
cutting. It had a gallery down one side on cast-iron stanchions
fitted to take line-shafting to drive the machines. w of the Plate

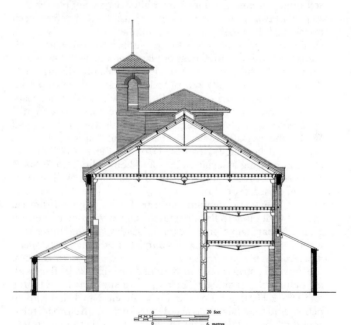

Burrell's Wharf, Plate House. Section

House, two long parallel ranges of workshops, now SLIPWAY and TAFFRAIL HOUSES. They were built 1906–7 by engineer *John J. Johnson* for Venesta Ltd, plywood manufacturers, on the adjoining Napier Yard but were later absorbed into this site. Facing them on the E side of the Plate House, more-or-less matching new blocks of flats. The conversion has retained an industrial aesthetic: wide bays glazed with close-set vertical bars imitate the original fenestration of the Plate House. Metal roofs and metal-mesh balconies. W of the Venesta buildings, a preserved section of the massive SLIPWAYS from which the *Great Eastern* (which was almost as long as the Thames is wide just here) was launched sideways into the Thames. What can be seen is the substructure of the S of the two slipways, built by *Treadwells* of Gloucester: they were 80 ft (24⅓ metres) wide and set 160 ft (48¾ metres) apart. The original horizontal timbers were fixed to timber piles and concreted between. Refurbished by *Livingston McIntosh Associates* and *Feilden & Mawson*. On Westferry Road (Nos. 264–266), an office block and adjoining house of the 1850s.

To the NE of Westferry Road, the housing is much longer established than that by the river, having been built pre-Second World War for the workers in the adjacent riverside industries and the docks. In HARBINGER ROAD and CAHIR STREET, straight rows of yellow and red brick flat-fronted artisan cottages of 1902–4. The N end of Harbinger Road, together with HESPERUS CRESCENT, describes a circle of Poplar Borough Council cottages and cottage flats with tight culs-de-sac opening from it: of 1929–30 by *Harley Heckford*, Borough Engineer. Simple cottage vocabulary in long terraces behind front gardens, whose walls of ceramic waste and brick rubble contribute a certain rusticity.

The CHAPEL HOUSE ESTATE, 1919–21, is linked to the E by footpath. It was the first public housing promoted by the borough as part of the government's post-war drive to provide Homes for Heroes. It is a much more sophisticated garden suburb essay than Hesperus Crescent, laid out by *Harley Heckford* but with houses built by *H. M. Office of Works* to designs by their Chief Architect, *Sir Frank Baines*. Stock-brick terraces and four-in-block cottage flats, cleverly styled in the manner of early C19 London houses. Some have round windows in the upper storey over bracketed hoods, others shell tympana over groups of three windows. The corner terraces of four houses set at an angle have straight parapets with sunk panels. In THERMOPYLAE GATE, blocks of three-storey flats with mansards round a square, unusual for such a scheme. The whole has the variety seen in a different style at Baines's pioneering Eltham Well Hall Estate. The subtleties and fine proportions deserve protection from creeping 'improvement'; fortunately, the estate is now a conservation area. 40

Thermopylae Gate opens N into East Ferry Road and from that into Spindrift Avenue, a new road giving access to the redeveloped S side of Millwall Dock, which was dominated until the dock closed in 1980 by its two staple imports, grain and timber.

Furthest E the housing at CLIPPERS QUAY is built round the former MILLWALL GRAVING DOCK, flooded as a barge berth in 1968. It was one of the largest dry docks on the Thames when made in 1865–8, founded on a series of inverted brick arches resting on concrete. The nine 'altars' or steps for the wooden supports for steadying a ship are now covered by walkways to moorings, and a high-arched, laminated timber bridge spans the dock entrance. This long, narrow slot of water makes an attractive setting for dull two- to three-storey houses of 1984–8 by *Robert Martin & Associates*. White-rendered blocks with pyramidal roofs emphasize the dock entrance. From here, a broad quayside walk leads N along the Millwall Dock to a grassed amphitheatre of open space, which terminates the E end of the dock and links it with parkland E of East Ferry Road. By *LDC Ltd* for the LDDC, 1992. As a landmark here, a lone tall CHIMNEY, the romantic relic of the unromantic refuse incinerator built here in 1952 by *Heenan and Froude*, engineers. Also, an *objet-trouvé* sculpture, a PUMP of 1924 salvaged from pneumatic grain-handling equipment in front of the flour mills at the Royal Victoria Dock. From here the view down the dock is stopped effectively at the W end by the spreading roof of the Docklands Sailing Centre.

TIMBER WHARVES VILLAGE, 1987–92, is grouped towards the W end of the dock. Built over the many acres previously used for the stacking of timber, it is one of the most extensive housing schemes in Docklands, built speculatively and acquired by the LDDC primarily to rehouse those displaced by the building of the Limehouse Link (*see* Limehouse). There is little of the village about it. The atmosphere of its relentless houses and flats (nearly 500) on a grid of streets and N–S walks is urban, but without shops or landmarks. Crisp but rather forbidding small-windowed blocks by *Barnard Urquhart Jarvis*. Closing the strong main axis, Ashdown Walk, a six- to seven-storey curved S block pierced by a tall central arch, the sort of monumental gesture beloved by the Italian Rationalists and their post-war imitators. In Spindrift Avenue, the DOCKLANDS MEDICAL CENTRE by *Jefferson Sheard*, 1990–2, with the same flavour as the houses. Further W on Westferry Road, the former St Paul Presbyterian Church (*see* Churches). A little further N by the river the remains of the original LOCK CHAMBER of the Millwall Outer Dock (*see* West India and Millwall Dock), and the pier-head social housing of 1997 by *Jestico and Whiles*: two blocks of flats linked by a sinuous terrace of houses.

NORTHERN MILLWALL lies N of the dock, which from here is fringed with commercial buildings developed as part of the LDDC Enterprise Zone (*see* Perambulation 3). Here, for example, on Westferry Road is the entrance to the huge West Ferry Printers, which backs on to Millharbour (*see* Perambulation 3), and TILLER COURT, four house-like blocks of business units by *Alan Turner & Associates*, 1988–90, on the corner of Tiller Road. Bronze metal-clad gables composed with some sophistication.

The PUBLIC HOUSING E of Westferry Road belongs to the pre-
LDDC Isle of Dogs. Some of it was built pre-Second World
War to replace decayed property, the rest post-1945 to repair
bomb-damage. The blocks of flats, by Poplar Borough Council
and the LCC, replaced terraces of houses developed from the
1840s. Alpha Grove had the largest and most respectable houses,
dating from the 1870s and 80s. The earliest council flats belong
to the Borough's Glengall Grove estate and are in TILLER
ROAD: Neo-Georgian, 1926–7 by *Harley Heckford*, Borough
Architect. Also in Tiller Road, HAMMOND HOUSE, 1937–8
by *Rees J. Williams*, one of the best examples of the Borough
Council's late 1930s streamlined housing, and some high-
density, informally laid-out houses by Tower Hamlets Borough
Council, typical of the 1970s. A few late C19 terraces remain N
of Tiller Road at the E end of MELLISH STREET, where it abuts
the commercial area (*see* Millharbour, Perambulation 3). W of
these, two blocks of flats, with striking cantilevered canopies, by
C. H. Weed, Poplar Borough's Principal Assistant Architect,
1946–50. Interesting metal FENCE of 1987 in front of the 1960s
John Tucker House. At Nos. 31–35, some of the prefabricated
ORLIT HOUSES built throughout the Glengall Grove estate by
the Ministry of Works in 1945–6: Orlit, a system of concrete
pier-and-panel construction, was just one of the many types of
prefabrication used for public housing post-war to counter a
shortage of homes and materials. RAWALPINDI HOUSE, also
built on the Orlit system by the Borough Engineer and
Surveyor, *W. J. Rankin*, 1947–8, was the first block of precast
concrete-framed flats in Britain and as such was much discussed
in the national and technical press. More Orlit houses nearby in
Tiller Road and ALPHA GROVE, where the conventionally built
but up-to-date post-war houses near the S end at Nos. 83–171
are probably also by *Weed*, 1951–2. On the JANET STREET
corner, ST HUBERT'S HOUSE (1935–6) for the Isle of Dogs
Housing Society by *Ian B. Hamilton* is worth more detailed
study. This is far more refined in detail and planning than contemporary LCC Neo-Georgian blocks: see the individual cast-
iron balconies and the shopfront to Cheval Street. Zigzag plan,
communal gardens and drying areas, where the posts with St
Hubert's stags are probably in Doulton's Polychrome Stoneware
by *Gilbert Bayes* (cf. St Pancras Housing Society estates, *London
4: North*, where Hamilton also worked). Mid- to late 1970s
modernization by *Max Lock & Co.* has rather spoilt Hamilton's
composition.

The BARKANTINE ESTATE, 1965–70 by the *GLC Architect's
Department*, towers over these modestly scaled developments.
Four twenty-one-storey, brick-clad point blocks replaced the
C19 terraces of Tooke Town and the Byng estate. Flat-roofed
red brick blocks of maisonettes form a more humane edge to
Westferry Road. Close to them, a row of shops, two-storey houses,
and a primary school (1968). The community centre was converted in the 1970s from a Gothic Wesleyan Chapel by *G. Limm*,
1887, and its hall of *c.*1926 by *Edwin Beasley*. Health centre

1983, and estate improvements, 1990, by the LDDC, the latter including a new entrance for the SIR JOHN MCDOUGALL GARDENS by the river on Cunard Wharf. First laid out by *Richard Sudell & Partners* for the GLC, 1968, these gardens were connected to the estate by a footbridge.

EXPRESS WHARF, by the river just N of the gardens, is the only wharf still working on the island. Here Freight-Express-Seacon have two huge sheds with canopies projecting over the river: the sheds are high enough to accommodate seven storeys within their concrete-framed structures. Constructed 1976 and 1986 by *I. W. Payne & Partners* in a bold attempt to stem the decline of the river traffic. N of these, No. 1 CUBA STREET was built in 1900–1 as the short-lived Millwall Working Men's Club and Institute; a plain brick building, by *William Bradford* for the brewers who sponsored the club, in use as a warehouse by 1906.

6. Cubitt Town: N *from Island Gardens*

The SE corner of the Isle of Dogs was developed from 1842, before the Millwall Docks opened, as Cubitt Town by William Cubitt, brother of the famous builder Thomas Cubitt. The land was leased mainly from the Countess of Glengall, daughter of William Mellish †1834, who hoped that Cubitt's embanking and development of the river would encourage house building on the rest of her estate in Millwall (*see* above). Cubitt established the timber wharves, sawmills, cement factories and brickfields necessary to his development, laid out roads, built a church, Christ Church, and terraces of houses, and developed wharves along the river, leasing them to a variety of industrial concerns. Nearly all his plain terrraces, built slowly up to the 1880s, were destroyed as a consequence of the Second World War. Now almost everything except Christ Church is post-war. The other Anglican church (St John Roserton Street by *A. W. Blomfield*, 1871–2) has gone. In place of Cubitt's houses there are council estates and, along the riverside, the housing begun from the late 1970s as industries closed, moved away or, from 1981, were relocated.

The perambulation begins at the DLR Island Gardens station by Island Gardens (*see* Public Buildings), with its breathtaking view of Greenwich Hospital on the s bank. The river can also be reached W of the station via JOHNSON'S DRAWDOCK, a well-designed slipway for small craft that opens a window on to Greenwich opposite. By *LDC Ltd* for the LDDC, 1989. Alongside it at Nos. 50–56 Ferry Street, DR BARRACLOUGH'S HOUSES, a highly individual group, the result of a special commission, unusual in Docklands, given in 1975 to *Stout & Litchfield* by a local doctor, Michael Barraclough. An emphasis on natural materials (white brick, Westmorland slate roofs, grey-stained casements, lead details) and expressionist forms (a series of peaked roofs, random elevations, upper storeys cantilevered out in sections). The fronts, which command a view of

49

Greenwich Hospital, cannot be seen from anywhere but the river. The rear is hidden by a C19 wall and long gardens along Ferry Street; at the w corner a C19 building is incorporated, a survivor from the paint factory formerly on the site. Timber salvaged from the demolished North Stacks of London Docks (*see* Wapping) predominates in the multi-level interior of Dr Barraclough's own house (N).

FERRY STREET runs W close to the river. Facing a river path, MIDLAND PLACE and LIVINGSTONE PLACE, with simple and nicely consistent housing by *Levitt Bernstein* for Circle 33 Housing Association, 1979–83, i.e. pre-LDDC. A restricted palette of buff brick, blue brick strings and pale-green profiled metal roofs. V-shaped layout: two-storey rows by the river walk, rising to three-storey houses with flats at each end behind. Bay windows, also set on the diagonal, under far-projecting roofs, open on to tiny individual gardens. After this, either side of Ferry Road, an unexceptional mix of social and low-cost speculative housing. First, Wates flats by *Wigley Fox* in FELSTEAD GARDENS, 1983–4 (S), and HORSESHOE CLOSE, 1987–8 (N). The former, with a big arch into a riverside garden, is on the site of part of the Port of London Wharf, the westernmost of those embanked by Cubitt & Co. Also N, another pre-LDDC housing association development, a severe three-sided court of red and yellow brick flats by *Grillet, Lyster & Harding*, 1974–80, with the monopitched roofs that were so popular in the 1970s. Turning the NW corner with a round tower and crude lantern, the sub-Regency DE BRUIN COURT (Nos. 17–31), completed 1988. The pub at the w end, the FERRY HOUSE, looks late C19 but the core may date back to 1748–9, when the Ferry House stood alone on this shore by the Greenwich ferry.

The riverside road, E of Island Gardens station, is Saunders Ness Road. The turning W past George Green School leads to GLENAFFRIC AVENUE and Christ Church, built by Cubitt for his new town (*see* Churches). Its surroundings are no longer Victorian though the WATERMAN'S ARMS, 1853, probably also built by *Cubitt & Co.*, survives. Cavernous neo-Victorian interior of 1972 by *Roderick Gradidge*. Along the rest of the SW side, neat and unaffected housing association flats and houses, banded in dark and yellow brick, by *Levitt Bernstein Associates*, 1993–4.

CUMBERLAND MILLS SQUARE begins the string of residential 81 developments along SAUNDERS NESS ROAD (formerly Cubitt's Wharf Road) that have replaced heterogeneous industrial buildings on the wharves. This complex group of flats is one of the most sophisticated in Docklands. By the former GLC architect *Donald Ball* of *Alan Turner & Associates*, 1987–9, it bears a strong resemblance in plan and materials to the GLC's Odham's Walk, Covent Garden, designed by Ball in 1972. This group has none of the colour and decoration of nearby speculative housing. Four sombre, brown brick cluster blocks, piled up with layers of balconies, rise from a central courtyard to nine and ten storeys with a commanding silhouette of monopitch roofs. A masterly interlocking spiral plan gives most flats a river view from oriel window or balcony. There is water on two sides: the NE block overlooks the former NEWCASTLE DRAWDOCK, part of Cubitt's initial development of the river in the 1840s. The dock is brick-walled with wooden fenders on both sides. The SCULPTURE here is by *Grenville Davey*, 1997 (Button Seat). A new park was laid out here in 1997, with remnants from a chapel which once stood on the site (bombed in the Second World War). They include a figure 're-erected 1882, F. W. Gunning', and three commemoration stones of 1862, 1878 and 1905. Beyond here between GROSVENOR WHARF ROAD and Empire Wharf Road, a pre-LDDC, council-built housing group, also laid out to give as many homes as possible a view of the river. Staggered terraces round courtyards of 1978–81 by Tower Hamlets Borough Council (project architect *Martin O'Shea*).

CALEDONIAN WHARF is an earlier, simpler scheme by *Alan Turner & Associates*, 1984–7, gathered round the river walk and the former Cubitt Town Dry Dock built in 1877 by ship-repairer Thomas Rugg on the site of part of Cubitt's cement factory; the dock is now an ornamental lake. Distinctive barrel-vaulted canopies over the balcony bays of the flats, and similar porches on the houses behind. Close to Caledonian Wharf, one remaining but disused (in 1997) industrial building at STORER'S QUAY, originally Cubitt & Co.'s own wharf where they established *c.* 1843–4 the sawmills, timber wharves, cement factory, pottery and brickfields that served their building operations. Though reduced in size in the 1870s, Cubitt & Co. continued on part of the site until 1882, when it was taken over by the neighbouring paint manufacturers, David Storer and Sons of Glasgow. PLYMOUTH WHARF, beyond, has well-laid-out but unremarkable speculative housing by *Lindsay Associates*, completed 1986.

COMPASS POINT, 1985–8, closes the N end of Saunders Ness Road. Here *Jeremy Dixon* has created a small world of its own, inspired not by the industrial past but by early to mid-C19 London suburbs. With its paired villas and terraces, mews and mixture of styles (from Late Georgian to Italianate and Dutch-cum-Jacobean), it has more in common with parts of Camden and Kensington than with any C19 development on the Isle of Dogs. The English picturesque layout exploits every advantage of the site, formerly Dudgeon's Wharf. Some of the house designs are reworkings of Dixon's previous interpretations of the London house; compare the Sextant Avenue houses with those in Lanark Road, Maida Vale, the riverfront terraces with St Mark's Road, Kensington, and the Chichester Way terraces with Ashmill Street, Westminster. All in purple-brown brick and thin off-white stucco, laid on like icing. Inventive details throughout, though perhaps because the scheme was carried out under a design-and-build contract (architects, *Jeremy Dixon/ BDP*; builders, Costain Homes), the execution frequently does not match the ambition. SEXTANT AVENUE, the main street with the largest semi-detached villas, ends w in THE CRESCENT, a curved neo-Nash terrace with an open central slot for access

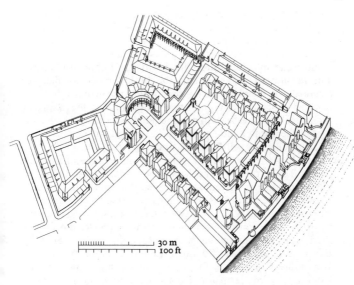

Compass Point. Axonometric view

to Manchester Road. At the E end, a view of the river is framed by tall blocks that repeat the emphatic uprights of silos on the far bank of the river. To the S, a slightly rustic boathouse-like block. To the N an obelisk gateway to the public river walk, shaded by a pergola. From here a terrace of three-storey houses, 78 set back behind gardens, looks out on the river. Stepped gables and bows, each topped by a balcony and glass canopy. Shaped gables to the separate blocks at each end. The houses are entered from MARINERS MEWS, through stuccoed porches alongside garages. Down CHICHESTER WAY, single-gable pairs face a terrace with full-height projecting triangles of windows. The vista back to the river ends in two gabled riverside blocks. A green alley runs between the gardens here and those in Sextant Avenue. Linking Saunders Ness Road with Manchester Road, BLYTH CLOSE and FRANCIS CLOSE, mews courts where the finishes look cheerless. Along Manchester Road, the old wharf wall, pierced by monumental stuccoed gateways.

Off the W side of MANCHESTER ROAD, a little to the S, the extensive but dull LCC MANCHESTER ESTATE of the 1960s, the houses in SEYSSEL STREET reclad by the LDDC c. 1990. To the N, set back behind their own garden, the cheerful JUBILEE 43 CRESCENT, flats for workers retired from the local ship-repairing firm R. & H. Green & Silley Weir Ltd (who had built a similar scheme at Falmouth, Cornwall). 1935 by *G. R. Unthank*. Five blocks, each of six two-room flats, that look like interwar houses linked at the first floor by a continuous concrete balcony. Otherwise brick and render with modest patterns of terracotta diamonds and rectangles. On the balcony relief portraits of King George V and Queen Mary. Beyond, FRIARS

MEAD, 1983–6 by *Ronald Quin Associates*, who with Comben Homes won an early limited LDDC design competition. A secluded, luxuriantly planted loop of semi-detached houses and four-in-a-block flats forming an island amid the would-be countryside of Mudchute City Farm (*see* Public Buildings). The inspiration is garden suburb, the low blocks of flats set diagonally on the plots, the houses cottage-style with overhanging pantiled roofs and dovecote-style ventilators. At the centre of each block of flats a staircase sheltered by a cascade of glass roofs. The smaller and simpler Nos. 105 and 107 belong to the adjacent Glengall self-build scheme, 1985–7.

Back on Manchester Road, E side, one more trace of the C19 Cubitt Town, the CUBITT ARMS, No. 262, a plain three-bay pub made plainer by removal of most of its stone dressings. It stands on the corner of the truncated OLIFFE STREET, the entrance to MILLWALL WHARF, which is undergoing development in 1997. Partially retained on the riverside, the former single-storey, twin-gabled warehouse units built 1901–2 by *Edwin A. B. Crockett*, Surveyor to the London Wharf and Warehouse Committee, for the storage of sugar and fibre by Cook & Co. Some of them may incorporate the remains of early C19 sheds. Also a plain brick warehouse dating from 1907–8. To its N, LONDON YARD, redeveloped in 1984–8 by Dutch developers VOM and Dutch architects *ED* (see the street names); scheme executed by *BDP*. Gabled flats and houses in brick with pantiles, conventional but quite well done and with a landscaped drainage lake at the centre. Unusually for such developments, there is one short street of small shops.

Here the private developments stop and pre-LDDC public housing dominates. To the W of Manchester Road, the ST JOHN'S ESTATE, the Borough of Poplar's only big immediately postwar estate except for Bazely Street (*see* Poplar, Perambulation). Multi-phase but started in 1952 (approved 1949), with the aim of creating a neighbourhood similar to the LCC's Lansbury. The first houses do have that Lansbury lightness of touch, e.g. in Castalia Square, where one finds the tough but not unfriendly community centre-cum-church, ISLAND HOUSE, put up by the Presbyterian Church to replace St Paul's (*see* Churches), but later United Reformed. 1971–2 by *Philip Pank*. It has an industrial flavour, dark brick inside and out, painted stanchions along the upper wall and an exterior staircase. Later phases of housing, e.g. Watkins House, are by *Adams, Holden & Pearson* (1964) and by *Co-Operative Planning Ltd* (1963–6, 1969–70). The last, e.g. Kingdon and Lingard Houses, are still brick but more brutal and tightly planned. Of this date too the ten-storey system-built block. On the E side of Manchester Road, the GLC's smaller SAMUDA ESTATE by *Sir John Burnet, Tait & Partners*, 1965–7, marked by a twenty-five-storey slab, heavily glazed, with narrow floor bands and a slightly separated service tower. Scissor-plan flats, a planning device used often in slab blocks by the GLC, cf. Pepys Estate, Deptford, etc. N again, the fantastic Storm Water Pumping Station (*see* Public Buildings) makes an immensely cheering sight. N again by the main entrance to the West India Docks, PIERHEAD WEST, by *Goddard Manton* (begun 1997), curves round a former graving dock and ends S in a landmark block of flats.

The QUEEN OF THE ISLE pub, back on Manchester Road in the angle between it and East Ferry Road, is an early Cubitt Town building, of 1855–6, extended 1875. Neat one-storey pilastered front projecting in a wedge from the three storeys of the rest. W and N from here the commercial buildings mostly built during the period of the Enterprise Zone (*see* Perambulation 3).

LIMEHOUSE AND RATCLIFFE RIVERSIDE
London Borough of Tower Hamlets

Limehouse and Ratcliffe, both riverside hamlets within Stepney parish in origin, have developed very differently since the C19. Ratcliffe has almost disappeared, leaving only the C18 warehouses at Free Trade Wharf and the house now occupied by the Royal Foundation of St Katharine as reminders of its significance. In contrast, the original, riverside part of Limehouse (the later part N of Commercial Road and East India Dock Road is outside the scope of this book) has been transformed from a decayed industrial area into an expensive residential one, especially along its picturesque riverside thoroughfare, Narrow Street. Here, surviving late C17–C18 houses and small C19 warehouses, built on the original narrow plots, give Limehouse a much more intimate character than its neighbour, Wapping. Away from the river stands Hawksmoor's noble St Anne, and, round it, as in many of these Thames-side hamlets, a fragment of a respectable residential neighbourhood, with some attractive though not grand C18 houses.

RATCLIFFE was the first landfall downriver with a good straight road to London. A wharf existed here in 1348, the first known exploitation of the riverside E of the City. By the C16 many famous voyages of discovery set off from Ratcliffe. The hamlet, originally restricted to the riverside, expanded in the C15 N along Butcher Row, the main route to Stepney and Hackney. In the early C17 it was the most populous of Stepney's riverside hamlets (about 3,500 inhabitants). Its riverside street was lined with sea-farers' houses and shipwrights' premises, but in 1794 a fire, which spread from an ignited barge of saltpetre at the East India Company's warehouses (later Free Trade Wharf), wiped out the S part of the built-up area and caused much rebuilding. Soon after this, Ratcliffe's character changed dramatically as its population expanded from about 5,000 in 1801 to 17,000 in 1861 (it became a parish distinct from Limehouse in 1840) and prosperous wharfingers and tradesmen gave way to seamen and dock-workers. Broad Street, now the E end of The Highway, became, like neighbouring Shadwell, a notorious slum. Much was gradually wiped out by waves of destruction: in the early C19 by the building of the Commercial Road and of the London and Blackwall Railway; in the C20 by the construction of the Rotherhithe

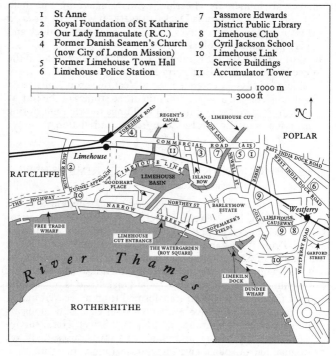

1	St Anne	7	Passmore Edwards
2	Royal Foundation of St Katharine		District Public Library
3	Our Lady Immaculate (R.C.)	8	Limehouse Club
4	Former Danish Seamen's Church	9	Cyril Jackson School
	(now City of London Mission)	10	Limehouse Link
5	Former Limehouse Town Hall		Service Buildings
6	Limehouse Police Station	11	Accumulator Tower

Limehouse and Ratcliffe Riverside

Tunnel and its approaches, and the laying-out of the King Edward
VII Memorial Park. This was followed by bomb damage, slum
clearance, road widening and the demolition of most of the riverside wharves. Now its E end is dominated by the giant portals of
the 1990s Limehouse Link and major roads cover most of the S
part of the former hamlet.

LIMEHOUSE, adjoining to the E, gained its name from the lime
kilns around Limekiln Dock, established by the C14 when chalk
was brought from Kent to serve the London building industry.
Stow in the C16 knew the hamlet as Lime Hurst. It then lay out in
the country and housed a busy seafaring community. Late in the
same century, it specialized in shipbuilding and provisioning, with
ropewalks out in the fields to the N of Fore Street (now the E end
of Narrow Street).

The hamlet more than tripled in size within a hundred years
(2,000 in 1610; 7,000 in 1710) and spread N. The surviving late
C17–C18 houses in Narrow Street and the magnificent St Anne
show the wealth and sophistication of at least some members of
the burgeoning population. By the early C18, London had spread
so far that Limehouse was now its easternmost suburb. In 1767–70
the Limehouse Cut was built to link the river to the Lea at
Bromley-by-Bow and it initiated industrial development in the
area. Then, in 1820 the Regent's Canal Dock (Limehouse Basin)

opened at the entrance to the Regent's Canal. It handled huge amounts of coal and timber. This, together with the establishment of new routes from the river and docks into London and beyond (the Commercial Road, its branches the West and East India Dock Roads, and the London and Blackwall Railway), destroyed the amenity of the hamlet and stimulated industry. By 1880 the riverside had been built up with small warehouses and industrial buildings. Shipbuilding, so vital throughout the C18, had by then dwindled to one yard on the Limehouse Cut, T. & W. Forrestt, which made lifeboats (though barge repairing survived into the second half of the C20). At the W end of Narrow Street the Regent's Canal Dock was still busy as a coal dock, while from 1909 – and particularly after 1937 when it was extended with a huge 350 ft (107 metre) high chimney – Stepney Power Station dominated the E end, its coal conveyed from Blyth's Wharf; previously the W end was part of the site of a steam-engine works. Limehouse became part of the industrial East End, notable mainly for its part of Chinatown centred pre-war on Limehouse Causeway (*see* also Poplar). It remained so until post-1960, when the Barley Mow Brewery closed (1960), the canal dock closed and was renamed Limehouse Basin (1969), riverborne trade waned, and the power station was mostly demolished in 1974.

Further change began when the first pioneers of gentrification moved into Narrow Street's C17–C18 houses in the late 1950s and set up home against a backdrop of industry and juggernauts. They were followed in the 1970s by others who converted decaying warehouses, attractive because of manageable size, at the W end of the street. The *East End News* complained about the influx of planning applications from wealthy individuals in 1977, the same year that the ILEA bought Free Trade Wharf with plans to house the City of London Polytechnic there. Though a few factories remained into the 1980s, the decision to free Narrow Street of traffic by building a relief road (projected since the 1930s) and to hide it beneath Limehouse Basin in a tunnel, has led to the riverside part of Limehouse becoming distinctly exclusive and residential. In 1982, when the LDDC drew up its development strategy, 94.6 per cent of homes in this area were still council-built. Since then the balance has changed dramatically, with the demolition of fifteen blocks of council flats (mostly for the Limehouse Link), and new speculative houses and flats joining those in converted warehouses and in refurbished council blocks.

CHURCHES

St Anne, Commercial Road. With Christ Church Spitalfields 7 and St George-in-the-East (*see* Wapping), one of *Hawksmoor's* three great East End churches. They were begun almost simultaneously in 1714. St Anne was furnished 1723–5 but not consecrated until 1730. The master mason for St Anne and for St George was *Edward Strong*. The composition here is as original as that of St George, but the vocabulary is more conventional and elaborate, the mouldings all exquisitely carved and enriched.

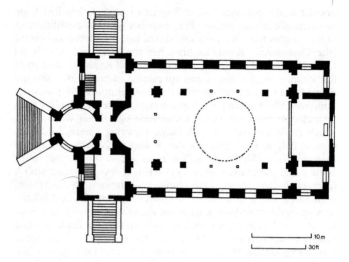

St Anne. Plan

Gutted by fire in 1850, the interior was reconstructed by *Philip Hardwick* and the local *John Morris*, 1850–1. Restoration (surprisingly faithful to the original) resumed under *P. C. Hardwick* in 1856–7 with reseating and pulpit by Hardwick's pupil, the young *Arthur Blomfield*. In 1891, as *Sir A. Blomfield*, he remodelled the chancel. Restoration 1983–93 by *Julian Harrap*, who added tubular steel trusses by *Hockley & Dawson*, consulting engineers, to support the C19 roof. This, with its wrought-iron hanger rods, closely resembles those used by the Hardwicks in the Great Hall of Euston Station in 1846 and conforms to a pattern favoured by the builder of the church, *William Cubitt*.

The W tower is a spectacular sight from a distance. It has nothing of the routine character or skimpiness which so often spoils the appearance of later Georgian towers. The tower is neither embraced by the body of the church, as at Christ Church Spitalfields, nor projects from it, as at St George. Instead it is incorporated in a 'westwork' of vestibules, with attics pedimented to N and S and, below these, strongly rusticated quoins. The front has no portico, but instead an apsidal projection, the expression of a circular vestibule within the tower base. (Colvin suggests the portico might have been inspired by one of Montana's published versions of ancient temples.) The upper part of the tower is like St George's in shape, rectangular and appearing from the W wider than it really is, by means of buttresses grouped with the tower's angle pilasters and far projecting to the N and S. A bell-opening, its arch rising above the main entablature, echoes the dome of the vestibule below. The octagonal top is the equivalent perhaps of a medieval lantern (Summerson), very Baroque in its changes of direction but with no sinuous flourishes at all. Even the finials and urns have a consistent angularity. The order applied to all stages is a dignified Doric. The sides of the church, also stone-faced, are very restrained in adornment, as always with Hawksmoor. Tall arched gallery windows over squarish ones, below which are windows to the high crypt, perhaps intended for use as a school and now a clubroom. E and W bays slightly recessed, expressing the internal arrangement; the E bays (vestries) also have rusticated angle quoins to match the 'westwork' and curiously brutal rectangular angle towers; their interlaced ornament seems to follow no historical precedent. Cockerell's pre-fire drawings show three recesses over the centre of the sides which are no longer there. E wall with a triumphal arch motif, repeating the Doric order of the front.

The circular vestibule is domed, stone-lined and lit with a clear even light from big arched upper windows. From it, a disappointing entrance to the church, oppressed by Hardwick's organ gallery. The interior, as was the case at St George, is less inventive than the exterior. It is developed from the cross-in-square plan of e.g. Wren's St Anne and St Agnes. To E and W an additional bay. The E one is filled by a broad, rectangular and tunnel-vaulted chancel, flanked by vestries; in the chancel walls, quartets of arched windows, pierced by *Blomfield*, 1891. His chancel seating has gone. The W bay emphasizes the longitudinal direction and hints at a narthex, perhaps a reference to the arrangements of Early Christian churches, in which Hawksmoor and contemporary theologians were interested. The Corinthian order is used throughout. The main columns and entablature are of stone, timber columns support the galleries. Hardwick's intervention is most obvious in the heaviness of the plasterwork and W gallery (screen beneath) carrying an ORGAN by *Gray & Davison*, which won a prize at the Great Exhibition of 1851 and was installed soon after. Fortunately unaltered. – FONT by *Hardwick* and *Morris*, 1853. Discordant neo-medieval stone bowl carved with big lilies. Neo-C17 font cover, post-1894. – PULPIT. By *Blomfield*, 1856, carved by *William Gibbs Rogers*. Faithful C18 style, unusual at this date. It originally stood further E and was reached from the chancel by a long flight of stairs. – COMMUNION TABLE. C18, small, oak. – STAINED GLASS in the E window: large and richly coloured scene of the Crucifixion, painted in enamels by *Charles Clutterbuck*, 1853. – MONUMENT. In the porch, high up in a niche, monument to Maria Charlesworth, apparently C19. Hope with her anchor. The CRYPT has beautifully constructed groin vaults in red brick.

The approach to the W front is via Newell Street, through a passage between houses, cf. St George-in-the-East. In the CHURCHYARD, the most interesting monument is a remarkable PYRAMID, NW of the church. Panelled in stone and inscribed with 'The Wisdom of Solomon' in English and Hebrew with a weathered armorial shield below. A mid-C19 print shows that it formerly stood on a square plinth, cf. the Raine monument at St George-in-the-East. – WAR MEMORIAL. Blessing Christ in bronze on a tall pedestal with a harrowing relief of a corpse-filled no-man's land. By *Arthur G. Walker*, unveiled 1921. –

Dozens of half-buried ledger slabs line the perimeter wall, taken from demolished tomb chests, an indication of the C18 affluence of this parish. – RAILINGS. Reproduced to original design in the 1980s.

ROYAL FOUNDATION OF ST KATHARINE, Butcher Row, Ratcliffe. A peaceful island in the midst of roads and railways, a reminder of the hamlet of Ratcliffe as it was in the late C18. The Foundation has occupied the site of St James Ratcliffe, bombed 1940, since 1949. It was by *Edward Lapidge*, 1837–8, Gothic; restored by *R.P. Day*, 1899–1901, and again by *Caröe*, 1932. The centrepiece now is the C18 house that faces Butcher Row. St James was built on its garden and the house was used until the war as the vicarage.

The Foundation is, remarkably, that founded as a religious community next to the Tower of London by Queen Matilda in 1147. It survived the Reformation as a Royal Peculiar, but was exiled to Regent's Park when its buildings were demolished in 1825 for the St Katharine Docks (*see* Wapping, Perambulation 1). Its original buildings were largely C14 and C15, but were much rebuilt by its first lay master, Sir Julius Caesar, in the C17. When it moved to Regent's Park, the Foundation was at first an almshouse only, but was reorganized in 1878 with a clerical master, three sisters, ten bedesmen and ten bedeswomen. The Foundation returned to the East End, first to Bromley Hall, Poplar, in 1914. Now home to the Community of the Resurrection.

The MASTER'S HOUSE is a plain, square, three-bay, two-and-a-half-storey Georgian house with a four-column Ionic porch to Butcher Row. It was built in 1795–6 as the house of a sugar refiner, Matthew Whiting. Whiting was a director of the Phoenix Assurance Company to which *Thomas Leverton* was surveyor. Whiting and Leverton worked together in the aftermath of the Ratcliffe fire of 1794, which had destroyed Whiting's previous house on this site. It seems likely that Leverton was involved here, though there are no distinguishing architectural features.

What is unique among surviving London merchants' houses is the extensive MURAL PAINTING of Claudian landscapes in the main ground-floor rooms on the garden front. In the former drawing room, in oil on plaster above the panelled dado painted in grisaille, a fictive Corinthian colonnade as the foreground to a landscape based on Claude's Landscape with Arch of Titus. Opposite the windows, a seascape based on his Coast scene with the landing of Aeneas in Latium: both pictures had been published as engravings in 1772. In the dining room, only two panels remain. The paintings on which they were based – C.J. Vernetone's Seascape showing coastal fortifications against Napoleon (namely a martello tower and Dover Castle), and Richard Wilson's View of the Tivoli Cascalette and Villa of Maecenas – were not engraved until the early C19, and the bow window seems to have been added to the room post-1819. All the murals could have been done at any time up to the mid

1830s. Besant says the painter was Italian but he has not been identified.

Linked to the house, a simple chapel and plain community buildings designed by *R. E. Enthoven* and built in 1950–2 as part of the Festival of Britain. The post-war CHAPEL, though simple inside too, has rich FURNISHINGS. The following come from the demolished chapel of St Katharine by the Tower, chiefly built 1368–77. The C17 work belonged to Sir Julius Caesar's refurnishing. The tomb of John Holland, Duke of Exeter †1447, is in the chapel of St Peter ad Vincula in the Tower of London (*see London 1: The City of London*). – CHOIR STALLS, C14, with ogee crocketed canopies, carved misericords and elbows; possibly the work of craftsmen from the royal workshops, they belong to a series beginning with those formerly in St Stephen's Chapel, Westminster (cf. also Gloucester and Lincoln). Set in the modern fronts, eight classical panels with busts in medallions. Three also in the altar frontal. – PULPIT. C17, carved with supposed views of the ancient hospital. Unusual. – STATUES of Edward III and Queen Philippa of Hainault, probably C19. – RELIEF PANEL. Adoration of Magi, C16, of alabaster? – Good collection of C17 and C18 WALL TABLETS in the cloister.

Post-war FITTINGS by *Keith Murray* (who, as a silversmith and designer, also worked as *Keith Fendall*) include a spare star-shaped forged-iron corona over the altar, which originally had a fabric covering, and a silver SANCTUARY LAMP in the same idiom. – ALTAR, 1954, carved with a long inscription and symbols from Roman catacombs by *Ralph Beyer*, who went on to work at Coventry Cathedral. – CARVINGS. Christ in Majesty in teak by *Michael Groser*, 1959–60, son of the first post-war Master of the Foundation, Father Groser. – CRUCIFIX made by *Edwin Florence* for an early performance of T. S. Eliot's *Murder in the Cathedral* (1935), in which Father Groser appeared. – ORGAN. An C18 chamber organ by *John Avery*.

OUR LADY IMMACULATE WITH ST FREDERICK (R.C.), Commercial Road. Begun 1926–8 by *A. J. Sparrow*, but not finished until 1934. Plain brick Early Christian basilica with an apse towards the road, a NW campanile, and an odd S turret crowned with a statue of the Sacred Heart, designed as a war memorial to be seen from the river.

Former DANISH SEAMEN'S CHURCH IN FOREIGN PORTS (now City of London Mission), Commercial Road and Yorkshire Road. A haven on this tight wedge of land hemmed in by road and railway. 1958–9 by *Holger Jensen* with *Armstrong & McManus*. Like the other Scandinavian missions to seamen, an admirably flexible arrangement of homely accommodation and a small church within an envelope characteristic of the seamen's own country. This crisp, blue brick building looks more modern than most British architecture of the date. The church, with butterfly roof and clerestory lighting, is linked to rooms enclosing a small central garden.

PUBLIC BUILDINGS

Former LIMEHOUSE TOWN HALL, Commercial Road. 1879–81 by *A. & C. Harston*. A white brick palazzo with stone dressings. Arched moulded windows, channelled angle piers, central pediment and strong projecting cornice; chimneys rising from stone aprons on the face of the building. Projecting doorcase with polished granite columns.

LIMEHOUSE POLICE STATION, West India Dock Road. Of *c.* 1940 by *G. Mackenzie Trench*, Metropolitan Police Architect. Large, handsome and well planned. Brick and streamlined in a pre-war Dutch way, but with up-to-date touches, see the bold angle tower with snapped headers to Birchfield Street. Courtyard with large section house behind.

PASSMORE EDWARDS DISTRICT PUBLIC LIBRARY, Commercial Road. 1900–1 by *J. & S. F. Clarkson*. Stone except for the yellow brick upper outer bays with shaped gables. Two storey with attics in gables. Behind, the main library looks post-1945. – Large MURAL of Limehouse Reach by *Claire Smith*, 1986. An androgynous angel broods over a Turneresque river with unpleasant flotsam. – In front, Clement Attlee, Prime Minister 1945–51 and member for Limehouse 1922–50. A touchingly prosaic portrait in bronze, 1988, by *Frank Forster*, who won a GLC competition in 1986.

LIMEHOUSE CLUB, Limehouse Causeway. A simple youth club and community hall that makes quite a bold statement on this prominent corner by the DLR Westferry station. Built by the LDDC for Tower Hamlets, 1994–5, architects *Michael Squire Associates*. Somewhat church-like, with clerestory-lit hall flanked by lower vaulted rooms. Glass bricks in the curved stair-tower which lights up as a welcoming beacon after dark, and in the vaulted spaces (the crèche) projecting l. of the entrance. Otherwise a friendly mixture of yellow brick, timber boarding and profiled metal. Inside, the hall's rear window opens on to a roughly sculpted climbing wall, studded with coloured roundels and protected by the gawky timber canopy standing up at the S end. A N gallery opens from a smaller hall over the entrance foyer and office.

CYRIL JACKSON SCHOOL has two interesting parts. In Three Colt Street, a hipped-roofed brick building, an early example of the softer, more vernacular approach adopted for some London schools in the 1970s; completed *c.* 1973 by the *GLC Architect's Department*. Later part (1991–5) by *Robert Byron Architects* in Limehouse Causeway next to the Limehouse Club, with which it forms a harmonious group.

LIMEHOUSE LINK. Built 1989–93 (engineers *Sir Alexander Gibb & Partners*) to link The Highway with new roads on the Isle of Dogs instead of the overground relief road proposed in 1976 which would have destroyed Limehouse. The 1 m. cut-and-cover tunnel, with its underground sliproads to Westferry Road and Canary Wharf, was exceptionally expensive. The deeply buried twin concrete box was constructed mostly top downwards, between diaphragm walls, but, across the Limehouse Basin, it was made bottom upwards behind an open cofferdam, all involving massive temporary works of strutting and dewatering and the removal of 1.8 million tons of spoil by barge. The work also involved rehousing 556 households of local people, many of whom were moved to Timber Wharves, Millwall (*see* Isle of Dogs).

The PORTALS, designed by *Rooney O'Carroll* with *Anthony Meats*, house the services and make a dramatic Postmodern statement in their surroundings, overemphatic near Westferry Road but appropriate to the scale of Docklands. The WEST SERVICE BUILDING closes the view down The Highway. Above its W PORTAL, a SCULPTURE, Restless Dream, by *Zadok Ben-David*, huge but lightly done in painted aluminium. A silhouetted sleeping figure dreams of dozens of tiny active figures whirling in a circle above him or her – a commentary on the frenetic activity of Docklands that could be viewed either positively or negatively. – On the E face of the EAST SERVICE BUILDING, over the sliproads to Westferry Road, impressive geometric monoliths of Kilkenny limestone by *Michael Kenny*, entitled On Strange and Distant Lands. On the NORTH QUAY PORTAL in Aspen Way, an untitled abstract of interlinked Cor-Ten steel bars by *Nigel Hall*. 56

ROTHERHITHE TUNNEL. *See* Rotherhithe.

LIMEHOUSE BASIN (REGENT'S CANAL DOCK)

The Limehouse Basin or Regent's Canal Dock began in 1812 as a proposed barge basin at the mouth of the Regent's Canal and later became an important coal dock and the gateway into the whole of Britain's canal system. It closed in 1969 but, though in decay, continued to be used by lighters and for the export of scrap metal until the 1980s. Its present role as a marina originates from the early 1980s when the British Waterways Board invited private developers for proposals. The mixed-use scheme they chose in 1983 was immediately decried as poorly planned and designed and too greedy of land (it proposed filling in 40 per cent of the basin). Fortunately, nothing except part of the housing element of the plan by *Richard Seifert & Partners* for Hunting Gate was carried out in 1985–7, and only moderate N and NW areas of water have been reclaimed above the Limehouse Link tunnel (*see* above). Slightly more appropriate speculative housing has been added since 1990.

The Regent's Canal Company was formed in 1812 to build a canal to link the Grand Junction at Paddington with the Thames at Limehouse. This was completed, including the Dock, in 1820. The original Act allowed for a proposed barge basin, but the scheme was enlarged in 1819 to receive ships, and again in 1852–3 to compete with Poplar Dock (*see* Isle of Dogs, West India and Millwall Docks) after the North London Railway opened there. Hydraulic power for cranes was installed then. In 1869 a new shiplock was built to take iron-built screw-driven colliers. Coal jetties and, later, low-rise warehouses stood all round it. The quay walls were mostly rebuilt in the 1900s; there were originally low timber revetments. In 1968 the Limehouse Cut (*see* below) was diverted into the dock; lighters continued to pass through it until the 1980s.

LOCK. Small, of 1988–9, within the former shiplock of 1869. – HARBOURMASTER'S STATION. 1989 by *Peter White* and *Jayne Holland* of the BWB. Timber and brick pagoda. Near it a bronze relief MAP of the basin, 1986, commemorating this first phase of redevelopment. – Marina PONTOONS 1994. – Across the dock entrance a SWING BRIDGE of steel box-girder construction, by *Husband & Company*, 1962. – To the N the first of the twin LOCKS on the Regent's Canal and a two-arched BRIDGE of 1820 under the Commercial Road.

The ACCUMULATOR TOWER, NE of the Basin in Mill Place, is the most impressive survival and, as renovated by *Dransfield Design* 1994–5, accessible to the public. The tower, octagonal with slit windows, and an octagonal N chimneystack attached to it, are the only remains of a hydraulic pumping station of 1868–9, i.e. contemporary with the new shiplock. It has a huge riveted wrought-iron weight case, 24 ft (7$\frac{1}{3}$ metres) high, which held some 80 tons of gravel. This weight-case, which was driven up the tower to maintain the hydraulic pressure by steam engines under the viaduct, has been fitted with a helical iron staircase to an exhibition area and, at the top, a viewing platform. This pumping station superseded the first one of 1852, which had a very early Armstrong accumulator, and stood, until 1994, on the W side of the Commercial Road locks. A third station (1898), was combined with back-pumping up the canal to refill the four nearest locks, and the wrought-iron PUMPING MAIN for this low-pressure water can be seen crossing the canal at the Commercial Road Bridge. These installations became largely redundant with changes of practice in the 1920s.

The VIADUCT, of brick with elliptical arches, is by *George & Robert Stephenson* and *G. P. Bidder* for the London and Blackwall (originally Commercial) Railway (*see* Blackwall), 1839–40. It crosses the canal and former branch dock in three magnificent segmental brick arches, each spanning 85 ft (26 metres). Original cast-iron railings. A similar but smaller bridge crosses the Limehouse Cut, W of St Anne. Originally run with stationary engines and cables, the railway terminated at Brunswick Wharf, Blackwall. In 1849, it was linked to the mainline railway system at Stepney (now Limehouse) station. The E chord (disused) was added 1880: it has a distinctive style of wrought-iron trussed BRIDGE, as used by the Great Eastern Railway. In 1984–7 the viaduct was refurbished for the DLR.

LIMEHOUSE CUT of the River Lee Navigation, 1$\frac{2}{3}$ m. long from Limehouse to the Lea at Bromley-by-Bow. 1767–70 by *Thomas Yeoman* upon the recommendations of *John Smeaton*. The tidal entrance lock was just E of the Regent's Canal Dock (*see* Perambulation 1). The Cut was diverted through the dock

1853–64 and more permanently in 1968. Beneath the Commercial Road a fine segmental-arched bridge of 1853, straddling a former flood lock.

PERAMBULATIONS

1. Ratcliffe to St Anne

FREE TRADE WHARF is the only remnant by the river of the 17 hamlet of RATCLIFFE. It is announced on THE HIGHWAY by a handsome gateway of 1796 (rebuilt 1934), bearing lions and the coat of arms of the East India Company, the original owner of the wharf, which housed saltpetre here, at a considerable distance from its main warehouses in Cutler Street (*see London 1: The City of London*). This precaution was wise. The two elegant warehouses, facing each other across a long paved court, were built in 1795–6, probably by *Richard Jupp*, Company Surveyor, after the previous warehouses were destroyed in the fire of 1794 (*see* p. 141). First enlarged in 1801 and again in 1828, the original brick piers and vaulting being replaced with iron and timber; this structure in turn was replaced in concrete and steel in 1935, though the queenpost roofs were retained. By 1838 the warehouses were being used by a ship chandler and in 1858 were renamed Free Trade Wharf.

Each yellow brick range is of nine bays, with a tenth bay 65 expressed as a pedimented two-storey pavilion to The Highway. The lowest two storeys are embraced by a tall arcade, open on the ground floor with the shops recessed. Above two more, lower storeys, not as original but altered to respond to the levels of the concrete floors inserted in the 1930s. Altogether very elegant elevations for such practical buildings. Converted in 1985–7 to flats over offices for Regalian by *Holder Mathias Alcock*.

To the w lies the modern part of Regalian's scheme by the same architects, a huge development of flats for which the various other warehouses along the rest of Free Trade Wharf were sacrificed, and with them a chance to create a more enjoyable mixed development. The design was an optimistic attempt to escape the derivative warehouse style. In fact, the piled-up red-brick flats with layers of balconies facing the Thames look old-fashioned for their date and overbearing in all river views. Big jetty here.

ATLANTIC WHARF, 1995–8, continues Regalian's riverside development E with five large design-and-build blocks of flats, their only distinctive feature the mannered roofs to the tall blocks along The Highway: initial design by *HMA Architects*. From here the view E is blocked by the entrance to the LIMEHOUSE LINK TUNNEL (*see* Public Buildings): with its striped Postmodern styling, this is easily mistaken at first glance for a 1930s supercinema. The remains of the ancient Butcher Row are crossed by The Highway here. To the N the Royal Foundation of St Katharine (*see* Churches), to the s the w end of Narrow Street.

NARROW STREET follows the river for nearly half a mile. Architecturally it has a bad start, especially on the N side. The S SIDE has the most interesting and sympathetic developments. Former warehouses along the riverside here, though of various dates, are all quite small, up to five storeys and only a few bays wide, and contribute to the intimate feel of the indeed narrow street. Nos. 22–28 were among the first to be converted for residential use in Docklands by the designer *Rae Hoffenberg* (with architects *Berman & Guedes*). They are especially significant as industrial zoning had to be overturned here to permit change of use (cf. Oliver's Wharf, Wapping). It was a phased development from 1976; the standard of design and detail far outstrips some of the later conversions. The interwar RATCLIFFE WHARF (No. 22) has been partly rebuilt and its riverfront courtyard filled with an atrium-like conservatory containing the lift. COMMERCIAL WHARF (No. 24) was the earliest conversion, completed 1980. Internal timber and ironwork retained. No. 26 is all new, heavily glazed to the river. No. 28 was also industrial, with its roof timbers retained in the rebuilt upper floor; see the interesting details in blue bull-nosed brick. To the river the centre is opened up with large arched windows, balconies and a broken pedimental gable between tall narrow chimneystacks: below Mean High Water the large circular outfall of an early C19 sewer. At SUN WHARF (No. 30), a lavish and unusual scheme by *Scott, Brownrigg & Turner*, 1983–5, for the film-maker, Sir David Lean. It shares the romantic approach to derelict industrial areas popular amongst landscape designers and architects in continental Europe. Four C19 warehouses, two of them burnt-out shells, have been turned into a house and large garden, the house and garage created from the three-bay, gabled W one and its unsound neighbour; the outer walls and some arched cross-walls of the other two used as garden walls and features, including a cottage against the E wall. After that a long stretch of Narrow Street has been spoilt by ostentatious speculative flats packed on to restricted sites, amongst which CHINNOCK'S WHARF, 1997, by *Michael Squire & Associates*, stands out crisply.

LIMEHOUSE BASIN (*see above*) opens up on the N side. The BARLEY MOW stands S by the entrance. It was the Regent's Canal Dockmaster's house of *c.* 1905–10; since 1989 a pub. Queen Anne style, red brick. Limehouse Basin is a wonderful site wasted, an almost landlocked pool walled in on the N by a handsome viaduct that demands an equally strong response from new buildings. It could have been a refreshing oasis with enjoyable facilities (proposals on these lines were drawn up by *Rae Hoffenberg* and *Phippen Randall & Parkes* in 1985). Instead, there is mediocre speculative housing all round, particularly regrettable on the W, where gabled low-rise houses and flats are crammed in round GOODHART PLACE. By *Richard Seifert & Partners*, part of a never-completed scheme for offices and houses by that architect, 1985–6. Gimmicky details, garish red and yellow brick, ugly paving. Round the E side, entered from

NORTHEY STREET, QUAYSIDE, a group of larger Italianate blocks by *John Thompson & Partners*, playing safe but more appropriate than Goodhart Place. Part of this group, completed 1997, the CRUISING ASSOCIATION HQ, also faintly C19 industrial.

Further down Narrow Street, on the S side beyond the speculative housing of Victoria Wharf and Victoria Lock, the disused bell-mouthed LIMEHOUSE CUT ENTRANCE (*see* also above), with a late C18 house (No. 48) and a wrought-iron girder bridge of 1865. The site of the lock, rebuilt 1865, is marked by a late C19 row of former LOCK-KEEPERS' COTTAGES (N). In Northey Street, preserved parapets of another bridge, *c.* 1865. PAPERMILL WHARF with its simplified Italianate tower is a reconstruction of early C20 Hough's Wharf which incorporates some of the outer walls of the former C19 Dover Wharf to the E. Victoria Lock (N) is on the site of the Limehouse Paperboard Mills, built in the first decade of the C20 on the site of late C16 Limehouse Bridge Dock and closed in 1986.

After this Narrow Street becomes interesting again on both sides, both for the surviving historic buildings and the good modern housing that has replaced the power station and the coaling wharf that stood opposite. On the latter, BLYTH'S WHARF (S), idiosyncratic but acceptable houses of 1985–6 by *Heber-Percy & Parker Architects*. Though set back behind a wall and trees, the terrace links in size and texture with the late C17 to early C18 row next along this side. Warm, deep golden brick, timber windows, horizontal in the intermittent gables, otherwise upright of various sizes. Slight bow over the passage to the former coaling island, built in 1923 for colliers delivering to Stepney Power Station. On the riverfront, alternate gables and bows along the projecting top floor, weatherboarding below, a mixture of formal and informal elements reminiscent of houses seen in views of the C18 riverside.

THE WATERGARDEN (a pretentious renaming of ROY SQUARE) faces Blyth's Wharf from the N side. This fine group, by *Ian Ritchie Architects*, 1986–8, is a more rigorous reinterpretation of Georgian urban housing on the site of Stepney Power Station. It is a long introverted courtyard of flats, raised on a tall carpark podium. Screening the podium along Narrow Street, the gridded bay windows of a row of studios and workshops. The entrance is via a narrow entrance slot of steps, edged with rills, which lead up to the courtyard garden, bisected by a canal and enclosed by crisp pavilions of flats and lower, glass-walled stair links. Tall, completely glazed rectangular bays embrace ground-floor flats and maisonettes above. Balconies on top of them serve the top two floors. The original planting was remarkable and slightly Eastern (the developer, Roy Sandu, is Hindu), the flats screened by lush stands of bamboo: mostly replaced 1996.

The street opens out into a charming wedge of open space, laid out by the LDDC, 1994, in the manner of a French *place*, with Indian bean trees, seats; screaming copper HERRING GULL on a coil of rope by *Jane Ackroyd*, 1994. Continuing the open space

to the E, ROPEMAKER'S FIELDS, in origin a street named after
the several ropewalks that lay N of Narrow Street before the C19
but now a park, landscaped by the LDDC and *Churchman
Associates*, who designed the sturdy rope-moulded railings and
the bandstand which incorporates cast-iron columns saved
from one of the former warehouses at St Katharine Docks.
Prominent on the N side of the *place*, a terrace of stock-brick
houses by *Proctor Matthews Architects*, 1992–6, well designed but
rather coarse-grained for its older neighbours opposite. It replaces
the LCC's Brightlingsea Buildings of 1904, demolished in
1982, and takes its cue from THE HOUSE THEY LEFT
BEHIND, the plain, Late Georgian-style pub that remains from
a previous mid-C19 terrace. Four houses paired by two-storey
window units and balconies in layers that distance them from
the street. Rooftop terraces and plain rear elevations with long
windows, relieved by the bold roll-moulding over the garage
doors. In the centre an angled slot makes a right of way through
to BRIGHTLINGSEA PLACE and the refurbished tenement,
Faraday House, built by Stepney Borough Council in 1931.

10 THE GRAPES introduces the long run of C17 to early C18 houses
(Nos. 78–94) on the S side of the *place*, with a slightly later two-
bay stock-brick façade. This row is one of the most picturesque
in Docklands, but the houses are chiefly remarkable as rare
survivals of this type of riverside dwelling in the area. Early
photographs show many of similar type in the other riverside
hamlets from Wapping to Rotherhithe, but all of those have
gone. These have well-preserved façades, the shuttered lower
floors formerly shops or stores, though many are now used as
garages. The backs, looking on to riverside gardens, have been
much altered.
  First (Nos.78–86), a ten-bay, slightly cranked row of four early
  C18 houses, apparently built *c.* 1718 by Thomas Wakelin of

Limehouse, view of the riverside.
Engraving by J. Boydell, 1751

Ratcliffe on the site of earlier houses. Stock brick, with red brick dressings including the strings. Flush segment-headed sashes on two storeys in pairs. In the attic, similar smaller windows centred over each pair and narrow blind panels between them. A variety of ground-floor treatments is unified by dark-green paint. Only No. 80 has a conventional rusticated ground floor with arched door and window, perhaps early C19.

No. 88 has a painted two-bay front, apparently a C19 recasting with moulded window surrounds and cornices on consoles poised over them: early C19 shopfront. No. 90 is plain, also early C19, and two-bay. No. 92 (BOOTY'S BAR), the least altered of these early houses, still has much original fabric (probably late C17), including the roof. The segment-headed sash windows have rubbed-brick voussoirs and keystones topped by a narrow moulding. One smaller window below a small central gable. Another plain gable to the rear, shown as a shaped gable in a late C19 photo though perhaps not as original. The plan seems late C17 too, with one-and-half flights of the original stairs flanking the central chimney. Original cupboards in the alcoves formed by the chimney.

Continuing the row of houses, an early C19 barge-building works (No. 94), where barges were repaired until the early 1950s. Dwelling over the double-height ground floor with a big archway through it. A timber mould loft straddles the yard on the riverside. DUKE SHORE STAIRS was the lowest point on this side of the river for passenger embarkation. Pepys came here in 1660 to be ferried upriver to the Tower of London. No. 98 has a sturdy early C20 shopfront and C19 No. 100 still has its original cast-iron windows and loading doors (with wall-crane) on the ground and first floors. At No. 102 a four-storey early to mid-C18 house, heavily restored, and at DUKE SHORE WHARF flats by *Barnard Urquhart Jarvis*, 1985–8, that pick up the arch motif from No. 94. At the back a big drum of flats with good and contrasting views that can be shared by pedestrians on the riverfront here: downriver those landmark blocks, Dundee Wharf and Cascades, and, upriver, the higgledy-piggledy backs p. 154 of Nos. 78–94 Narrow Street.

Beyond Duke Shore Wharf is a new residential development presently named Dunbar Wharf, the western part of which is over the Limehouse Link. This carefully avoided Nos. 136–140, the well-converted original DUNBAR WHARF, a two- to three-storey mixture, with cast-iron and sash windows, loading doors, wall-cranes; and sail loft the rear boarded at No. 136. These small early C19 warehouses back on to the tidal inlet LIMEKILN DOCK and formerly belonged to Duncan Dunbar & Sons which ran a famous fleet of fast sailing ships to India, Australia and North America. At ST DUNSTAN'S WHARF of 1878 at No. 142, just the gable front, with decorative moulded brick plaque, remains; the rest has been rebuilt. Nearer the head of the inlet, LIMEHOUSE WHARF (Nos. 148–150) still conveys atmosphere. It is mid C19, of three storeys and five bays, with original loading doors and cast-iron windows. Last on this side at the corner of

Three Colt Street, a former pub of *c.*1850 (No. 154), still with its pilastered front and Corinthian aedicules round the upper windows.

THREE COLT STREET is also one of the original streets of Limehouse. In the boundary wall of LIMEKILN WHARF, a replica of the doorway from the famous LIME HOUSE, which was built in 1705 and demolished in 1935 (with the adjacent last remaining lime kiln) for a builders' merchant (see the converted office block to the N). The round-headed timber doorcase, with narrow neck supporting a miniature pediment, was moved to the boundary wall and replaced with the replica in 1988 when it was donated to the Ragged School Museum, Stepney. The site of the lime kiln and its adjacent limehouse is now part of a block of flats with quirky details by *John Brunton Partnership*, *c.* 1989. From the public walkway to the N good views of LIMEKILN DOCK and the backs of the former warehouses in Narrow Street. Housing has now replaced industry entirely in East Limehouse.

87 DUNDEE WHARF stands between here and the river. Furthest N, the late C19 classical office building, in red and yellow brick, of the original Dundee, Perth, and London Shipping Co. Galleon in the pediment and a cupola on the roof. To the S the new flats, part of a large group of housing by *CZWG* (1995–7) make a massive landmark to answer the same architects' Cascades further downriver. Though less original, this block is nearly as theatrical. The vocabulary of quayside engineering is dramatically expressed; giant 'hoppers' top the service towers towards the horseshoe-shaped rear court, enclosed with lower blocks and flats and houses and a drum of leisure facilities. Sinister crane-like attachments support balconies along the sheer river façades and form an eleven-storey free-standing tower at the angle. The flats here are some of the largest in Docklands, each filling a whole floor of the angle block. From here a wonderful FOOTBRIDGE by *YRM/Anthony Hunt Associates* for the LDDC, *c.* 1995, takes the Thames path in a sinuous curve across the mouth of Limekiln Dock and is stayed by a single mast.

Back N to Narrow Street and Limehouse Causeway, the W end of the latter realigned and widened in 1904 and with public housing N of it. Prominent just W of Three Colt Street is the BARLEYMOW ESTATE which replaced the Barley Mow Brewery, founded in 1730. When built in the 1960s, the estate was one of the few examples in Tower Hamlets of the *GLC*'s flirtation with industrialized building. Now the towers and lower blocks are crisply white-clad, the result of an energy-efficient refurbishment by *ECD Architects* for the LDDC and Tower Hamlets, 1989–93. The blocks of various heights edge Three Colt Street, as it continues N of Limehouse Causeway. Beyond the railway viaduct, facing the large leafy churchyard of St Anne (*see* Churches), the mildly Baroque pink terracotta front of the former LIMEHOUSE CHURCH INSTITUTE by *W. H. White*, 1903–4, now flats with ugly additions. Its neighbour, the FIVE BELLS AND BLADE BONE, has an unaffected C19 pub exterior.

NEWELL STREET can be reached by crossing the churchyard. The terrace of mid-C18 houses on the E side is the remains of the smart quarter round the church. No. 11, on the corner of St Anne's Passage, is the largest house, though in other respects it is like the others. Open-pedimented doorcase with delicate brackets to the side, a bow to the front. Nos. 13–23 are all two-to three-bay; No. 21 is stuccoed. Opposite (W), overlooking Limehouse Cut, an early C19 detached villa at Nos. 2–4, at one time used as a sea-training establishment for boys. The E façade still has a tin plaque reading 'British and Foreign Sailors' Society'. The entrance is off-centre through a low forebuilding, articulated to the street with a row of blind arches. Later C19 N extension with paired, arched first-floor windows. Built into the S boundary odd little post-war houses (Nos. 6a–b) roofed in big pantiles and with an Italianate tower.

2. St Anne Limehouse to Westferry station

COMMERCIAL ROAD crosses the N end of Newell Street. It was built as a toll road in 1802–4 to provide a direct route between the City and the East and West India Docks and was unusually wide (70 ft, 21½ metres) to take heavy traffic. Only its E end lies within the LDDC area but this includes Limehouse Town Hall on the corner of Newell Street and, W of the canal, the Passmore Edwards Library and the R.C. church (*see* above). In ISLAND ROW there is a short length of STONEWAY, two lines of smooth granite slabs either side of a sett-paved horse-path, similar to that laid along the S side of West India Dock Road and Commercial Road for the heaviest traffic (engineer *James Walker*) in 1828–30 and taken up in 1871.

THE MISSION looks E towards the Docks from the corner of Salmon Lane, with a stripped Perp exterior on a cathedral-like scale. It was the Empire Memorial Sailors' Hostel, designed by *Thomas Brammall Daniel & Horace W. Parnacott*, 1923–4. Salmon Lane wing 1932. The stone-clad façades, with vertical strips of window and seaweedy foliage carving, masked completely plain interiors round a courtyard; subdivided as flats in 1989. The far superior PASSMORE EDWARDS SAILORS' PALACE, further E on the S side at No. 680, was the HQ of the British and Foreign Sailors' Society and must have been Daniel & Parnacott's model. It is an unusually pretty building of 1901 by *Niven & Wigglesworth*, two architects always worth watching for. The façade's chief motif is the very Arts and Crafts 'gatehouse' (cf. Townsend's earlier Bishopsgate Institute and Whitechapel Art Gallery on the E fringe of the City of London). Octagonal flanking turrets, a flat three-storey rectangular oriel and lavish carving on a nautical theme, including a regal figurehead keystone (presumably Britannia) grasping two galleons, flanked by the names of the winds finely lettered. Over the arch a rope moulding twisted round the names of Continents. The label-stops are delicate reliefs of seagulls touching down lightly on the waves. Anchors, dolphins, shields etc. embossed on the metal panels here and on the side to Beccles Street, which is articulated by flattened bays projecting slightly over a segmental arcade of windows. W wing rebuilt c. 1960. Converted into flats 1983–4 by *Shankland Cox* for Rodinglea Housing Association. Next door in BECCLES STREET, plain early C19 houses, which look like a pair, but have only one doorway.

WEST INDIA DOCK ROAD turns off at the major road junction to the former West India Docks (*see* Isle of Dogs). At its start, W side, the former German Sailors' home of c. 1906 (No. 14), red brick and stuccoed, some relief garlands in the gabled bays and a tiny oriel within the entrance arch. On the E side, THE SAILMAKER BUILDING, erected 1860 as a sailmakers and ship chandlers, according to the lettering on the stringcourse. Three-bay pedimented façade like a tall Nonconformist chapel.

WESTFERRY ROAD at this end belongs in character to modern Docklands. Much post-1981 building around Westferry station, including, just to the W in Limehouse Causeway, the Limehouse Youth Club (*see* above). Marking the gateway into the Isle of Dogs, DRAGON'S GATE, a reminder of the Chinese community that first settled round here in the late C19: 1996 by *Art of Change*. More powerful as a landmark will be (post-1997) the giant lettering incorporated into the brick-faced wedge of *CZWG*'s 'live-work' building facing the station. A novel type of building (for the Peabody Trust), incorporating commercial units to the street and living-and-working spaces above. Also bold but more conventional the intensely coloured PREMIER PLACE by *Chassay Architects*, 1995–8, speculative flats on the corner of Garford Street: rendered, with bright-blue attic storeys. Just in GARFORD STREET, S, on the site of St Peter's church (by *Ewan Christian*, 1882–4), the pre-LDDC MARY JONES HOUSE, social housing for the single by *Christopher Beaver Associates*, succeeded by *Prior Manton Tuke Partnership*, 1978–9. Collegiate in style with a Kahn-inspired red brick perimeter heavily modelled with staircases; generous bay windows to the courtyard garden. For the rest of Garford Street *see* Isle of Dogs, Perambulation 1.

NORTH WOOLWICH
London Borough of Newham

North Woolwich is a very small but distinct neighbourhood. Until absorbed in Metropolitan London in 1889, it belonged, not to Essex like its East Ham neighbour, but to Kent. Maps of the early C19, before the present settlement developed, show two pockets of riverside land marked 'Kent' cutting into East Ham Level, towards Barking Creek. This anomaly was of very long standing. 'Kent in Essex' probably had its origins in the land held in 1086 by Hamon, Sheriff of Kent, which extended both N and S of the Thames. W of Hamon's land by East Ham Creek lay the manor of Hammarsh, owned by Westminster Abbey from at least the C11 to 1846. There was a chapel and hamlet at Hammarsh until the late

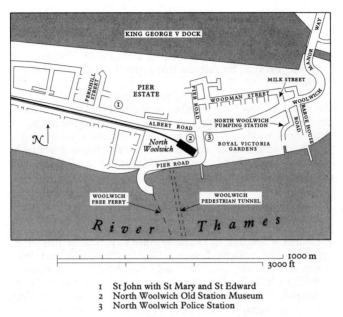

1   St John with St Mary and St Edward
2   North Woolwich Old Station Museum
3   North Woolwich Police Station

North Woolwich

Middle Ages, when it seems to have been inundated. The land was used for grazing until the mid C19, when G. P. Bidder bought hundreds of acres of farmland from Westminster Abbey, and promoted a new railway and ferry to Woolwich, which in turn increased the prices of his North Woolwich Land Co. as industry was attracted to the area.

The name North Woolwich was coined when the new steam ferry to Woolwich from this part of 'Kent in Essex' was opened in 1847, replacing a crossing further w. The railway line to it was an extension by the North Woolwich Railway Co. of the Eastern Counties and Thames Junction Railway line to Thames Wharf on Bow Creek, built to carry coal in 1844–6. The companies, only nominally separate, amalgamated in 1847. Ferry passengers and those who had disembarked here on their way to and from Gravesend used the railway, but it quickly declined as a passenger line when Woolwich got its own line into central London in 1849. In order to attract custom the Royal Pavilions Gardens were opened as a privately run pleasure resort in the early 1850s, with ballroom, dining room and dance floor.

The amenity of the river bank was soon spoilt. Opened up for industry by the railway and the contemporary road to North Woolwich, the first commercial concern was established just w of the ferry in 1859 and, until the late 1970s, took up much of the riverfront. Henley's, an offshoot of the rubber industry (*see* Silvertown), made and laid transatlantic cables. Workers and goods began to use the line after industry spread all along the river and the docks opened in 1855 and 1880. In 1889 the LCC opened the Woolwich Free Ferry to bring workers from the s bank to work on the N. In 1890 they converted the decayed pleasure gardens into the public Royal Victoria Gardens to serve the housing that had grown up between the rail and ferry termini and the Royal Albert Dock.

There are few C19 buildings now. North Woolwich, like the Royal Docks, was badly bombed in the Second World War, and almost completely rebuilt with public housing in the 1960s. In 1997 there are few signs of new development apart from the British Telecom satellite station established on the site vacated by Henley's, and a relandscaped riverfront which the LDDC have scattered with marine relics.

CHURCHES AND PUBLIC BUILDINGS

St John with St Mary and St Edward, Albert Road. Joint Church of England and R.C., planned as part of the Pier Estate (*see* below). 1968 by *Laurence King & Partners*. A dark brick box with a broad, lower aisle and linked by a glazed corridor to the church centre. Over the altar a square lantern supporting a thin, white flèche. In the spacious sanctuary, floored with black slate, the large, square ALTAR of green stone sits beneath an octagonal metal corona. The wide aisle allows a high degree of flexibility in the seating arrangements. – FONT. Movable. A copper cooking pot from Africa set in a wooden frame; given by the architects.

27 North Woolwich Old Station Museum, Pier Road. A small station, but quite elaborate befitting its role as the terminus of the Eastern Counties and Thames Junction Railway. Completed in 1854, it replaced the previous terminus, which had been built in 1847 and which stood further E. Converted to the museum of the Great Eastern Railway in 1984, after it was superseded in 1979 by a smaller station alongside the former goods yard.

Italianate front with rich detail especially on the projecting wings, where the columned and rusticated archways look quite Baroque. A single tripartite window in each wing, the balustrade beneath their sills continuing as a parapet to the central one-storey ticket hall. Plain five-bay platform façade with round-headed ground-floor openings. The timber canopy is a restoration and the supporting cast-iron columns with strapwork decoration come from Goodmayes Station, Essex. The axial arrangement of a locomotive turntable, within a walled enclosure, is unusual and has been restored. The ticket office has been returned to its interwar form. The RAILWAY PIER, to the S, was rebuilt in 1900 but has largely been dismantled.

Woolwich Free Ferry. The free ferry allowed vehicles and workers to cross from one bank to another and was maintained free of toll from 1889 by the LCC, then the GLC and now the London Borough of Greenwich. The terminals designed by *Husband & Co.*, 1964–6, with steel-trussed ramps adjustable to

. Bermondsey, St Saviour's Dock showing footbridge by Whitby & Bird and
Nicholas Lacey & Partners, 1995 and New Concordia Wharf, converted
by Pollard Thomas & Edwards in succession to Nicholas Lacey &
Partners, 1981–3

2 Rotherhithe village with St Mary, by John James, 1714–37, tower by
Lancelot Dowbiggin, 1747–8, and the Thames Tunnel Mills, from the
1860s

3 Bermondsey, Shad Thames, flanked by the later nineteenth-century
warehouses of Butler's Wharf

4 Wapping, Pier Head, with houses by D.A. Alexander, 1811–13, Oliver's
Wharf, by F. & H. Francis, 1869–70, and (background) tower of St John,
1756

5 Royal Docks, Royal Victoria Dock, 1850–5, from the south-west, with
twentieth-century Stothert & Pitt cranes

2 | 4
3 | 5

6. Poplar, St Matthias, Woodstock Terrace, interior, 1652–4, with windows inserted by W.M. Teulon, 1870–6

7. Limehouse, St Anne, by Nicholas Hawksmoor, 1714–30, from the south

8. Wapping, St George-in-the-East, by Nicholas Hawksmoor, 1714–29, from the south-east

9. Limehouse, St Anne, by Nicholas Hawksmoor, 1714–30, approach to west front
10. Limehouse, Narrow Street, south side, including Nos. 78–94, of the late seventeenth to early eighteenth century
11. Wapping, Raine's House, Raine Street, 1719
12. Rotherhithe, Nelson House, Nelson Dock, Rotherhithe Street, c.1730–40

9 | 11
10 | 12

13. Wapping, St Paul, Shadwell, by John Walters, 1820–1
14. Poplar, All Saints, Bazely Street, by Charles Hollis, 1820–3
15. Isle of Dogs, Isle House, No. 1 Coldharbour, by Sir John Rennie, 1825–6
16. Wapping, Pier Head, the west terrace by D.A. Alexander, 1811–13

17. Limehouse, Free Trade Wharf, warehouses attributed to Richard Jupp, 1795–6, converted with additional housing by Holder Mathias Alcock, 1985–7

18. Wapping, Tobacco Dock shopping centre, former New Tobacco Warehouse, by D.A. Alexander, 1811–14, converted by Terry Farrell Partnership, 1984–9

19. Isle of Dogs, West India Docks, Import Dock North Quay (now West India Quay), warehouses, by George Gwilt & Son, 1800–3, altered by Sir John Rennie, 1827

20. Isle of Dogs, West India Docks, Import Dock North Quay (now West India Quay), Dock Office, by George Gwilt & Son, 1803–4, remodelled as the Ledger Building by Sir John Rennie, 1827

21. Bermondsey, Butler's Wharf, warehouses by James Tolley & Daniel Dale, 1871–4, converted by Conran Roche, from 1983
22. Wapping, St Katharine Docks, Ivory House, by George Aitchison Sen., 1858–60, converted by Renton Howard Wood Associates, 1972–4
23. Bermondsey, Hay's Galleria, warehouses by William Snooke and Henry Stock, 1851–7, roof etc. by Michael Twigg Brown & Partners, 1982–6
24. Wapping, John Orwell Sports Centre, Tench Street, converted by Shepheard Epstein & Hunter, 1977–80, from a nineteenth-century dock workshop

25. Royal Docks, Royal Victoria Dock, W Warehouse, by Robert Carr, 1883
26. Isle of Dogs, Burrell's Wharf, off Westferry Road, Plate House by
    W. Cubitt & Co., 1853–4, flats by Jestico & Whiles, 1987–9
27. North Woolwich, North Woolwich Old Station museum, Pier Road,
    completed 1854

28. Blackwall, Hydraulic Pumping Station of the former East India Dock, East India Dock Wall Road, 1857, extended 1877–8

29. Wapping, Wapping Hydraulic Pumping Station, Wapping Wall, 1889–93, enlarged 1920s

30. Isle of Dogs, former St Paul Presbyterian Church in England (now The Space), by T.E. Knightley, 1859

31. Wapping, St Patrick (R.C.), by F.W. Tasker, 1879, from the north-west

32. Silvertown, St Mark, by
    S.S. Teulon, 1860–2,
    from the south

33. Isle of Dogs, Christ
    Church and St John,
    pulpit painted by John
    Melhuish Strudwick,
    c. 1914

34. Poplar, former Poplar
    District Board of Works
    Offices, Poplar High
    Street, by Hills &
    Fletcher with A. & C.
    Harston, 1869–70

35. Wapping, River Police
    Station, Wapping High
    Street, by John Dixon
    Butler, 1907–10

32	34
33	35

36. Isle of Dogs,
    Scandinavian
    Seamen's
    Temperance Home
    (now Grieg House),
    Garford Street,
    by Niven &
    Wigglesworth,
    1902–3
37. Limehouse, Empire
    Memorial Sailors'
    Hostel (now The
    Mission),
    Commercial Road, by
    Thomas Brammall
    Daniel & Horace
    W. Parnacott, 1923–4
38. Royal Docks, Royal
    Victoria Dock,
    Custom House,
    properly Dock
    Directors' Access
    Centre, by Sir Edwin
    Cooper, 1920–4
39. Bermondsey, St Olaf
    House, Tooley Street,
    by H.S. Goodhart-
    Rendel, 1929–31

44. Bermondsey, Most Holy Trinity (R.C.), Dockhead, by H.S. Goodhart-Rendel, 1951–61
45. Rotherhithe, Finnish Seamen's Church, Albion Street, by Cyril Sjöström (Mardall) of Yorke Rosenberg & Mardall, 1954–9
46. Bermondsey, Most Holy Trinity (R.C.), Dockhead, by H.S. Goodhart-Rendel, 1951–61, interior looking west

44 | 45
   | 46

47. Poplar, Thornfield House, Birchfield Estate, by the LCC Architect's Department, 1960–2
48. Poplar, Robin Hood Gardens, by Alison & Peter Smithson for the GLC, 1966–72, from the south-east
49. Isle of Dogs, Dr Barraclough's Houses, Ferry Street, by Stout & Litchfield, commissioned 1975
50. Isle of Dogs, Maconochie's Wharf, off Westferry Road, by the Great Eastern Self-Build Housing Association with architects Stout & Litchfield, 1985–90

51. Isle of Dogs, Heron Quays, South Dock, by Nicholas Lacey, Jobst & Hyett, 1981–9, and (background) Canary Wharf, 1987–91
52. Isle of Dogs, Canary Wharf DLR station, by Cesar Pelli & Associates with A.S.F.A. Ltd, 1987–91, interior
53. Isle of Dogs, floating footbridge, Import Dock, West India Docks, by Future Systems, engineers Anthony Hunt Associates, 1994–6

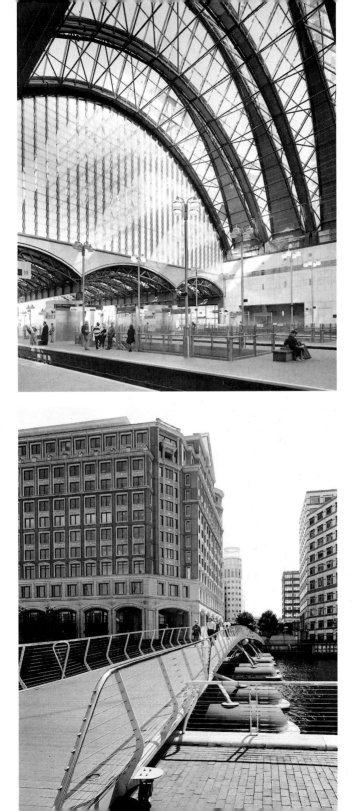

61. Bermondsey, China Wharf, Mill Street, by CZWG, 1986–8
62. Bermondsey, Horselydown Square, by Wickham & Associates, 1983–90, entrance from the north-west
63. Bermondsey, The Circle, Queen Elizabeth Street, by CZWG, 1987–9

4. Bermondsey, Vogan's Mill, Mill Street, late nineteenth century, converted by Michael Squire & Associates, 1987–9

5. Wapping, Gun Wharves, Wapping High Street, c. 1920, remodelled by Barratt East London, c. 1985

6. Bermondsey, Design Museum, Shad Thames, converted from a 1950s warehouse by Conran Roche, 1989, Invention by Eduardo Paolozzi

7. Limehouse, Free Trade Wharf, warehouses attributed to Richard Jupp, 1795–6, converted by Holder Mathias Alcock, 1985–7

68. Isle of Dogs, Cabot Square, Canary Wharf, 1987–91, landscaping by Hanna Olins, consultant Sir Roy Strong
69. Isle of Dogs, No. 10 Cabot Square, Canary Wharf, by Skidmore, Owings & Merrill (Chicago), 1987–91, arcade
70. Isle of Dogs, No. 25 The North Colonnade, Canary Wharf, by Troughton McAslan with Adamson Associates, 1987–91
71. Isle of Dogs, No. 10 Cabot Square, Canary Wharf, by Skidmore, Owings & Merrill (Chicago), 1987–91

72. Blackwall, former Financial Times Printing Works, East India Dock Road, by Nicholas Grimshaw & Partners, 1988
73. Wapping, No. 2 Pennington Street, offices by Rick Mather, 1989–92
74. Isle of Dogs, Isle of Dogs Neighbourhood Centre, Jack Dash House, Marsh Wall, by Chassay Architects, 1988–91
75. Blackwall, Reuter Technical Services Centre, Blackwall Way, by Richard Rogers Partnership, 1989, with Blackwall Tunnel ventilation stacks, by Terry Farrell for the GLC, 1960–7

76. Wapping, remains of the Western Dock, 1801–5, with original quay wall by John Rennie, landscaping by Paddy Jackson Associates, 1982–5, and housing (Thomas More Court) by Boyer Design Group, 1987–90
77. Wapping, Shadwell Basin, housing by MacCormac, Jamieson, Prichard & Wright, 1985–7
78. Isle of Dogs, Compass Point, off Saunders Ness Road, by Jeremy Dixon and BDP, 1985–8
79. Rotherhithe, Riverside Apartments (formerly Prince's Tower), Rotherhithe Street, by Troughton McAslan and Tim Brennan Architects, 1986–90

80. Isle of Dogs, Cascades, Westferry Road, by CZWG, 1985–8, detail
81. Isle of Dogs, Cumberland Mills Square, Saunders Ness Road, by
    Donald Ball of Alan Turner & Associates, 1987–9
82. Isle of Dogs, Cascades, Westferry Road, by CZWG, 1985–8, east
    elevation

83. Isle of Dogs, Burrell's Wharf, off Westferry Road, flats by Jestico & Whiles, 1987–9

84. Rotherhithe, The Lakes, Norway Dock, Greenland Dock, by Shepheard Epstein & Hunter, 1988–96

85. Rotherhithe, Wolfe Crescent, Surrey Quays, by CZWG, 1988–93

86. Beckton, Ambassador Gardens, off Tollgate Road, by Form Design Group, 1987

87. Limehouse, Dundee Wharf, housing by CZWG, 1995–7,
footbridge by YRM/Anthony Hunt Associates *c.*1995, from
the north-west

a 30-ft (9-metre) tidal range, replace the floating landing-stages of 1889.

WOOLWICH PEDESTRIAN TUNNEL, Pier Road. 1909–12 by the engineer *Sir Maurice Fitzmaurice* for the LCC. Similar to the Greenwich Foot Tunnel (*see* Isle of Dogs). The entrance rotunda here is smaller. Red brick, paired sash windows with segmental heads in recessed panels and wrought-iron grilles. Copper dome with little conical-roofed lantern on top. Entrances with glass canopies on cast-iron columns with foliated caps, decorated bargeboards. An earlier subway here, begun in 1876 by *J. H. Greathead*, was not completed.

NORTH WOOLWICH POLICE STATION, Albert Road and Pier Road. 1904 by *John Dixon Butler*, the Metropolitan Police architect, in his characteristic Free Style. Red brick striped in Portland stone. Pretty and no doubt useful corner oriel with domed cap. Hooded stone porch with battered sides. Shaped gables.

PERAMBULATION

The N part of Pier Road (originally High Street) at the junction with ALBERT ROAD forms the hub of the settlement. Here there are still a few pre-war buildings. At the junction, the Police Station and opposite it the ROYAL STANDARD (No. 116), dated 1898. Simple Baroque details all in brick. Lush Art Nouveau iron overthrow to the saloon entrance. Further E two other pubs which must have served the docks, the CALIFORNIA at the corner of Milk Street, 1914 by *Robert Banks-Martin*, with Baroque details precociously turning Deco, and the C19 striped brick ROUND HOUSE curving round the corner into Woodman Street. The ROYAL VICTORIA GARDENS stretch along the river bank. In the gardens, a small STEAM HAMMER from the blacksmith's shop of the ship-repair yard in the Royal Albert Docks. By *R. Harvey* of Glasgow, 1888. The gardens reach E to the little S tail of the old road from the river N to East Ham, WOOLWICH MANOR WAY; N of Albert Road it was improved in 1896 and post-1981. At the S end the NORTH WOOLWICH PUMPING STATION, built by the LCC *c.* 1900 in connection with main drainage. Red brick, very plain, with arched panels in a pedimental gable end. Closer to Albert Road, artisan cottages and another row, more Baroque in style, E in BARGE HOUSE ROAD; all early council housing built by Woolwich Council, 1901. The rest of North Woolwich, N of Albert Road, is now post-war public housing.

The PIER ESTATE stretches W of PIER ROAD to Fernhill Street. A mixed development planned in 1962 by the *GLC Department of Civic Design and Housing*, with small squares along a tree-lined pedestrian route. Round the squares three brick-faced towers, nineteen- and twenty-storey, quite sculptural with balconies at each projecting corner, and brick two-storey houses refurbished with pitched roofs and coloured Postmodern details. The GLC's designs are tinged with Brutalism and more aggressively up to date than *East Ham Borough Council's* estate

E of Pier Road, which, though almost contemporary (opened 1965), is still in a more approachable 1950s idiom and clad mainly in brick. Flats above shops along Pier Road roofed in a series of barrel-vaults. Also five slab blocks of flats, and lower maisonettes.

POPLAR

London Borough of Tower Hamlets

Poplar can claim to be the heart of London Docklands. Within its C19 parish lay the most extensive system of enclosed docks in Europe – the West India and Millwall Docks and the East India Docks – two-thirds of which, though no longer used for their original purpose, survive as beautifully constructed basins of open water at the centre of a huge new commercial district. The parish was established in 1817; the Metropolitan Borough, which covered almost exactly the same area, in 1900: the borough was combined with Stepney and Bethnal Green into one London Borough, that of Tower Hamlets, in 1965. Topographically and historically, the former parish and borough of Poplar falls into three sections, all of which are treated individually in this volume: the Isle of Dogs, marshland into which the West India and Millwall Docks were cut; Blackwall, a peninsula at the Leamouth where the East India Company's C17 shipyard was followed in the C19 by the construction of the East India Docks; and, on the highest gravelly ground, the remains of the original hamlet of Poplar, which developed along Poplar High Street and spread in a triangle N of the East India Dock Road. This triangle, redeveloped post-war as the Lansbury estate, falls outside the Docklands area as designated in 1981 and is not discussed here.

For Blackwall and the East India Docks *see* p. 83.

For The Isle of Dogs and the West India and Millwall Docks *see* p. 90.

For Poplar hamlet (Poplar High Street N to the East India Dock Road) *see* below.

In the mid C17 the hamlet of Poplar, with a population of about a thousand, was only a double row of houses lining the road from the much larger Limehouse to Blackwall (qq.v.), where the East India Company had just established their shipyard. The company dominated the hamlet from the mid C17 to 1866. In 1628 it bought a stretch of land on the N side of the road, including a house which it gradually developed into large almshouses (they were replaced by the Council Offices and the recreation ground in 9, p. 1866). It also allowed a proprietary chapel, later St Matthias, to be 172 built in 1639 within the grounds of the almshouses to serve Poplar and Blackwall, both then within the parish of Stepney. Though respectable in the C17 and C18, the hamlet was never rich, for local merchants and shipbuilders, who mainly had their premises to the W along the river at Limehouse Hole, preferred to retreat to more rural parts of Essex.

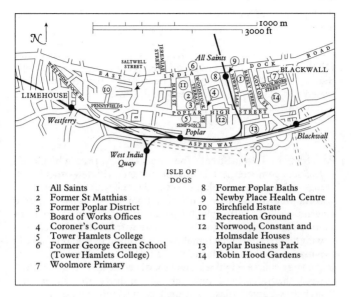

Poplar

1	All Saints	8	Former Poplar Baths
2	Former St Matthias	9	Newby Place Health Centre
3	Former Poplar District Board of Works Offices	10	Birchfield Estate
4	Coroner's Court	11	Recreation Ground
5	Tower Hamlets College	12	Norwood, Constant and Holmsdale Houses
6	Former George Green School (Tower Hamlets College)	13	Poplar Business Park
7	Woolmore Primary	14	Robin Hood Gardens

The High Street grew more commercial after the opening of first the West India Docks in 1802 and then the East India Docks in 1806. The population rose sharply in ten years, from 4,493 in 1801 to 7,708 in 1811, necessitating the creation of the parish of Poplar in 1817. The parish church, All Saints, was built with the 14 help of contributions from the dock companies in 1820–3 close to the East India Dock Road (*see* Limehouse), which had opened in 1812: a residential quarter was soon laid out around it. In the middle of the C19 the population mushroomed (28,432 in 1851 to 43,529 in 1861). Poplar Chapel was recast and reseated as the church of St Matthias in 1865–75, offices erected next to it in 1866–7 to house the reformed District Board of Works and, in 34 1870–1, a town hall for public events (demolished) was built close to All Saints. Though the population continued to grow until about 1900, little more housing was built after 1870. Prosperity was distinctly reduced after 1880 by the decline in fortune of the docks and the building of a new large dock downriver at Tilbury, which opened in 1886. Poplar High Street lost its shops, and the alleys off it soon degenerated into slums.

Little was done physically to improve the housing situation until the 1930s, when many blocks of streamlined Borough Council 41 flats were built. Then, after the Second World War, the E and W ends of the neighbourhood were rebuilt. Public housing still dominates a High Street affected very little by the enormous upheavals within Docklands since redevelopment began in 1981. The streets to the N still have a good proportion, despite bombing, of their original C19 houses but to the E is the fearsome 1960s approach to the Blackwall Tunnel (*see* Blackwall) and next to it

the high walls of housing built soon after at Robin Hood Gardens.
The High Street, cut off from the redeveloped West India Docks
not only by the railway, built as early as 1840, but also by the
post-1981 main road, Aspen Way, is tenuously connected via the
54 DLR and its glamorous footbridge, spanning between Poplar
Station and West India Quay. The contrast between modestly
scaled old Poplar and the new gigantism at Canary Wharf is
almost surreal.

CHURCHES

14 ALL SAINTS, Bazely Street. The parish church, 1820–3 by *Charles
Hollis*. A competent design by an architect with few other buildings to his name. Greek, in Portland stone with a w steeple still
composed in the Wren-Gibbs tradition of at least a hundred
years earlier. Tetrastyle fluted Ionic portico, based on the
Athenian Temple on the Ilissus. The w front turns the corners
with two pilasters which make the transition to side porticoes in
antis (cf. Gibbs's St Martin in the Fields), which gave access to
the large staircase lobbies (now social centre and vestry). Otherwise, the sides have two tiers of windows, the upper ones
arched. Coupled pilasters at the E corners too, before the E wall
curves round to the slightly projecting, slightly curved chancel;
lower, square vestry (N) and former lobby (S) fitted in the angles
between nave and chancel. On the E wall a consecration plaque.
The tower has a Corinthian order. First stage above the roof
square with coupled pilasters and attached columns in antis
flanking the bell-openings: antefixae. Then, resting on a clock
stage, a circular tempietto which has detached coupled columns
projecting in the diagonals carrying projecting entablatures. Tall
obelisk spire.

   The interior, originally plainer and galleried with a flat ceiling
on coving, dates mainly from a post-war reconstruction of 1951–3
by *Wontner Smith*, succeeded by *Cecil Brown*, the restorer of
St Lawrence Jewry (*see London 1: The City of London*). Wide
nave, now without galleries. Flat, deeply beamed ceiling carried
on four piers near the corners, linked to the walls by means of
arches to form a compartment at each angle in a faint echo of a
cross-in-rectangle plan. Corinthian pilasters applied all round.
Plain chancel arch. In the chancel, a 1950s BALDACCHINO, cut
back as part of alterations and repair by *Triforium Architects*,
1981–9, which also included the conversion of the crypt into a
parish centre. The ALTAR, of Oberammergau work, dates from
1897 when the *Rev. Arthur Chandler* raised the E end (since
reversed) and blocked the E window. The original cast-iron
ALTAR-cum-parish safe, now in the NE chapel, looks like an
elegant piece of Neoclassical furniture. – Boldly curved w gallery
with a C19 ORGAN by *Hunter* from Clapham Congregational
Church, south London, rebuilt by *Noel Mander*. – Baluster
FONT, apparently C17 and *ex situ*. – Handsome Neoclassical
railings round the S side of the large CHURCHYARD, made into
public gardens in 1865–6 but still with a few tombs. Two similar

headstones with reliefs of mourning women to George Ramage
†1838 and to Alexander & Matilda Mace.

Former RECTORY, opposite the W front. A dignified Neoclassical design by *Hollis*, 1822–3, in yellow brick with bold and
precise stone cornices. The exterior clearly expresses the simple
ground plan of four large rooms and narrow staircase hall.
Recessed centre filled by the pilastered porch, with delicate
cobweb-patterned balcony over. Two-storey segmental bows
emphasize the outer bays. Blind windows to the first two side
bays. In the centre of the house a plaster cross-vault between
entrance hall and staircase.

Former ST MATTHIAS, Woodstock Terrace (now a community
centre). The exterior is by *William Milford Teulon*, 1870–6, and
of an uncompromising eccentricity more usually associated
with W.M.'s older brother Samuel Sanders Teulon. It exhibits
plenty of Kentish rag, a bell-turret of unprecedented Victorian
shape, bold pastry-cutter tracery, N and S porches and a chancel.
But all this is only a superficial skin enclosing the handsome,
red brick C17 Poplar Chapel built to serve the hamlets of Poplar
and Blackwall: it is the only Interregnum church still standing in

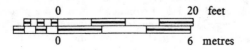

Former All Saints rectory. Elevation

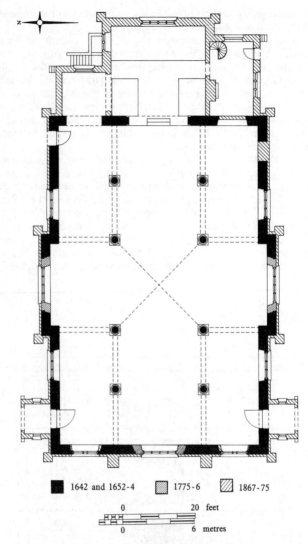

N

| ■ 1642 and 1652-4 | ▨ 1775-6 | ⬚ 1867-75 |

0   20 feet
0   6 metres

Former Church of St Matthias. Plan

London, and so of exceptional importance. Laid out in 1639 in the grounds of the East India Company almshouse (*see* Perambulation), but not built until 1652–4, i.e. after the Civil War, it was closely based on the just-completed Broadway Chapel, Westminster (1635–8), then a rare model of Protestant church building. Like its predecessor, it had a predominantly Gothic exterior with some classical features and a thoroughly Palladian interior, which survives. The East India Company, who effectively took the chapel over in 1657, made it look more conventionally classical in 1775 and 1805. The present guise dates from its transferral to the Diocese of London in 1866. The interior modified by Teulon's reseating in 1867–8 (since removed): this involved the removal of the N and S galleries and the cutting back of the W one, and the addition of a conventional chancel in 1875–6, supervised by Teulon's partner *Edwyn Evans Cronk*. Restored for LDDC 1990–1 by *Peter Codling* (*Roger Taigel*, job architect); closure in 1976 had led to dereliction.

The body of the church is rectangular. Within it a symmetrical 6 Latin cross of nave and transept, with aisles to complete the rectangle. Nave, transept and aisles are clearly differentiated outside by separate roofs, very early examples of a Continental type of kingpost roof introduced to England in the C17, perhaps by Inigo Jones: especially complicated and experimental construction over the crossing. Inside, the nave and transept have elliptical vaults which meet in a depressed cross-vault, with the arms of the East India Company in plaster at the centre. The vaults are carried on columns (all timber except one of stone) of an incorrect Tuscan order and by entablatures which, because continuous from W to E, stress the longitudinal axis. There is no other eastward emphasis and no evidence of how the furnishings were laid out. Unpretentious moveable screens of 1990–1 now divide the interior according to function. – MOSAIC Evangelist symbols below E window, 1903. – SCREEN to former choir vestry, N aisle, by *W. Charles Wheeler*, 1927. Tudor-style panelling. – STAINED GLASS. E window: Crucifixion, 1875 (*c.* 1868 design) by *N. J. H. Westlake* for *Lavers & Barraud*, who had fitted other windows (see nave NE and SE) in 1870–2. – N transept, by *Cakebread, Robey & Co.*, 1920. – The only remarkable MONUMENT, one of *Flaxman*'s best-known works, has been moved and is to be put on public display in London. George Steevens †1800, son of an East India Company director and Shakespeare scholar. Simple epitaph with a relief in a roundel. Steevens comfortably seated and looking at a bust of Shakespeare on a pedestal; an unaffected composition of great ease.

In the large CHURCHYARD: Daniel Coppendale †1722, malt distiller. Urn-topped obelisk on ball feet upon a pedestal with an armorial relief. – John Smart †1777, distiller of Limehouse. Elegant Neoclassical sarcophagus with reliefs of tear vases on pilasters. – Hugh Mackintosh †1840, dock contractor. Heavy Egyptian sarcophagus of granite. – Best is the monument to Captain Samuel Jones †1734. Pedestal with relief of a man o' war and a naval trophy upon a tall base, erected to a naval officer who distinguished himself against the French in 1706–7. Much restored in the late C19. – Also a number of C18 and early C19 tomb chests. – The GATEPIERS are shared with the former Board of Works Offices (*see* Public Buildings).

PUBLIC BUILDINGS

Former POPLAR DISTRICT BOARD OF WORKS OFFICES, 34 Poplar High Street. 1869–70 by *Hills & Fletcher* (both of whom had served as Assistant Surveyor to the Board), in collaboration with *Arthur & Charles Harston*, also local. Italian Gothic in red brick, subtly polychrome with tile decoration and richly carved Portland stone cornice, friezes etc. Tall and eye-catching octagonal tower with spire-topped dome; it stands almost detached within the angle of the S and E wings. The E wing is more elaborate, with granite-shafted columns marking the first-floor boardroom, subdivided with a mezzanine into offices by *Peter Eley*, 1987.

CORONER'S COURT AND MORTUARY, Poplar High Street. 1910–11 by the *LCC Architect's Department*. Like a sweet little Arts and Crafts house, in red brick with stone mullioned windows, gables and a moulded chimneystack. Courtroom to the W, mortuary behind, i.e. the usual London arrangement devised by *Thomas Blashill* in 1893. Alterations 1937 and 1982 do not affect the façade.

TOWER HAMLETS COLLEGE, Poplar High Street. A long range of buildings, the chief of which is the former School of Marine Engineering and Navigation by the *LCC Architect's Department*, 1902–6: *Percy Ginham* may have been the dominant designer. Portland stone-clad front, Mannerist and asymmetrical. Paired columns and arched windows mark the first-floor class- and lecture-rooms in contrast with bold functional drawing-office and lab windows in the mansard above. Main doorcase carved with cherubs and sea-creatures by *Bertram Pegram*. Extended E 1929–31; more conventional Neo-Georgian but with a flat roof for students' use. Another E extension 1951–5 by *Pite, Son & Fairweather*. W extension, opened 1991, by *John R. Harris Partnership*, with prefabricated bays and yellow-brick walls oddly combined; the top storey opens as a balcony.

The former POPLAR CENTRAL LIBRARY (No. 126) has been incorporated E: 1893–4 by *John Clarkson* (District Suveyor) of *J. & S. F. Clarkson*. Tall central block of yellow brick unified by an arched centrepiece and unrelated low wings with wavy parapets, a clumsy composition explained by the fact that the centre was designed for a narrow site on East India Dock Road and adapted for this one.

Former GEORGE GREEN SCHOOL (Tower Hamlets College), East India Dock Road. 1883–4. Designed for the endowed school founded 1828 by George Green †1849, shipbuilder of the Blackwall Yard, who was a prominent local Nonconformist philanthropist. He also paid for a seamen's mission (*see* East India Dock Road) and the demolished Trinity Congregational Chapel nearby. By (*Sir*) *John Sulman*, better known for his rather emphatic, sometimes clumsy Congregational chapels. This design has a Northern European picturesqueness and, despite the bold High Victorian stripes of brick and stone, Arts and Crafts feeling in the asymmetrical fenestration and areas of blank walling. E tower with a Rhenish roof forms the girls' entrance and screens the NE classroom block. Boys' entrance tower central with a gabled timber lantern. To its E and rising behind, the galleried Hall. Thin decapitated gallery stair-tower, W. NE lab block by *William Clarkson*, 1902.

WOOLMORE PRIMARY, Woolmore Street. 1912–6 by the *LCC*

Architect's Department. Neo-Georgian block distinguished by a strict row of tall chimneys and elegantly bracketed eaves. Round the corner in Bullivant Street, the LCC manual training centre, 1910, now St Matthias Centre. Single storey, with shaped gables.

Former POPLAR BATHS, East India Dock Road (a training centre since *c.* 1988). 1931–4 by *Harley Heckford*, Poplar Borough

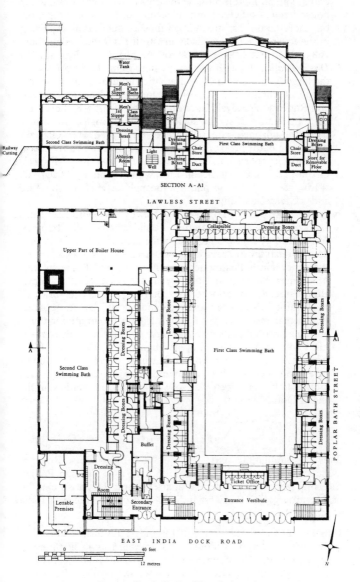

Former Poplar baths. Plan and section

Engineer and Surveyor, the design probably by *D. L. Dick* with
the engineer *R. W. Stanton.* Not immediately recognisable as
baths. Its grey-brick front, reminiscent of contemporary Dutch
buildings, looks like a cinema or like one of the factories sited
on arterial roads out of London. The towered centrepiece, with
Art Deco overtones, screens the first-class swimming bath. To
the l. a more functional coda (mainly slipper and second-class
baths) and an E projection, with strips of windows, designed to
house lettable offices. Familiar layout for baths of the period,
but more luxurious, streamlined finishes than usual, especially
in the foyer, faced hygienically in vitrolite. On the ceiling since
1985, three PAINTED SCENES of the history of the baths by
David Bratby. Though the rest is steel-framed and brick-clad,
42   the large bath is spanned by dramatic elliptical concrete arches
supporting stepped clerestories, a formula taken from Easton
and Robertson's Royal Horticultural Hall of 1927–8. This is the
first appearance of such a structure over an English swimming
bath, though ferro-concrete arches were used over Glasgow
swimming baths pre-1914. When floored over the bath became
a theatre or sports hall. In front a bronze STATUE of Richard
Green †1863 of the Blackwall Yard, with his dog. By *Edward W.
Wyon,* 1865–6. On the plinth atmospheric reliefs of the Yard
and a Green-built ship.

NEWBY PLACE HEALTH CENTRE, Newby Place and East India
Dock Road. 1993–5, a design-and-build scheme with architects
Janka & Tony Mobbs. A reprise of the Neoclassical rectory next
door, though the informal composition, the ugly pre-cast cornice
and other faintly Postmodern details give the real date away. It
supersedes the SOUTH POPLAR HEALTH CENTRE in Poplar
High Street (Nos. 260–268, to let 1997). This prefabricated
steel-framed, steel-clad box, composed of sixteen separate
rectangular modules, was adapted from a prototype for trans-
portable hospital units by *Derek Stow & Partners,* built 1978–9.

DLR POPLAR STATION, Poplar High Street. One of *ABK*'s
stations on the Beckton line. It flies high above a frighteningly
54   cave-like concrete substructure and has a dramatic suspended
tubular link over Aspen Way to West India Quay station on the
Isle of Dogs.

PERAMBULATION

This perambulation starts on the West India Dock Road at
Westferry DLR station. It follows the old road through Poplar,
diverting N into the residential quarter round the parish church,
and returning W to the West India Dock Road via the East India
Dock Road.

PENNYFIELDS is the W end of the old route from Limehouse
through the centre of Poplar to Blackwall (q.v.), disrupted in
1802 when the Commercial Road (later known along this part
as the West India Dock Road) was cut through. Here one
immediately gets the flavour of the neighbourhood, whose C19

housing and commercial property was almost entirely rebuilt with council housing after both World Wars. Only a sprinkling of shops is left along the length of Pennyfields and Poplar High Street. Pennyfields became the home of the East End's Chinese community, after it moved from the slums of Limehouse Causeway when these were replaced early in the 1930s. None of the C18 houses and modest C19 terraces colonized by the Chinese have survived comprehensive post-1945 rebuilding. Along the N side and N to East India Dock Road, the BIRCHFIELD ESTATE by the *LCC Architect's Department*, 1955–64. Four-storey brick-clad flats and one slab block, THORNFIELD HOUSE, 1960–2, 47 quite elegant with an abstract concrete relief running up the full height. Some other, then fashionable, mural decoration on other blocks, e.g. the tiles with abstracted Docklands motifs at GORSEFIELD HOUSE, facing East India Dock Road. Along Pennyfields itself four-in-a-block maisonettes by *Stewart, Hendry & Smith* for the GLC, 1963–6.

POPLAR HIGH STREET starts in the same vein but first, at the corner of Saltwell Street, the WHITE HORSE (Nos. 9–11) on a long-established site: 1927–8 by *E. A. Sewell,* with a nostalgic faience corner panel. At this W end of the street, which has been well landscaped by the LDDC, the first of the series of council estates. On both sides the standard LCC tenements (1934–7) of the WILL CROOKS ESTATE, continued S in 1955–7 (Dingle Gardens scheme) and in 1973–5 to the W, with some town houses round Saltwell Street.

Next on the N SIDE the RECREATION GROUND, created 1866–7. Its extent gives some idea of the prominence of the East India p. 172 Company's property before 1866. On the S edge facing the High Street were the company's almshouses, developed from a pre-existing house remodelled by *Edward Carter* in 1627, extended in 1798–9 and completely rebuilt in 1801–2 by *Henry Holland,* the Company Surveyor. The chaplain's house at No. 115 (MERIDIAN HOUSE) is all that remains; it formed the centre-piece of Holland's composition. Simple three-bay front with small upper windows and the company's arms on the tiny stone pediment on consoles which interrupts the top cornice. Big doorhood on skinny columns by *Cecil Brown*, 1964, in place of a plain porch of 1826 by *William Wilkins*, then Company Surveyor. Incongruous bay window 1878. Gothic rear extension by *H. J. Tollit*, added in 1868 when the house became the vicarage of St Matthias (*see* Churches). W of No. 115, the POPLAR PLAY NURSERY, a neat little monopitch-roofed building, extended in more colourful fashion by *Proctor Matthews Architects*, 1992–3. To the E the former District Board of Works Offices (*see* Public Buildings), built in the mid C19 on the S E corner of the alms-house site. St Matthias lies behind, entered from WOODSTOCK TERRACE, which is lined on the E with mid-C19 terraced houses.

On the S SIDE, the long ranges of Tower Hamlets College (*see* Public Buildings), which incorporates the former public library, and, just beyond to the E, the VIETNAMESE PASTORAL CENTRE at No. 130, built as the youth club of the R.C. settlement

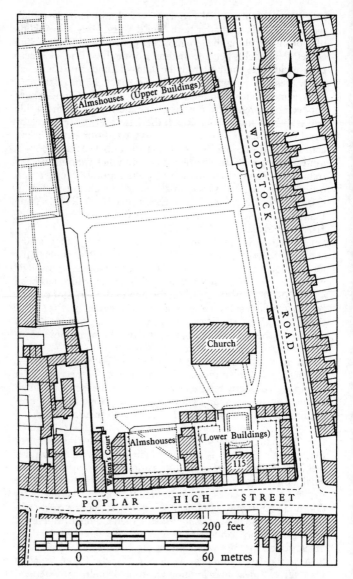

Former Church of St Matthias and East India Company Almshouses.
Site plan *c.* 1870

of the Holy Child (now gone). Minimal Neo-Georgian with
slight invention on the end wall and large pantiles. 1955–6 by
Adrian Gilbert Scott, who built the impressive R.C. church in
Lansbury N of the East India Dock Road in 1950–1.

The streets off this side are stopped very short by the former line
of the London and Blackwall Railway (*see* Blackwall), which

divided Poplar from the West India Docks when it opened in
1840. Beyond the tracks, now used by the DLR, rise the gleaming blocks of Canary Wharf, in complete contrast to these
narrow, sadly stunted little streets. Tucked into a small site in
SIMPSON'S ROAD, a group of flats with splendidly uplifting
names built by the Presbyterian Housing Scheme. First blocks
by *T. Phillips Figgis*, the scheme's surveyor and architectural
adviser to the Presbyterian Church in England. At the far end
GOODSPEED HOUSE (1926–9), almost indistinguishable from
contemporary LCC tenements. GOODWILL HOUSE (1932),
NE of it, is playfully Italianate. The other blocks on the E side of
Simpson's Road form a small court with Goodspeed House.
WINANT HOUSE was built in 1951 as an outlier to the LCC's
Lansbury estate (N of the East India Dock Road), itself begun
in 1948 as the Festival of Britain Live Architecture Exhibition
(1951). Very close in style to the Lansbury buildings, with flint-
faced brick, shallow-pitched roofs, snapped headers as decora-
tion etc., and designed, like GOODFAITH and GOODHOPE
HOUSES of 1955, by *Harry Moncrieff* and *Edna M. I. Mills* of
Co-Operative Planning Ltd.

NORWOOD HOUSE by *Trevor Dannatt*, 1965–72, continues the
public housing along Poplar High Street beyond Simpson's
Road. It has handsome sculpted red brick and shuttered-
concrete façades articulated in distinct units that relate to
maisonettes within. This approach is clearly very different
from that used by the Poplar Borough Council for their interwar blocks just to the E. Here, on CONSTANT HOUSE and 41
HOLMSDALE HOUSE of 1936–8 by *Rees J. Williams*, Borough
Architect, the impression of individual flats is effaced by streamlining achieved by solid balconies and continuous strings, dividing storeys of subtly different red bricks. Such streamlining was
quite widely adopted by Poplar Borough Council in the later
1930s and can be seen again on the N side further E. Still on
the S side, by the railway bridge at No. 212, a former goods
manager's office for the North London Railway Co., 1876–7,
and near the E end, Nos. 246–245, the only surviving, uninspiring row of C19 houses along the whole of the street, *c.* 1812 in
origin but much rebuilt later in the C19; converted to flats by
Stephen George & Partners, 1984–5. Behind them, the neat, grey-
clad, one- and two-storey units of the POPLAR BUSINESS
PARK; 1987–8, by *YRM* for the LDDC.

ROBIN HOOD GARDENS lies beyond the end of Poplar High 48
Street by the Blackwall Tunnel approach. Of 1966–72 by *Alison
& Peter Smithson* for the GLC, the apotheosis of public housing
in the borough and an icon for the Smithsons' admirers. It is a
late expression of the Smithsons' early 1950s ideas about 'the
building as street', cf. their unbuilt designs for Golden Lane
housing (*see London 1: The City of London*), and the first built
expression of those ideas by the Sheffield City Architect at Park
Hill, Sheffield, in 1956–61. Over 600 people live (at a density of
141.8 per acre, more than the GLC's then-average of 136) on
this horrible site flanked by two trunk roads full of thundering

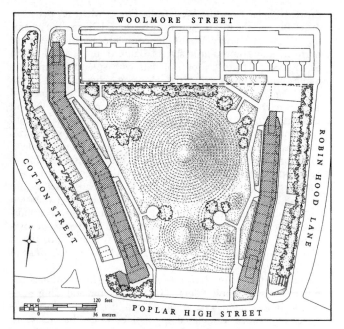

Robin Hood Gardens. Site layout

traffic. These two long, high walls of stark grey concrete flats bend to follow the curve of the roads. Their finish is rough and tough shuttered concrete precast in big pieces on the Swedish SUNDH system. The Cotton Street section was cast *in situ*, because there was no access for large cranes. Though impressively monumental, the scheme is ill-planned to the point of being inhumane. The 'streets' are only decks cantilevered off the cross-walls of the reinforced concrete box-frame, much narrower than those at Park Hill and with a grim aspect towards the traffic. They buffer the living rooms which open off them. Bedrooms and kitchens face inward to a sculpted open space, but on this more peaceful side the tiny balconies are too small to enjoy and can be used only as fire escapes. Below in a dry moat is parking and storage.

Now back w to BAZELY STREET (originally Bow Lane) and through 1950s council housing N to All Saints, where there is still a substantial fragment of the respectable neighbourhood created round All Saint's churchyard as soon as it appeared. MOUNTAGUE PLACE, along the s side, was laid out in 1822 by *James Mountague*, District Surveyor for the North Division of the City of London. It was built up piecemeal, 1822–c. 1826, with a row, rather than terrace, of plain two-bay houses of which Nos. 5–12 survive. No. 7 has one bay of wider windows, No. 8 is a storey higher, and No.12 has a Greek Doric porch round the corner in Bazely Street, originally matched by

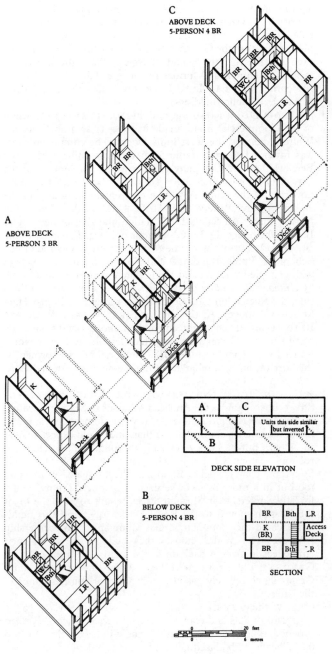

C
ABOVE DECK
5-PERSON 4 BR

A
ABOVE DECK
5-PERSON 3 BR

BR BR Bth
LR

BR K BR

K

Deck

Deck

BR BR
WC
Bth
BR
LR

K

Deck

A	C	
		Units this side similar but inverted
B		

DECK SIDE ELEVATION

B
BELOW DECK
5-PERSON 4 BR

BR	Bth	LR
K (BR)		Access Deck
BR	Bth	LR

SECTION

0   20 feet
0   6 metres

Robin Hood Gardens.
Cut-away, elevation and section

another at No.1 which turned into Newby Place. Diagonally opposite in Bazely Street, a uniform terrace with first-floor balconies (Nos. 45–51) built in the 1830s. A little further down, the neat front of the GREENWICH PENSIONER of 1827. Facing each other across the N end of Newby Place the handsome façades of church and former rectory (*see* Churches). On the NW corner with East India Dock Road, Newby Place Health Centre (*see* Public Buildings).

EAST INDIA DOCK ROAD was built in 1806–12 as an E extension of the Commercial Road, made in 1802–11 as a link between Whitechapel and the West India Docks. The completed route was intended to take traffic from the East India Docks (*see* Blackwall) to the Company's Cutler Street warehouses in the City of London (*see London 1: The City of London*). The road is now part of the grimy A13. The few remaining houses of the earlier C19 are at the W end. At the E end on the S side, after Newby Place, All Saints DLR station and the former Poplar Baths, which face the LCC's famous post-war Lansbury estate (*see* above). Further W on the N side, the bulky George Green School (*see* Public Buildings) and No. 153, a lone villa of 1834 with canopied veranda and Doric porch, converted to a hostel by *Anthony Richardson & Partners*, 1983–4. Opposite, on the S side, the Recreation Ground that goes through to Poplar High Street (*see* above). At this end, a FIRST WORLD WAR AIR RAID MEMORIAL to eighteen children, mostly aged 5, killed by bombs from a German aircraft which fell on the Upper North Street LCC school in June 1918. Memorial plinth crowned by the sort of angel familiar from C19 cemeteries. Signed *A. R. Adams*, a local undertaker.

POPE JOHN HOUSE (No. 154) wraps round the corner of Hale Street. It was built as the Anglican Missions to Seamen Institute by *Sir Arthur Blomfield*, 1892–4. Jacobean domestic-style in red brick, more like a country house than one would expect so near the Docks but perhaps a reassuringly solid English refuge for roaming seamen. Chapel and chaplain's house 1898, SE in Hale Street; the plain chapel by Blomfield, the house possibly by him too but in a more relaxed, vernacular manner. Trinity House for lady workers, W, in Shirbutt Street, rebuilt 1934. In the 1930s the Mission moved to the Royal Docks (q.v.) and this building became the Commercial Gas Company's Co-partnership Institute. The modest houses they built to the W for their employees in 1934–6 back on to the main road from MALAM GARDENS: three rows of cottages along three private lanes. Originally completely gas-powered: still-working gas lamps in the lanes.

Further W the URBAN LEARNING FOUNDATION (No. 56), a courtyard of flats and teaching rooms by *Paul Hyett & Partners* (opened 1992), discreetly and lovingly detailed. Smooth red brick façade with glazed green tile strings linking simple steel-lintelled windows. Set into the brick, lead roundels with symbols and tools of learning (letters, numbers, notes of music). Continuous row of windows under the upswept eaves. Sturdy gate with good lettering within the gateway into the courtyard, which has simple elevations except for a glass-roofed gallery. To be extended w in 1997 by *PRP*, with new facilities for this teacher-training centre. Its neighbour is a former branch of the London and County Bank (No. 52), 1885 by *Zephaniah King*, very old-fashioned but dignified. Attached Greek Doric columns round the ground floor and for the corner porches. A terrace (Nos. 2–50) of ordinary houses continues up to the junction with West India Dock Road. 1850–60, perhaps by *George Alexander*, architect to the Conant estate, whose property this was. There was originally an almost-matching terrace on the N side.

On the N SIDE No. 133 appears to be a stuccoed Late Georgian terrace, much altered. There is now no clue to its original role as a seamen's home, built by George Green of the Blackwall Yard in 1839–41, nor to its former dignified appearance, with Doric colonnade and balcony filling the recessed five-bay centre. Well converted to social housing *c.* 1983 by *Anthony Richardson & Partners*. Another seamen's home, the QUEEN VICTORIA p. 45 SEAMEN'S REST (Seamen's Mission of the Methodist Church) fronts the road from Nos. 121–131 with a long block of 1951–3, which builds up in the centre in a 1930s way. Chapel plain except for stained glass by *Goddard & Gibbs*. Facing E to Jeremiah Street, the earliest part of 1901–2, free C17-style with a cupola on the entrance tower. w extension 1932. All parts of the mission are by the same practice, called *Gordon & Gunton* in 1901–2, *Gunton & Gunton* by 1932. Beyond, the well-landscaped fringe of the HIND GROVE ESTATE, the western-most housing site (completed 1952) of the Lansbury estate, runs w to the junction with West India Dock Road. It replaced, after war-time bombing, an interesting collection of buildings along what was then the most prosperous residential stretch of the East India Dock Road. Among the losses, the large Dec St Stephen, 1865–6 by *F. & H. Francis*, and the classical Trinity Congregational Chapel, built for George Green by *William Hoskings*, 1840–1.

RATCLIFFE see LIMEHOUSE

THE ROYAL DOCKS
London Borough of Newham

The Royal Docks were the last group of docks to be built in London, between 1850 and 1921, and the last to close, in 1981. Compared with their predecessors they are vast, stretching along the river for over three miles E of the River Lea. The huge cargo ships and liners which the docks were built to accommodate have gone, together with the warehouses and transit sheds that lined the seven miles of quay. What remains are the great shining stretches of water, silent and still except for the dwarfed pleasure craft to which the docks are now devoted.

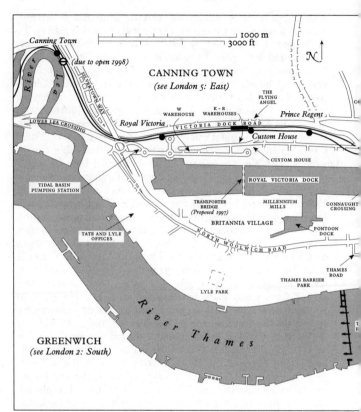

The development of the Royal Docks 1850–1981

The railway engineer and promoter *G. P. Bidder* saw the potential for the undeveloped Plaistow levels. First he built a branch from the Eastern Counties Railway at Stratford to the first railway coal wharf on the Thames, alongside Bow Creek (River Lea), in 1846, then extended it to the ferry at North Woolwich in 1847. Next he proposed the Victoria Dock. This was designed to be linked with the railway, making the dock's distance from the City immaterial, and to berth the increasingly large iron steamships for which the earlier docks were too small. The dock promoters, who included Bidder, acquired enough land to build not only the Victoria Dock but to allow for future expansion. They planned to sell the dock as soon as it was constructed. In 1864 it was bought by the recently merged London and St Katharine Dock Co., who went on to build the Royal Albert Dock in 1875–80.

As the docks grew, so did the railway system. When the Victoria Dock was built, the dock company provided an avoiding line to the E for the Eastern Counties Railway and took for itself the old line where it went over a swing bridge across the original dock

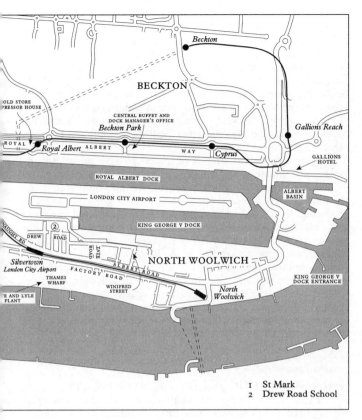

Royal Docks and Silvertown

entrance (W). The old line, called the Silvertown Tramway, can partly be traced in the footpath the LDDC has laid along what remains of it. Stations opened on the new line at Victoria Dock station (later Custom House) in 1855, Tidal Basin (gone) in 1858 and Silvertown in 1863. When the Royal Albert Dock was built, with a new E entrance to serve both docks, the dock company constructed a tunnel for this main line beneath the Connaught Passage (between the docks) to avoid delays at the new swing bridge. The dock company used the high-level route and also built its own passenger line for dock workers to Gallions Reach, with stops at Connaught Road, Central and Manor Road (Way); it was also used by ship passengers, for whom they built a series of related facilities. This line joined the main line at Custom House, whence ran a single workers' line to Beckton.

On some of the reserved land S of the docks, the newly founded Port of London Authority (PLA) built the King George V Dock in 1912, with an entrance large enough for, exceptionally, the 35,000 ton liner *S.S. Mauretania*. The railway links, and the ample storage space that existed elsewhere, put increasing emphasis on goods in transit. There was an ever-growing throughput of food, especially from the Empire and later the Commonwealth. Technology helped, with the use of hydraulic power from 1855, arc lighting from 1880, and electric mechanical handling equipment from the early and mid C20. Warehousing became concentrated and steadily increased in the Royal Victoria Dock, including a large complex for tobacco. The Royal Albert Dock acquired the world's largest cold store in addition to transit sheds. In the C20 major dockside flour mills were built. Also within the docks were important ship-repair facilities, notably the Pontoon Dock of the Royal Victoria Dock.

The reasons for the decline of the docks were many. But the first disadvantage to be felt was the poor road connections, as road transport gradually became as important as rail. Road traffic within the docks was held up by numerous swing bridges and level crossings: the elevated Silvertown Way was constructed in 1932–4 over the Royal Victoria Dock's w entrance to improve both situations (see Silvertown). After post-war modernization, record tonnages were being handled in the Royal Docks c. 1960. Liners still docked there though gradually air travel began to be preferred. But the twin revolutions represented by the shipping container and the bulk carrier demanded total reinvestment in the mid 1960s and this was concentrated at Tilbury. After that, the Royal Docks were superseded even more rapidly than had been predicted by the PLA in 1973, and closed in 1981.

Redevelopment 1981–97

From 1981 the LDDC gradually acquired the Royal Docks from the PLA, encouraging the establishment by the developers Mowlems of a STOL (short take-off and landing) airport between the Royal Albert and King George V Docks. The Corporation's other proposals were countered by a 'People's Plan' backed by the GLC. In 1987 the LDDC agreed to three elements of a new plan: a regional shopping centre, the London Dome, a North American-style arena, exhibition space and leisure facilities by *Ron Labinski*, and an agreed provision of social housing. A masterplan for the Royal Albert Dock, drawn up by the *Richard Rogers Partnership* for Rosehaugh Stanhope, was selected by the LDDC in 1988. It proposed three business parks within parkland along the N edge of the dock; a huge shopping centre at the far E along the line of the Albert Basin, related to a marina with boat exhibition area, museum, hotel etc. on the basin itself; and high-quality housing along the Thames with 700 units of social housing on a polluted site round Beckton DLR station (see Beckton). The social housing, planned by *Chris Wilkinson Architects*, has been built and now forms Winsor Park, and one of the business parks has been laid out. Most of the other elements of the scheme were abandoned in 1993, though the form of the great upturned saucer-dome of the shopping centre has been reincarnated as the Millennium Dome for the Greenwich exhibition site.

The docks themselves have been reduced almost to a *tabula*

rasa. All the warehouses, except a group on the N side, have been demolished and the quayside carefully landscaped according to the landscape strategy commissioned by the LDDC from *The Gillespies Practice*, executed by *Keyside Hard Landscapes – Gillespies* c.1990. The hard landscaping and dockside furniture is of high quality and subtly varied according to its location. The Royal Victoria Dock is now devoted to sailing, the Royal Albert to rowing.

New roads have been laid out along the N side of the docks, a new road bridge built to span the Connaught crossing and public open spaces landscaped between the road and dock edges, linked to the stops on the DLR line. This has been extended to Beckton and some handsome new stations, designed by *ABK* (1992–4), provided along the route. The remaining warehouses and the late C19 hotels and offices built along the dock company's passenger line have been carefully restored. In 1997 plans are in hand (or have begun) for an international rowing centre, a huge exhibition centre, a park to link docks and river, and a campus for the University of East London, as well as an urban village and a business park.

ROYAL VICTORIA DOCK

Built 1850–5 by the Victoria Dock Co. formed by the railway con- 5 tractors, Samuel Morton Peto, Edward Ladd Betts and Thomas Brassey with the engineer *G. P. Bidder*. Their aim was to sell it quickly, but it was not until 1864 that the newly amalgamated London and St Katharine Dock Co. bought the dock, spurred on by lack of space in the old docks and by the fact that the Victoria Dock had taken much of the tobacco trade away from the London Docks. Renamed the Royal Victoria in 1880 when the Royal Albert Dock was opened.

The dock was an advance on earlier docks in several ways, apart from size ($1\frac{1}{4}$ m. long, 94 acres of water): it had its own railway system, connected to the main railway system by marshalling sidings on the N side; hydraulic power from the start, with machinery by *W. G. Armstrong & Co.*; and a novel construction with, on the N side, five finger jetties (previously experimented with at the London Docks) to increase capacity. It was built economically with earthen banks, but the entrance lock and some other parts used cast-iron piled and panelled walls backed with concrete, a technique used before by Bidder at Brunswick Wharf (*see* Blackwall). The finger jetties were also of iron piles, with horizontally arched brick walls between them, supporting two-storey brick warehouses with basements. Other warehouses were added along the N bank (*see* K and W Warehouses below).

The dock was extensively reconstructed from 1935 into the 1940s, the tidal basin amalgamated, and the north quay rebuilt (1937) S of the original dock edge, with new projecting false quays in place of the C19 finger jetties. Three-storey reinforced-concrete warehouses with transit facilities were built on the N and S quays. Though the building of Silvertown Way meant that ships could no longer use the W lock, it was rebuilt in 1963–7.

For the Pontoon Dock *see* below.

Buildings: North Quay W *to* E

An excellent view of all these buildings can be gained during a journey along the DLR from East India station to Beckton and back. The main group of surviving dock buildings lies close to Custom House station near the centre of the N side. A fringe of public housing, together with a few groups of C19 buildings including pubs, survives along Victoria Dock Road, once the busy main thoroughfare of a 'sailor town' on this side of the dock.

58 TIDAL BASIN PUMPING STATION, Tidal Basin Road, 1986–90. Like a colourful piece of sculpture NE of the roundabout. To handle drainage for the Royal Docks area. Engineers *Sir William Halcrow & Partners*, who were also responsible for the Stewart Street station (*see* Isle of Dogs). Two circular chambers, a main chamber and a screen chamber behind. The main chamber has two concentric drums rising about 39 ft (12 metres); inside an 82 ft (25 metre) shaft lifts waste water from new underground channels to a high-level discharge from where it run into the Thames. What we see is by the *Richard Rogers Partnership* in a characteristically industrial manner. White polycarbonate sheet as semi-opaque curtain walls are encased in an external steel grille. Royal-blue-rendered drums and steelwork in primary colours.

CUSTOM HOUSE STATION opened in 1855 as Victoria Dock station on the 'avoiding line' to North Woolwich made necessary by the construction of the dock (*see* above). The DLR station now shares the site and its footbridge links Victoria Dock Road and the dock. For details of this and the other DLR stations *see* Introduction.

THE FLYING ANGEL, No. 287 Victoria Dock Road, N of the station. 1934–6 by *Petch & Fernand* to house the Anglican Missions to Seamen Institute which moved here from Poplar (*see* Poplar, Perambulation). A big, eight-storey building of seamen's accommodation in red brick and white render. Tower-like blocks to N and S. Centrepiece of tiered attics carrying a hint of 1930s commercial buildings such as Joseph's Shell-Mex building, Victoria Embankment, Westminster. On the top there is a square-arched lantern that originally housed a flashing light. Centre of the building, including the originally irregular E side, reorganized in the conversion to shared serviced flats for Newham's single people by *Jefferson Sheard*, 1985–8.

38 CUSTOM HOUSE, near the station to which it gave its name. 1920–4 by *Sir Edwin Cooper*, architect of the PLA's headquarters in Trinity Square (*see London 1: City of London*). An early example of Cooper's post-war stripped classical style in a red brick building with white stone dressings. Two and a half storeys landward, one and a half to the dock, with an attic to the five centre bays. The end elevations have semi-Venetian windows, i.e. with blocked heads and sides. Properly called the Dock Directors' Access Centre, it was intended by the PLA as warehouse and office premises for letting to the railway company and tobacco importers. The landward ground floor contained a refreshment

room and canteen. Restored 1994–5. There is another smaller office by Cooper of 1931 within London City Airport (*see* King George V Dock).

K–R WAREHOUSES, to the w. With a smaller neighbour, the W Warehouse, now the only C19 warehouses left. Of enormous size. The SE section is the original three-storey K Warehouse, a bonded store for tobacco of 1859 by *Bidder*. It was originally as long as the whole of the present building. Internally of two storeys plus loft, with a basement ventilated by arched brick areas. It has the usual timber floors on cruciform cast-iron columns but its trussed timber roof is of unusual design, with iron hanger rods, and of large central span. Attached to its w, but now demolished, was another warehouse of similar length divided by a central firebreak wall.

At the back of K, the K Annexe, the pitched-roofed range with tall upper windows above a row of smaller ones, lighting a single large hall used for the high stacking of tobacco casks; added in 1919 by the PLA in yellow stock brick, despite their usual preference for red. In 1925 major reconstruction of the w part of K, following a fire, involved the party wall being taken down and new roofs and party walls constructed to form the series of tall but single-storey hipped-roofed sections (O–R). All these sections have steel trusses on tall steel or concrete columns carrying crane rails. Warehouses restored for the LDDC by *Rees Johns Bolter Architects*, 1994–5, and fitted for future use as a public hall and exhibition space. The letters K etc. remain from the PLA's series of warehouse names.

W WAREHOUSE, nearest the dock. 1883 by the company engineer 25 *Robert Carr*. Narrow and four-storey, with three-storey giant arcades in the earlier style of the St Katharine Docks warehouses. Before the N quay was altered, it stood over the dock edge with its s wall on brick arches supported on cast-iron screw piles. Timber floors on cast-iron columns, queenpost roof. Restored by *Feilden & Mawson*. In front a row of *Stothert & Pitt* portal quay CRANES (1962 design in welded tubular construction) answers the cranes on the s quay.

To be re-erected here, a late C19 gentlemen's URINAL. Cast-iron, by the *Lion Foundry* of Kirkintilloch, the only surviving circular example left in London. It originally stood by the Connaught Tavern near the Royal Albert Dock (*see* below).

TRANSPORTER BRIDGE (begun 1997). In 1995 *Lifschutz Davidson* and *Techniker* won an LDDC competition for a pedestrian bridge to span the Royal Victoria Dock from Britannia Village (*see* Silvertown) to transport people to the proposed London Exhibition Centre (ExCeL) on the N side. The design is for a cable-stayed bridge, with lifts in the masts up to a transporter car suspended from the 418 ft (127½ metre) main span. Supported by an ingenious succession of cable-stayed cantilevers, each springing from the previous one. ExCeL, designed by *Moxley Jenner & Partners* with *Chris Wilkinson Architects*, is planned in 1997 to be a giant exhibition and leisure centre in the setting of ROYAL VICTORIA SQUARE by *EDAW/Patel Taylor*.

55 PRINCE REGENT DLR STATION. One of *ABK*'s distinctive stations for this line (*see* Introduction pp. 39 and 54). To Connaught Road, a fine piece of popular art, a steel FRIEZE with lively silhouettes of dockland scenes and people by *Brian Yale*, 1995.

CONNAUGHT CROSSING *see* Royal Albert Dock below.

South Quay and Pontoon Dock

On the South Quay a huge housing development, Britannia Village (*see* Silvertown), predominates. It lies W of the PONTOON DOCK, another of *Bidder's* promotions, built as the Victoria Graving Dock when work on the main dock was already well advanced. Here there was a revolutionary hydraulic ship lift, first used in 1858 and invented by *Edwin Clark*, who had hydraulically lifted the tubes of the Britannia Bridge over the Menai Straits, 1850. Each ship was lifted out of the water on pontoons which were raised by hydraulic jacks. Drained of its ballast water, the pontoon then floated the ship into one of the eight finger docks for repair. Run by the Thames Graving Dock Co. until 1896 by which time the size of ships had exceeded the capacity of the lifting equipment. Subsequently the dock was used for the transhipment of grain. Corrugated-iron silos were built by the London Grain Elevator Co., 1898, but damaged in the Silvertown explosion (q.v.) of 1917. One was rebuilt in reinforced concrete in 1920 as D SILO. Refurbished as a monument *c.* 1995, alongside the one remaining finger dock. Planar, white-painted concrete walls with small windows, some of them circular, distinctly symmetrical with octagonal plant rooms on top. Bulk grain was lifted from ships and barges into the central cube of silos and the two side towers, both by bucket and by suction elevators, and loaded through weighing machines into other barges.

Four FLOUR MILLS were constructed on the main dock, just to the W, from 1905–7 on. These and their huge silos, as extensively rebuilt and extended in reinforced concrete, were monuments on a remarkable scale. They included the striking horizontal-banded C.W.S. MILLS, 1938–44 by *L.G. Ekins*. They were mostly demolished in the early 1990s, though most of Spiller's MILLENNIUM MILLS have been kept and await a new use in 1997. Gabled W wing dated 1933: formal N side a little later. Also surviving the tall mid-C20 brick CHIMNEY of Rank's Empire Mills. Four pneumatic GRAIN ELEVATORS of the 1930s which also stood in the dock on dolphins in front of the flour mills have also gone but one of their large air pumps is to be re-erected as a feature.

ROYAL ALBERT DOCK

Built 1875–80; 85 acres of water, the main dock, of 71 acres, being 1¼m. long. Built for the London and St Katharine Dock Co. to provide a new, larger E entrance to the Victoria Dock to accommodate the larger ships developed during the previous twenty years. It was initially intended to be a ship canal, over a mile long, running W to the older dock, with a quay along the N side to allow ships to berth. Only during construction was it decided to wharf the S side as well. Engineer *Sir Alexander Rendel*. There was electric light, by arc lamps, from the beginning.

The dock was used chiefly for transit. Railway sidings lining the quays were almost entirely built up with large single-storey metal sheds. Built in 1882, these twin-span structures made by *Westwood, Baillie & Co.* had frames of wrought-iron trusses on cast-iron columns and corrugated-iron sheet cladding, and were linked by covered areas into six groups. They represented the important change in dock warehousing from long-term storage to transit facilities. Cold stores were later added at the NW corner for the large frozen meat trade. Nearly all the buildings were cleared in the 1980s, along with the former Great Western Railway goods station of 1900, of very early reinforced concrete, which lay just E of the Connaught Tavern. Two major dry docks for ship repairs are now beneath the London City Airport, as is a third belonging to King George V Dock.

Dock structures

DOCK WALLS, 40 ft (12 metres) high, mostly of concrete; 18–19 ft (5½ metres) thick at the bottom, reducing to 5 ft (1½ metres) at the top, with an up-to-date and technically efficient stepped rear face and projecting toe at the base. Entirely of Portland cement concrete, one of the first occasions that this was used for quay walls without a protective brick facing.

CONNAUGHT PASSAGE, linking the docks; 1880, deepened 1935–7, widened 1958 except through the bridge. The concrete copings belong to the 1990s landscaping. The North Woolwich railway was diverted through a steep TUNNEL beneath. Dated 1878 on the tunnel portal. It is marked by two brick circular ventilation shafts and a lantern-roofed octagon over the pumping shaft. Approach cuttings walled in mass concrete, with strainer arches in brick and concrete strainer arches, visible from Silvertown. Excellent natural exposed aggregate finish.

CONNAUGHT CROSSING. A swing road bridge, by *Sir William Halcrow & Partners*, 1990 for LDDC. Cable-stayed, steel box girder, with control cabin perched on the central pylon. Concrete approach spans on pilotis. A two-leaf swing FOOTBRIDGE echoes the main bridge with the curved soffit of its box girders. The old SWING BRIDGE of 1879 was one of the largest such bridges (90 ft, 27½ metre, span) and took two rail tracks and a single-lane road between three hog-backed plate girders. Main cross-girder and its hydraulic operating gear preserved.

ENTRANCE BASIN AND LOCKS. Originally of 9 acres (now 13), i.e. about the same size as the whole of St Katharine Docks. The 1880 lock, mostly filled in *c.* 1960, was the largest of its time: 500 ft (152 metres) long, 80 ft (24 metres) wide, 30 ft (9 metres) deep to admit any ship then afloat. A new entrance lock further N was built 1884–6, 36 ft (11 metres) deep, to compete with the new Tilbury Docks, downriver in Essex. Small-craft lock constructed within it 1980. 1950s electrically driven gate operating gear preserved. Red brick IMPOUNDING STATION of 1911, its prominent chimney demolished 1980s.

Associated buildings

HOTELS AND DOCK OFFICES. The London and St Katharine Dock Company provided passenger facilities along its railway line, following the opening of the Royal Albert Dock. The Connaught Tavern (1881), the Central Buffet and Dock Manager's Office (1881–3), and the Gallions Hotel (1881–3) survive but The Ship at the w end of Royal Victoria Dock, The Manor Way, and some semi-detached dock officers' houses have gone. They were all designed by *George Vigers & T. R. Wagstaffe*. Wagstaffe was appointed surveyor to the dock company in 1881, Vigers had been a student at the Royal Academy Schools when Norman Shaw taught there. Shaw's influence is obvious. The buildings look like transplanted fragments of Bedford Park. Although originally surrounded by dockside buildings and railway activity, they now stand dwarfed by the immensity of their empty surroundings. Central Buffet etc. all restored for LDDC 1994–5 by *The Conservation Practice*; Connaught Tavern and Gallions Hotel by the *Brian Clancy Partnership* (1996); awaiting new uses in 1997.

CONNAUGHT TAVERN, Connaught Road. Isolated in the road system leading to the Connaught Crossing. 1881. Tall (the published designs show it a storey lower) and made taller with high ribbed chimneystacks. Tile-hung gables, a central Dutch gable, and canted bays rising from a ground-floor projection with timber balustrade, extended later to form a terrace. Brick ship relief to the side.

CENTRAL BUFFET AND DOCK MANAGER'S OFFICE, Royal Albert Way, by the Beckton Park roundabout and station. 1881–3. Though plainer than the other traditionally constructed buildings, these are of especial interest. Here the apparently conventional Domestic Revival exteriors conceal the largest known use of a concrete system of construction patented by the builder *W. H. Lascelles* in 1875 and first used at his house at No. 266 Sydenham Road, Croydon. The system, which involves walling slabs screwed to timber uprights, was recommended by Wagstaffe.

The buffet, with its bold central bow, is very plain compared with the Gallions (*see* below), though published drawings show lavish pargeting in the gables and round the bow. The use of concrete is most obvious in the base of the concrete blocks; the rest is rendered. Inside some concrete and some timber joists; cast-iron columns helped support the upper floor. The office looks more domestic, like an H-shaped manor house with jettied wings and a central cupola. The basement is of rough concrete covered with concrete bricks. The chimneys have a mix of red brick and narrow concrete bricks laid in an Arts and Crafts way.

Central Buffet, Royal Albert Docks. Elevation (not as built)

Other details, door and window surrounds also concrete, some of it to resemble gauged brickwork. The details on both buildings are of moulded concrete. The panels were mostly through-coloured with a red iron pigment, but in the restoration have been painted for economy.

GALLIONS HOTEL, Gallions Road, N of the Albert Basin, close to Gallions Reach DLR station. 1881–3. Long rendered front with a jettied upper storey, an ogee-capped tower, and 'Ipswich' windows like those used by Norman Shaw at the Tabard Inn, Bedford Park, two years before. The rich plaster frieze in blue and white is by *Edward Roscoe Mullins*. The first-floor billiard room opened on to a balcony over the station platform canopy. Cast-iron columns on ground and first floors. The building, intended for liner passengers, was originally surrounded by railway tracks.

COLD STORE COMPRESSOR HOUSE, N side near Royal Albert station, s of Royal Albert Way. Handsome red brick building of one tall storey, with a bold stone cornice and the PLA badge, built as the compressor house of a multi-storey reinforced concrete cold store of *c.* 1914–17 which housed 305,000 carcasses. Unusual concrete lattice-beam roof structure, supporting a concrete water-retaining roof for the cooling process. The trusses dominate the single-volume interior, retained in the restoration by *Rees Johns Bolter Architects* for use as a visitors' centre, 1994–5. To its s by the dock, the Royal Albert Business Park, planned by *Aukett Associates*, is being laid out in 1997.

Additional buildings

ROYAL ALBERT BUSINESS PARK. *See* above.

REGATTA CENTRE. Planned in 1997 for the NW corner of the dock, a boat store and clubhouse by *Ian Ritchie Architects* for an Olympic standard rowing course. High Tech with a whiff of angular Deconstructivism in the two long, intersecting buildings of steel set within wedges of concrete walling. It will lie along the water's edge to form a focus for the dock's rowing activities and a landmark in these great open spaces.

UNIVERSITY OF EAST LONDON CAMPUS, NE end centred on

Cyprus DLR station. Masterplan by *Edward Cullian Architects*; phase one from 1997. A wall of teaching buildings parallel to the dock, fronted by coloured free-standing cylinders of residences.

KING GEORGE V DOCK

Of 1912–21. Begun by (*Sir*) *Frederick Palmer*, the Port of London Authority's first Chief Engineer, completed by (*Sir*) *Cyril Kirkpatrick*. The only one built of the two docks planned for N and S of the Royal Albert Dock, by the London and India Dock Co., who obtained an Act in 1901. The PLA took over the proposals when they were established in 1909. The plans for the N one, though never carried out, prevented development of the land until 1980.

Of 64 acres of water, only five-eighths the size of the Royal Victoria Dock. Concrete quay walls. Some original capstans dated 1916. On the N side were two-storey transit sheds, of reinforced concrete with brick infill. Distinctive Warren-trussed concrete girders bridged the roadways between them. Travelling cranes hung from the roofs. There were also sixty-six electric cranes with Toplis Patent level-luffing gear. This type, with a counter-balanced jib, became most common throughout the docks; examples 5 remain along the Royal Victoria Dock. The whole N side and the W dry dock, as well as the integral graving docks at the SW end of the Royal Albert Dock, were obliterated by the formation of the City Airport (*see* below).

ENTRANCE LOCK. 800 ft (244 metres) long, 100 ft (30½ metres) wide and 45 ft (14 metres) deep below high tide, much larger than the Royal Albert entrance locks. Now the oldest operational lock in unaltered state in the Port of London. It had three pairs of steel gates, some of which remain. Hydraulic machinery, not removed until 1989, now on display alongside.

LIFTING BRIDGE, taking Woolwich Manor Way over the lock. Attractive classical red brick and stone abutments of *c.* 1920. The present bridge, replacing *c.* 1990 a pair of steel trussed bascules renewed after war damage, is of steel box girders, their soffits gently curved and footways elegantly cantilevered on raking struts.

LONDON CITY AIRPORT, Hartmann Road, a STOL (short take-off and landing) airport, 1982–7, aimed particularly at business travellers to European airports. Runway on the quays between the Royal Albert and King George V Docks; extended since 1990 to allow the use of small jets.

The TERMINAL by *Seifert Ltd*, completed 1987, is little more than a dreary shed clad in grey-blue coated metal panels with grey fascia and blue tinted glazing. Control tower to one side. All stuck in an unpropitious corner with minimal landscaping, parking and other facilities. King George V DOCK OFFICE BUILDING, 1931 by *Sir Edwin Cooper*, now the airport transit office. Rather Soanian in yellow brick with mostly blank walls and top-lighting. Round arches and round windows away from the dock. Also by *Cooper* the tiny DOCKMASTER'S OFFICE, 1922–4, derelict in 1997. Both of Cooper's buildings deserve better surroundings.

SHADWELL RIVERSIDE *see* WAPPING

SILVERTOWN*
London Borough of Newham

In 1954 Pevsner wrote in his Buildings of England volume on *Essex*: 'Silvertown in spite, and partly because, of its heavy war damage, has much poetry. The mixture of the vast ships in the docks, the vaster factories and mills (C. W. S. Warehouses, 1938–44 by *L. G. Ekins*; Messrs Spiller's Millennium Mills; Tate & Lyle's premises), the small, mean, huddled and not uncomfortable houses, the scrubby vegetation of the bombed sites, and the churches cannot fail to impress.' He found Teulon's St Mark's church 'As horrid as only he can be and yet of a pathetic self-assertion in its surroundings. No lived-in house seems anywhere near.'

Only the poetry of the vast expanse of water in the Royal Docks remains the same: the last ships left when they closed in 1981. Teulon's church is still there (though opinions about it have changed) and so are some terraces of small houses, but they have been joined by big public housing schemes of the 1960s, when Silvertown became part of Greater London (1965). Only one or two relics of the vast dockside grain mills survive though some industry still thrives along the river. The LDDC's intervention since 1981 can be seen in the grand scale of the quayside landscaping, the planning of the new Britannia Village on the S side of Royal Victoria Dock, and the City Airport established between the Royal Albert and King George V docks.

Silvertown began soon after the (Royal) Victoria Dock was started in 1850, and grew up as a few streets round the rubber and telegraph works of S. W. Silver and Co., founded 1852, demolished in the 1960s. It was known as Silvertown by 1859, with St Mark (1860–2) and a station (1863) soon built close to the works. In 1867 there were still only about 360 houses, but by 1900 the narrow strip between the dock and Albert Road had been built up with plain terraces. This housing was grouped into two distinct neighbourhoods, the original Silvertown, of which a fragment survives, and West Silvertown, beyond the Pontoon Dock, replaced by tower blocks after the war and rebuilt again in the 1990s as Britannia Village.

Chemical, engineering and food-processing industries quickly extended E and W along the Thames. Established firms from elsewhere were attracted by the lack of restriction on noxious industries, and by the river, docks and North Woolwich Railway, which brought in bulk raw materials and distributed their goods to a world-wide market. Chemical manufacturers came from Germany after 1870 and several of the food processors from the west of Scotland, including Abram Lyle & Sons, who began to make Golden Syrup at Plaistow Wharf in 1881. Henry Tate & Sons, whose firm began in Liverpool, established themselves at Thames Wharf in 1878 to manufacture the recently patented cube sugar, and in 1921, though they retained their two sites, the firms amalgamated.

Silvertown was badly damaged in both the First and Second World Wars. In 1917 the terrible Silvertown Explosion, caused by a fire in the TNT plant at Brunner Mond, damaged 60,000–70,000 properties throughout West Ham and killed seventy-three people. In the Blitz of 1940, the industrial plant all along the river was badly damaged or wiped out and houses destroyed. Most of the industrial premises are now post-war, and only a few terraces near St Mark still date from the C19.

CHURCH AND PUBLIC BUILDINGS

32 ST MARK, Connaught Road (formerly a museum store for Newham). 1860–2 by *S.S. Teulon* and a building that has provoked strong, opposing reactions. For Teulon's biographer, Matthew Saunders, it is a 'masterpiece' and 'a triumph of decorative brickwork'. Pevsner in 1954 found Teulon's work 'as horrid as only he can be'. But, when *The Ecclesiologist* reviewed the design in 1860, it was quite mild in its rebuke, noting that 'there is much ingenuity and facility in this design, although it recals too strongly the works of the same architect.' In fact in 1860, when polychromy was so much in vogue, this exotically treated church probably seemed less surprising than it does today. It was built on a site given by the dock company and, with its now-demolished vicarage and school, made a sharp contrast with the grim surroundings in the best Victorian town church tradition.

The most striking features are the materials employed, the angular geometry and use of some decidedly innovative tracery. Extensive use is made of hollow bricks of buff terracotta and stock brick, with red and black bricks supplying decorative detail. The building is dominated by a hefty tower placed over the choir (a Continental plan introduced by Butterfield at St Matthias, Stoke Newington, in 1849–53). The E end has a rounded apse, the aisles are lean-to but above them rise three large clerestory windows that break dramatically through the eaves into gables of their own. Their treatment mirrors that in the tower where the louvred belfry windows are forced up into gables set against the slated spire, thus creating a helm-spire effect. At the SE angle of the tower is a Germanic turret combining a staircase and chimney. The window treatment is varied throughout with square heads in the aisles and pointed everywhere else and an amazing display of tracery in the tower windows.

The interior is no surprise after the outside but is slightly quieter. It was badly damaged by a fire in 1984 but *Julian Harrap* carried out a careful restoration, completed 1989, including a faithful replacement of the hammerbeam roof. The details are generally fairly conventional (e.g. the octagonal piers and arches to the arcades) but the character is set by the exposed materials which are the same and as strong as outside. The centre of gravity is the choir, set between corbelled arches from the nave and into the sanctuary, and with pairs of arches on the N and S (each pair with twinned octagonal piers in the middle). Most surprising internally are the details of the tower windows and the decoration over the W doorway. There is a distinctly Islamic feel to all this, as there is in the horseshoe arches he used in St Mary, Ealing (1866–74): although Teulon is scarcely likely to have had unchristian models in mind, these exotic features show the strange lengths to which the mid-Victorian architectural imagination could go.

DREW ROAD SCHOOL. *See* Perambulation.

SILVERTOWN WAY, from the A13 to North Woolwich Road, with a 1300 yard long reinforced concrete viaduct crossing existing roads, the railway and the former W entrance of the Royal Victoria Dock. 1932–4 by *Rendel Palmer & Tritton*, consulting engineers. Sliproads to the Lower Lea Crossing added 1991. A related development, avoiding the busy Silvertown level crossing with bowstring-arched concrete bridge, was the Silvertown by-pass, opened 1935, demolished 1995.

THAMES BARRIER (Silvertown to Charlton). One of London's most ambitious civil engineering works, mostly hidden below water, but with the sculptural silver shell-like roofs of the machinery rooms making a memorable visual impact. It was necessitated by the increasing height of surge tides in the Thames estuary, to protect London from catastrophic flooding. Designed by *Rendel Palmer & Tritton* for the GLC Department of Public Health Engineering, under the Act of 1972. Construction began in 1974 and was effectively completed in 1982.

There are four navigation openings each of 200 ft (61 metres; the same width of opening as Tower Bridge), two subsidiary openings of 103 ft ($31\frac{1}{3}$ metres), and four side spans also of 103 ft. While the side spans have radial gates which fall from above, the navigation openings have rising sector gates, a novel feature. Of a narrow D-shape in section, and pivoted at each end, they will rotate into a vertical position when a flood warning is given, but normally lie flat on the river bed. Beneath the gates and shaped to their curve, cellular pre-cast concrete sills span from pier to pier. Dimensions are huge. The main gates, of welded steel, are 66 ft (20 metres) tall in the vertical position, designed for a differential head of 28 ft ($8\frac{1}{2}$ metres), and each weighs 1,300 tons without the counterweights. The concrete piers, supporting the gates and their hydraulic operating machinery, are founded on the underlying chalk, requiring excavations some 90 ft ($27\frac{1}{2}$ metres) below water level. The piers are capped with boat-shaped roofs of laminated timber clad with stainless steel. On the S bank a tall control building with sculpted roof and viewing galleries, by the *GLC Architect's Department*. The river walls and banks for many miles downstream have also been extensively raised.

THAMES BARRIER PARK, on the site of a tar works. Planned to run down from West Silvertown Urban Village (*see* below) and to create physical and visual links between the village, the dock and the Thames. In concept the S part of the band of parkland that runs all through Beckton, but very different in character. This will be Britain's first Postmodern park, the result of an international competition in 1995 for a phased master-plan. The landscape architects are *Groupe Signes*, the architects *Patel & Taylor*. *Alain Provost* of Group Signes was a consultant to the Parc Citroën, developed on a similar riverside industrial site in Paris from 1972. Like the Parc Citroën it has been designed on a bold framework with strong diagonal routes shooting through the underlying geometry, and will incorporate a series of cultural references. The strongest image is perhaps the 'Green Dock', a 1312 ft (400 metre) strip of lush planting hollowed out of the central plateau to link the Royal Victoria Dock with the Thames Barrier. The perimeter of the park on two sides will be residential. To be completed 1999.

PERAMBULATION

The only fragment of C19 Silvertown lies along CONNAUGHT ROAD and to its N and E. St Mark (*see* above) still stands defiantly by the railway line, the only Victorian church S of the docks to survive the Blitz. On ALBERT ROAD, opposite Silvertown mainline station, a Victorian former pub, and, further E, at the corner of Wythes Road, the Norman Shaw-style TATE & LYLE SOCIAL CLUB, 1887, designed by a Mr *Lewis* as the Tate Institute, with amenities such as a reading room, billiard room and hot baths for the local inhabitants. Altered inside; it was a public library from 1938 to 1961. To the N, amongst very modest terraces and some sympathetic late C20 infill, the DREW ROAD SCHOOL, 1895, in the reduced Queen Anne style of most West Ham Board Schools, stock brick with red brick dressings.

The pre-1965 boundary with North Woolwich (q.v.) was just E of Tate Road but weatherboarded council housing in informal clusters of the 1970s now extends to Winifred Street and incorporates the KENNARD STREET COMMUNITY and HEALTH CENTRE. The former is contemporary with the housing, the latter was added in 1990 by *Form Design Group*, redeveloped in 1996 in forticrete blocks and with lean-to conservatories each side. N of this, King George V Dock and the London City Airport (*see* The Royal Docks).

TATE AND LYLE'S huge sugar refinery lies due S of Silvertown station on Thames Wharf. Mostly rebuilt post-war. In the style of the 1950s, the bulky tower and a long frontage with decorative tiles and canopies over the lower windows and bold original lettering to FACTORY ROAD, parallel with the railway. TAY WHARF, the site of Keiller & Sons' jam factory in 1880–1967, closes the w end of Factory Road, with the restored remains of its monumental gateway, dated 1900.

TATE AND LYLE'S Plaistow Wharf site lies further w along NORTH WOOLWICH ROAD. This has a handsome Portland stone-faced framed building in stripped classical style, built in 1946–50 to plans of the 1930s. Giant pilaster order on the E entrance block, which contained drawing office and boardroom. On the tower-like w end, the firm's trademark in relief: the lion killed by Samson surrounded by bees and, from Judges XIV, the answer to Samson's riddle 'Out of the strong came forth sweetness'. Well-preserved interior complete with lightfittings, signs, and the trademark in plaster and bronze. Faience walling in the entrance hall, Soanian vaulting in the boardroom. To the w the open-well staircase and a managers' dining room panelled in early C18 style on the second floor. To the S, ARDESCO HOUSE has as its core a three-bay, two-storey wharf manager's villa of pre-1860, i.e. when Plaistow Wharf was used for oil storage. By the wharf, off Bradfield Road, the wellhidden pocket of LYLE PARK, provided by Lyle's for the Borough of West Ham in 1924. Further w still, CHARRINGTON'S Brutalist ensemble, with much board-marked concrete, designed as the canteen, offices and weighbridge of British Oil and Cake Mills Ltd by *Munce & Kennedy*, 1964–5.

BRITANNIA VILLAGE stretches along the Royal Victoria Dock N of North Woolwich Road, the first part of the WEST SILVERTOWN URBAN VILLAGE conceived by the LDDC as a self-contained community within an urban setting, with shops, pub, a village common, a village hall and a primary school. Most of it will resemble a giant housing estate, with 777 homes built for sale by *Wimpey Homes* in a predictable manner and 235 of the total number of dwellings designed for social housing. Ambitious plans, which included leisure and exhibition facilities and which proposed reusing the huge granaries then all still standing by Pontoon Dock (*see* Royal Docks), were put forward in 1987 by *Conran Roche*, and more modest ones, mainly for housing, by *Form Design Group*. The w part of the site is finally being developed from 1995 broadly along the lines of a masterplan devised by the *Tibbalds Colbourne Partnership* (now *Tibbalds Munro*), which includes some public amenities and leisure facilities on Thames Barrier lands to the S (*see* the Thames Barrier Park). Building began, 1995–7, at the far w end of the dock with the first phase of Wimpey homes for which Tibbalds Munro are the architects. The layout follows the masterplan: pavilions of flats along the quay and conventional streets of terraced houses leading from a central crescent. The buildings themselves, in yellow brick, are unexceptional, encompassing variations on the theme of the London terrace house or warehouse block but with lots of unnecessary tricks. Two pairs of *Stothert & Pitt* cranes make a dramatic accent on the quayside. To the E, social housing, designed for the Peabody Trust, East Thames Housing Group, Newham Council and Hunting Gate by *Broadway Malyan*, will fill one-third of the site.

A new low-rise community round a village common will replace
BARNWOOD COURT, a pair of twenty-two-storey tower blocks
of 1966, linked by crescents of shops, community rooms etc.,
designed for West Ham Council by *Stillman & Eastwick-Field* to
rehouse the isolated community of West Silvertown. Unmourned.
For the Pontoon Dock *see* Royal Victoria Dock, Royal Docks.

WAPPING AND SHADWELL RIVERSIDE
London Borough of Tower Hamlets

Wapping, though on the fringe of the City of London, was for
over 150 years a territory known well only by those who lived and
worked there. The London Docks and the St Katharine Docks,
developed there in the early C19, covered most of Wapping. They
were private territory, well secured from the idly curious, and they
cut the riverside settlement off from the City and the rest of the
East End, breeding a special 'island' culture and loyalty. Before
the docks closed in 1968, the tourist was restricted to the riverside
thoroughfare walled-in by towering warehouses, interspersed with
dozens of dockers' pubs and with glimpses of the river only available at the narrow riverside stairs, and to the few residential streets
squeezed between the warehouses and the forbidding dock walls.
Wapping lost its intense brooding quality in the aftermath of
closure, when shipping and industry departed and the docks and
many of their particularly magnificent warehouses were destroyed
in the replanning of the neighbourhood. What remains of the
docks and warehouses has been welded into a more conventional
though good-hearted neighbourhood, much of it on a suburban
scale, threaded through with parks and gardens.

Wapping was originally mainly marshland. Perhaps named after
the Saxon Waeppa, it was probably first settled N of the river on
higher ground, close to where St George-in-the-East now stands
at Upper Wapping. Two causeways, later called Gravel Lane and
New Gravel Lane and now known as Garnet Street and Wapping
Lane, led across the marsh from Upper Wapping to the river.
Draining of the marsh and building of river defences seem to have
begun by 1327. These encouraged the growth of a new riverside
settlement that soon eclipsed the more northerly one. In 1395 a
wharf was built on Wapping Wall next to a mill, on land owned by
the hospital of St Thomas of Acon. During the early C15 wharves
spread all along this stretch of the river, so much so that in 1417
there was an ordinance to allow the local inhabitants access to the
shore – a foreshadowing of C20 arguments.

Much further W, by the river close to the City wall where the
St Katharine Docks now lie, was the Royal Foundation of St
Katharine, founded as a hospital in 1147 by Queen Matilda.
Further N in East Smithfield was another religious foundation,
the Cistercian Abbey of St Mary Graces, also known as East
Minster, founded by Edward III in 1349 as an easterly rival to
Westminster Abbey: it became the site of the Royal Mint in the
early C19. In the mid C15, building began to spread E from the

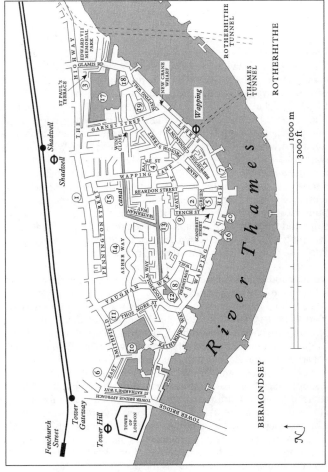

1 St George-in-the-East
2 St John
3 St Paul
4 St Peter
5 St Patrick (R.C.)
6 Former Royal Mint
7 Police Station
8 Hermitage Primary School
9 John Orwell Sports Centre
10 St Katharine Docks
11 Former Entrance to London Docks
12 Hermitage Basin
13 Spirit Quay
14 News International
15 Tobacco Dock
16 Wapping Pier Head
17 Shadwell Basin
18 Wapping Hydraulic Pumping Station
19 Prospect Place
20 Wapping Old Stairs

Wapping

City along the river, giving rise to a new hamlet within the parish of Whitechapel, known as Wapping-Whitechapel. It was separated by marsh from the older hamlet further E, known as Wapping-Stepney, which was centred on Wapping Wall and New Gravel Lane. By 1536 the marsh had been drained by *Cornelius Vanderdelft*, and divided to become rich farmland. Building now spread more quickly along the riverside, though the development of wharves was slowed briefly by the establishment of the City's Legal Quays in 1558. Stow refers to the new road, now Wapping High Street, laid out *c.* 1570 through Wapping-Whitechapel, as a 'filthy straight passage' with 'alleys of small tenements and cottages, inhabited by sailors' victuallers'. By 1615, Wapping-Whitechapel warranted a chapel-of-ease. This was elevated to a parish church in 1694 and rebuilt in 1756 on the other side of the High Street, almost at the N limits of the settlement. Wapping-Stepney remained within Stepney parish until St George-in-the-East was built in 1729. The whole riverside was increasingly devoted to ships and shipping. Royal ships had been refitted and victualled at Wapping Wall since the early C16 and, more than a century later, Pepys saw ships being built there. In the C18, there were still prosperous houses as well as shipbuilders, wharves and inns, but wealthy householders gradually moved away from the riverfront as it became increasingly industrial.

The C16 Thames frontage at Wapping was divided into narrow plots. The C19 story is of the amalgamation of these plots and redevelopment of the warehouses, many of which had grown from C18 houses. For example, the big warehouses along Wapping Wall absorbed fifteen plots of C16 size. In 1885 Timbs wrote that 'the wood-built wharf and house fronts towards the river are fast disappearing.' Some of these amalgamations have obliterated river stairs and alleys. Until the mid C19 there was a great mix of uses along the riverfront. Although most of the plots were called wharves they housed a variety of crafts and trades – biscuit and rope makers, ship builders, engineers, chandlers etc., as can be seen from the street directories for Wapping Wall – and some had small buildings on them as late as the Second World War.

In parallel with the development of the riverfront came the establishment and growth from 1805 of the enclosed, secure and private docks – the London Docks just inland N of Wapping High Street and St Katharine Docks. The building of the London Docks caused a diminution in the population of St John's parish (from 5,889 in 1801 to 3,313 in 1811) and the overcrowding of the surviving inhabitants into the remaining houses, which soon deteriorated into slums. The poor condition and isolation of the area was recognized in the 1850s when a mission (later St Peter London Docks) was set up from St George-in-the-East. Very little was done about the condition of the property until between the wars. Then in 1926 all of the housing between the London Docks and Wapping High Street was swept away in a huge clearance scheme. Old property, including plain but handsome C18 and early C19 houses, was replaced with sensitively designed LCC flats. A similar scheme replaced the houses alongside St Katharine Docks in the 1930s.

Incendiary bombs in the Second World War devastated some areas, particularly the E part of the St Katharine Docks, the S side of the Western Dock of the London Docks, and the W end of Wapping High Street. After repairs the remaining dock and riverside warehouses continued in use much as before, until their labour-intensive handling methods became uncompetitive in the 1960s.

The closure of the docks to shipping in 1968 wrought a huge change. The St Katharine Docks were developed commercially immediately from 1971, but the 103 acres of the London Docks lay untouched for years. In 1968 the GLC and Tower Hamlets saw the site as valuable for rehousing once the docks had been infilled. Instead, in 1973, following the studies on the future of the docks commissioned by the government in 1971, the PLA began filling them in prior to intense redevelopment with offices. This scheme caused an outcry, and in 1976, under the influence of the strategic, community-biased plan published that year by the Docklands Joint Committee, and a property market depressed by the oil crisis, the PLA sold the mostly infilled London Docks to the London Borough of Tower Hamlets. The borough began redevelopment following a masterplan drawn up in 1977 by *Shepheard Epstein & Hunter*. The plan involved 200 acres and 1500 dwellings, some to be designed by the architects, the rest by Tower Hamlets Borough Council.

The Wapping envisaged by Tower Hamlets was not exactly suburban but it did include low-rise housing at garden suburb densities (most for rent, some for sale), generous open space and wedges of green giving access to the river. The conservation area, new gardens and sports centre are part of this plan, but neither the pedestrianized shopping centre and piazza meant for the lower part of Wapping Lane and the High Street to its W, nor the main W–E thoroughfare on the line of Green Bank and Prusom Street, were realized. Shadwell Basin and Hermitage Basin were the only two stretches of water retained, the former for watersports. The council's employment of a private firm for the masterplan and much of the architectural design was hotly debated. The few buildings actually built to Shepheard Epstein & Hunter's designs range from sensitive conservation (John Orwell Centre) to small, simple houses (Wine Close), built on the S edge of the infilled Eastern Dock, which, unsuitable for buildings, was planted with Wapping Wood. The first local amenity, the sports centre, was created over the Western Dock entrance basin.

Alas, News International acquired a large slice along the N side of the former Western Dock and, though the plan designated only general light industry there, in 1981 erected its gargantuan printing works, which involved the demolition of the best dock warehouses. This was a black period for the magnificent dock buildings and the enclosing dock wall, which were seen by the Council and by many residents as not only redundant but also as oppressive reminders of a depressed past.

The LDDC's strategy of 1983, slightly revising Shepheard Epstein & Hunter's plan and providing for a majority of houses for sale, not rent, has created a new and very distinctive landscape of waterways and broad, well-planted quays within the former docks. The low-rise housing built here by private developers, though mostly crude in design, with the notable exception of that around Shadwell Basin by *MacCormac, Jamieson, Prichard & Wright*, nevertheless fits comfortably into the LDDC's overall urban design.

Though the dock warehouses have gone, many of the private riverside warehouses have, encouraged by the LDDC, been converted into housing. Extensive and immediately impressive, they and some equally massive new blocks line the whole length of Wapping Wall and Wapping High Street E of Wapping Pier Head. Moves to reuse the abandoned warehouses predated any official plans by several years. Several were colonized with artists' studios in the late 1960s and 70s, especially at the St Katharine Docks and on Wapping Wall at Metropolitan Wharf. As in New York's SoHo, where artists led the way, developers followed, encouraged in Wapping by gradually changing attitudes to conservation and a popular appreciation, even if superficial, of historic buildings. Oliver's Wharf was the first warehouse to be converted into housing in 1970–2 by a group of enterprising young architects, *Goddard Manton*, and their associates. Developers on a larger scale then moved in to create luxury flats of a kind beyond local pockets. Among the best were *Conran Roche* who, at New Crane Wharf from 1989, created a well-designed mixed development of flats, shops and workshops, parallel with their much larger but comparable development on the S bank at Butler's Wharf. Their example was not followed and, though some of the conversions are good (for example, *PRP*'s Prusom's Island), mixed uses are missing except along the old shopping street, Wapping Lane.

THE LONDON DOCKS

LONDON DOCK opened in 1805. It was the second of London's enclosed docks: its Act was passed in 1800, only a year after that enabling the West India Docks. Wapping had been suggested as a site for docks dealing with the West India trade in 1793, and work had proceeded far enough for a plan to have been drawn up in 1794 by *John Powsey*, and a Bill to have been prepared in 1796. The Wapping scheme and that planned for the Isle of Dogs continued as rival projects until 1799 when Wapping was finally abandoned by the West India merchants and their partners, the City Corporation, in favour of the Isle of Dogs (q.v., West India and Millwall Docks). But the site, so conveniently near the City, was immediately exploited by another consortium of merchants, who formed the London Dock Company. They obtained a twenty-one-year monopoly to deal with all vessels trading in rice, tobacco, wine and brandy, except those ships coming from the East and West Indies. Gradually expanded between 1805 and 1858, the docks grew from W to E, until they eventually comprised six basins and docks stretching from just E of the St Katharine Docks to Shadwell. The several entrance basins had locks at both their outer and inner ends, and these feature prominently in the preserved remains.

The original LONDON (later WESTERN) DOCK of 1801–5 by *Daniel Alexander*, surveyor, and *John Rennie*, civil engineer, was a rectangle of 20 acres with a S entrance basin and an entrance lock at Wapping Pier Head across Wapping High Street. An additional SW entrance through Hermitage Basin, created in 1811–21 by Rennie, was closed in 1909 and an impounding station built. Rennie's quay walls were of brick with a stone rubbing band, similar in design to the West India Docks. Across the main entrance lock, the world's first cast-iron swing bridge was built by *Rennie* in 1803–4, followed by several others around the docks; the last remaining of these was destroyed in 1976. Along the north quay were *Alexander*'s five North Stack warehouses, 1805, their noble façades shamefully emasculated in the mid C20 before demolition in 1979 to make way for News International. Kept but altered were the five Pennington Street sheds, built in one line parallel to the North Stacks on the N side and completed in a single storey *c.* 1811–13, but demolished, just before 1976, the South Stacks of 1806 on the S quay which had been raised from two to four storeys in 1810–11. The North Stacks, of four storeys over vaults, were constructed with timber posts but the South Stacks were given new cast-iron cruciform columns, early for London and still with wooden heads. One of the most remarkable features was the extensive system of basement liquor vaults, which ran under the warehouses and the roadways. They were ventilated by a perimeter tunnel, open to the air, and by narrow slots in the boundary walls, still to be seen in Reardon Street.

Provision was made to raise the Pennington Street sheds to four storeys and connect them to the North Stacks on archways, but this was not done, though Portland stone springings can still be seen. These mirrored a similar provision on the North Stacks. A few of the queenpost roof trusses, of over 50 ft (15¼ metres) span, have been kept, but not the most impressive ones which spanned diagonally. To their E the major part of a building of even more adventurous construction, which fortunately still survives: the New Tobacco Warehouse (now the Tobacco Dock shopping centre, *see* below) was built in 1811–14 by *Alexander*: this originally surrounded on three sides the small dock, known as the TOBACCO DOCK when it was made in 1811–13 by *Rennie*. It was extended as the link between the Western Dock and the projected EASTERN DOCK, E of Wapping Lane when that was added in 1824–8 by *William Chapman*, consulting engineer, and *Alexander*. An E entrance from the Thames was provided via the SHADWELL OLD BASIN of 1828–32 by *J. R. Palmer*, while the SHADWELL NEW BASIN of 1854–8 by *J. M. Rendel* was built in parallel, with larger locks and novel quay walls, and linked to the older basin.

Very extensive five- and six-storey warehousing was built to the W of the Western Docks in the 1840s and 50s by *William Nesham*, with the builder *William Cubitt*, on the site of a maze of earlier sheds, while a long jetty with transit sheds was constructed in 1838 to increase the quay length of the Western Dock. This jetty was replaced by a larger one in reinforced concrete in 1912, and several reinforced concrete transit sheds were also built then. All these constructions were swept away in the 1970s.

Much of the form of the London Docks is still traceable. Though the docks were crudely infilled in the 1970s, the Western Dock was infilled again in 1980 more carefully in preparation for house building and the construction of a new loop road, Vaughan Way. The top 10 ft (3 metres) of the s quay walls of the Western Dock and Tobacco Dock were left exposed, revealing their excellent construction. The walls were used as the s edge of a new channel dug to link, notionally, the Hermitage Basin with the Shadwell Basin to the E. The channel is interrupted by the site of the Eastern Dock, totally infilled and planted as Wapping Wood.

18 TOBACCO DOCK (formerly the New Tobacco Warehouse, later known as the Skin Floor) is one of the most remarkable of the surviving dock buildings. It was rescued by Tobacco Dock Development Ltd, after News International had claimed its warehouse neighbours, and converted 1984–9 by *Terry Farrell Partnership* into a shopping centre.

It was built in 1811–14 by *D. A. Alexander* as the New Tobacco Warehouse, a bonded store for tobacco above wine and spirit vaults (furs and skins replaced tobacco only later). A vast building (originally 210,000 sq. ft, 20,000 sq. metres, it extended s of the Tobacco Dock); about two-fifths have been lost in C19 and C20 demolitions. The structure is as impressive as the scale. It belongs to an evolutionary phase in the combination of timber and cast iron for spanning horizontally, before the widespread use of cast-iron arched beams.

What remains is enclosed on two sides by solid brick walls, which are the outer walls of the dock at its NE corner. The covering is six parallel lines, 370 ft (112 metres) long, 54 ft

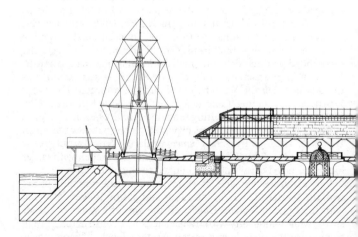

(16½ metres) span, of queenpost lantern roofs of particular elegance. They are supported not by intermediate walls but on lines of stanchions of an astonishing tree-like form. In raking views these columns form a veritable forest. There are twice as many roof trusses as stanchions, which stand at 18 ft (5½ metre) centres. Each stanchion, resting on a stone base, branches into two at mid-height and carries at its head a wooden bolster which supports the twin gutter plates (the longitudinal valley beams, originally timber, now steel) and a pair of trusses of the adjacent roofs. From just below the bifurcation spring two other struts, themselves Y-shaped, which meet their neighbours mid-span in curvilinear crown-pieces; these carry the gutter plates and intermediate roof trusses on brackets. The struts act compositely with the beams, to form balanced cantilevers. (The arrangement of raking struts is a three-dimensional refinement of the arched-braces used in *Alexander*'s entirely timber Old Tobacco Warehouse of 1805, destroyed in the Second World War. This had long-span roof trusses in a similar arrangement, and groin vaults beneath on an exceptionally adventurous 26-ft (8-metre) grid.) All the cast-iron members are of a slim cruciform section, except for every sixth column which is hollow, circular and acts as a rainwater downpipe. Laterally, stability is imparted to the structure by inverted quadrant braces of cast iron which rise from the floor to the longitudinal fire-break wall. The lanterns have cast-iron side-lights.

Under the Skin Floor run the wine and spirit vaults, shallow brick groin vaults on waisted, octagonal stone pillars, with some lines of barrel vaults to give stability. Foundations are on timber piles which rely for their preservation on a locally high water table, which is now specially augmented with run-off from the roofs. The vaults are on an 18 ft (5½ metre) square grid.

Farrell has tried to create a second Covent Garden Market, 8 adopting a similar approach by making several wells in the floor

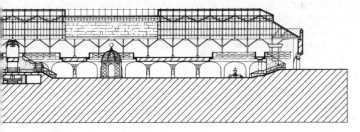

Tobacco Dock. Section

into the vaults beneath, and openings in the two lines of roofs above these wells, as a fire precaution. The three eastern roof bays, demolished after war damage, have been reinstated using trusses dismantled for the voids in the roof and others from one of two western bays that were taken for the adjoining carpark. New stanchions were cast to make up the numbers. There are suitably subtle breaks in the daunting brick wall for entrances, their elliptical arches on thick Doric columns with a warehouse flavour but actually derived from Ledoux. Unnecessarily massive, Postmodern staircases in concrete to the vaults. Otherwise the C19 structure has been left to speak for itself, with shopfronts just sheer planes of glass in bolted metal frames. This treatment continues on to the quayside front, where the solid wall had long ago been demolished. In the vaults, heavier, more classical shop units. Intended as a tourist attraction and local shopping centre, Tobacco Dock became a collection of factory shops in 1993 with forecourt carparks designed by *Danell Smith*. In 1997 one or two cafés and pubs are open but nothing else.

To the s of the Skin Floor the remains of the small Tobacco Dock (*see* above). Now just a canal, spanned by a steel swing bridge of 1912.

Also surviving, parts of the DOCK BOUNDARY WALLS, including the former main entrance and original customs offices (now London Dock House, *see* Perambulation 2a). Originally more spectacular, and standing up to 20 ft (6 metres) above street level though truncated for safety and curtailed for recent developments, were the boundary walls around the s and e sides of the Western Dock. Beside the Wapping and Hermitage entrance locks may be seen the icicle-rusticated springings of the former gateways through the walls (*see* Perambulation 2a), while lengths have been retained at their original heights in Tench Street and Wapping Lane. The ventilation slits through the walls to the former spirits vaults behind are best seen in Reardon Street (where the walls themselves have been severely cut down). The great level change of some 10 ft (3 metres) between the quays and the original ground on the s side can best be observed in that area. Few dock buildings survive. Other than the impressive New Tobacco Warehouse and the re-roofed Pennington Street Sheds, there is only the group of dock officials' houses at Wapping Pier Head; the pump houses of the Hermitage Basin (for all these *see* Perambulation 2a); and a former maintenance shop (now John Orwell Sports Centre, *see* Public Buildings). Of other structures, two bascule bridges survive at either end of Shadwell Basin (*see* Perambulation 2c).

For St Katharine Docks *see* Perambulation 1.

CHURCHES

St George-in-the-East, The Highway. One of the churches built as a result of the New Churches Act of 1711 as a parish church to serve Wapping-Stepney and the area to its N. Designed

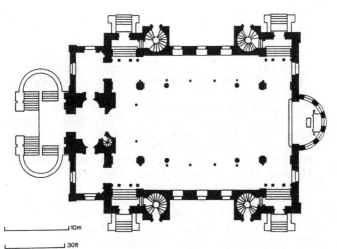

St George-in-the-East. Plan as built

by *Hawksmoor* and mainly built by the mason *Edward Strong* in 1714–18, followed by the building of the tower 1720–3, the plasterwork 1723–4, and the pewing and carving in 1724. It was not consecrated until 1729. The most original of Hawksmoor's three contemporary East End churches, though not perhaps as mighty as Christ Church Spitalfields further w in Tower Hamlets.

The exterior survives intact. All the planes are peculiarly sheer and flat, in Portland stone. All the details are idiosyncratic, angular and unmoulded, with window openings simply recessed. The inside is new, rebuilt after bomb damage in 1941. Hawksmoor's plan was a variation of St Anne Limehouse (q.v) with groups of piers and columns marking out a rectangle within a rectangle. The sense of the Greek cross achieved by Wren at St Anne and St Agnes (*see London 1: City of London*) etc. must have been clearer here with lower corner bays and the centre marked by a shallow plaster cross-vault (a pyramidal roof to express the centre externally was also projected). As at St Anne, Limehouse, there were additional E and w bays; here they were separately vaulted and clearly acted as transepts leading to the side doors.

There is a w tower but no w portico; instead an arena-like platform in front of the church, now approached by a single wide flight of steps, a C19 alteration: could it have been by *George Dance Sen.* who altered the rectory in 1802–6? Hawksmoor's design had steps approaching the platform on each side, with the door to the vaults straight ahead. The lowest stage has coupled Ionic pilasters and an arched doorway with an oculus over instead of a portico. The flanking vestries are linked by big volutes. The three stages above have windows deeply set in sharply cut recesses. On top an octagonal lantern reminiscent of

Perp churches like Fotheringay or Boston, but with pinnacles in the form of Roman altars, both features that occur earlier in Hawksmoor's unbuilt early designs for his first Commissioners' church, St Alfege, Greenwich. He had at first intended a turret similar in design to those which he eventually added to crown the staircase projections in the second and sixth bays of the side elevations. These are almost certainly deliberate paraphrases of those at King's College Chapel, Cambridge, but they are also close to an early design for the tower of St Mary-le-Bow (in the City) and their effect is similar to that which Archer at the same moment was making the chief motif at St John Smith Square (Westminster). The small doors in the projecting bays have Hawksmoor's typical heavy keystones (cf. St George, Bloomsbury, *London 4: North*) on a complicated surround that encloses an *œil de bœuf*. The lower nave windows, which sit high above the tall basement, also have oddly shaped and exaggerated lintels and keystones; the upper windows are plainly arched. The E apse continues the cornice line of the sides below the main roof pediment.

The post-war reconstruction, 1960–4, is by *Arthur Bailey* of *Ansell & Bailey*, who built a smaller church within the outer walls, leaving a courtyard within the W end flanked by flats on the site of the aisles. A hall was created in the vaults. Bailey's W façade looks like that of a conventional though modern 1960s church, the centre of the W wall glazed with hexagonal panes. Inside, the plain concrete structure has been left exposed in stark contrast with the C18 apse plasterwork and mosaic panels of 1880. Plain furnishing of 1964, except for the C18 FONT. Octagonal bowl identical to that in St George, Bloomsbury (probably by *Strong*) on a baluster stem.

The CHURCHYARD is a large public garden (laid out 1886, relandscaped by the LDDC early in the 1990s) consisting of the original parish burial ground with the former burial ground of St George's Methodist Church, Cable Street (dem.), joined together in 1875. All headstones were cleared to the sides in the 1870s, with the more picturesque examples along the S wall. – Former parish MORTUARY of *c*. 1880, inscribed 'Metropolitan Borough of Stepney Nature Study Museum'; opened as a museum in 1904 under the direction of the rector, with living specimens so that East End children could observe nature at first hand. Closed in 1939 and subsequently reduced to a shell. – GATEPIERS, W ones dated 1815: originally very good cast-iron gates as well. – WAR MEMORIAL of the First World War, tall neo-Grec cross of Portland stone, its E side embellished with a sword in the manner of Blomfield's 'cross of sacrifice' design. – MONUMENTS. Raine monument in memory of Mrs Sarah Raine (†1725) Mrs Elizabeth Raine (†1732) and Mr Henry Raine, brewer (†1738), who founded the school in 1719 in Raine Street *see* p. 222. Square pyramid (formerly urn-capped) upon a two-stage base. The pyramid and upper base are of Portland Stone while the large pedestal is of two sorts of marble, veined and statuary. The S face sports an achievement of arms. On the N face a relief of a semi-reclining draped woman, her right arm and face (now smashed off) directed towards heaven; clearly a variant upon conventional effigial sculpture of the period, this is a highly unusual example of an outdoor effigy. The other two sides have inscriptions. – Andrew Wilson †1844, near NE gate to main part of churchyard. Portland stone sarcophagus surmounted by a draped urn. Doric frieze with triglyphs, rosettes and repeated AW monograms. – NW of the church, a grey marble sarcophagus of *c.* 1740, carried on ball and claw feet with acanthus decoration; gadrooning to the base and lower edge of coved cover. Armorial cartouches on the cover. Unusual and lavish. – Alexander Wyllie †1741, against the S wall SE of the church. Headstone almost certainly of northern manufacture, judging by style and sandstone brought to London by sea.

Until the Blitz in 1940, there were always houses along The Highway screening the S side, which may account for the wild, eye-catching towers and S doorways. Hawksmoor tried to persuade the Commissioners to demolish the houses, perhaps intending to replace them with more appropriate precinct buildings, based on his designs for 'A Basilica for the Primitive Christians'. Various proposals have been made since to re-establish the enclosure by building along the S boundary, e.g. by *Price & Cullen* in 1990, and in 1992 by *Stanton Williams* as part of their plans for remodelling the interior of the church. The W approach is still constricted by walls. On the N the former RECTORY, 1726–9, the only part of the precinct plan achieved. *Edward Strong* and others of the church craftsmen worked on it and the accounts were approved by *Hawksmoor* and *John James*, but this plain two-and-a-half-storey red brick box gives away nothing as to the hand of its architect. Ugly C19 additions removed and façades repaired in 1996. Porch of *c.* 1800 on slender columns.

ST JOHN, Scandrett Street. 1756. The former parish church of Wapping, the successor to the first one, which was built as a chapel in 1615–17 on the S side of Wapping High Street. Except for the tower only a fragmentary rectangular shell survived the Second World War. As in many of these Thames-side hamlets, the neighbourhood of the church remained residential and still has some attractive though not grand C18 houses. In 1997 the nave is to be filled with housing. The tower, restored in 1964 by the LCC, has a handsome Continental-looking lead top. In outline above the clock stage, a concave receding stage and then the convexity of the cupola: a somewhat old-fashioned Baroque design. His obituary in the *Gent's Magazine* claims that the church was designed by *Joel Johnson*, who was trained as a carpenter as so many C18 church designers were. The original designs may have owed something to *Boulton Mainwaring*, surveyor to the London Hospital, for whom Johnson worked. Mainwaring gave evidence before the House of Commons in 1756 concerning the rebuilding. – Opposite, the former CHURCHYARD, hemmed in by the former dock wall, was made into a public park in 1951. Portland stone CHEST

TOMBS to the Staple children, *c.* 1730, and to John Robinson. *c.* 1750, are among the few left *in situ.* – STREET NAME TABLET, affixed to the Turk's Head, opposite on Scandrett Street. Inscribed. 'Bird Street Erected Anno Dom 1706'.

ST MARY GRACES. *See* Royal Mint.

ST PAUL, The Highway, Shadwell. 1820–1. Plaques read '*J. Walters*, Architect: Rebuilt 1820: *R. Streather*, Builder'. John Walters †1821 had been a pupil of D.A. Alexander, architect of many buildings in the London Docks. His church replaces a chapel of 1656.

Economical and straightforward: Pevsner in 1952 thought it was designed without fire. Yellow stock brick with stuccoed pilasters on the simple Greek Revival w front. Blind niches flank a big w door; inscription tablets over. Plain side elevations, five bays, two storeys, with a bold stone stringcourse below the parapet. All the windows rectangular, the upper ones with cornices. Chancel with angle pilasters as on the w front. In contrast the much richer stone steeple above, which evokes Wren, especially St Mary-le-Bow, via George Dance's St Leonard, Shoreditch. The base, with plinth and cornice broken out in response to paired Corinthian angle columns, looks particularly Baroque. Corinthian columns also form a circular tempietto above. Obelisk top stage.

Square galleried nave with a saucer-dome, a centralized plan, even more obvious when there was still an E gallery carrying the organ (now in the w gallery). The galleries, w, n and s, are of dark wood on squat Tuscan columns. Projection w for porch and gallery stairs flanking the tower and E for shallow vaulted chancel between vestries. The present tripartite E window is the result of alterations by *Butterfield* in 1848, modified (Butterfield's chancel arch and vault removed) by *W.C. Waymouth* in 1931. Brick crypt with burial vaults: now a community centre, created during restoration by the LDDC, 1983–4. – COMMUNION TABLE, C17, walnut, and RAILS, C17, *c.* 820. – PULPIT, of bombe form, oak, *c.* 1700. – ORGAN. Early C19 but a large part dates from 1714, one of the few surviving works of *Abraham Jordan.* – STAINED GLASS. Post-war E window by *John Hayward*, 1964.

CHURCHYARD – Good early C19 iron railings and lamp brackets. – On the s side the dock wall, pierced by a doorway to Shadwell Basin. Landscaping of the churchyard and terraces by the LDDC 1983–4.

The former CHURCH SCHOOLS, within the churchyard (w), look like a pair of semi-detached houses, three (l.) and four bays plus broken-forward entrance bays. Late Georgian but with Italianate ambitions. Along the top floor, a row of closely-set, segment-headed windows. Blank stone plaque over the round-headed ground-floor windows. To the w on The Highway (No. 298) the plain three-bay, still-Georgian RECTORY, *c.* 1820.

ST PETER, Wapping Lane. Begun 1865–6 by *F.H. Pownall* for Father Charles Lowder, and important in the rise of Anglo-Catholicism. It originated as a mission from St George-in-the-East under the auspices of the Society of the Holy Cross in 1856 with a chapel in Calvert (now Watts) Street. This was the first such mission to the poor in the East End and, under Father Lowder, was famous for its advanced ceremonial of the kind that led to notorious riots at St George-in-the-East in 1859. Unfortunately Pownall's church lay unfinished until the 1930s, though the clergy and sisters' houses were built in 1881; architect *Bowes A. Paice*. The W end, with baptistery, mortuary chapel, and tower designed 1884–94 by *Maurice B. Adams*, editor of *Building News*, was not completed until 1939, and then without the top of the tower and the W gallery. The whole church was damaged by bombing the year after (the sisters' house was destroyed) and much reconstructed 1948–50, with new stained glass.

A muscular exterior, originally hemmed in by other buildings and screened from the street by the sisters' house (l., rebuilt 1950 without its gabled top floor) and clergy house (r.) linked by a pair of squat Gothic arches with an image bracket and domestic Gothic window over. Lining the passage to the courtyard, hygienic glazed red and white tiles. The church is in what Father Lowder described as 'later First Pointed Gothic'. Stock brick, black-brick patterning and touches of red, except for the later and more genteel red brick W front and stump of SW tower, which can be seen from Raine Street. It has nave, chancel and transepts, all equally high. N and S aisles and S chapel. Bold plate tracery except on the blank N aisle where houses formerly abutted. The E façade almost blank too except for the very elaborate wheel window high up, probably so it could be seen over St George's workhouse and the dock wall beyond, which originally came quite close here. Big circles with quatrefoils and cinquefoils as the S windows. More cinquefoils in the N chancel clerestory, large and with rows of smaller quatrefoils below.

The interior is equally muscular in red and black brick, its Ruskinian toughness exaggerated by the huge blocks of uncarved stone where capitals and corbels were left unfinished. Fine carving on the two finished crocketed capitals: one chancel capital includes an angel. Additional polychromy in the nave columns of cold blue Pennant stone and in the red and green of the modest iron chancel screen and rood beam, planned in 1880 in memory of Father Lowder, incomplete until *c.* 1925. Stone wall shafts carry a crown-post nave roof; painted wagon roof in chancel. Adams's W end has a baptistery in the vaulted tower base, with a stone stair intended to lead to a W gallery.

Though the general impression is harmonious, the FURNISHINGS are later or imported. – PULPITS. One from the ritualist Margaret Street Chapel (Westminster), plain and not used. The main pulpit, on columns but now without its sounding-board, from Blomfield's Anglo-Catholic St Barnabas, Jericho, Oxford. – Undistinguished, sub-Wren High Altar REREDOS by *Lawrence King.* – In the N aisle REREDOS (pre-war), Our Lady of Wapping by *Trevor Griffin*, dated 1948. – Many easel PAINTINGS, those in the S chapel fitted into timber panelling, which seems to match the reredos here. Best are Crucifixion, *School of Guido Reni* (High Altar), and Taunting of Christ, Flemish C16 (s aisle). – IRON GATES. Baptistery and Sacred Heart chapel, 1949 by *Romilly Craze*, made by *Fred Sage & Co.* from ironwork salvaged from the church. – STAINED GLASS. s chapel E window. The Good Shepherd to a *Burne Jones* design; post-war. – By *M. E. Aldrich Rope*: w and s transept windows, strips of grisaille medallions (The Sacraments), 1937–40, from St Augustine, Haggerston; chancel E, in medievalizing reds and blues, 1949; s chapel, with circular illustrations of the work of past vicars, charming and well fitted to the cinquefoil windows within their stumpy arcade, 1950. – NAVE. Ugly Saints signed by *Hardman*. Post-war.

ST PETER'S CENTRE, on the other side of Wapping Lane, w of the green, was the C19 Reardon Street School, attractively converted *c.* 1990 by *Architype* for the LDDC.

31 ST PATRICK (R.C.), Green Bank, immediately E of St John. A remarkable, knowingly rustic Italian design by *F. W. Tasker*, 1879. Unusual for its date, perhaps directly influenced by Cardinal Manning who developed a taste for things Italian and was a family friend. Classical and very straightforward, with big shady pediments each end and an overhanging cornice, all of stone. Almost blank yellow brick walls with clerestory windows, perhaps because it lay close to the dock wall. Projecting s an apsidal and half-domed baptistery. Elegant arcaded narthex. Attached to the s, the presbytery round a charming informal courtyard. Restored externally by *Simon Crosse* and *Roger Jorgensen* of *Feilden & Mawson*, 1987–8.

Interior with giant Ionic columns dividing the flat ceiling of the aisles from the coffered timber barrel-vault of the nave. The chancel is differentiated by the change to a plaster vault on Corinthian columns. Some of the FURNISHING was done 1892–1902 at the expense of Pugin's patron, Charles Willcock-Dawes of Burton Hill, who also paid for the gateway. – HIGH ALTAR. Quattrocento-style marble altar with grotesques finely painted on the frontal. The altar table, possibly C18, came from Cardinal Newman's first oratory in King William Street, Westminster. Pedimented retable. The painting of the Crucifixion is by *Greenwood c.* 1892. – LADY ALTAR similar with a Spanish oil painting. – SACRED HEART ALTAR. Descent from the Cross after Rubens from the previous Wapping R.C. chapel in Virginia Street.

PUBLIC BUILDINGS

Former ROYAL MINT, East Smithfield. Though it lies just beyond the boundary of Docklands as drawn by the LDDC, it is important in the development of the area and makes a prominent neighbour to the St Katharine Docks at one of the most important gateways to Docklands.

The Royal Mint moved here from the Tower of London in 1809. The new buildings were designed *c.* 1805 by *James*

Johnson, Surveyor to the Mint 1794–1807, and built 1807–12 by Johnson's successor as Surveyor, *Sir Robert Smirke*. The main building looks like a government palace and was indeed partly residential originally, with apartments for the deputy master, the assay master and the provost of the moneyers, as well as bullion stores and the Mint office. Blocks round the courtyard behind housed minting machinery installed by *Matthew Boulton* and *John Rennie*. Since the Mint moved out between 1965 and 1975, these blocks have been replaced and the interior of the main building swept away for open-plan offices behind a retained façade. Architects *Sheppard Robson* and *RMJM*, the latter master planners and executive architects, 1985–9, for the whole complex, which includes social housing, and architects for the conversion and the new offices behind.

The façade of the main block is long, rather flat and of stone: Johnson's Palladian composition was old-fashioned in 1805 (Britton says: 'little that is novel or striking'). Ground floor of channelled rustication, broad central pediment, with the royal arms, carried by six attached Roman Doric columns, end bays marked by four pilasters. The crisp Greek metope frieze must surely be due to Smirke. The whole building is set well back behind railings. Two lodges, set diagonally opposite the Tower, announce it from the street. Elements of Smirke's dignified classical interiors have been reused.

To one side the former Seamen's Registry, also designed as staff houses in 1805 by *Johnson*. Stepped façade extended by RMJM. Channelled rustication to the stone ground floor; very plain brick otherwise. Along the w and n perimeter huge later additions, many of them c20 Neo-Georgian. The large new office blocks by RMJM have boldly articulated concrete frames: the housing along the e perimeter, by Sheppard Robson, is quite traditional.

The remains of the Cistercian ABBEY OF ST MARY GRACES were excavated (1972 and 1986–8) during the removal of the Mint and the conversion work. They lie under the entrance court and fragments can be glimpsed under a parking platform. The site was granted by Edward III to the Cistercians as a foundation endowment for a new Royal Free Chapel of St Mary Graces on Tower Hill in 1350. It was the last Cistercian abbey founded before the Dissolution and was mostly complete by the 1390s. The plan was unusual for a Cistercian church, perhaps influenced by the layout of properties along Tower Hill and affected by its late date. It had a large central tower and no transepts. Originally it probably had a T-shaped e end modelled on Fountains Abbey (North Yorks), but n and s chapels were added later making it rectangular. The n chapel was a Lady Chapel added by Sir Thomas Montgomery before 1489; there are no other Lady Chapels in Cistercian churches. On the s side, there were a series of small chapels or rooms, perhaps including sacristy and vestry. The cloisters seem to have been detached, suggesting a courtyard or second set of cloisters in the usual place immediately s of the church. The

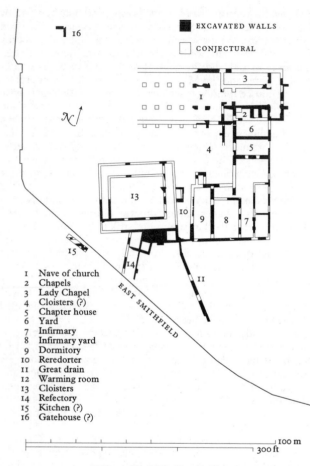

1 Nave of church
2 Chapels
3 Lady Chapel
4 Cloisters (?)
5 Chapter house
6 Yard
7 Infirmary
8 Infirmary yard
9 Dormitory
10 Reredorter
11 Great drain
12 Warming room
13 Cloisters
14 Refectory
15 Kitchen (?)
16 Gatehouse (?)

Abbey of St Mary Graces. Plan

chapter house was separated by a small yard from the E end of the church and the infirmary to its S was separated by another yard from the dormitory which adjoined the cloister (SW).

In 1542–3 the buildings were granted to Sir Arthur Davey †1560 who pulled the church down and retained the S range, perhaps as a house. In 1560 this was sold to the Crown and became victualling yards for the Navy. In 1634–5 there were a bakehouse and ovenhouse in the dormitory and infirmary yard, a barrel staves store in the infirmary, a coopers' workshop in the chapter house. The remains of the church were called the long storehouse. After 1748, when the Navy moved entirely to Deptford, the buildings became government warehouses, until in 1805 they were demolished for the Royal Mint. On the N part of the site a CEMETERY was found, containing 762 victims of the Black Death.

RIVER POLICE STATION, No. 98 Wapping High Street. By *John* 35 *Dixon Butler*, Metropolitan Police architect, 1907–10 for the Thames Division (river police). Brick and stone; Norman Shawish. Flats for officers along the street. River front more elaborate with tiered oriels in the outer bays and moulded stone gables, cf. the similar but earlier and slightly simpler Cold-harbour Police Station by John Butler the elder (Isle of Dogs, Perambulation 3). The river police was founded in Wapping in 1798; the building now contains a museum. Further w, the launch maintenance works of 1973 by the *Metropolitan Police Chief Architect*, clad in GRC-panels boldly moulded in a sculptural relief, rudely disrupts the riverside harmony.

HERMITAGE PRIMARY SCHOOL, Vaughan Way. By the *ILEA Architect's Department*, 1985–9. The central octagonal lantern tower makes this low-key school a modest landmark. The composition builds up from a single-storey s wing, with veranda to the classrooms, to two storeys at the back where there is street access to both levels. Yellow brick, slate and lead.

Former RAINE'S FOUNDATION SCHOOL. *See* Perambulation 2b.

Former ST JOHN'S SCHOOL. *See* Perambulation 2b.

JOHN ORWELL SPORTS CENTRE, Tench Street. An early and 24 very successful venture into the reuse of a London Docks building, by *Shepheard Epstein & Hunter*, 1977–80 for Tower Hamlets Borough Council. The entrance is just a discreet doorway in a stretch of wall that formerly surrounded London Dock. Inside an activities hall converted from a machine-tool workshop, which hugged the curve of the dock wall at the edge of the dock entrance basin; the basin has been infilled for sports pitches. Long and gently curved with full-height arched w windows. At the N end a new sports hall, kept as low and discreet as possible by means of a slate mansard. Round the hall a covered walkway carried on salvaged cast-iron stanchions.

ST GEORGE'S POOLS, The Highway. 1965–9 by *R. H. Uren*. Engineering-brick plinth with three storeys of white mosaic and glass bands.

EDWARD VII MEMORIAL PARK, between The Highway and the river. Planned 1910, opened 1922. At that time, the only park in Stepney. The s part of the site had been the Metropolitan Fish Market, a marginally successful venture opened in 1885 and sold to the City of London in 1901. Parts of it were used as the main working site for the Rotherhithe Tunnel works. The park obliterated the old centre of Shadwell (*see* Perambulation 2c) teeming slums by then.

Landscape restored and improved by *Cooper Partnership* for the LDDC in the 1980s. – FOUNTAIN by *Sir Bertram McKennal*. On axis, a plain stone CENOTAPH (N) and a roofless, classical brick ROTUNDA, the air shaft of the Rotherhithe Tunnel (*see* Rotherhithe), which has a twin in Rotherhithe. Of 1904–8, it predates the park. In front of it, a roughly hewn MEMORIAL stone to 'Sir Hugh Willoughby ... and other navigators who in the latter half of the sixteenth century set sail from this reach of the River Thames near Ratcliffe Cross'. Erected by the LCC, 1922. Porcelain plaque painted with galleons. – From the embankment, a magnificent view up- and downriver. One can see, on the opposite bank, the rows of speculative housing in historical guise along Rotherhithe Street, and, in the centre of the view E, the clustering blocks of Canary Wharf.

THAMES CROSSINGS. For London Bridge, Tower Bridge, Tower Subway *see* Bermondsey Riverside. For the Thames Tunnel *see* Rotherhithe.

The EAST LONDON RAILWAY, 1865–76 by *(Sir) John Hawkshaw*, from Shoreditch to New Cross, passes through the earlier Thames Tunnel (*see* Rotherhithe). From Wapping southwards it was opened in 1869. Northwards, twin bores were constructed beneath the Eastern Dock of the London Docks in a coffer dam, and the underpinning of a warehouse on the N quay was a major operation. The double tiers of massive cast-iron flying shores in the ventilation wells at Shadwell and Wapping stations convey a little of the magnitude of the work, through water-bearing ground. Oval ventilation stacks stand in open spaces along the route.

PERAMBULATIONS

1. The St Katharine Docks and St Katharine's Way

The scene at the ST KATHARINE DOCKS is lively but chaotic. Redevelopment for a multiplicity of leisure, residential and office uses following its closure in 1968 (an early example of planned mixed development) has given it new life and preserved its unique enclosed form but, with the exception of one warehouse and the dockmaster's house, has not saved its architecture.

This was the smallest group of enclosed docks in London yet, despite that, the last of the early C19 wave of dock building. It was built in 1825–9 by the St Katharine Dock Company, a consortium of seamen and city merchants, on the very constricted site of the Hospital of St Katharine by the Tower, established in 1147 by Matilda, wife of King Stephen, as a Royal Foundation. The Foundation moved away, first to splendid new premises in Regent's Park (*see London 3: North West*) and later to Poplar; it is now in Ratcliffe (q.v.). The dock company's speculation, considered at the time to be greedy and heartless, involved not only the demolition of the Hospital, with its fine C14 church, but also the obliteration of over 1,000 dilapidated houses, the refuge of out-casts and the very poor who were protected by the Foundation's status as a Royal Peculiar.

Although the warehousing was generous and desirably near the City, the water area was very small and made no provision for the as yet unforseen revolution in ship size that the use of iron would bring. By the mid C19 the lock and passages were proving to be too small: the company reacted by merging in 1863 with the London Dock Company, which bought in 1864 the huge new Victoria Dock downriver. The joint company went on to build

the Royal Albert Dock in 1875–80 (*see* Newham: The Royal
Docks). Though the Blitz of 1940 destroyed the three warehouses
round the Eastern Dock, together with the fine offices at the
NW corner, the Western Dock retained, post-war, its sense of
enclosure and unity of scale until the 1970s.

The St Katharine Docks did not close until 1968, and a competition for their redevelopment was launched in 1969 by the
GLC. The site was awarded on a 125-year lease to Taylor
Woodrow because they agreed, as encouraged in the competition,
to conserve at least two remaining warehouses round the West
Basin, as well as to provide a mixture of publicly and privately
owned housing, offices, shops, hotel, chapel and recreational facilities. Instead, the Western Dock is lined with frankly modern hotel
and office buildings of the 1960s to 80s, including a crude version
of one of the original warehouses, and the Eastern Dock is devoted
to housing, some still being completed in 1997. The range of uses
is about that prescribed in *Renton Howard Wood Associates'* original
plan of 1968. None of the C20 architecture, designed in a peculiar
medley of styles, is distinguished, but the one remaining mid-
C19 warehouse still stands as the *pièce-de-résistance*, in a crucial
position for picturesque effect.

THE DOCKS, with two docks linked by a single entrance basin
almost as big, were designed by *Thomas Telford*, engineer. By
the use of two linked basins he increased the amount of
wharfage in this very restricted space. Only single pairs of
stop gates, rather than full locks, were provided in the passages
to the dock basins (*see* Introduction), and retracting footbridges were provided to save space. The quay walls (brick
with gritstone copings) in the docks have mooring rings recessed
into their face, an unusual feature to reduce congestion on
the quay. The Western Dock opened in 1828, the Eastern in
1829.

The warehouses by *Philip Hardwick*, designed 1826–7, were
unique in the London docks. Six stacks of them originally surrounded and enclosed the basins. Because of the restricted site,
these warehouses were placed on the edges of the quays on colonnades (an arrangement suggested in 1799 by Ralph Dodd for
extension to the Legal Quays in the City and used later at Liverpool
docks from 1843). Goods could be hoisted straight from ships into
the warehouses or sorted for other destinations behind the colonnades. Along the quays were Tuscan Doric columns of hollow
cast iron, 18 ft (5½ metres) apart and 16 ft 9 in. (5 metres) tall,
carrying a plain Portland stone entablature with concealed cast-iron
beams. Above this, five or six storeys of simple, well-proportioned
brickwork, with broad cast-iron framed windows and pilaster
strips finishing in semicircular arches, beneath an inconspicuous
Portland stone coping. Certain bays were recessed for cranes
which served the quay; on the landward side there were deeply
recessed yards for carts, so breaking up the long façades. Conventional construction of cruciform cast-iron columns and timber
floors above extensive brick groin-vaults also on cruciform cast-
iron columns.

The best overall first impression of the docks is gained from the entrance lock, best reached by the pedestrian route from Tower Hill station, via the landscaped walkway below the level of Tower Bridge Approach, to the river terrace by the TOWER THISTLE HOTEL. The hotel is by *Renton Howard Wood Associates*, 1970–3, a huge overdevelopment of this narrow site, scaled to the river and Tower Bridge rather than the docks. Its bulk is somewhat disguised by the cruciform plan and the way in which brutal, brown concrete-panel-clad storeys cascade down from sixteen to nine. Multi-storey foyer, layered with galleries. In the angle of the s façade a pool with a spiralling group of a flying GIRL WITH A DOLPHIN, by *David Wynne*, 1973. It stands on the jetty from a former wharf; see the mid-C20 capstan and bollards. To the E the quay wall of St Katharine's Wharf, 1829, with gritstone cornice. Further E, a functioning TIME PIECE by *Wendy Taylor*, also 1973, more literal than her later work. Studded stainless-steel ring supported on rigid chains and pierced by a spear-like gnomon. Here Tower Bridge looms up close to.

The ENTRANCE PASSAGE into the docks is flanked on the E side by the DOCKMASTER'S HOUSE of *c.* 1828, which like the others of its type has a bow facing down the river. At the lock original cast-iron BOLLARDS, inscribed 'St Katharine Docks, 1828', not to be confused with the ornamental ironwork of the 1970s. The ENTRANCE LOCK is of 1828, its upper walls now refaced and its mitre gates and sills replaced by flap gates in 1957. Telford provided an elegant double-leaf cast-iron swing bridge, replaced in 1895. In the ENTRANCE BASIN, two recesses in the quay walls for the bowsprits of sailing vessels awaiting the tide. Minimalist lifting FOOTBRIDGE by *Powell-Williams Architects* and engineers *Robert Benaim & Associates*, 1996, and, carrying the road, a crisp welded-steel LIFTING BRIDGE by *Ove Arup & Partners*, 1973.

At the PASSAGES to the dock basins are the recesses for the former stop gates, and the original bollards. A unique double-leaf RETRACTING FOOTBRIDGE of 1829 crossed the eastern passage and is now preserved on the quay to the s. Its canti-levered leaves, meeting in the middle, are of wrought-iron bars in an unbraced construction, springing from cast-iron counter-weight boxes which ran on rails and retracted into recesses in the opposite quays. A contractor's design, by *John Lloyd*, in substitution for one in cast iron by Telford's assistant Thomas Rhodes. Rails and railway wheels are C19 replacements – probably double-flanged wheels ran on ribbed cast-iron rails, which are preserved among the ballast. One of the earliest moveable iron bridges remaining in Britain. On the original site, a replacement bridge on similar principles, with elegant tubular steelwork. 1994 by *Brian Morton*, one hand winch of 1829 in situ. Across the W passage, a wooden, Dutch-style LIFTING FOOTBRIDGE also by *Ove Arup & Partners*, 1983. Moored in the Western Basin, handsome Thames spritsail barges: the rest of the docks harbour more modern boats.

The view of the Western Dock takes in immediately the battle of styles. INTERNATIONAL HOUSE, designed for the World Trade Centre (now defunct) by *Watkins Gray Woodgate International*, 1977–83, walls in the W side. It replaces the last 1820s warehouse. It incorporates the idea of the dockside colonnade with double Doric columns (salvaged from Hardwick's warehouse) and the bays; otherwise, misleadingly semi-historical. On the N side, EUROPE HOUSE, of precast-concrete units by *Andrew Renton & Associates*, 1962–4, predates the regeneration scheme for the docks and replaces the dock company's handsome Greek Revival offices of 1828 by *Hardwick*, demolished after war damage. To its E, COMMODITY QUAY designed for the London Commodity Exchange, 1984–5, by *Watkins Gray International*. Not unlike International House but even more routine. Blank towards the street, a late alteration to the design to accommodate two trading floors. Between the Entrance Basin and the Western Dock, the CORONARIUM, begun in 1977 by *Hurden, Gill & Dent* as a chapel to commemorate the Queen's Silver Jubilee on the supposed site of the church of the Royal Foundation of St Katharine. Eight Doric columns, salvaged from the A Warehouse (on the site of the hotel), ring a glass-walled, domed rotunda, a lumpen reminiscence of a garden temple.

THE IVORY HOUSE, so-called, thrusts forward between the basins. 22 It is the only warehouse still standing, large and T-shaped on a T-shaped jetty which effectively divides the docks into their three basins. Only the N front of the W wing stands directly above the water. It was designed by *George Aitchison Sen.*, Hardwick's successor in 1827 as architect and clerk of works to the St Katharine Dock Co., and replaced a wooden two-storey export shed of 1828 in 1858–60. Converted to flats with business facilities and shops in 1972–4 by *Renton Howard Wood Associates*. The original incombustible construction has brick jack arches on wrought-iron beams, circular cast-iron columns and brick outer walls, and was perhaps inspired by Fairbairn's then-recent *On the Application of Cast and Wrought Iron to Building Purposes* (1854, revised edn 1857). Wrought-iron roof trusses. It has a plain S front with a big arched passageway through to the rear wing, which faces the N gateway with a pedimented three-bay end façade. On this N side also an Italianate tower. The lowest two of the five storeys are embraced within big arches, carried on stanchions and spanned by iron beams: the warehouse was largely open at ground level. Inserted beneath the beams, bowed shop windows. An original mezzanine of York stone slabs on wrought-iron beams and a similar S canopy have been renewed in reinforced concrete. The upper windows, originally of cast iron and uniform size, have also been altered; re-entrant balconies are cut into some of the openings. All the semicircular openings on top floor were originally blind. Beneath, the last of the 1828 VAULTS, brick groin-vaults on cast-iron columns.

The DOCK WALL runs along East Smithfield. Original vermiculated gatepiers; modern elephants in GRC. To the E, round the

N and E sides of the Eastern Dock an intensely developed wall of yellow brick flats, six storeys high with taller penthouses and many clichés typical of the date, 1995–7. The architects are *Renton Howard Wood Associates*, who, twenty years earlier (1975–7), were responsible for the public housing piled up in the SE corner, flats of a type made popular in the 1970s by the Marquess Estate, Islington. Of buff brick with slate-hung boxy upper storeys and multi-level access. They continue the 1930s LCC St Katharine's Estate, which extends to St Katharine's Way. In contrast, along the S quay right on the water's edge, a terrace of silly folksy cottages in weathered brick and weather-boarding by *APT Partnership*, 1982, apparently built in response to the DICKENS INN, another odd interloper, to which it is connected. The pub's present beguiling, weatherboarded and galleried exterior by *Renton Howard Wood Levin Partnership*, 1974–6, is a fantasy. The structure is genuinely old but never appeared in this guise. It is about one-third of the timber internal frame of an early warehouse that predated the docks; extended post-1978 in imitation. The warehouse dated from *c.* 1793–9 but had been remodelled by *Hardwick*. The brick exterior was demolished in 1974 and part of the frame moved on rollers from its original position 180 ft (55 metres) SW. Four storeys and steep-pitched queenpost roof; diagonal struts to the upper floors. The building had a complex early history, probably as a bean store. From the piazza (Marble Quay) in front of the inn, another effective glimpse of Tower Bridge.

TOWER WALK, the mongrel-Regency crescent of houses SW of the pub, confuses the historical picture further. Built in 1987 (architects *Watkins Gray International*) and inspired, according to the developers, by the terraces of Regent's Park, to which the Foundation of St Katharine moved in 1826. It has colonnades of hefty, warehouse proportions. Nearer the river, Devon House (*see* below); and back to the W at the entrance passage yet another incongruity, the ST KATHARINE'S YACHT CLUB, 1985 by the same architects; much timber and two belvedere turrets.

ST KATHARINE'S WAY starts here and follows the river behind new blocks of offices and flats and the few restored warehouses. First, DEVON HOUSE, part of the St Katharine Docks development; offices of 1987 by *Watkins Gray International*. Centrepiece of channelled rustication. U-shaped court to the rear with big Neo-Regency bows to the river. After this *Goddard Manton Partnership*'s PRESIDENT'S QUAY (No. 72, Royal Naval Reserve with flats above), built 1984–5 on South Devon Wharf. Like a warehouse, six storeys with full-height arched bays, curved balconies within the arch heads. To the river glazed bays resembling loading bays rise into glazed gables, attics and atrium roof. The same height but one storey less, the cranked front of MILLER'S WHARF, the former British and Foreign Wharves G warehouse of *c.* 1860–70, gently converted 1986–7 by *Terry Farrell & Partners*, though without its fixed iron windows and with a glazed atrium bursting through the roof. Then a completely modern intervention at No. 84, the small office block, SUMMIT, of 1984–5 by *Goddard Manton Partnership*, replacing a stuccoed C19 pub. Refreshing off-white metal cladding and sheer upper storeys of dark glass cantilevered from the steel frame. Simple forms: a cylindrical projecting stair-tower to the street, a curved office projection to the river and a barrel-vaulted penthouse. It stands alongside ALDERMAN'S STAIRS, where the water laps in a sinister way, even on the brightest day; at each end a gatepier topped by a spiked metal ball. On the far E side of No. 84, a passage to a broad riverside terrace on the long Carron and Continental Wharf, with a wonderful view of the s bank from Tower Bridge right round to Rotherhithe village (q.v.). Behind the river walk, the flats of TOWER BRIDGE WHARF, by *BUJ Architects* 1985–6, composed to suit the bend of the river but otherwise a messy ensemble with very distant warehouse echoes. The next perambulation starts due N of here at the former main entrance to the London Docks (*see* Perambulation 2a).

2. Wapping and the remains of the London Docks

The next three perambulations trace what remains of the old centre of Wapping, the warehouses along the river and the fragmentary survivals of the infilled London Docks (*see* also the London Docks above), as transformed by C20 development.

2a. The remains of the London Docks

This tour starts at the NW corner of the former LONDON DOCKS where EAST SMITHFIELD and Thomas More Street meet. Here the former MAIN ENTRANCE, set within longish stretches of dock wall, now opens into a prominent office development, THOMAS MORE SQUARE. Flanking the rebuilt gateway LONDON DOCK HOUSE, two blocks of simple Neoclassical dock offices by *Daniel Asher Alexander*, 1805, each of three pedimented bays by five, with round-headed windows on the ground floor and no other articulation. Until *c.* 1840 they served the Customs and Excise and consequently stood just outside the docks: then they were extended by two single-storey wings and the dock wall was brought round to enclose them. Restored and extended as offices by *Thomas Brent Associates*, 1986–8, following a scheme of *c.* 1975 by *Pollard Thomas Edwards* to reinstate the façades. Asher's offices introduce the first court-yard of Thomas More Square, designed by *Sheppard Robson* for Scandinavian developers Skanska, 1988–90. Beyond, two inter-linked courtyards of six mirror-clad blocks, rising from four and five storeys nearest the St Katharine Docks to twelve-plus storeys on the E. The lower blocks are minimal but the taller ones have slick cream metal cladding and greenhouse roofs capping full-height atria. At ground level grey striped granite and suspended curved metal trusses used as canopies. Along the s boundary, a nod to mixed development: a SAFEWAY store

and behind it, facing s to STOCKHOLM WAY, yellow brick flats
with glass bricks to stair projections and balconies. – SCULPTURE,
commissioned by the developers. First court: Angel Musician
by *Carl Milles*, one of Sweden's best-known sculptors. Delicate
bronze figure poised on one foot, like Gilbert's Eros; a cast
from the original which is in Stockholm. – Second court: Geese
Landing, by *David Norris*, an artist well known for his studies of
flocks of birds in flight; 1990, bronze. – Third court, outside
Safeway: To Meet Again, 1990, by *Michael Beck*; an abstracted
bronze encounter of two figures.

Where Thomas More Street meets WAPPING HIGH STREET,
some more dock walls, once of impressive height (up to 27 ft,
8 metres) but now truncated. They enclose the sw end of the
HERMITAGE BASIN, added to the London Dock by *Rennie* in
1811–21, on either side of the entrance lock. Two sets of
gatepiers with the stalactite rustication that Alexander used
throughout the London Dock. By the w gate a former red brick
Neo-Georgian IMPOUNDING STATION of 1913–14, the first of
a standard PLA type. The remains of the entrance, with fine
sandstone ashlar facings, can be seen on the riverside; the lock
was closed off in 1909. By the lock, a former hydraulic PUMP-
ING STATION of the London Dock Co., 1856 (derelict 1997).
This end of Wapping High Street was damaged in the Blitz. The
housing development planned in 1997 for HERMITAGE WHARF
by Berkeley Homes (adapted from a competition-winning mixed-
use scheme by *Andrew Cowan*) aims to incorporate a riverside
garden as a memorial to the civilian victims of the bombing.
Round the Basin itself, flats and houses by *Jestico & Whiles* for
Barratt, with standard elevations but quite a bold layout.

76 Hermitage Basin is the start of a narrow CANAL that, accompanied by a pedestrian route, runs through the former Western
Dock and transforms late C20 speculative development into
something distinctive and visually rewarding. This imaginative
infrastructure was designed by *Paddy Jackson Associates*, 1982–5,
and the canal excavated from the infilled dock against the s
edge of the dock basin, where *Rennie*'s original QUAY WALL,
built of yellow stock brick with a limestone rubbing band, has
been retained. Canal and path begin at the former Hermitage
INNER ENTRANCE LOCK, adapted as a subway to pass beneath
Vaughan Way. Fine ashlar, with recesses shaped to two leaves of
the cast-iron swing bridge, stolen in 1976. Within the former
dock there is a striking contrast between the high and solid quay
wall and the new, lower and stepped N quay, an effect reinforced
by good paving and planting and by the neat and consistently
gabled rows of houses down each side.

Raised on the s quay, now SPIRIT QUAY, houses by *Form Design
Group*, pre-1987, which stretch s to the contemporary Vaughan
Way. Big arched windows form the controlling motif towards
the canal. The broad paved piazza of Spirit Quay fills the former
passage to Wapping entrance basin. The original inner entrance
lock, flanked by massive, curved sandstone walls, has been
turned into an impressive landscape feature by a grand flight

of steps and, on axis, a bronze Neoclassical-style BUST of John Rennie, twice life-size, by *John Ravera*. Along the much lower N quay opposite Rennie's wall, terraces of gabled, yellow and red brick three-storey houses raised above a protective embankment of front gardens. The centre bay of each restrained elevation is enclosed by a tall arch. The houses here, and those facing the small courts behind, belong to THOMAS MORE 76 COURT, 1987–90 by *Boyer Design Group* for Heron Homes. Behind, in ASHER WAY, QUAY 430, by *John Brunton Partnership*, 1986, is an undulating wall of flats that builds up in sections from three to ten storeys, to screen the intimidating bulk of NEWS INTERNATIONAL'S monstrous printing works and offices (by *Wimpey* with *Grove Consultants*), which in the late 1970s replaced *Alexander*'s marvellous North Stacks (*see* the London Docks above). The so-called Fortress Wapping forms a frustratingly impenetrable barrier to free passage N–S through Wapping.

To the E, alongside the canal as it runs N, a neo-vernacular group of houses that might well have strayed here from rural Essex. By *Ronald Toomey & Partners*, 1983–5. Along the spine of WATERMAN WAY, where the E quay wall is left upstanding like an old town wall, elevations in rough ochre brick with much grey slate-hanging and rows of W gables with mock chimney finials face the canal. A white-rendered, more cottagey group marks the entrance to the inner part of the scheme, which links through to the brash and brightly coloured housing of EAST QUAY, by *Pinchin & Kellow c.* 1990, on the S quay of the former Tobacco Dock.

The main canal path, lined with shady horse chestnuts, runs along the N side of the narrow TOBACCO DOCK, which was built to link the old London Dock (subsequently known as the Western Dock) with the new Eastern Dock (*see* the London Docks above). It still has a section of tall brick and granite quay wall between granite-walled dock passages, widened *c.* 1912. A steel swing bridge of the date recalls the original cast-iron bridges. On the N side is Alexander's huge tobacco warehouse, which formed the E end of his great stacks of warehouses between the dock and Pennington Street (*see* the London Docks: Tobacco Dock). Along WAPPING LANE, its forbidding E wall doubled as the wall of the dock. Further N, where Wapping Lane meets The Highway, BABE RUTH'S bar, a bold, white, Modernist rendering of the corner pub by *Blair Eastwick Architecture*, 1995–6. On the N side of The Highway, and so just outside the Docklands area, a far more remarkable landmark – Hawksmoor's St George-in-the-East (*see* Churches).

PENNINGTON STREET runs W from in front of the Tobacco Dock centre to the main gate of Fortress Wapping (at No. 1), with, on the S side, the blank rear wall of the Pennington Street Sheds (*see* London Docks). Facing Fortress Wapping from No. 2, an office block by *Rick Mather* 1989–92, protectively 73 stepped back with a wall studded with projecting triangular windows, into a courtyard landscaped by *Georgie Wolton*.

THE HIGHWAY façade makes an exhilarating interlude for the motorist. Big projecting canopy pierced with holes, a 1930s Modernist feature (cf. e.g. Simpson's, Piccadilly). Below, a skin of narrow Danish bricks gradually peeled back to transform pilotis (E) into full-height columns (W); behind the pilotis, a wavy glass wall. Shooting through the cornice at the centre, an angled glass screen. Further W between Pennington Street and The Highway, TELFORD'S YARD is a bulky five-storey former wool warehouse of 1882, converted into flats c. 1985 by *CZWG*.

VAUGHAN WAY turns s a little further on, and takes traffic through the infilled dock, passing first the commercial development of the N part, then through some of the housing already discussed, and then over the entrance to Hermitage Basin. Beyond this, on the SW side, the bold group of the Hermitage Primary School (*see* Public Buildings) and to its s on HERMITAGE WALL (Nos. 20–40), a crisp group by *Austin-Smith Lord* (1988) that continues s into Hellings Street and encloses a courtyard. Yellow brick, engineering brick in geometric patterns, nautical balconies. The N façade is undulating, with a strip of attic windows, a top-floor corner drum, overhanging eaves and slim pilotis. Regular terraces of tiny Neo-Victorian houses, built by Tower Hamlets, and blocks of flats, inspired with varying degrees of faithfulness by the C19 warehouse, stretch from here down to Wapping High Street at Wapping Pier Head.

4 WAPPING PIER HEAD was originally the main entrance from the river into the London Dock (*see* the London Docks above). The ENTRANCE LOCK of 1805, in handsome gritstone ashlar still partly visible, was only 40 ft (12 metres) wide and 170 ft (52 metres) long: infilled and first made into a garden in the early 1960s, it is flanked by two handsome terraces of dock officials' houses. The houses are of 1811–13 by *Daniel Asher Alexander* and more subtle in design than the average speculative housing

16   of the date. Three-storeyed, except for the SW terrace rebuilt in four storeys of offices after the Blitz. Both end s in larger five-bay houses, with broad three-bay bows facing each other and suggesting a gateway to the river. This pair has Doric porches. Both s terraces have tall basements with rusticated heads to the windows and, on the ground floor, doors and windows in arched recesses. The other houses are narrow, of two and three bays. On the E side, No. 6 has a groin-vaulted entrance hall; top-lit stairs at Nos. 5–9. At the end of the E terrace (No. 5), a discreet extension facing the river ends in a triangular brick room and drum-like conservatory, geometrical planning in the manner of Botta or the late Stirling. Of 1982–3 by *Goddard Manton Partnership*, who converted the adjacent Oliver's Wharf (*see* Perambulation 3). No. 11, facing Wapping High Street, belongs with the group. All the houses of the W terrace were renovated as a single block of flats by a developer in 1971. The lower terraces N of Wapping High Street are reconstructions from 1981 by Tower Hamlets, except for Nos. 12–16; very unconvincing details. At this end, remains of the dock wall with stalactite gatepiers; modern continuation across the lock.

2b. The old centre of Wapping

The interesting part of Wapping High Street, still lined with warehouses, starts E of Wapping Pier Head (*see* Perambulation 3). There is almost nothing of pre-C19 Wapping along Wapping High Street except the old river stairs, but to the N a few fragments of the old village can be found, both E and W of Wapping Lane.

SCANDRETT STREET turns N off Wapping High Street a few yards E of the Pier Head. Here is clear evidence of the C18 village: the tower of St John (*see* Churches) and the former parish school, restored by *Dransfield Design*, 1994–5, as four houses, two in ST JOHN'S OLD SCHOOL, two more in its extension, THE LANTERN HOUSE. The school was founded *c.* 1695 and rebuilt, together with the church, in 1756–60. It is of two and a half storeys plus basement, and five bays. The central bay, very broad and pedimented within the attic, has a double doorcase and, in niches above it, *Coade* stone figures of a boy and a girl. One first-floor room is now lined with the panelling salvaged from the rest of the building. The S extension of *c.* 1840 is also of five bays. The three central first-floor windows are linked by arched stone heads and cornices. Two doorways with stone festoons on consoles. The attic, pierced with *œils de bœuf*, and square lantern are new, and make the whole composition look more C18. TENCH STREET continues the line of Scandrett Street N, lined on the W side by remains of the E wall of the London Dock and, behind it, an early C20 ship-maintenance shop turned into the John Orwell Sports Centre (*see* Public Buildings).

GREEN BANK runs E past St Patrick (*see* Churches). The WAPPING ESTATE (LCC, *c.* 1926) extends E along it in a narrow band, originally constrained by the dock wall, from Reardon Path behind Wapping High Street as far as Garnet Street; they follow Prusom Street and Cinnamon Street E of Wapping Lane. Small-scale and rather refined yellow brick tenements with early C19 overtones in the arches over the windows; the impression of height has been reduced by designing the top floor as a mansard with dormers. On the NE side of WATERSIDE GARDENS (transformed from a derelict site by *Cooper Macfarlane* for the LDDC, 1989), TOWER BUILDINGS face BREWHOUSE LANE. Built in 1864–5, they are important as the second major project of Alderman Sydney Waterlow's Improved Industrial Dwellings Co., founded 1863 (his first was Langbourne Buildings, Finsbury). Waterlow's buildings were better than most contemporary standard tenements: no courtyard, better ventilation, and access to individual flats via balconies. Architect unknown: Waterlow claimed not to need them. To the S, facing Wapping High Street, a second slightly later block.

Green Bank emerges on Wapping Lane (for the S part of which, *see* Perambulation 3). On the E side a little to the N is St Peter (*see* Churches) and, N of it in RAINE STREET, a length of the London Docks Eastern Dock wall and another fragment of the

old settlement – the former Raine's Foundation School (now
RAINE'S HOUSE, offices of the Academy of St Martin-in-the-
Fields). Built in 1719 as a charity school by Henry Raine, who
lived in Wapping 1679–1738, it has a Baroque façade of high
quality. Two storeys and a basement in yellow brick with
rubbed red brick dressings and finely carved stone details. Red
brick pilasters divide a narrow entrance bay from broader three-
window-wide flanking bays. Oddly shaped doorcase (rather in
Hawksmoor's or Archer's style), linked to a shaped stone plaque
forming the apron of the arched window above. Arched windows
repeated in the outer bays of the first floor, alternating with
niches, which have stone open pediments on Corinthian pilasters
within relieving arches. Two-storey wings with panelled attics,
the l. one the schoolmaster's house, the r. one a replacement
c. 1985 by the GLC. A bigger boarding school for girls (Raine's
Asylum), built to the N in 1736, has gone: it was very similar in
form but more modern in style. The whole school moved to
Stepney, first to Cannon Street Road in 1883, then to Arbour
Square in 1913. RAINE'S LODGE, E of the old school, is Queen
Anne style, post-1883 and heavily altered in 1996–7 by the
Borough of Tower Hamlets as flats for the elderly. To its E, on
the site of the boys' school built in 1820, a tall block of flats con-
verted from the remains of the ST GEORGE-IN-THE-EAST
WORKHOUSE. According to the datestone this block is of 1886
by *Wilson, Son & Aldwinckle*, architects, *Charles Cox*, builder.
The workhouse stood on the SW edge of the now-infilled Eastern
Dock (*see* Perambulation 2c).

2c. The site of the Eastern Dock, including Shadwell Basin, and Shadwell

The EASTERN DOCK, added to the original London Dock in
1824–8, lay E of Wapping Lane. It was infilled post-closure and
mostly built over with small houses. But further E, Shadwell
Basin, added from 1828, survives as a stretch of open water.

The canal is continued E of Wapping Lane just N of Raine Street
as a shallow pond. It ends at an informal park, planted with
trees and known optimistically as WAPPING WOOD. This covers
the E part of the former dock, left as open space in *Shepheard
Epstein & Hunter*'s masterplan for the area (*see* Wapping:
Introduction). To the s a friendly enclave of simple brown brick
houses and flats by those architects. Along the s edge of
Wapping Wood, the former quay wall has been incorporated as
the lowest part of the N wall of the flats. Along GARNET
STREET, the houses on the E side of WINE CLOSE shelter
behind the remains of the dock boundary wall, which the architects pierced with garden gateways. Similarly round the NE
corner of the dock, ventilation grilles to the Rum Vaults in the
faces of the quay walls behind RUM CLOSE, and the original
boundary wall along Garnet Street.

SHADWELL BASIN, the final extension E of the Eastern Dock (*see* the London Docks above), is reached via the remains of the Inner Entrance Lock of 1858, 60 ft (18 metres) wide and 350 ft (107 metres) long. The steel LIFTING BRIDGE of Scherzer rolling bascule type, 1930s by the PLA, was restored by the LDDC as a fixed bridge pre-1987. Cascade of ponds beneath. There is another such bridge over the outer entrance lock. The present basin is the New Shadwell Basin of 1854–8 by *J. M. Rendel*, its quay walls constructed with mass concrete piers and brick relieving vaults. Amalgamated on the S side, the OLD SHADWELL BASIN of 1828–32 by *H. R. Palmer*.

The HOUSING round three sides of the basin, scaled to its 77 quite modest size, is by *MacCormac, Jamieson, Prichard & Wright*, 1985–7. Theirs is an original design which acknowledges, though not slavishly, the forms of C19 dock buildings, for instance in the quayside colonnades. The terraces of flats are not single bulky blocks like warehouses, but clearly articulated into portal-like sections rising from Venetian openings of an arch flanked by two narrower sections on the ground floor to split gables at the top. Balconies between these slight projections. Galleried top-floor studios are incorporated in the uppermost flats, services cluster round the staircase cores. Smaller, similar houses at the NE corner. Some alterations during the design-and-build project have detracted in detail but only the scarlet and ultra-marine trim (in place of the London Dock colours of Venetian red and dark blue) really grates.

In the centre of the N side, a broad gravelled terrace, created by the LDDC to reveal the dock wall and a gateway to the churchyard of Shadwell parish church (St Paul, *see* Churches) high above the level of the basin. E of the basin less ambitious housing in PEARTREE LANE stands beneath the high dock wall that runs S of The Highway and down Glamis Road. In the NW corner, below the retaining wall of the churchyard, Nos. 1–3 ST PAUL'S TERRACE, a row of tiny, one-bay artisan cottages of *c*. 1820, originally accessible only via an alley from the dockside. E of Glamis Road is the pier head of the New Shadwell Basin. On the N side of the pier head, the SHADWELL PROJECT, a community sailing centre by *Bowerbank Brett & Lacy*, 1980s for LDDC; brick with a little leaded lookout. On the S side Thames Path turns into a big circular deck projecting for a prospect of the river; the path itself continues E to Limehouse (q.v.) and W to Wapping Wall, where Perambulation 3 starts.

The building of the New Basin encroached upon the hamlet of SHADWELL, reducing the population from 12,000 (1851) to about 9,000. This riverside hamlet within Stepney was virtually unknown before 1600, though the Romans guarded the easily accessible shore with a watchtower, probably part of a mid- to late C3 A.D. campaign against priacy, and Roman burials have been found on the site. It grew rapidly between 1630 and 1650, with the establishment of numerous industries and the building of terraces by the progressive speculator Thomas Neale. He established a chapel in 1656. By the time Shadwell became a separate parish in 1669, about 8,000 lived there, many of them mariners. Shadwell market house (also built by Neale, 1681–2) lay just E of the church. The centre, with its timber-framed houses, degenerated into notorious slums in the C19 and was swept away after the First World War for the Edward VII Memorial Park (*see* Public Buildings). The church, rebuilt in 1821, still stands on The Highway which divides the old riverside part from the later C19 spread (this lies outside the Docklands area).

3. Wapping Wall and Wapping High Street W to Wapping Pier Head

The last perambulation follows the river back to Wapping Pier Head, taking in the development of the riverside with C19 and C20 warehouses.

29 It starts at the E end of WAPPING WALL where WAPPING HYDRAULIC PUMPING STATION of 1889–93 marks the junction with Glamis Road. Tall, single-storey red brick buildings, the rear one housing the boilers, the front one the engines. Tall tower with miniature temple fronts rising above the parapet. Engineers' house adjoining. This was the last working station of the five built by the London Hydraulic Power Company to provide power for cranes, lifting bridges etc. throughout inner London, and is the best surviving (cf. Renforth Street, Rotherhithe). Closed in 1977, twenty years later it still awaits a new use. It was perhaps laid out by *E. B. Ellington*, engineer to the Hydraulic Engineering Company of Chester who supplied machinery, and was originally steam powered. An engine house with timber and iron Polonceau-truss roof: extension S in the 1920s, when the power was augmented by electricity; it became totally electric during the 1950s. Raw water was raised – originally from the Shadwell basin and later a well – filtered, and passed by gravity into the underground reservoir from where it was pumped into the mains. The tower housed two accumulators. Cast-iron tanks for clean and raw water form the roofs of the large rear block, centred on the boiler house. This was raised with a clerestory 1923–5, for larger boilers. Filter house in lean-to. Truncated square chimney. Original fittings of the inlet and filtration plants; and cast-iron hydraulic mains.

PROSPECT WHARF, opposite, is a huge development of flats by *Shepheard Epstein & Hunter*, 1985–7, that closes the view E down Wapping Wall with dumb brick walls rising sheer to a skyline of irregular gables. Similar façades face a big hollow landscaped court and a concave river front. Its neighbour is the famous inn, THE PROSPECT OF WHITBY, which may date from *c.* 1520 and have been named after a ship that moored here in the C18. It is still the narrow width of the C16 riverfront plots. C19 façade with very small-scale classical features – pedimented first-floor windows, tall attic with the name in bold letters and lion masks; informal and rambling at the back. The oldest obvious feature is some C18 panelling, probably not *in situ*. PELICAN WHARF at Nos. 58–60 makes a great contrast with the pub and with the massive riverside neighbours that continue E. Surprisingly fashion-conscious for *Shepheard Epstein & Hunter*, 1986–7. The yellow brick façade is split, deeply recessed and filled with semicircular green metal balconies, like a half-open atrium sheltered by a glass canopy high up. Simpler river façade with a half-hipped roof over recessed penthouse, curved balconies. Lightwells cut in on flanks. There is no river access here except for the narrow Pelican Stairs.

From here WAPPING WALL has the best stretch of large C19 riverside warehouses left on the Thames, in 1997 only part converted. Metropolitan, Great Jubilee and New Crane Wharves form a continuous wall between street and river. The street retains a crisp, industrial feel.

First the huge METROPOLITAN WHARF, utilized as small offices and workshops and still grittily industrial in 1997. At first the name (which appeared in 1865–6) referred to only Nos. 70–74, the largest single block; more was amalgamated later. From E to w: Warehouses N and O (Nos. 65–69) of 1898–1900, seven storeys and ten bays, modern-looking with their rolled-steel lintels though still with cast-iron windows. King James Stairs remains a broad passageway through the building. Warehouse A (No. 70) is perhaps the oldest warehouse along Wapping Wall, built *c.* 1862–3 by *William Cubitt & Co.* Originally four storeys, the top two floors probably added *c.* 1900. The six-storey Warehouses B and C (Nos. 72–74) were added 1864–5 and designed by *John Whichcord* the younger, as twin warehouses to extend Warehouse A. Here, as in A, a prominent modillion cornice on the street frontage, and deep, rendered name bands front and rear. Plain pediment with occuli on B and C and two magnificent forged-iron wall-cranes. On the riverside the ground floor is open, with cast-iron Doric columns and a riveted girder entablature. Inside, cross-section iron columns with console-shaped flanges to their caps and 'shoe' heads housing the timber beams. Warehouse D (No. 75) of 1898–9, was built by *Holland & Hannen*. Only three bays but seven storeys with giant arched niches and an occulus gable. Mid-C20 concrete-framed block opposite at the corner of Monza Street, being converted into flats in 1997 by *Nicholas Grimshaw & Partners*. Squeezed in between here and Shadwell Basin, some small-scale housing, quite pretty in PROSPECT PLACE, where the introverted group with an enjoyable central courtyard is by *Nigel Clarke*, *c.* 1989.

Metropolitan Wharf encroached 40 ft (12 metres) into the river, plus a C20 jetty, whereas the next block w perpetuates the post-medieval river wall-line. The newly named GREAT JUBILEE WHARF is now a single block of flats by *BUJ Architects*, 1996–7, unifying the façades of three former warehouses. The E half, previously Jubilee Wharf (Nos. 76–77) was mid C19, three-storeyed with a plain stucco entablature, now raised in line with its neighbours. Five bays plus one recessed to the street; loading bays with three forged-iron wall-cranes. Cruciform iron columns retained. The w half was previously Lusk's Wharf and Lower

Oliver's Wharf (Nos. 78–80), built in 1890 in four storeys and six bays with white brick window heads within giant arcades. Contemporary wrought-iron wall-cranes, with a large one to the river. Curious gablets for former transverse roofs have now been repeated across the E half, and a glass-and-timber attic storey added.

The warehouses of NEW CRANE WHARF have been transformed freely 1989–90 by *Conran Roche* (job architect *Stuart Mosscrop*) into shops and flats with new, plain grey metal steps and balconies and small-paned timber windows. Round the corner at the w end, the long paved yard, now NEW CRANE PLACE, makes a picturesque coda to Wapping High Street. s of the yard, a line of four riverside warehouses first built 1873, burnt out and reinstated in 1885; probably of both periods now. Six storeys, thirteen bays, corbelled brick cornice, white brick window heads. Its partner to Wapping Wall uses more blue brick with concrete lintels. By 1914, when the four-storey block across the E end (on the site of an ice depot) was also being rebuilt. At the NW corner a white-rendered, Neo-Modern section in place of a pub. New Crane Wharf is the only part executed of a plan by *Tom Hancock c.* 1980 for a new urban quarter along Wapping Wall, integrating workplaces and housing. A crescent of housing was planned opposite, to extend as far as the Hydraulic Power Station (*see* above), which Hancock intended to be a museum.

WAPPING HIGH STREET starts with new development. On the s side the underground station (at the end of the Thames Tunnel, *see* Rotherhithe). Most interesting of the otherwise dreary warehouse-style flats are ST HILDA'S WHARF, by *Shepheard Epstein & Hunter*, 1988–90, and TOWERSIDE, which belongs to a successful Wates development of 1985–7 designed by *Phippen Randall & Parkes*. It continues on the N side of Wapping High Street with PRUSOM'S ISLAND, No. 135, where a mid- to later C19 five-storey warehouse has been cheerfully converted with colourful loading doors and warehouse-style windows in timber, replacing cast-iron ones. Large two-storey wagon entrance. The new-build houses, round a formal courtyard, have blue under-eaves panels.

In WAPPING LANE, on the E side between Wapping Dock Street and Cinnamon Street, No. 105, CORBETT'S WHARF (now Gulliver's Wharf), early C19, quite a rare survival; three storeys with cellars and loading doors. Opposite, with a bowed corner to Brewhouse Lane, Nos. 78–80, a small later C19 warehouse, converted to a restaurant *c.*1984. Single storeyed on a semi-basement opened up through a well. Aisled, with cruciform columns carrying king-rod timber trusses on a riveted iron-trussed valley beam. For Wapping Lane beyond here *see* Perambulation 2b. The high tea and spice warehouses of GUN WHARVES now close in at the s end of the lane and on both sides of WAPPING HIGH STREET. They were all much changed by *Barratt East London* before 1987. The E, F, G and H Warehouses, which line the N side of Wapping High Street and turn the corner into Wapping Lane, were built in the 1930s, though the last two bays were added as late as 1937. Concrete stringcourses and window mullions, original loading bays. Ersatz balconies give the refurbishment away. The warehouses along 65 the river, less heavily altered, date from *c.* 1920. In style they are still C19 but with artificial-stone dressings and reinforced-concrete floors. The thirteen bays to the river are treated as a giant arcade through six storeys, with channelled rustication on the ground-floor piers. The pilasters, some coupled, have fluted neckings. The original windows were two-light and mullioned.

Then along the river come warehouses that date from the mid and later C19: first the tall warehouse of KING HENRY'S WHARF, with pilasters to the loading bays; then a smaller twin-gabled warehouse (No. 112), once a four mill, of 1840 by *Sidney Smirke*: its cast-iron columns have unusual tri-branched heads. Converted to flats *c.* 1996. It stands close to EXECUTION DOCK, once a sinister spot where pirates were hanged at low-water mark until 1830; Captain Kidd met such an end here in 1701. Then a pair of early C18 houses (Nos. 108–110), each of three storeys and three bays. These, probably chandlers' shops, are representative of riverside buildings before the spread of warehouses. Imaginative re-creation of shopfronts by *Russell Wright c.* 1988. Behind, the former workshop converted into the CAPTAIN KIDD pub in 1988–9 by *Goddard Manton Partnership*. ST JOHN'S WHARF was once part of a more extensive complex. The tall twin-gabled warehouse had its upper parts destroyed by fire and was reconstructed in 1984–6 round a glass-roofed central court by *Goddard Manton Partnership*. The unrestored (in 1997) OLD ABERDEEN WHARF (Nos. 94–96 w of the police station) has a unique monumental stucco river façade, like a West End theatre or club. It was built in 1843–4 as Sun Wharf for the Aberdeen Steam Navigation Co. Plinth with panelled pedestals carrying giant Tuscan columns to the centre five bays and end pilasters. The columns originally carried segmental pediments along the attic. Between the columns tall, blind arched panels visible from the wooden riverstairs next to the police station (*see* Public Buildings). The riverside wall of buildings is interrupted here first by the Waterside Gardens, then by the River Police boatyard.

In Waterside Gardens, a BANDSTAND built by the LDDC, reusing upside down some cruciform cast-iron columns salvaged from Hardwick's warehouses of 1828 at St Katharine Docks.

On the land side, between Reardon Path and Dundee Street, is THE SANCTUARY, a development in a strange mixture of styles left incomplete after the 1990 property crash. It incorporates remains of a six-storey granary of *c.* 1880 (No. 79), with white-brick window heads and a new, highly sculptural wall-crane in welded steel. Derelict three-storey rear wing with timber stanchions and queenpost roof, in 1997 the only such building on the N bank.

Then No. 73, DUNDEE COURT, an eight-bay, six-storey warehouse of the 1870s, converted to offices and flats. Imposing stucco cornice (renewed) and white-brick stringcourses which arch over the cast-iron-framed windows. Rusticated stone doorway to former office. Wrought-iron lattice-trussed gangways, the last in Wapping, span the street at two levels to the smaller No. 78 on the riverside, and its simpler neighbour, No. 80, both carefully converted.

Then ORIENT WHARF by *Shepheard Epstein & Hunter*, 1987–9, occupies the next prime site, an unusual advantage for social housing. Built for the Toynbee Housing Association, it is very plain, absolutely so to the street. To the river its irregular gabled façades round a court are well composed to frame a view of St John's tower. In a strip beyond, a survival of the narrow C16 plots, the TOWN OF RAMSGATE pub, perhaps older than it looks and once one of over three dozen pubs along the street. Alongside another early and rare survival, WAPPING OLD STAIRS, one of the few remaining passages down to the river. The perambulation ends with the most architecturally sophisti-
4   cated warehouse in the street, OLIVER'S WHARF (No. 64), the first warehouse in Wapping to be converted into flats; by *Goddard Manton*, 1970–2. It was designed as a tea warehouse in 1869–70 by *F. & H. Francis*. To the river an especially elaborate Venetian Gothic face, six storeys, the attic windows with paired arches in red brick, the four below tied together by giant segment-headed arches. Sandstone dressings. Cast-iron columns and timber beams inside.

DOCKLANDS:
SOUTH OF THE THAMES

Docklands south of the river lies within the London Borough of Southwark. In character it is rather different from Docklands north of the Thames and not only because of its much more limited extent. It includes the part of Docklands which, except for the St Katharine Docks at the opposite end of Tower Bridge, is most visited by tourists: they come to Shad Thames chiefly to visit the shops, museums and restaurants of this regenerated quarter of Bermondsey but also to see the street itself, a rare survival now of the gloomy canyons walled in with high warehouses that, until the 1970s, could also be found further E and in Wapping, N of the river. In Bermondsey the Docklands boundary, as drawn in 1981, takes in little more than the riverside, with its wharves and warehouses; further E it embraces the whole of the Surrey Docks peninsula, including the remains of the Surrey Commercial Docks which closed in 1970.

The Surrey Commercial Docks, the only significant trading docks established on the S bank, were themselves very different in character from the earliest docks, which had been designed for the secure unloading and storage of valuable goods like rum and sugar. The Surreys dealt mainly with timber and other bulky goods of relatively low value. They evolved gradually throughout the C19 from London's very first dock, the C17 Howland Great Wet Dock, into a network of ponds and basins, and lacked the tightly controlled layouts of the West India, London and St Katharine Docks, with their high enclosing walls and splendid, well-integrated dock architecture. As the dock basins fell idle – and before they were infilled in the 1970s – they returned in spirit to the original marshy landscape, becoming a haven for wildlife.

Unlike the tiny riverside hamlets N of the river, both Bermondsey and Rotherhithe originated as medieval parishes with substantial medieval churches, since rebuilt. Bermondsey grew up, not by the river, but along the road from London Bridge to Bermondsey Abbey and thence into Kent, so its centre and its parish church lie S of Docklands (*see London 2: South*). The monks of Bermondsey Abbey exploited the natural inlet of St Saviour's Dock for river-borne trade, while the rest of the riverside developed gradually until the C18, when there was a relaxation of trade restrictions outside the City of London. From the C19 the wharves dealt almost exclusively with spices and foodstuffs and Bermondsey became known as the larder of London. Industries on Rotherhithe's long shoreline were always more varied: shipbuilding and related trades, begun in the C16, remained important, alongside the establishment of huge granaries and flour mills and the opening of the docks.

Present-day Bermondsey and Rotherhithe still reflect their different histories. Most of the wharves and warehouses still survive in Bermondsey, though those that lie nearest to the City of London have been colonized since 1980 by commercial overspill from the N bank. E of Tower Bridge dense urban texture has resulted from the retention and conversion of warehouses to a mixture of uses, combined with some imaginative infill. Further E the riverside is gap-toothed, infilled with small-scale housing and open spaces, before the impressive scale of warehousing resumes round the church at Rotherhithe, where it forms the river edge to the close-knit and picturesque village centre. This, with its C18 parish church, tall C19 warehouses and interwar council housing, has a configuration very similar to the centre of Wapping, to which it is joined by the earliest tunnel under the Thames (opened in 1843).

The main part of the Surrey Docks peninsula is different from any other part of Docklands. As in Wapping, infilling and redevelopment with low-rise public housing started soon after dock closure in 1969–70: here the many acres of available space, combined with the mainly naturalistic landscape into which the housing has been interwoven, have given the whole area a relaxed, almost rural atmosphere and in its flattest, most watery parts it retains an intense flavour of the marsh it once was. Post-1981 speculative housing now dominates the riverside but has not entirely wiped out all evidence of Rotherhithe's long maritime history.

BERMONDSEY RIVERSIDE
London Borough of Southwark

The territory described below is only a sliver of Bermondsey. It takes in the remains of riverside industry but little of the housing built for the workers employed in it. One can only get a taste in the E part beyond Tower Bridge Road round Tooley Street and the interwar Dickens Estate of the phases of philanthropic housing built from the mid C19 to replace the terrible slums described by Dickens, Mayhew and Charles Kingsley. Pre-C19 relics of Bermondsey have almost vanished from the riverside, though names still give clues to the past, for example Bermondsey, probably signifying the Saxon Beormond's *ea* (island) amidst low-lying marsh. Evidence of Roman settlement in the form of potsherds and cremation burials has been found w of Wilson Grove and s of Bermondsey Wall East.

The royal manor of Bermondsey was granted in 1089 by William II to the monks of La Charité-sur-Loire, the mother house of Bermondsey Priory, which was founded in 1082 by Alwin Child. Rotherhithe (q.v.) was not mentioned in Domesday and presumably formed part of the royal manor of Bermondsey.

In the Middle Ages, the main roads from London Bridge veered SE towards Dover, SW to Croydon, and E (as the present Tooley Street) and then SE (as Bermondsey Street) to Bermondsey

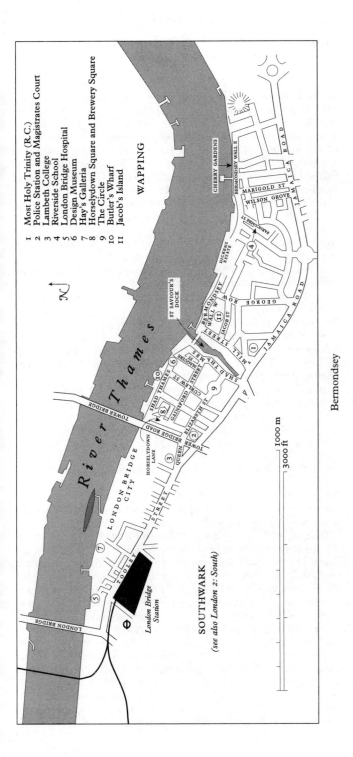

1 Most Holy Trinity (R.C.)
2 Police Station and Magistrates Court
3 Lambeth College
4 Riverside School
5 London Bridge Hospital
6 Design Museum
7 Hay's Galleria
8 Horselydown Square and Brewery Square
9 The Circle
10 Butler's Wharf
11 Jacob's Island

WAPPING

River Thames

TOWER BRIDGE

LONDON BRIDGE

ST SAVIOUR'S DOCK

CHERRY GARDENS

BERMONDSEY WALL E

MARIGOLD ST

WILSON GROVE

JAMAICA ROAD

AMAICA ROAD

GEORGE ROW

DICKENS ESTATE

BERMONDSEY WALL W

MILL STREET

JACOB ST

SHAD THAMES

GAINSFORD ST

CURLEW ST

ELIZABETH ST

QUEEN ELIZABETH ST

TOWER BRIDGE ROAD

HORSELYDOWN LANE

QUEEN STREET

TOOLEY STREET

LONDON BRIDGE CITY

London Bridge Station

SOUTHWARK
(see also London 2: South)

1000 m
3000 ft

Bermondsey

Abbey and the parish church of St Mary. The land just to the N was reclaimed by the monks for cultivation. E of the present Tower Bridge Road the riverside was at first owned by the Knights Templar, Shad Thames supposedly being a corruption of St John at Thames, and from the C15 by Magdalen College, Oxford. In Tooley Street lay a church dedicated to the Norwegian invader and saint, Olaf or Olave (rebuilt 1738–9 by *Flitcroft*, demolished 1928 for St Olaf House; see a turret from the tower s of Docklands in Tanner Street Recreation Ground), and three important clerical residences, or inns. Some remains of the medieval property have been found E of Hay's Galleria, including remains of the Abbot of Battle's Inn beneath the E range of the Galleria, traces of Edward II's 'Rosary' palace of the 1320s and of Sir John Fastolf's moated house of the 1440s.

Mid-C16 maps show the riverside built up as far E as where Tower Bridge now stands. Beyond lay Horselydown with, until the C17, an isolated beerhouse on the site of Sir John Falstolf's medieval property. Wharves grew up gradually in the C17 along this bank and round the mouth of the River Neckinger, once used as a port for Bermondsey Abbey and known as St Saviour's Dock at least as early as 1747. Beyond that, tenements and smarter houses were built from *c.* 1700, just below the old flood bank which was called Rotherhithe Wall and later Bermondsey Wall. Wharves encroached on the foreshore for timber yards, a few ship repairers and, to an increasing extent, granaries. The concentration of the grain trade probably originated with the several tidal corn mills in Bermondsey and Rotherhithe. These were driven at low tide by water penned up in the marshland drainage channels and they helped feed the City in the post-medieval period. Some worked until the early C19 when steam milling began to take over. The stagnant watercourses around Jacob's Island, E of Mill Street, received human and industrial waste from the leather-tanning district just inland. In the mid C19, until the main drainage was formed in the 1860s, this was one of the foulest areas of London. The terrible slums, described with horror by journalists and novelists alike, were mostly replaced by industrial premises though a few houses survived until after the Second World War.

The wharves and warehouses along the s bank just E of London Bridge flourished in the C18, when the intense congestion of the Legal Quays, across the river in the City, had forced a relaxation of their Elizabethan monopoly over imported goods. Despite the opening of the enclosed docks in the early C19, the further growth of these wharves was assured by rapidly increasing national prosperity and the freeing of trade. Imposing six-storey warehouses were built at Fenning's Wharf and Cotton's Wharf in the 1830s and around Hay's Dock in 1851–7; they continued w after the great Tooley Street fire of 1861. Warehouses of a similar or greater bulk were erected in the 1870s at Butler's Wharf in Shad Thames and extended progressively landward to create the densest warehouse group in London. There and elsewhere the landside blocks were connected by footbridges at high level across the narrow streets and cartyards. Further E, clustered round St Saviour's

Dock, were steam mills processing wheat flour, rice, split peas, pearl barley, pepper and spices, while granaries and mills at a slightly lower density lined the river as far as Rotherhithe. Bermondsey came to specialize in foodstuffs. Tea clippers once headed for Hay's Wharf, which also led in the provision of cold stores for imported butter, cheese and bacon. Founded by a brewer, Alexander Hay in 1651, the Hay's Wharf Company was still building new multi-storey warehouses in the 1930s and 40s. 23, 39

The district entered a precipitate decline in the later 1960s, centred on changes in goods handling methods. Extensive demo-litions soon created a semi-desert along Bermondsey Wall, where a decline had set in earlier, but even in the denser w areas much stood empty or in partial use until the 1980s property boom and beyond. By then, the rise of the conservation movement had secured some protection for the most distinctive buildings. Overspill of offices from the City first affected the warehouses by London Bridge, where there was in the 1970s strong resistance to the spread of office building along the whole s bank. Development, accelerated from the early 1980s, was halted abruptly by the reces-sion in the first half of the 1990s, and in 1997 a number of sites w of Tower Bridge are still to be restored or built over.

CHURCH AND PUBLIC BUILDINGS

MOST HOLY TRINITY (R.C.), Dockhead and Jamaica Road, just E of St Saviour's Dock. 1951–61. An eclectic design of pre-war type by *H. S. Goodhart-Rendel* †1959 which betrays his passion for Victorian architecture in the patterned brickwork of its exterior and the banded stonework within. Completed under the supervision of *H. Lewis Curtis*. It replaced, on a slightly different site, a Gothic church of 1834–5 designed by *J. J. Scoles*. 44

Bold westwork of late Arts and Crafts form, twin-towered and with a deep and high central arch. The crossing is taller than the nave but not quite a tower, and is marked by a trans-verse roof. Windows concentrated on the s side where they are full height to a stringcourse and arched above it, forming a clerestory. The plan is worked out on the basis of an equilateral triangle, symbolizing the Trinity, and the hexagon, hence the hexagonal form of the w towers and the triangular section of the nave. The exterior is all of brick including brick mullions and parapet. The polychrome brick patterns are inventive and in places create an almost three-dimensional illusion.

In contrast the interior is quiet. It is plastered, whitewashed, and in the sanctuary banded with stone of three types in gentle polychromy: white Portland, brownish York and blue Forest of Dean. Concrete construction, reinforced with delta metal and subtly modelled in the barrel vaults with diaphragm arches. The aisled nave is well lit from the tall windows with plain glass in varied patterns of leading, and the tall narrow crossing is even more brightly lit, throwing the E end into contrasting dimness. – PANELS of the Creation, Nativity and Pentecost on the E wall above the altar, and round the nave STATIONS OF THE CROSS: 46

all by *Attri Brown* in glazed terracotta, that favourite Victorian medium. High on the E wall an emblem of the Trinity. – Projecting from the N wall a curved stone PULPIT banded in grey and white. – CAPITAL on a bracket. C12? from Bermondsey Abbey, found during building work in Abbey Street.

The CONVENT OF MERCY 1839 by *Pugin* (according to the then Reverend Mother) adjoined the former church. It was destroyed in the war, along with the presbytery of 1845. A new PRESBYTERY was built adjacent to the new church to *Goodhart-Rendel*'s designs: completed post-1959 by *H. L. Curtis*.

POLICE STATION AND MAGISTRATES COURT, Tooley Street. By *J. D. Butler*, 1904, quite spectacular for its date, with a large Baroque centrepiece. Broken curved pediment and an outward-curving balcony, and a doorway with a curved hood on elongated brackets.

LAMBETH COLLEGE, Tooley Street branch. Former St Olave's and St Saviour's Grammar School, founded 1571. 1893–6 by *E. W. Mountford*, the architect of the Old Bailey, the Battersea Polytechnic, the Northampton Institute in Finsbury etc. A handsome Queen Anne building in red brick striped with white stone. The hall forms the centre of an H-plan: stoned-faced, with large windows between Ionic columns and a central segmental pediment. On the roof a tall cupola. The wings are articulated in broad bays also topped with segmental pediments: good sculpture on the street façade. The entrance is in an outer L formed by an additional, W wing. Curved portico, more Baroque than the rest of this part with its shaped gables, big chimneys and ogee-capped stair-tower.

RIVERSIDE SCHOOL, Farncombe Street. 1874 by *M. P. Manning* of *Gale & Manning*. An early and fine example of London School Board architecture on a cramped site that involved providing a ground-floor playground (quite common on inner-city sites); it opens to the front in an arcade. Charming Gothic details such as the decorative brickwork in the pointed window heads.

LONDON BRIDGE HOSPITAL, Tooley Street. *See* Perambulation 1, p. 239.

66 DESIGN MUSEUM, Shad Thames. The successor to The Boilerhouse, Sir Terence Conran's showcase for C20 design in the Victoria and Albert Museum. Housed in one of the properties cleverly redeveloped by *Conran Roche*, in 1989. This white Corbusian box, stepped down towards the river, was an unprepossessing 1950s warehouse. One floor has been taken out to make a double-height first-floor gallery and a new top floor, used for the Blueprint Café (extended on to the terrace in 1997). The ground floor, part-foyer, part-shop and bar, still looks utilitarian though with good views of the river from the wall of windows, and a stair which invites progression to the gallery. The gallery has an ad-hoc air despite neat display cases by *Stanton Williams*. So far (1997) a predictable choice of objects (Camden Market often has better) though exhibitions can be enlightening. – SCULPTURE on the broad piazza. By

Paolozzi for the Conran Foundation. On the theme of Invention and inspired by James Watt, Isaac Newton and Leonardo da Vinci, this lump of complex machine-like parts resolves itself into an elegant bronze head.

LONDON BRIDGE STATION. The earliest London railway station, opened 1836 as the terminus of the London and Greenwich line but rebuilt many times since. The main part of the station lies s of the area covered here (*see London 2: South*) but part of its substructure dominates the s side of Tooley Street at its w end. What one sees is mainly a widening of 1893–4, with the contemporary sliver of the SOUTH-EASTERN RAILWAY COMPANY OFFICES in red and yellow brick with terracotta diapering below the windows, and the earlier viaduct, *c.* 1862–4, extending westward. Carrying an extension of the station concourse across Joiner Street (out of Docklands), a remarkable Warren truss BRIDGE of 1850 by *P. W. Barlow*. Girders of cast-iron triangular frames bolted together, with bottom chords of pin-jointed wrought-iron tension bars, an instructive example of a composite structure from a fast-evolving period of bridge design. The brick and stucco arcade in the E abutment was the frontage of the London & Croydon railway station of 1839, i.e. one of the earliest fragments of railway architecture in London. Further s along Joiner Street, the rusticated segmental-arched entrance to the original arcade under the London & Greenwich station of 1836.

THAMES CROSSINGS

LONDON BRIDGE, Southwark. 1967–72 by *Mott, Hay & Anderson* with *Lord Holford* as architectural adviser. Prestressed-concrete cantilevers form three slender spans, founded on concrete piers dug deep in the clay. It is successor to a series of bridges spanning between the City of London and Southwark close to this point.

The first was almost certainly ROMAN. The river crossing lay close to the line later adopted by the medieval structure, i.e. immediately downstream of the modern bridge. A ferry may initially have been preferred but was apparently supplanted later by a timber construction. A timber structure found near Fish Street Hill in the City in 1981 may have been a bridge pier base built *c.* A.D. 85–90, although this is uncertain.

A crossing was restored by *c.* 1000, and twice replaced in the C11–C12. Timber gave way to stone in the next rebuilding, by the chaplain *Peter of Colechurch*, 1176–1209; this MEDIEVAL BRIDGE, much altered, lasted until the 1820s. It had nineteen arches, a drawbridge at the Southwark end, and a chapel built out over one of the central cutwaters. It was also famously lined with houses, first mentioned in 1201; they burnt down in 1633 and 1666 but were rebuilt. Only in 1758–62 did *George Dance* and *Sir Robert Taylor* clear them away and replace the two central arches with a single navigation span; they also built stone alcoves on each pier. Examples of the piers are preserved in Guy's Hospital, Southwark, and at Victoria Park, Hackney. From 1581 to 1828 some of the arches housed waterwheels which pumped drinking water from the Thames.

The C19 BRIDGE replaced the medieval one further E. It was built 1823–31 to *Rennie*'s design by his son, *(Sir) John Rennie*, and widened in 1903–4 by cantilevering the footways. Five quite ambitious elliptical masonry arches of up to 152 ft (46⅓ metres) span rested on slightly troublesome timber-piled foundations. On its demolition in 1968, the granite facework was sold and re-erected at Lake Havasu City, Arizona, USA. Remains of its screen walls may be seen by the Fishmongers' Hall (*see London 1: The City of London*) and a land span in Southwark (*see London 2: South*).

TOWER BRIDGE. 1886–94 (Act of 1885) by *Sir John Wolfe Barry*, engineer, and *Sir Horace Jones*, architect. The lowest bridge on the Thames, its form was governed by navigational requirements: the Pool of London was still intensively used by ships and barge trains, and a clear passage was stipulated of 200 ft (61 metres) width and 135 ft (41 metres) headroom, to remain unobstructed for two hours at each high tide. This was relaxed after the bridge was built. The towers contain passenger lifts and support two high-level footbridges, for use when the bascules were raised. At their bases, across the footways, disused turnstiles and decorative gates.

In the architect's words, the towers are 'steel skeletons clothed with stone'. The Gothic style was required by Parliament, in deference to the neighbouring Tower of London; the barren detailing was performed after Jones's death, however. The side spans are hung from curved lattice girders. The use of the suspension principle follows here from the provision of towers (needed for the high-level footbridge), rather than vice versa. The stiffening by trussing of the suspension members rather than the suspended deck is unusual. The bascules were electrified in 1976, but some of the magnificent hydraulic machinery by *Armstrong Mitchell & Co.* is preserved, including the tandem cross-compound steam pumping engines under the S approach viaduct. Yellow brick POWER HOUSE with boiler chimney and accumulator tower, stern and sentinel-like, alongside. On the W side, a discreet and sleek entrance and ticket office to the museum by *Michael Squire Associates*, 1992. Built against the bridge approach, the early C18-style BRIDGEMASTER'S HOUSE, dated 1906, by *Anthony Perks*, with the Tower Bridge workshops below and under the arches. The wrought-iron gate leads to steps down to them.

TOWER SUBWAY (Vine Lane, off Tooley Street, to Tower Hill). 1869 by *P. W. Barlow*; *J. H. Greathead*, contractor. This small tunnel, 6 ft 8 in. (2 metres) internal diameter and 1,340 ft (408 metres) long, introduced three features with a profound effect on later tunnelling under London, paving the way for the tube railway network: it was dug in the dry, deep in the London Clay; it was lined with cast-iron segments; and it used the cylindrical 'Greathead' shield, developed from patents by

Barlow. Originally conveying a cable-hauled tramcar, part of a system of underground transport envisaged by Barlow, it was soon converted to a foot tunnel, and closed in 1896 after Tower Bridge was opened. Now carrying water mains, it is marked by a small round entrance building of 1926 in Tower Hill.

PERAMBULATIONS

1. Bermondsey Riverside: London Bridge to Tower Bridge (London Bridge City)

London Bridge City, a single ribbon of development between the Thames and Tooley Street, was developed as a wave of office building, mainly for financial concerns, spread out from the City to colonize its fringes to the E and along the S bank opposite. The Company of the Proprietors of Hay's Wharf, who from the mid C19 owned much of the riverside along here, closed their wharves at a stroke in 1969. They began to redevelop their own property but were superseded as developers in 1980 by the St Martin's Property Corporation, for whom *Michael Twigg Brown & Partners* produced a masterplan in 1982. The first phase (1984–6) stretches from London Bridge E to Hay's Dock and was subject to a lengthy planning enquiry. It has involved redeveloping the Listed premises, all attractively close to London Bridge station, and slotting in new buildings. The second phase, which stretches from Battle Bridge Lane to Tower Bridge, has been delayed mainly because of the economic recession but partly because the site's sensitive position opposite the Tower of London engendered a huge planning battle. Here there are fewer riverside Listed buildings of note and so more scope for contemporary architects. First into the fray in 1988, with a mock-Gothic scheme parodying the Houses of Parliament and reminiscent of their PGG Plaza, Pittsburgh, were *John Burgee* with his former partner *Philip Johnson*, perhaps commissioned in an attempt to outdo the North Americans at Canary Wharf. Two other proposals were drawn up, one by *Twigg Brown* and another, for a 'Venice-on-Thames' in the Quinlan Terry scene-setting mode, by *John Simpson & Partners*. This wrapped five blocks of modern offices with standard large floor-plates in fancy dress, but was, surprisingly, recommended at the planning enquiry of 1989–90, only to be abandoned in favour of proposals of 1996 by *Chapman Taylor Partners* (originally brought in to work with Simpson) for cladding the blocks in late C20 commercial-modern style. In 1997 these have in turn been superseded by others designed by the North Americans *Swanke Hayden Connell*.

The first phase can be comprehended at a glance from London Bridge. It reveals a mixture of C19, pre-war, and new buildings with pastiche C19 elements. Apart from No. 1 London Bridge, the fronts of the modern blocks maintain the height of the pre-existing warehouses while building up behind to considerable height. Though the buildings have a certain uniformity from the front, they are all curiously shaped to fit into the wedge between street and river. Land access was originally from Tooley Street; the riverfront, used for the unloading from ships, was private. Now much is made of the riverside walk and the routes back and forth through the buildings, even underground, linking No. 1, Cotton's and Hay's Galleria (hints of North American cities such as Houston where office workers need never emerge into the overground world). On the river walk, corporate identity is reinforced by London Bridge City monogrammed on lamp standards.

By the bridge, No. 1 LONDON BRIDGE, by *John S. Bonnington Partnership*, completed 1986, a typical boom building of minimum-cost, high-quality offices, related to the river but not to the historic approach to London Bridge. Simple geometrical forms and smooth façades in pink polished granite with regular, flush windows of standard Postmodern type. The pentagonal w tower invites access from the bridge by a deep recess cut into eight storeys of its thirteen; a lower ten-storey hexagon mediates between this tower and the adjacent warehouses. The two are linked by a slope of glass roof that continues over the riverside walk. The form is derived from the 1967 Ford Foundation, New York, but has only a modest foyer not the true atrium of Roche & Dinkeloo's pioneering building. No. 1 replaced FENNING'S WHARF which, although externally c20, incorporated a timber-stanchion warehouse of 1836 by *George Allen*, Surveyor to the parish of St Olave, who published *Plans and Designs for the Future Approaches to the New London Bridge*, 1827–8.

39 ST OLAF HOUSE with its gleaming white Portland stone-clad façade holds the attention from the bridge – 'hard and cornery' as *H. Goodhart-Rendel* himself described it. 1929–31 for the Hay's Wharf Company, whose name in angular gilded metal lettering crowns the façade. Goodhart-Rendel fitted his building on to the constricted site of St Olave's Church, demolished by the company in 1928. His was both a practical and a decorative solution. It should be viewed both from the bridge and from Tooley Street. Projecting windows on the landward side catch all the available light, legs raise it to allow access for loading vehicles to the quay. On the front, best seen from the river, several more practical refinements: the windows, sawtooth so casements can open out of wind, are graduated upwards from tall to narrow bands, responding to the increase of natural light. Skylights to the drawing office. What catches the eye is the broad band of black granite framing boardroom and directors' common-room, which make two floors in the midst of three. It is patterned with bronze faience reliefs by *Frank Dobson*, representing the chain of distribution (see the chains, bales, crates etc.). The back to Tooley Street has smooth, Mendelsohnian stair-towers: on the curved w corner, a linear black-and-gold mosaic of St Olaf by *Colin Gill*. Only minor decoration, though the bronze glazing bars were originally gilded: above the doorway enamelled copper arms of chief families concerned with

the development of the Wharf. Exterior restored by the *Rolfe Judd Partnership*, 1982–3, the streamlined interior by *Bacon & Woodrow*. These are enriched with veneers and Birmabrite, an early form of stainless steel. There was originally specially designed furniture.

LONDON BRIDGE HOSPITAL, to the E of St Olaf House, was converted from Chamberlain's Wharf *c.* 1985 by *Llewelyn-Davies Weeks*. The warehouse just post-dates the great Tooley Street fire of 1861, which began in a warehouse at Cotton's Wharf (*see* below). Handsome Doric-pilastered river front, the name of the hospital lettered in old style along the broad stone cornice. Stone-faced ground floor given an arcade of segmental arches during the 1980s reconstruction. Interior all new with nine floors related to the sill heights (facsimile windows) and the centre opened up as an atrium with a glass barrel vault. The landward façade is original with minor alterations as on the river front. Walkways link it to Denmark House and Emblem House which face Tooley Street. DENMARK HOUSE (No. 15), 1908 by *S. D. Adshead* for the Bennett Steamship Company, faces W. It has a Scandinavian look and rich nautical reliefs, composed on the smooth red brick façades in the elegant manner Adshead used for the Duchy of Cornwall in Lambeth (*see London 2: South*). EMBLEM (formerly Colonial) HOUSE (Nos. 17–25) by *C. Stanley Peach* of *Peach & Reilly*, 1900–3, is less inventive, late C17 English style in brick and terracotta. Nos. 29–33 is Italianate, a former warehouse of *c.* 1840 (see the side loading bay). On the corner a neo-Rococo plaque by *S. H. Gardiner* commemorating the London fire chief, James Braidwood, who died in the Tooley Street fire of 1861. He had been a vociferous advocate of better fire protection in buildings.

The COTTON CENTRE lies further E, an office complex of 1982–6 by *Michael Twigg Brown & Partners*, named after Cotton's Wharf where the 1861 fire started. A public route leads from the deep rear courtyard through a glass-walled atrium with North American-style watery landscaping and giant, spirited Dancers cut out of painted metal by *Allen Jones*, 1987. The public space continues outside as a broad piazza linked to London Bridge City pier. The building is really an assembly of two huge side blocks and two lower ones to Tooley Street, the size disguised by the stepping-down of the front blocks to the median eaves height along the river. Modernist treatment, crude in detail with bands of tinted glazing and ugly yellow-tinged cladding. All that remains of Cotton's Wharf, originally part of the development that survives next door as part of Hay's Galleria, is the landward range, Nos. 47–49 Tooley Street.

HAY'S GALLERIA is a shopping arcade in C19 style, created by 23 *Michael Twigg Brown & Partners*, 1982–6, out of the long, narrow, mid-C19 Hay's Dock and the elegant warehouses that walled it in. Shoppers now walk on the pavement built to cover over the dock and beneath a steel and glass roof inserted to span between the warehouses. The dock is used as an underground carpark (the dock gates have gone), the warehouses as flats and offices above shops. The yellow brick warehouses, built in 1851–7 by *William Cubitt* for the Hay's Dock Co. to the designs of *William Snooke* and *Henry Stock* (Surveyor to the Board of St Olave's Parish) are in a style widely used in the riverside warehouses of the period, above and below London Bridge. They are of six storeys plus vaults and lofts, with windows and former loading doors within two tiers of giant arches, the lower ones now opened into ground-floor arcades. Upper arches and entablature of stucco. The W range was rebuilt in the same form after the Tooley Street fire; the river front is a facsimile of the 1980s, the original warehouses having been replaced by cold stores in 1947. The arched 'galleria' is C19 pastiche in steel, laid out like the warehouses on an odd, cranked plan following the line of the dock, a shape perhaps determined by the greater width of Beale's Wharf at the NE corner. Though Beale's Wharf was rebuilt in 1856 as part of the unified design, the details are slightly different, betraying different ownership. Too whimsical for these dignified buildings, the Heath Robinson-style ship by *David Kemp* (The Navigators). The warehouse interiors are mostly new. Only in the middle of the E side has the 1850s structure been retained: the cruciform cast-iron columns are visible on the ground floor, the timberwork is concealed. There were originally timber floors alternating with brick jack-arched floors on cast-iron columns throughout, a device to circumvent building regulations with regard to compartmentation against fire but actually ineffective. In the basement of the W range, a portion of chalk rubble wall from the medieval Abbot of Battle's Inn. In the S range, a double-height auction room over the entrance arch. Attached to this range and facing Tooley Street, matching warehouses by the same architects, 1887. Counter Street passed beneath it via archways. The ground-floor arches have been opened here as well, to form an arcade sheltering shops, almost Parisian in flavour.

The substructure of London Bridge station dominates the S side of Tooley Street at the W end (*see* Public Buildings). The S side of Tooley Street beyond the station belongs with the rest of Southwark (*see* London 2: South). This stretch was widened in 1877–84 and, despite extensive demolition along the N side in connection with London Bridge City Phase II, still has a few pubs, warehouses and houses that give hints of its former mixed character. (The most notable losses were Symon's Wharf, 1936–9 by *Hay's Wharf Estate Department*; the four-storey Anning and Chadwick warehouse, 1856, with unusual circular ground-floor windows, in Abbot's Lane; the DUKE OF CLARENCE (No. 69), classical and of the 1870s; Nos. 71–73 Tooley Street, a stationer's warehouse, 1870; and Nos. 75–81, an early Victorian wholesaler's warehouse, small Egyptian pediment.)

Further on a few buildings await incorporation into the new development, including Nos. 115–121, a jolly office building of the New Scotland Yard type by *Aston Webb*, the only remains of Boord's Gin Distillery, 1889–1901, which stretched to the river in an impressive complex of distillery and warehouses. The distillery was faced in a distinctive diaper brick pattern, repeated on the rebuilt rear elevation of the offices. Then more modest four-storey C19 warehouses and houses, the small, Gothic former Southwark FIRE STATION of 1879 at Nos. 139–141 and a good early to mid-C19 pub, THE ANTIGALLICIAN, at No. 155.

The former St Olave's and St Saviour's Grammar School (*see* Public Buildings) stands close to the junction with Tower Bridge Road. In the roadway opposite it, a STATUE by *Sydney March* of S.B. Bevington †1907 in mayoral robes as first mayor of Bermondsey, and a bronze BUST of Ernest Bevin M.P. †1951, who was a dockworkers' union official before he became Minister of Labour: 1955 by *E. Whitney-Smith*. At the important junction of Tooley Street and Tower Bridge Road, two large brash buildings that followed the building of the Tower Bridge approach and perhaps anticipated the creation of Tower Bridge Road in 1902. On the NW corner, the former London and County Bank (No. 201), 1900 by *William Campbell Jones* in his favoured free classical style, much more refined than the former Tower Bridge Hotel (NE) by *Latham A. Withall*, 1896–7, in coarse Jacobean style with no accents except the dome.

2. Bermondsey Riverside: Tower Bridge to Rotherhithe

The Bermondsey riverside from Tower Bridge to Rotherhithe preserves the dusted-down remains of its industrial past in combination with, in its W part, some of Docklands' best new buildings. Most of the wharves and warehouses lay abandoned throughout the 1970s, though a few with better road links continued longer. Perhaps following the lead of the pioneers of warehouse conversion in Wapping and Limehouse, a very young entrepreneur, Andrew Wadsworth, began developing this less accessible part of the riverside, then at an inconvenient distance from the City. He seems to have given those with larger purses and reputations the confidence to invest in the conservation and reconstruction needed here. Wadsworth's conversion of New Concordia Wharf 1 from 1981 was the first project of his Jacob's Island Company, which carried out ambitious plans for the extensive Courage brewery site by Tower Bridge, and conceived others for Jacob's Island further E on which Spillers' dogfood factory then stood. Another consortium, the Butler's Wharf Company, led by (Sir) Terence Conran, entered the game in 1984 with the conversion of the massive Butler's Wharf warehouse and a mixture of conver- 21 sion and new build along Shad Thames.

The different styles and generations of Wadsworth and Conran are clearly apparent, though the architectural and townscape quality of both developments is high and uses, though predominantly residential, are mixed: it set a standard that, alas, has been followed only patchily throughout the rest of Docklands. Neither scheme has been completed due to the economic recession in the early

1990s. Though Wadsworth's initial scheme for New Concordia
Wharf was a model of careful conservation, his new buildings by
61–3 *Julyan Wickham* and *CZWG* have a Postmodern verve – even
rebelliousness – and colour lacking from the monochrome, recti-
linear Modernist designs by *Conran Roche*, *Michael Hopkins* and
Allies & Morrison for the Butler's Wharf Company. Thank good-
ness neither company controlled the whole area, and what a pity
that CZWG's masterplan for the Jacob's Island was not carried
out.

All the converted warehouses are mid C19 and later. Though
wharves, timber yards and houses had already appeared
along the river by the mid C16, nothing pre-Victorian now
remains. C17 and C18 houses survived on Jacob's Island until
after the war. The oldest surviving warehouses are now
1 among those that line St Saviour's Dock, a 330 yd (300 metre)
long tidal inlet developed early from the mouth of the River
Neckinger and the granary of Coles Upper Wharf further w at
Wheat Wharf.

2a. From Tower Bridge and the Anchor Brewhouse s to Tooley Street

The perambulation starts from Tower Bridge (*see* Thames Crossings
above), with an excellent view of the warehouses facing the river
3, 66 from Shad Thames as far E as the Design Museum (q.v. Churches
and Public Buildings). It goes then from the Anchor Brewhouse s
across the rest of the brewery site to Tooley Street.

The ANCHOR BREWHOUSE, best seen from the bridge, can be
approached from there by the E steps. It is the remains of a
huge brewery that extended s to Gainsford Street, with more
buildings w of Horselydown Lane and stables to the SE. It
was founded in 1787 by John Courage who bought a small
brewhouse here on the w edge of Horselydown. Courage's
brewery closed in 1982. This riverside range was refurbished
by Andrew Wadsworth with *Pollard Thomas & Edwards* as
flats and offices; completed 1989. The river façade, reconstructed
in the central section which had been altered in the mid C20,
is now much as *Inskip & McKenzie* recast it in 1894–5, though
of necessity opened up with windows and so less industrial
looking. The w and central parts were further rebuilt after a
fire in 1891. In the lowest two storeys arcading. The centre
part was the fermentation block. Now its upper parts are
freely treated to replace mid-C20 brick and casements, which
in turn themselves replaced timber louvres. The w part was
the malt store, formerly mostly blind. It has an octagonal
cupola and projecting gabled hoist which are little altered.
The gabled New Brewhouse, which included steam boilers,
is very different in style and is of 1894–5. On the landward
side, small windows to five floors plus an inserted one. The
upper parts are treated as a giant arcade. Through the w
end (which may have extended further w), a passageway con-

tinues Horselydown Lane to HORSELYDOWN OLD STAIRS, modern but shown on Roque's map of 1746.

HORSELYDOWN SQUARE and Brewery Square, which lie E of 62 Horselydown Lane and S of Shad Thames, were developed on the rest of the brewery site and designed with zest by *Wickham & Associates*, 1983–90. Horselydown Square opens from the informal Tower Bridge Piazza with round Constructivist towers: from within the square the towers frame a dramatic view of Tower Bridge. The main square has an affluent Continental, perhaps German or Dutch, urbanity in its concentration of different uses (shops and offices, flats above), and its unabashed modern forms and colour (stock brick with panels of terracotta render, blue balconies and windowframes). Just off centre, a bronze fountain of Renaissance-cistern shape, surrounded by undersized nymphs disporting themselves: WATERFALL, 1991, commissioned by the architects from *Anthony Donaldson*. Between Horselydown Square and the narrow, more private BREWERY SQUARE, S, another gateway made by twin turrets of flats. Suitably tall and elongated sculpture, also by *Donaldson*, 1991, of a bronze female TORSO raised iconically on a tall cone of Cor-Ten steel slats. Brewery buildings have been incorporated here, a C19 one at the SW corner and a handsome Neo-Georgian interwar building, THE COOPERAGE, facing Gainsford Street. At the corner of Copper Row, the C19 ANCHOR TAP pub, tiny with a curved corner.

QUEEN ELIZABETH STREET, further S, has another interesting group of converted warehouses at its W end. These are of *c*. 1900, mostly in red and white brick with classical details, and on a large scale. On the S side, No. 20 (Albion House, now offices) and another on the corner of Boss Street (Nos. 2–16), attached to a later block that extends S to Tooley Street (Nos. 227–239); both the latter now flats by *Michael Ginn Associates*, 1994–7. On the N side, a similar block on the corner of Lafone St (now SSAFA Forces Help) with what looks like new detailing over the windows. On the E side of Lafone Street HORSELYDOWN MANSIONS (though much altered 1997) is one of the few groups of tenements of *c*. 1900 that survive amongst the warehouses, outliers of the extensive groups along the S side of Tooley Street. Further E, N side, the FLAG STORE, handsome premises of 1899 built by Black and Edgington, flag and tent manufacturers, imaginatively converted into offices with flats above by *Dransfield Design*, 1991–3. Two and a half storeys, the long, segment-headed windows arranged in distinct pairs. The double-height top-floor flats with mezzanines are lit by two rectangular lanterns linked by a platform with a flagpole. Central passage with salvaged iron gate leads to the CANVAS HOUSE, also part of Dransfield's conversion. Originally two warehouses, one of the 1840s, the other of *c*. 1890, where tents were stored.

THE CIRCLE by *CZWG*, 1987–9, breaks suddenly and brilliantly 63 blue into the narrow and slightly oppressive street further E. One of the most extravagant pieces of architectural whimsy in

London, rich enough to keep it from palling. Four big quadrant blocks, w of Curlew Street, their inner curves faced in ultramarine glazed bricks and linked in two pairs to make a circular piazza. The design plays on a circle in plan, in three dimensions (The Circle reads like a cylinder) and in elevation too, resulting in odd owl-like ears to each block. Down each façade, bold slashes of metal balconies carried on timber 'logs', or perhaps sections of mast; also diagonal the glazing bars on the bronze-coloured steel windows. The other façades take up the area's prevailing yellow brick. They have undulating parapets and bigger balconies. In the circular piazza JACOB, a bronze drayhorse by *Shirley Place*, 1987, a reminder of the early C19 stabling for brewery horses which this complex of 302 apartments, with eight office suites, a swimming pool, shops, a restaurant (unlet in 1997) and parking replaced. It belongs to the Jacob Island Co.'s redevelopment of the Courage brewery premises. The jokiness of the exterior is not carried into the flats, some of which have necessarily odd floor plans. Back now to the w end of Shad Thames.

2b. Shad Thames to Gainsford Street: the Butler's Wharf Estate w of Curlew Street

3 SHAD THAMES follows the river E from Tower Bridge until it is deflected s along the side of St Saviour's Dock. Until the early 1980s it was the most dramatic industrial street surviving in London, the atmosphere excitingly gloomy and still faintly perfumed with spices and tea. The redevelopment of the 1980s has done its best to exploit rather than destroy this flavour: despite smart shops and restaurants at the w end and conversions to flats further E, Shad Thames retains a claustrophobic, slightly melancholy air. The street still runs at first in a canyon between the massive blocks of the Butler's Wharf warehouses.

Butler's Wharf Ltd was the dominant force in this area for well over a century. The limited company was formed in 1872, at the time when the riverside range of their extensive block of warehouses was rebuilt. Under the vigorous management of Henry Lafone, the landward blocks were subsequently rebuilt in the 1880s and 90s, generally to six storeys high. This created the densest warehousing in London, extending 150 yards (140 metres) inland to Gainsford Street. These warehouses are all in the familiar and simple idiom of yellow stock brick, with window heads in paler brick, cast-iron window frames, and timber floors on cast-iron columns. Goods hoisted through the river front were carried landward on barrows across high gangways. During the C20 the company's ownership spread E towards St Saviour's Dock, acquiring many of the earlier irregular buildings that characterized the E part of Shad Thames and building (and rebuilding after the war) six-storey warehouses in brick and concrete. After the last ship had berthed in 1972, the company changed hands more than once, with redevelopment in prospect. What materialized in the 1980s boom, though incomplete, is more ambitious than the earliest redevelopment proposals.

The first part of BUTLER'S WHARF extends S to Gainsford Street, w of Curlew Street. The RIVERSIDE RANGE of warehouses on 21 the N side of Shad Thames is unified by a majestic façade to the river, best seen from Tower Bridge. It was restored to close to its original appearance in the conversion to flats by *Conran Roche* for Butler's Wharf Ltd. Before 1983 it had a more rackety appearance, due to the many alterations since the warehouses were built in 1871–4 to designs by *James Tolley & Daniel Dale*. The handsome symmetrical façade in the debased classical style common to many C19 warehouses fronts a block a full 480 ft (146 metres) long, originally constructed in sections of varying length. Twenty-eight unadorned bays stretch between two pavilions, one storey higher than the six-storey rest: the centre-piece is similar but narrower. Ends and centre are emphasized with rusticated quoins, stuccoed attics and entablatures (mostly renewed). The massive end entablatures, boldly lettered to be read from afar, had two storeys of lofts behind them from the beginning; they and the heightened pediments now conceal a new full attic storey, exposed along the rest of the roof. The windows are the original shape, the balconies new but discreet. On the ground floor towards the narrow jetty, an open colon-nade of cast-iron columns and brick piers carrying an iron-girder entablature: now glazed behind them for shops and restaurants. In the centre a two-storey wagonway with good cast-iron gates to Shad Thames. Double tiers of lattice metal footbridges span the street to carry the high-level barrow runs.

For conversion into flats the riverside block was given a new concrete structure, which replaced basement jack arches on cast-iron columns, later enclosed in polygonal concrete casings, and various combinations of timber and cast-iron columns on the upper floors; two blocks were entirely of timber posts and beams. Some of the timber elements probably came from previous warehouses on the site, and some posts have been employed inside the flats to give them those saleable warehouse features.

The CARDAMON BUILDING, 1884–92, is the modern name of 3 the later landward range of warehouses on the S side of Shad Thames. On an axis with the passageway through the riverside block of Butler's Wharf, a doorway (now to a passage) with an ornate stone surround including date 1891–2. Just to its w, in the part of the building dated 1884, the former company office, marked by square cast-iron columns between large windows with neat cast-iron mullions. The structure of this block had cast-iron columns and supporting timber floors and mainly steel joists. More similar landward warehouses to E and W of the Cardamon Building. To the w on the corner of Lafone Street a block of 1889, now called EAGLE WHARF, and to the E along Curlew Street, a retained four-storey façade awaiting develop-ment behind. Facing GAINSFORD STREET (s), another element of the Butler's Wharf scheme, an LSE STUDENT RESIDENCE by *Conran Roche*, completed 1989. A long façade in pale yellow brick like the warehouses, punctuated by four ranks of grey metal balconies. Pleasant, uncontroversial street architecture.

2c. Shad Thames E of Curlew Street

Beyond Curlew Street, the canyon of warehouses stops. The failure of the Butler's Wharf redevelopment due to the recession left an empty site, the former Coles Upper Wharf, on the riverfront until 1997 and put paid to ambitious plans of 1992 by *Conran Roche*, which would have extended an enjoyable mixed development as far as the Design Museum. SPICE QUAY, in the white, steel-framed manner of their Saffron Wharf (*see* below) was planned to stand here and to straddle Shad Thames with office, shopping and exhibition space. Now the site is to be filled with flats by *BUJ Architects*, who intend to convert the surviving landward building of Coles Upper Wharf (known as WHEAT WHARF) to flats as well. This was the largest granary in Bermondsey in the mid C19. Its four-storey N and E frontages date from 1903–4 and were designed to redress the severe tilt of the whole building, which is entirely timber-framed with five aisles of square posts and spreader caps carrying timber floors. The queenpost roof trusses are over 60 ft (18 metres) long, constructed as part of the loft and supported from below. Open timber staircases. The original rear wall has small windows and the remains of two lucams. Conran Roche wanted to move the whole structure 330 ft (100 metres) S for Spice Quay and link it with the Butler's Wharf Business Centre S in Gainsford Street via an amphitheatre-like open space and apartments. In 1997 it is to have a less dramatic fate as flats and a restaurant. Just behind the granary in MAGUIRE STREET, the glazed red brick and terracotta of the SHAD THAMES PUMPING STATION disrupts the quietly coloured surroundings. Built 1906–8 by the *LCC* for storm drainage and originally driven by gas engines.

Shad Thames now passes under the rear part of the Design Museum, then turns sharply S along the W side of St Saviour's Dock. E of the Design Museum at the mouth of the Dock, a plain but well-built warehouse of 1922, Butler's Wharf BUILDING 15, threatened with replacement in 1997. On the quay in front of the warehouse, as if carelessly abandoned, a rough lump of pink granite split open like a fruit to reveal seeds or perhaps a Greek anthemion: EXOTIC CARGO, 1995 by *Peter Randall-Page* for Conran Restaurants and the LDDC.

1 A magical FOOTBRIDGE, with a delicate web of stainless steel supported by a central stay, crosses the head of St Saviour's Dock at this point, and glimmers against the sombre walls of warehouses and the water. 1995 by *Whitby & Bird*, engineers, with *Nicholas Lacey & Partners* for the LDDC. The footbridge is the most exciting way to approach Jacob's Island (*see* Perambulation 3), but our perambulation continues along Shad Thames where the buildings show their backs to the W side of the street and their faces to the dock. At the N end of this stretch they belong to the Butler's Wharf development, and have the same combination of careful conservation and crisp modernism. Behind the Design Museum and in the same spirit, the CLOVE BUILDING (No. 9 Maguire Street), converted like

the museum from a post-war warehouse. *Allies & Morrison*, 1988–9, retained the concrete structure, exposing the mushroom columns inside, but created a lightwell and a new, part-open top floor. To Shad Thames the ground floor opens to shelter an undulating wall of shop windows. On the E side, next to the back of Building 15, CINNAMON WHARF, an early and totally transforming conversion to flats, completed 1987 by *Conran Roche*. Next a particularly successful group. On the W side, the former DAVID MELLOR BUILDING, No. 22, designed as workshops for the industrial designer by *Michael Hopkins & Partners* 1990–1. The form is a simple box, glazed both back and front, but the materials, exposed concrete and lead-wrapped side panels, are both tough and subtle. Clearly expressed top-floor flat. It replaced an earlier C19 granary, the landside warehouse of which remains on the W side at No. 15, to be converted to flats. Four storeys and four bays, gable end to the street, small granary windows with original shutters. Substantial wooden stop-chamfered stanchions, with particularly large, tapering spreader caps. The iron 'queen-rod' hanger in the roof trusses indicates a mid-C19 date. SAFFRON WHARF (No. 18) on an axis with Gainsford Street, was designed by *Conran Roche* at the same time as No. 22 but entirely as offices; alas in 1997 it too may become residential. It is crisper and more obvious than its neighbour, with a very simple framework clad in white stove-enamelled steel panels. Between the two a parking court giving a glimpse of the dock. On the corner of Gainsford Street, the CORIANDER BUILDING, an early C20 warehouse, divided by a new service core and courtyard garden.

Shad Thames S of Gainsford Street is characterized on the E side by the grain and pea and spice mills which surround St Saviour's Dock. They date mainly from the second half of the C19 but follow the narrow plots of earlier wharves. Many of them are boldly lettered in a traditional manner though some of the names have changed or wharves amalgamated. Almost all of them have been reconstructed internally though they originally had a wide variety of types of construction. Those to note are, first, a crude 1980s reproduction at JAVA WHARF of post-1894; then the former Crown Wharf (now part of Java Wharf), probably a recasing of c. 1840 and, if so, an important early survival before it was gutted. Distinguished by the arcaded recesses framing (enlarged) windows and loading doors, and by the C20 steel footbridge over the street. ST ANDREW'S WHARF 'A' (post-1857) and 'B' (perhaps of c. 1840) have also been gutted though B retains some of its granary character: gable ends front and rear with recessed giant arches. Though there are now small windows only in the loft floor, it still has an early to mid-C19 cast-iron footbridge linking the landside mills at No. 11. This complex was built, probably in the 1830s, as rice and oil mills, but when it closed in 1995, as the last working mill in Docklands, it was a spice mill (the Butler's Grinders). The street frontage of the complex is the BURMA(H) WAREHOUSE, probably the original 1830s rice mill. Five storeys, cast-iron window sills and wall tie plates. Timber floors on stout circular cast-iron columns, supplemented with timber stanchions when converted to a rice warehouse in the later C19. Hipped queen-post roof with loft. Water-tower for fire-fighting *c*. 1900. Behind, the former beam-engine house, two storeys, narrow, with an octagonal chimney: in 1857 this contained the largest steam engine of all the Bermondsey mills. Various C19 mill buildings behind contained remains of late C19 edge-runner spice milling equipment. The last, late C19 flourmills on the E side have been much altered, though ST GEORGE'S WHARF, *c*. 1870, has a distinctive toothed cornice and bands of blue brick linking the small, and originally even smaller, cast-iron windows; and JAMAICA (formerly No. 2) WHARF, dated 1883 and at the dockhead, still has a timber and slate hood over the loading doors.

3. St Saviour's Dock (E side) and Jacob's Island E to Rotherhithe

Where Tooley Street crosses the dockhead, a good view can be caught of the waterside fronts of the warehouses along the W side down to the sharp W bend of the dock. Their cantilevered metal enclosures reproduce the metal-clad hoods or lucams over the hoists of the former mill-warehouses. The buildings along the E side have their landward faces to Mill Street. The N block on the E side of Mill Street is still known as Jacob's Island. This area was first built over *c*. 1700 and evidence for that period survived until 1950 when a delightfully wealthy house dated 1706 with curved gables of C17 type and a shell hood was demolished. It stood at the N end of George Row and there was also a row of houses beyond the Island in East Lane. In the early C19 there were timber yards, superseded by mid-C19 warehousing. By then the C18 houses had deteriorated into some of the worst slums in London, decried by Dickens in *Oliver Twist* as embodying 'every imaginable sign of desolation and neglect'. Much of the W part was developed *c*. 1905 by Spillers as a factory for ships biscuits, later dog food. Almost all demolished in 1995, including an early reinforced-concrete structure on the *Hennebique* system. The architect *William T. Walker* was a friend of Hennebique's UK licensees.

MILL STREET starts N with modern warehouse-style infill. First of interest is LLOYD'S WHARF, with a late C19 biscuit-factory façade. Then UNITY WHARF, *c*. 1850, each face with a truncated gable and a forged-iron wall-crane above the loading doors. Mill Wharf has been incorporated in the major reconstruction for flats in 1987–9 by *Michael Squire Associates*, known as VOGAN'S MILL. Apart from the entrance block with cartway and cast-iron columns, only some of the outer walls remain of this late C19 pea and barley mill. The façade N of the entrance block is facsimile. A slender seventeen-storey tower, capped with a jaunty penthouse, shoots up from the warehouses – an exhilarating change of scale. It replaces and echoes the mill's concrete silo. Another new block, joining tower and warehouses, appears on the waterfront as a serene white structure with metal balconies.

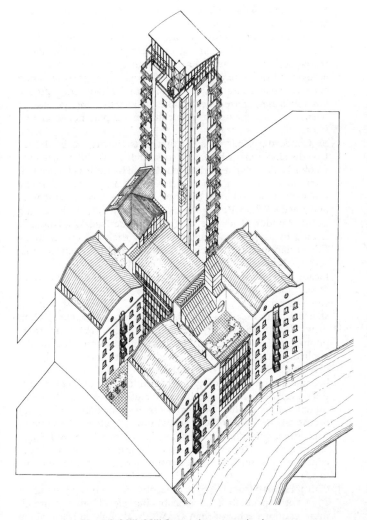

Vogan's Mill, Mill Street. Axonometric view

The six-storey ST SAVIOUR'S WHARF, c. 1860, is more in the general warehouse style, its nine-bay front with three loading doors. On the dock front wall-mounted lattice-jibbed cranes. Its cruciform cast-iron columns are visible on the ground floor.

NEW CONCORDIA WHARF is last on this side. Here in 1981–3 Andrew Wadsworth pioneered the conversion of South Bank warehouses to mixed use in an imaginative way sensitive to the fabric. This re-use predates that at Butler's Wharf and the Anchor Brewery. The architects were *Pollard Thomas & Edwards* in succession to *Nicholas Lacey & Partners*, the engineers *Alan Baxter & Associates*. The courtyard of buildings formed part of

St Saviour's Flour Mill, established in 1882 and reconstructed in 1894–8 after a series of fires. The mill itself is marked by its water-tower and chimney, truncated in 1979. A long façade to the dock: windows, their glazing bars imitating the original, paired and single in arched recesses and simple metal balconies across the loading bays. Electric wall-cranes of 1937, when grain gave way to tea. Timber jetty renewed to the traditional pattern. On top a new glazed penthouse. Inside, the original timber beams on cruciform cast-iron columns support new concrete floors.

New Concordia Wharf was the first phase of the Jacob's Island Co. development, which was to stretch E of Mill Street over Jacob's Island, with a bold mixed scheme by *CZWG* focused on a circular piazza (cf. The Circle). *CZWG*'s CHINA WHARF (1986–8), squeezed in on the riverside between New Concordia and Reed's Wharf B, has some of the bright colour and daring of the abandoned scheme. Each of the sides speaks a language related to its surroundings, not a new trick but one used by Edwardian architects such as Lutyens, and by Postmoderns, such as Venturi at the National Gallery. White concrete rear façade with deep flutes, intended to echo nearby grain silos (since gone); windows angled in the flutes for privacy and sun. The brick side wall responds to Reed's Wharf, with which it shares an entrance and lift. The river front, accessible through New Concordia Wharf, is the most memorable and most photographed. It is mostly of glass but is dominated by the applied centrepiece of red-painted concrete scallops – further play on CZWG's favourite circle motif. The lowest balcony has become a surreal boat disappearing under the building between thick black legs. More lighthearted nautical details in the communal spaces inside. Originally scissor-plan flats, with living rooms on the front, offices below; now all offices. The line of Mill Street continues under REED'S WHARF B to Mill Stairs and the river. The warehouse itself is mid C19 and only part converted in 1996. Timber floors and circular cast-iron columns inside.

JACOB'S ISLAND from the river to Jacob Street is being built up in 1997 with speculative housing by Berkeley Homes, a much more cautious scheme than CZWG's, though with a striking landmark block angled out on the riverfront at JACOB'S WHARF. Red brick, butterfly roof poised on a glazed penthouse, glazed angles with projecting balconies, adapted from a design by *Lifschutz Davidson*. S of Bermondsey Wall West, an open court, BUTLER'S SQUARE, of simpler, yellow brick flats with a glazed attic. Facing JACOB STREET, at its W end, the only remaining part of Spiller's factory of *c.* 1905 (*see* above), in origin probably the early to mid-C19 front block of the stave yard formerly on the site.

BERMONDSEY WALL WEST, pre-war, resembled Shad Thames, a dark narrow passage of warehouses spanned by gantries and gangways. Beyond Jacob's Island at No. 29, a WAREHOUSE of *c.* 1870, with distinctive small wooden granary windows, a central loading door and wagon entrance. On the river front a wall-mounted lattice-jibbed crane. Timber floors and posts inside. No. 33, near the corner of East Lane, is a converted grist mill of 1866, disused in 1997. It has a flat-topped hipped roof to which a curious pyramidal extension has been added, perhaps for a pneumatic grain-elevator. Full-height loading doors, hooded to the river. Wooden mullioned windows. Timber structure with spreader-capped posts; open timber staircases. Wooden chutes, with weighted-box braking. Near it the plain but prominent Nos. 38–40, early to mid C19, shown as a pub on the 1872 OS map.

Bermondsey Wall stops abruptly at the huge mostly interwar DICKENS ESTATE, where one gets for the first time some of the flavour of the way in which rehoused dockers lived in the shadow of their employment. The impression is especially vivid near the river close to the forbidding bulk of CHAMBER'S WHARF COLD STORES of the late 1930s, its decorative brick-work on the s side in polite acknowledgement of the neighbouring flats.

BERMONDSEY WALL EAST continues Bermondsey Wall beyond the estate. Once densely and evocatively packed with riverside warehouses, it is in 1997 only partly developed with small houses, open spaces and a few remaining converted industrial buildings. Near the w end just s in FARNCOMBE STREET, the DUFFIELD SLUICE, a puritanical two-storey wedge built on a former drainage outfall for the local Commissioners of Sewers. See the plaque inscribed: Sewers Surrey and Kent, Duffield Sluice, 1822. This, now offices, was one of the drainage outfalls, discharging by gravity at low tide, which provided the sole means of draining the area until the construction of interceptor sewers, approved by Parliament in 1858.

On the foreshore by Fountain Stairs, the remains of two GRIDIRONS for barge repairs, the earlier one incorporating C18 ship's timbers. Further along at CHERRY GARDENS, a broad riverside promenade and garden of cherry trees created 1988–9 for the LDDC by *RMJM*, who also designed the modest low-cost red brick terraces and blocks of flats behind. The SCULPTURE by *Diane Gorvin* is a sentimental depiction in bronze of Dr Alfred Salter (1873–1945), seated on a bench, greeting his daughter who stands by the river wall. His daughter died aged nine; the piece is entitled Dr Salter's Dream. Salter, local MP and Quaker, was instrumental in the creation of the oasis of garden-city cottages just to the s in EMBA STREET, WILSON GROVE etc. and E to MARIGOLD STREET. Built in reaction to the tenement tradition of the area, they are U-shaped pairs of 1928 by *Culpin & Bowers*, with arched entrances to doors in the brick ground floors; render above.

NAYLOR'S AND CORBETT'S WHARF, the latter named so on a big stone cornice to the river, stand beyond Cherry Gardens; windows in full-height segmental-topped recesses. Converted 1982; plain balconies added and the ground floor opened for parking, with the cast-iron columns exposed. Bermondsey ends imperceptibly where Bermondsey Wall East ends. Beyond lies Rotherhithe, including the site laid out with the medieval moated manor house, though the start of Rotherhithe Street (*see* Rotherhithe) has been reduced to a tiny stump cut off from the rest of the village by King's Stairs Gardens.

ROTHERHITHE AND SURREY DOCKS
London Borough of Southwark

Rotherhithe, though a separate ecclesiastical parish and manor in terms of landownership, was from the C12 part of Bermondsey, with which it was politically merged in 1900. Its w boundary was a mill stream on the line of West Lane, Bermondsey, its s one the border between Surrey and Kent at Deptford. The church lay close to the river, with the centre of the village mostly to the w of it. Most remarkable among its buildings was the moated manor house, which stood, with its own wharf, also close to the river. It was probably a royal property greatly enlarged in the mid C14 by Edward III; its remains can be seen near Cherry Garden Pier.

By the C16, Rotherhithe Street was a ribbon of intermittent development over 2 m. long, which reached almost to the border of Deptford, that is, to the Naval Victualling Yard and Royal Naval Dockyard, both founded there in 1513. The Pilgrim Fathers' *Mayflower* may have been moored at a wharf near St Mary Rotherhithe before it set sail in 1620; certainly its captain lived in the parish and was buried in the churchyard. At the end of the century Pepys still called Rotherhithe by its old name Redriffe, i.e. cattle haven. By then streets of smart houses, occupied by master mariners, such as Prince's (later Mayflower) Street, had been laid out w of the church; these were demolished in the mid 1960s.

Shipbuilding, first mentioned in the late C16, was well established by the C18, with much of the riverside devoted to ship and barge building, ship repair and breaking, and the landing of timber. By the 1660s there was a dry dock next to where the Howland Great Wet (later Greenland) Dock was dug in the marshes in 1696–9 to provide secure winter moorings for ocean-going vessels with repair facilities on hand. By the C18 dozens of shipyards were in operation: several of them were devoted to building and repairing warships for the Royal Navy. Best known was the still-surviving Nelson Dock, which in 1754 marked the s limit of Rotherhithe: the shipbuilder's Nelson House still gives an idea of local affluence. The C18 also saw the rebuilding and fitting of the medieval church and the expansion of the charity school. Horwood's map of 1799 shows a few streets to the s of the church as well, for example Adam Street obliterated in the C19 by the construction of the Rotherhithe Tunnel and Brunel Road. Ropewalks, sailmaking and other maritime industries grew up in the hinterland from the mid C18, as well as early mechanical engineering works, but much of the marshy land inside the bend of the river was until the C19 used for market gardens, osier beds and tidal millponds.

The first proposals for docks at Rotherhithe were made in 1796 by the surveyor *Charles Cracklow*, but development began in earnest in the first decade of the C19 with the conversion of the Greenland Dock into an import dock by the Commercial Dock Co., who began to build subsidiary docks. Others soon opened in competition mainly for grain and timber traffic. The various dock companies were amalgamated as Surrey Commercial Docks from 1865. Meanwhile, riverside granaries, overspilling from Bermondsey, crowded around St Mary Rotherhithe from the early C19 and others, of huge size, were later built on certain wharves downstream, for example Globe Wharf and Canada Wharf.

The creation of the docks, and the opening of the first Thames tunnel from Rotherhithe to Wapping in 1843, of course affected the surrounding area. The centre moved to Lower Road, SW of the Surrey Docks, where the main public buildings were built. These have all gone as has the workers' housing round the former dock fringes, replaced in the 1930s and post-war by Bermondsey Borough Council. Most of the C19 churches, including one by Butterfield of 1870–2, have also gone or been replaced. Several of the surviving C20 churches were founded in the C19 to serve the transient communities of Finnish, Norwegian and Swedish seamen, 45 associated with the docks' timber trade.

The Surrey Docks closed in 1969–70, the canal in 1971. This and the decline of riverborne trade threatened the future of the area. Following a Department of the Environment Report on the historic area in 1973 and another on historic buildings by Southwark Council, a few pioneers took on the conversion into workshops, theatres, flats etc. of the warehouses round St Mary. These modest but admirable efforts, and the half-hearted 1960s gentrification of the riverside round the Angel Inn, were overtaken in 1981 when the LDDC was established. Since then the parish has fallen into new patterns. The old village of Rotherhithe is an introverted 2 enclave of old and attractive buildings. Beyond it Rotherhithe Street, divested of its noisy industries, is lined with converted warehouses, speculative housing and refurbished council flats. To the SE the nucleus of the post-war, pre-LDDC community survives round Albion Street. The new inhabitants of the former Surrey Docks, encircled by a new main road parallel with Rotherhithe Street, look SW to yet another focus, Surrey Quays Shopping Centre. The influence of the Jubilee Line station at Canada Water, to be opened in 1998, may reinforce this southwards focus and link the area firmly to adjoining Deptford.

CHURCHES

ST MARY ROTHERHITHE, St Marychurch Street. The rebuilding 2 of the medieval church began in 1714–15 to designs by *John James*, but was still incomplete in 1737. The medieval W tower stood within the W end of the nave, where traces of its foundations survive in the vaults. A new C18 tower, W of the nave, was not built until 1747–8 by *Lancelot Dowbiggin*, architect of St Mary, Islington (*see London 4: North*), who probably based his designs

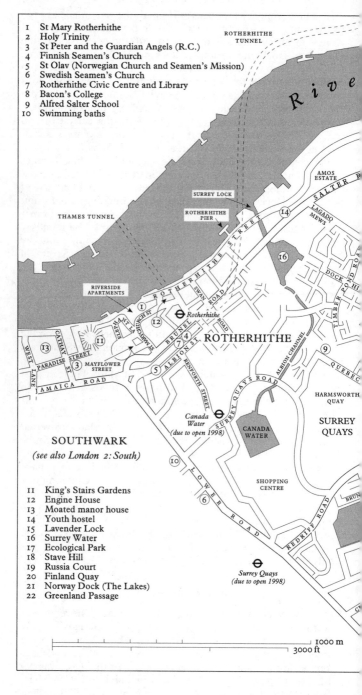

1   St Mary Rotherhithe
2   Holy Trinity
3   St Peter and the Guardian Angels (R.C.)
4   Finnish Seamen's Church
5   St Olav (Norwegian Church and Seamen's Mission)
6   Swedish Seamen's Church
7   Rotherhithe Civic Centre and Library
8   Bacon's College
9   Alfred Salter School
10 Swimming baths

ROTHERHITHE
TUNNEL

River

AMOS
ESTATE

SALTER R

LAGADO
MEWS

SURREY LOCK

ROTHERHITHE
PIER

14

16

DOCK POND
TIMBER POND

THAMES TUNNEL

SURREY
STREET

ROTHERHITHE
STREET

SWAN
ROAD

RIVERSIDE
APARTMENTS

1

Rotherhithe

12

ELEPHANT
LANE

SILWOOD
CHURCH ST

BRUNEL
ROAD

ALBION
ROAD

ROTHERHITHE

WEST
LANE

CATHAY
STREET

11

13

PARADISE
STREET

3

MAYFLOWER
STREET

4
7

ALBION ST

9

QUEBEC

ALBION CHANNEL

5

RENFORTH
STREET

JAMAICA   ROAD

Canada
Water
(due to open 1998)

SURREY QUAYS ROAD

CANADA
WATER

HARMSWORTH
QUAY

SURREY
QUAYS

SOUTHWARK
(see also London 2: South)

10

6

LOWER   ROAD

SHOPPING
CENTRE

REDRIFF ROAD

BRUN

11 King's Stairs Gardens
12 Engine House
13 Moated manor house
14 Youth hostel
15 Lavender Lock
16 Surrey Water
17 Ecological Park
18 Stave Hill
19 Russia Court
20 Finland Quay
21 Norway Dock (The Lakes)
22 Greenland Passage

Surrey Quays
(due to open 1998)

|_____| 1000 m
|_____| 3000 ft

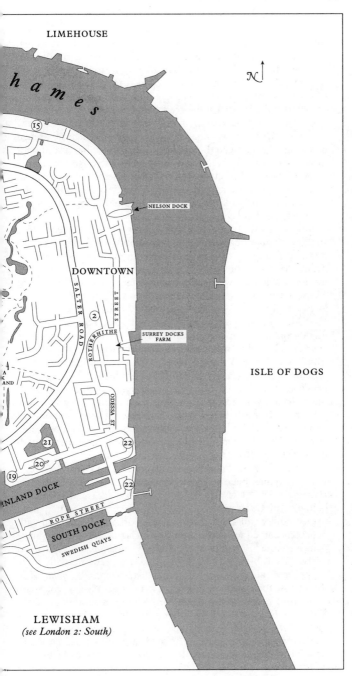

Rotherhithe and Surrey Docks

on existing ones by James. *Benjamin Glanville*, Surveyor of Works to the Naval Victualling Office and Inspector of Repairs to the Admiralty, was also consulted in 1746 but not, it seems, employed. C19 alterations included an extensive restoration between 1873 and 1889 by *Butterfield*, the main work being done in 1873–6. Tower underpinned in 1913 for the Rotherhithe MP and major landowner, Hubert William Carr-Gomm.

Yellow brick with rubbed red brick and stone trim round windows in two tiers, arched above, segmental headed below, except on the tower where all but one of the openings are arched including the rusticated doorways. The tower has prominent quoins, a low top balustrade and within it a stone steeple (rebuilt 1861). Thin circular top stage of detached Corinthian columns and an octagonal obelisk spire on a base pierced by ovals, more conventional than Dowbiggin's Islington steeple. Pedimented chancel, E.

Interior of three unequal bays, the E one narrower, and a shallow chancel recess. Tall Ionic columns carrying a shallow segmental vault over the nave, flat ceilings over the aisles. Simple plaster friezes as the only decoration, that round the nave quite modern. W gallery with a big Doric entablature (cf. James's St Mary, Twickenham) and good staircases with twisted balusters, in two flights before *Butterfield* removed the N and S galleries. He added the surprisingly tactful wrought-iron screens, possibly made from C18 ironwork, in the E bays to form a more spacious chancel. His redecoration scheme (mostly painted over) was far from subtle: Indian red walls and columns, banded in painted ornament; fictive ashlar and figurative paintings in the sanctuary; encaustic floor tiles. In the windows blocked by the addition of the N vestry, similar ashlar and figures on canvas, perhaps the remains of Butterfield's scheme. The original chancel is an odd shape, made almost apsidal by means of squinches, and probably also Butterfield's work. Segmental sanctuary arch enriched with freely handled Rococo plasterwork.

FURNISHINGS. There is still much fine C18 work, though some of it has been adapted for new purposes, probably by *Butterfield*. The REREDOS, made by *Joseph Wade* (*see* Monuments below) and *Gale*, carvers, and *John Dunnington*, joiner, lines the sanctuary walls and seems to be as original. Pilastered with delicately carved festoons etc. The panels, usually covered, have paintings after Reynolds by *Florence T. Nicholson*, 1925, instead of the C18 Tables. – COMMUNION RAILS, made up with a few of the original turned or twisted balusters made by *John Mell*, the rest of the balusters reused in CHANCEL PEWS, which are built from pieces of panelling, perhaps the dismantled gallery fronts. – Nave SEATING, apparently cut-down box pews. – LECTERNS. N aisle, made from big late C17 or C18 consoles. – Nave, made up from daintier C17–C18 carvings. – PULPIT. Plain, C18. – ORGAN CASE erected 1764. Splendid work in mahogany with Rococo carving including herald angels and musical instruments, related in style to that shown in Chippendale's *Director* (1762). Organ by *John Byfield II*, 1764–5. – Carved

ROYAL ARMS, now above vestry door. – Brass CHANDELIERS in the nave, C18 by *William Johnson* (centre) and *George Phillips* (side). – STAINED GLASS, E window. Assumption of the Virgin, C16 German, imported *c.* 1810.

MONUMENTS, N aisle. Peter Hills, one of the Elder Brothers of the Company of the Trinity, i.e. The Corporation of Trinity House at Deptford Strand, and two wives, 1614. Figurative brass. – Christopher Jones †1622, Master of the *Mayflower* which set sail from Rotherhithe to found the earliest permanent English colony in the New World. Commemorative plaque below the headstone of Anthony Wood †1625, carved with a sailing ship (moved from the churchyard). – Joseph Wade, S aisle, King's Carver in His Majesty's Yards at Deptford and Woolwich, †1743. Delicious quite asymmetrical Rococo cartouche, first-class workmanship.

In the CHURCHYARD, tree-ringed but mostly paved, TOMB CHEST of Prince Lee Boo †1784. Plain with good inscription, erected by the Honourable East India Company in memory of a prince of the Pelew Islands, whose father had treated the crew of the shipwrecked East Indiaman *Antelope* with great humanity in 1783. Lee Boo returned with the captain to Rotherhithe, only to die of smallpox. – MEMORIALS. Edward Blick, Rector, †1867, Gothic. – Captain Christopher Jones (*see* above). St Christopher, carved as a figurehead emerging from the prow of a tiny boat, by *Jamie Sargeant*, 1995.

HOLY TRINITY, Rotherhithe Street, Downtown. 1959–60 by *T. F. Ford.* Small, undistinguished. Domestic-looking gambrel roof with green pantiles. Gabled bays interpenetrate as semi-circular vaults and alternate with segmental ones in the passage aisles. – MURAL, E wall, by *H. Feibusch.* Crucifixion in his usual mildly Expressionist style. This church replaces Kempthorne's of 1837–8, destroyed in 1940, to which the former SCHOOL, 1836 (now hall) belonged. Prettier than the present church. Pedimented fronts to S and W. Windows in arched recesses.

ST PETER AND THE GUARDIAN ANGELS (R. C.), Paradise Street at the corner of King's Stairs Gardens. 1902 by *F. W. Tasker.* Simple, barn-like Gothic in yellow stock brick. At the W end a big round window, attached at the E a three-storey presbytery – an unusual solution. Thin hammerbeam roof. Chancel remodelled in Early Christian style in the 1930s, with marble walled platform and baldacchino. Stripped in style and progressive for the date: who was the architect?

FINNISH SEAMEN'S CHURCH, No. 33 Albion Street. Designed 45 in 1954 as a successor to the first Finnish Mission in London of 1887 by the half-Finnish *Cyril Sjöström (Mardall)* of *Yorke Rosenberg & Mardall*, built 1957–9. It faces the Civic Centre, also by YRM but later (*see* Public Buildings). It is a plain white box, containing the mixture of ecclesiastical and social functions common to seamen's missions, to which the detached, spindly, framed bell-tower gives an obvious churchiness. Contrast between the W front, where the division between church and auxiliary spaces, including a second-floor parson's flat, is clearly marked, and the well-windowed street front detailed with Portland stone and slate-hanging. Inside, free-flowing spaces, nicely done, with slate facing to the church part in Scandinavian taste. The first-floor refectory and the reading room below it both open into the church to make it larger when necessary. Basement sauna designed by Mardall's wife, *June Park*.

ST OLAV (Norwegian Church and Seamen's Mission), No. 1 St Olav's Square, Albion Street, by the entrance to the Rotherhithe Tunnel. 1925–7 by *John L. Seaton Dahl*, marrying English and Norwegian late C17 styles. At the front a pretty hipped-roofed block like a house, containing snooker room, library, reading room and flats above. In the centre of its façade, a tower with a copper spire topped by a Viking-ship weathervane; a minia-ture version of the tower of Oslo Cathedral. The church lies behind, wrapped round with ancillary rooms, those at the E end by *Genzler & Associates*, completed 1996. Dahl's interior is rest-ful, panelled in fine-quality timber. The reading room opens almost directly into the simple church, dominated by its arch-braced timber roof and STAINED GLASS by *Goddard & Gibbs*. – In the E extension, panels of stained glass from the second Norwegian church in London, the Ebenezer church of 1871 which stood further S in Rotherhithe. – REREDOS. The Epiphany. Oil painting by *Martinez*, C17, Spanish. – SCULPTURE. In entrance hall, St Olav, patron saint of Norway, †1030. Hand-some modern bronze, a copy of that outside Norway House, Trafalgar Square. By *Gustav Laerum*, 1921. – Vestibule. Bust of Rev. Ulrik Frederick Rosing, priest in London 1807–11, also by *Laerum*, 1929.

SWEDISH SEAMEN'S CHURCH, No. 120 Lower Road. A quiet, very Swedish design by *Elkington Smithers* and *Bengt Jörgen Jörgenson*, 1963–6, that repays attention. To the street a hostel in high-quality, typically Scandinavian materials of yellow brick, timber, slate and copper (for the folksy lettering) that continue in the cosy interior and the well-designed church fittings. Space flows back from the hostel foyer into the reading room and from there into the older chapel behind. Hostel and reading room replace predecessors of *c.* 1900. From the street the tall, hipped-roofed chapel is advertised by an open timber bell-tower with a slated spire and large copper weathercock.

PUBLIC BUILDINGS

ROTHERHITHE CIVIC CENTRE AND LIBRARY, Albion Street. By *Yorke, Rosenberg & Mardall*, 1970–5, for Southwark Borough Council. Designed to partner the same architects' earlier Finnish Seamen's Church, which it faces across a paved piazza. No obvious relationship except that the concrete banding echoes the storey heights of the seamen's rooms. An unadorned red brick cube, well finished but with an uninviting plainness. Inside, two equally plain assembly halls as well as the library. – In the piazza, a SCULPTURE, Bermondsey Boy by the musician, *Tommy Steele*; of celebrity value only.

SCHOOLS, Surrey Quays. Best of an uninspiring selection: BACON'S COLLEGE (a City Technology College), Timber Pond Road. Basic, low, yellow brick buildings bent round a forecourt. Low-pitched metal roofs and blue cladding panels at intervals. By *Newman Levinson*, 1992. ALFRED SALTER SCHOOL, Quebec Way. By *Southwark Borough Council*, 1995. Postmodern in yellow and red striped brickwork with a curved end wall. Former PETER HILLS SCHOOL (St Mary Rotherhithe Free School), *see* Perambulation 1.

SWIMMING BATHS (Seven Islands Centre), Lower Road and Gomm Road. 1963–5 by *W. S. A. Williams* of *Sir F. Snow & Partners* for Bermondsey Borough Council. Baths, assembly hall and cafeteria in a U round a sunbathing area. Transformed by a MURAL designed by *Rita Harris* for the LDDC, i.e. post-1981. Building-size wave painted by the *Bermondsey Artists' Group*.

KING'S STAIRS GARDENS, a post-1981 extension to the riverside of Southwark Park, on the S side of Jamaica Road, which was laid out in 1865–9 by *A. McKenzie* (*see London 2: South*).

SURREY DOCKS FARM. *See* Perambulation 2

SURREY DOCKS. *See* Perambulation 3

UNDERGROUND STATIONS. Jubilee Line extension (1993–8): CANADA WATER. 1993–7 by *Herron Associates*, completed by the Jubilee Line Extension's own staff for opening in 1998. A 72 ft (22 metre) deep cut-and-cover box in complex T-plan with multi-level concourses.

East London Line (1865–9): ROTHERHITHE. Of *c*. 1869. Single-storey booking hall in a style characteristic of this line. Across the railway cutting, massive cast-iron struts between tall arcaded retaining walls. By (*Sir*) *John Hawkshaw*, 1865–9. SURREY QUAYS. Substantial cast-iron columns and beams support the 1869 road bridge above the platforms; one of the few remaining substantial cast-iron beamed bridges left. New bus station by *Eva Jiricna*.

THAMES CROSSINGS

THAMES TUNNEL (Rotherhithe to Wapping), Bermondsey. The first tunnel to be built underwater through soft ground, it passes within a few feet of the bed of the Thames. The Cornish engineer *Robert Vazie*, who in 1805 began construction from Rotherhithe towards Limehouse, was replaced by *Richard Trevithick*, who completed 1,000 ft (300 metres) of timbered pilot tunnel by 1808, when an inundation and an adverse opinion from the engineer William Jessop caused the proprietors to abandon the project. In 1825 (Act of 1824) a revised scheme on a new line was begun by (*Sir*) *Marc Isambard Brunel*, using a tunnelling shield he had patented in 1818, the first of its kind. It had twelve rectangular cast-iron frames placed side by side and 22 ft (6¾ metres) high, supporting three working platforms and the roof. Tiers of boards supporting the earth face in front were strutted from the frames by screw jacks. Each board in turn was removed, excavated behind and screwed forward by 4½ in.

($11\frac{1}{2}$ cm), until a frame could be jacked forward by that amount and the process repeated. The brickwork of the permanent structure was constructed at the rear at the same slow rate. Without such a device, the project would have been impossible. There were five major inundations, counteracted by dumping clay on the river bed, and from 1828 to 1835 work was suspended for lack of finance. With government assistance and remarkable perseverance, the tunnel was opened in 1843.

The tunnel is 1,200 ft (366 metres) long. Two parallel vaults, of horseshoe section, 13 ft (4 metres) wide and 16 ft (5 metres) high, are joined by frequent cross-arches. They form the interior of a brick box. For the N half the tunnelling shield was exchanged for a new one in a remarkable mid-river operation. All brickwork was laid in Roman cement. The inner orders of the cross-arches rose from Greek Doric half-columns, while the main vaults had pilaster strips and impost bands, all formed in stucco upon a tiled and brickwork lining containing a concealed drainage system. These features were mostly removed when the tunnel was strengthened in 1996, but they were reproduced in a new lining of high-quality reinforced concrete. 100 ft (30 metres) at the S end, left in a largely unaltered state. Spiral ramps for carriages were never constructed and it remained a foot tunnel until it was converted in 1865–9 for the East London Railway. For *Brunel*'s engine house, *see* Perambulation 1.

ROTHERHITHE TUNNEL (Rotherhithe to Ratcliffe). By *Sir Maurice Fitzmaurice*, 1904–8, renovated 1979–81. 4,860 ft (1,480 metres) long, excluding the approach cuttings, with 3,740 ft (1,140 metres) of driven tunnel. Generally similar to the Blackwall Tunnel (*see* Isle of Dogs); 27 ft (8 metres) internal diameter. The flanged and bolted semicircular cast-iron entrance arches at the ends of the approach roads are the cutting edges of the two tunnelling shields, imaginatively re-erected as loading gauges. The lining segments are of different design. Portal also similar to those of Blackwall Tunnel. All in polished pink granite. Circular red brick drum of an AIR SHAFT in Rotherhithe Street, by the Surrey Lock (Perambulation 2); stone dressings, no roof. Contains a staircase down to the tunnel with four later ventilation fans at low level. Grilles in the openings incorporate the LCC monogram. In Brunel Road, another CONSTRUCTION SHAFT of 1900, with a conical roof.

PERAMBULATIONS

Rotherhithe Street follows the curve in the river, hugging the shore. It begins just w of King's Stairs Gardens with a tiny stump of Rotherhithe Street and the excavated site of the medieval royal manor house of Rotherhithe, and continues E of the gardens with the remains of the old village round the parish church (Perambulation 1). Further E a fringe of old houses and warehouses along the river, interspersed with interwar public estates and Docklands housing (Perambulation 2). The inner

ring, Salter Road, links small-scale, unintimidating recent public
housing schemes on the perimeter of the former Surrey Docks,
themselves redeveloped with a park, private housing and a commercial centre (Perambulations 3 and 4).

1. The Remains of the Village

The simple and friendly C18 parish church of St Mary in its 2
churchyard with old trees preserves the atmosphere of what was a
busy riverside village. Close around it stand the remains of the
warehouses and granaries. Some of these were converted very
early to studios and workshops for the arts, crafts and theatre
(earliest in the mid 1970s were Hope Sufferance Wharf, Grice's
Granary, and No. 99); others are still derelict in 1997. To the w,
C20 housing both public and private on the site of C18 streets and
riverside warehouses. Further w still, beyond King's Stairs
Gardens, the start of Rotherhithe Street. To the s the shopping
street, Albion Street, which really belonged to Surrey Docks and
now seems oddly isolated, psychologically divorced from the
village centre by Brunel Road and the Rotherhithe Tunnel cutting.
The street originally ran along the N boundary of Albion Dock,
opened in 1860.

We start E of the church in ROTHERHITHE STREET, where it
meets Tunnel Road, at *Sir Marc Isambard Brunel's* ENGINE
HOUSE. This contained the steam pump for his Thames
Tunnel of 1825–43 (*see* Thames Crossings). It is a small building, probably built in 1842 and altered several times. Restored
in 1979–80 when the raised brick-paved piazza was added.
Near-replica of the wrought-iron chimney reinstated 1993 on its
existing tapering brick base; slightly too narrow when compared
with contemporary engravings. Construction shaft of the tunnel,
adjoining, is of reinforced brickwork, sunk partly as a monolith
in 1825.

GRICE'S GRANARY, of *c.* 1796–1800, is one of the oldest granaries
left in Rotherhithe and lies between the Engine House and
church. It is divided inside by brick party walls into three units;
timber floors and posts, reinforced on the ground floor by
timber hanging knees. Kingpost roofs. Red brick s extension of
c. 1880. It is linked to the mid-C19 GRICE'S WHARF (No. 119),
converted to flats. This has timber storey-posts and a kingpost
roof.

The much higher wall of warehouses to the N between church
and river starts low with the single-storey TUNNEL WHARF
(Nos. 121–133), converted from a shell to a flat above workshops, 1974–82 by *Nicholas Lacey*: threatened with more intensive redevelopment (flats by *CZWG*) in 1997. Then the
MAYFLOWER INN (No. 117), alas only a picturesque pastiche
created by *H. G. Clinch* in 1958 after a war-time bomb had
removed the top floor of the apparently entirely C19 Spread
Eagle and Crown. It is dwarfed by the six- to seven-storey
THAMES TUNNEL MILLS (Nos. 111–115), a complex of 2

flour-mill buildings and warehouse, first built in the 1860s and converted quite early, 1980–3, by *Hunt Thompson Associates* to seventy housing association flats and a communal meeting room. New structure inside the walls replacing mostly timber floors on cast-iron columns; top-lit atrium flanked by balcony-access flats. The façade of the lower w block has window bays recessed between pilasters; octagonal NW chimney-stack over the boiler house. Roof-top cast-iron water tank for fire-fighting.

The street (w) then narrows dramatically to become a flagged passageway with gangways bridging between warehouses on either side. First at HOPE (SUFFERANCE) WHARF, an early C19 granary on the landside running a long way back beside a sett-paved courtyard. Three storeys and attics, timber storey-posts and hipped queenpost roof with eaves to the front. *Duffy Lange Giffone Worthington* carried out a pioneering conversion to managed workspace *c*. 1975, but in 1997 the building is due to become flats. The riverside building (No. 107) still has a hydraulic crane of 1930. Next is BOMBAY WHARF with an unusual late C19 Dutch gable to the river (No. 105), then EAST INDIA WHARF (Nos. 99–103), alias Archer's Wharf, with five-storey early to mid-C19 granaries. No. 103 is entirely timber inside, with a kingpost roof (large C20 wall-crane); No. 99 has cruciform cast-iron columns. Distinctive bracketed shelters to the loading doors above the street. The large, four-storey land-side warehouse (No. 124) is of the 1890s (note the white glazed bricks), yet with a fine timber frame of pitch pine, granary-style windows and tall queenpost roofs.

The narrow passage emerges into Docklands housing, built where some of the smartest streets of the village were once sited. The hinge between old and new is RIVERSIDE APARTMENTS (formerly Prince's Tower), by *Troughton McAslan*, executed 1986–90 by *Tim Brennan Architects*. A slender block of flats, eight storeys in all, with the smooth Modernism of the 1930s, as expressed, say, in the Bexhill Pavilion (Troughton McAslan worked on its restoration). Specially striking in the long view from the river. To the street a lantern-topped stair-tower and curved corner of windows, echoed by the tall bow lighting river-facing living rooms. Metal-mesh balconies also curved. White cladding on a proprietary steel frame, an updating of the experimental concrete and steel of early Modernism, and instead of smooth Crittall curves on the bow, simple window units making unsatisfactory faceted curves.

ELEPHANT LANE starts here. Riverside warehouses and small streets have been replaced by housing to forceful designs by *Corrigan Soundy & Kilaiditi*: a riverside four-storey terrace, blocks of flats like large villas and lower terraced houses further N. The designs, with strong buttresses of engineering brick and metal balconies, are crisp and logical. The aim was to look urban but the houses and the open, well-planted layout resemble Victorian suburbia and respond to the adjacent park rather than the intimate group to their E. Douglas Stephen was an adjudicator in this early LDDC competition, 1983, for housing for first-time buyers: the result has something of his forthright style. This scheme ends in MAYFLOWER STREET, dramatically changed from its origins as a smart gated street of sea-captains' residences in the 1720s. It is now lined with two parallel blocks of offices, crude reminiscences of warehouses, with saw-toothed gables and windows within tall arched panels. They are scaled to the main Lower Road roundabout.

To see the rest of the W part of the old Rotherhithe one has to cross King's Stairs Gardens to the W stump of ROTHERHITHE STREET. At No. 21 the ANGEL INN, established by 1682 but on a different, neighbouring site. In its present incarnation it is earlier C19, brick and stucco to the street, with a picturesque, partly weatherboarded front to the river.

The remains of a C14 MOATED MANOR HOUSE are a surprising find on the plot diagonally opposite the Angel Inn between Rotherhithe Street, Cathay Street and Paradise Street. They were first recorded in 1902 when a warehouse was built here: the warehouse was demolished in 1978 and the site partly excavated 1985–7. What can be seen are the footings and earth-works of a moated stone house with two courtyards. The inner court (N) of stone buildings, 100 ft by 66 ft (30 metres by 20 metres), was surrounded by a moat. There is evidence of a NW tower, four ground-floor N windows and internal division into small rooms. To the S lay an outer court of which few details have been found. The remains accord with accounts of an existing medieval house as expanded by Edward III from 1353. In 1361 it was described as having a hall, kitchen, chambers, a gatehouse and garden, and a wharf linked to the house by a bridge over the moat. From c. 1638 to 1663, this site was occupied by a pottery as part of Rotherhithe's delft manufacture.

PARADISE STREET leads back to the Gardens past No. 23, a plain three-storey, three-bay villa of stock brick of 1814, later used as a police station; nice ironwork lampholder, fret on doorcase; on the l. a four-bay addition, built for the Metropolitan Police in the 1850s by C. Reeves. Due E, beyond the Gardens, Cottle Way takes one to the church through the ST MARY'S ESTATE, simple brick council housing of 1954 by S. O. Hayes, Director of Housing and Architecture, Bermondsey District Council.

ST MARYCHURCH STREET skirts the S of the church and has the oldest village buildings. Facing the churchyard from the S side, the former PETER HILLS SCHOOL (St Mary Rotherhithe Free School), founded 1613, expanded 1739. The original school, rebuilt 1746, lay next to the church. This tall, narrow three-bay, three-storey red brick house with stone quoins must date from c. 1700, though the school moved into it only in 1795. Two pretty little figures of schoolchildren on first-floor consoles. Raised brick panels below the windows which have original sashes. Late C18 doorcase, delicate with a decorative fanlight. Attached to the W, the WATCH HOUSE, one of a matching pair of two parish buildings dated 1821 on the N boundary of St Mary's churchyard extension, created 1800. The FIRE ENGINE HOUSE, further W, has had its back removed to form a children's shelter. To the E, St Mary's RECTORY, planned in 1803 by *Martin Cole* and *David Laing*, author of the much-reprinted *Hints for Dwellings* ... (1800); enlarged 1869. Simple classical style, with the sort of pedimental gable made a cliché since the 1980s by speculative builders. Interwar council housing next, still modest, the Adams Gardens Estate by *H. Tansley*, Bermondsey Borough Architect, 1934.

Now back via Tunnel Road to Rotherhithe Street E of the Engine House. BRANDRAM'S COURT (Nos. 127–131) is a warehouse of *c.* 1870–80 converted to housing association flats 1984–8 by *Levitt Bernstein Associates*. The street wall is now just a screen to an internal courtyard. In the end wall the steel stanchions of the W part are revealed where balconies have been created. The E end had cast-iron columns. On the riverside, pilaster strips and the name Brandram's Wharf. Next E at No. 135 a rare mid-C19 barge-building and repair works, established 1789. Clerestory lighting and a queenpost truss roof. By it a riverside pocket park to mark the supposed position of the *Mayflower*'s mooring. Populist SCULPTURE by *Peter Mclean*, 1991, for the LDDC. A Pilgrim Father looks over the shoulder of a Bermondsey Lad reading about the United States in his *Sunbeam Weekly*.

The SWAN ROAD ESTATE, off the S side of the street, was built by the LCC in 1902–3 to rehouse those displaced by the construction of the Rotherhithe Tunnel. Red and yellow brick, quite handsomely classical: refurbished by *Robinson, Kenning & Gallagher c.* 1996 for the LDDC. New-build flats facing the river and two-storey red and yellow brick houses behind go with these. BRUNEL ROAD can be reached via Swan Road. On the corner the brick drum of an AIR SHAFT, 1908, for the Rotherhithe Tunnel which runs just below (*see* Thames Crossings). In the S half of SWAN ROAD, more of the Swan Estate, here terraces of four-in-a-block flats.

ALBION STREET runs parallel with Brunel Road and the tunnel. It, and not the historic enclave round the church, is the neighbourhood centre: here are churches, public buildings and shops in a casual low-rise mixture of dates and styles. Halfway along, facing each other across a paved piazza the Civic Centre and Finnish Seamen's Church (*see* Public Buildings; Churches). Also on the N side, a modest C19 house and next to it the cast-iron overthrow and lamp lighting the steps down into the start of the Rotherhithe Tunnel: at the W end of the street St Olav stands against its entrance portal.

RENFORTH STREET leads S. Near the beginning a PUMPING STATION, built by the London Hydraulic Power Co., 1902–3, to power warehouse machinery; closed 1977. Yellow, white and red brick. Tall arched windows to the pump room. Tapering octagonal chimney on a tall base. Accumulator tower with blind arcading. Lower N blocks supporting cast-iron settling tanks carried on a steel frame internally. Further S the CANADA ESTATE, which stands at the NW corner of Canada Water, created from the former Canada Dock (*see* Perambulation 3). By the *LCC Architect's Department*, 1962–4, with the tough concrete detailing typical of that time (cf. the same design on the Wyndham Estate, Camberwell, *London 2: South*). Low maisonettes and two lumpy twenty-one-storey towers with every fourth floor recessed (two-room flats between the three-room ones).

2. *Rotherhithe Street* E *from Rotherhithe Pier*

ROTHERHITHE PIER at Clarence Wharf was built in 1882 as a coal jetty for the South Metropolitan Gas Works, which had premises on the s side of Rotherhithe Street and in the Old Kent Road. Its remains preserve the original cast-iron columns: the four at the w end with bottle-shaped tops and ears (curved brackets) were added in 1908. (Similar but larger columns exist on the gasworks jetty of 1883 at North Greenwich.) New, lower deck, to improve public access, by *Clague*, for Bellway Homes, who developed the adjacent BRUNEL POINT housing, 1994–6.

ROTHERHITHE STREET, beyond the pier, continues to loop round the bend of the river with a mixture of Docklands housing, interwar public housing and a few remaining warehouses. It crosses the SURREY LOCK, the entrance to the Surrey Docks (now Surrey Water, *see* Perambulation 3). Opened in 1860 (engineers *George Bidder* and *Joseph Jennings*), it was largely infilled as a sluice channel in the 1980s. The curved dam incorporates the original iron lock gates, with the arms of the early C20 hydraulic gate rams reinstated. Cast-iron capstans and bollards, and a mid-C20 rolling-bascule lifting bridge. In the river a DOLPHIN, i.e. an anchor post for manoeuvring ships, of unusual cast-iron plate construction *c.* 1860. The original lock of 1807, which lay about 200 ft (60 metres) E, and Neoclassical-style Dock House were demolished *c.* 1939–45.

Just beyond, the most glamorous YOUTH HOSTEL in Britain fills the angle between Rotherhithe Street and Salter Road. By *Alan Turner & Associates* for the YHA, 1989–92. The w side, which makes such a distinctive statement with its clearly expressed elements of accommodation and circulation, was not designed for such exposure. The larger mixed-use group, Island Yard, of which it should have formed part was a casualty of the 1990s recession, and has been superseded by very ordinary housing.

After this bold gesture, Rotherhithe Street is dominated for about half a mile by the intervention since 1986 of the house-builders Barratt, who have not only built new homes but as *Barratt East London* have refurbished Southwark's rundown interwar council housing, in partnership with housing associations and Southwark Borough Council. The AMOS ESTATE is the most westerly of these refurbishments (architects *A & Q Partnership*). *Barratt*'s new housing, all whimsically historicist, shows that popular taste of the 1990s revels, as it ever did, in false grandeur. First PRINCE'S RIVERSIDE of *c.* 1996, scene-setting with neo-Edwardian domed and balconied towers on a prominent river bend. The blocks replace granaries and flank a former grain dock. They are dwarfed by GLOBE WHARF (No. 205), a massive, partly dismantled, brick grain warehouse of *c.* 1883, with giant blind arcades. At twenty bays wide and thirteen bays deep, it was one of the largest along the river. Converted to a rice mill in 1934; conversion to flats projected in 1996 by *PRP Architects*. Beyond it, the seemingly endless curving wall of Barratt's SOVEREIGN VIEW, 1992–5: 300 homes in a depressing adaptation of the Regency terrace to the demands of modern life. Thin pilastered and pedimented centrepieces stretched to bizarre proportions. Cramped courtyards and individual gardens between the street blocks and the lower ranges toward the river.

The remains of LAVENDER LOCK, built in 1863 to serve a timberpond that belonged to the Surrey Docks, can be seen along the riverfront here. LAVENDER POND, S of Rotherhithe Street, has been naturalized by the LDDC as a small wildlife pond at the head of the Ecological Park, which opens out to the S (*see* Perambulation 3). The former PUMPING STATION, a standard PLA design of 1928–9, converted *c.* 1981–2 and in 1997 used as the Rotherhithe Heritage Museum. Yellow brick with gauged arches. On Rotherhithe Street close to the lock, a FIRE STATION of 1903, the LCC's plainest.

Beyond Lavender Lock, more Barratt housing. PAGEANT STEPS, by *Lawrence & Wrightson*, 1994–5, repeats on a smaller scale and in more robust fashion the classical themes of Sovereign View. The terraced houses facing the river imitate stable blocks with cupolas. In contrast on the S side, ADMIRAL PLACE and HERON PLACE have irregular piled-up roofs, brashly modern in the style of much French New-Town housing. Also on this side, following a row of LCC cottages of 1920, ACORN WALK, a crescent of balcony-access flats with pantiled roofs looking inward to a courtyard. It is a survivor from the ACORN ESTATE, one of the most distinctively designed of the interwar estates round Surrey Docks, refurbished 1986–7 for Barratt (East London) etc. by *Swinhoe Measures Partnership*.

CANADA WHARF (No. 255) and COLUMBIA WHARF (part of the Holiday Inn, *see* below) lie opposite by the river, a pair of converted C19 granaries of great technological interest; this was the first site in England to store grain in bulk silos. Both buildings were originally known as Canada Wharf and both were designed for the Patent Ventilating Granary Co. by *James Edmeston*, better known for his Blackheath Conservatoire and Concert Hall (*see* Greenwich, *London 2: South*) of 1894. Columbia Wharf (furthest downstream) was the first silo in a British port, 1864–5. Four storeys, the walls strongly buttressed and with a variety of window shapes, including polychrome lozenges on the top floor: plain riverside façade, built pre-1914 when the building was converted to an ordinary warehouse. Inside it was originally divided into four compartments, each with fifty-six perforated iron boxes or shafts: each box could contain 50 tons of bulk grain. Cold air was blown through them to prevent spontaneous combustion. At the SE corner, two-storey offices, originally the engine house, with Moorish upper windows and shouldered arches below.

Canada Wharf (upstream) was a second silo, added in 1870–1. Five storeys, massively buttressed with linking stringcourses, it further develops the theme of polychromatic openings. Before its conversion to flats in 1995–6 by *Michael Ginn Associates*, the N flank wall was particularly distinctive, with lozenges and lancets: now drastically fenestrated with Moorish windows like those previously on the river front and with new twin lozenges in the formerly shallow parapet round the new attic floor. A tall hipped roof was lost in the Second World War: the new one contains obtrusive rooflights. Towards the road, conventional warehouses, rebuilt in the 1900s, have been converted to flats in the same scheme. Alongside, the BLACKSMITH'S ARMS, here in 1871 but also rebuilt with a half-timbered front.

Buildings belonging to the historic NELSON DOCK begin beyond the pub. Here are the only extant remains of Rotherhithe's once-thriving shipbuilding industry. The name is possibly from the 1820s but the yard was first mentioned in 1687. A dry dock may have been in use by 1707. Major warships and East Indiamen were built and rebuilt on this site, and, in the later C18, Randall & Brent's yards here and round the Greenland Dock entrance might be compared in importance with the Blackwall Yard (*see* Blackwall). In 1850 Thomas Bilbe took over the yard and built the mechanized slipway on the site of a neighbouring yard. Developing composite iron and timber construction, Bilbe was until 1866 a major builder of tea clippers, which for a while competed with iron and steam in the Far Eastern trade. The yard, by then used for ship repair, closed in 1968.

The WORKSHOPS of the 1860s, r. of the pub, have pedimented gables and recessed panels. The tall narrow bay with circular windows contained a forge. Next, the three-storey ENGINE HOUSE at the head of Thomas Bilbe's SLIPWAY, 1855–9, pedimented and with round-headed windows. The hydraulic machine, which hauled the ships up the patent slipway, is preserved, its cylinder probably re-cast *c.* 1900 but to an earlier pattern. The ships were carried in a cradle on iron rails. Unusually, to save space, the slipway is partly a dry dock with (renewed) mitre gates.

The original Nelson Dock site lies within the HOLIDAY INN complex. NELSON HOUSE (No. 265; now the hotel's business 12 centre) was built *c.* 1730–40. Its helps one visualize the comfortable life of a well-to-do C18 shipbuilder. From the rear of his mansion the proprietor had direct access to his shipyard; from his rooftop he could survey both yard and river. The house is of five bays and two-and-a-half storeys plus basement and has a broad octagonal, ogee-capped belvedere between its bank of chimneys. The façade is dominated by the handsome Baroque centrepiece of stone, now painted. It is tripartite both in width and height: on the ground floor a plain Doric doorway, on the first an Ionic Venetian window with blind balustrade, in the attic an oculus under an eyebrow of cornice flanked by volutes as a crowning feature. Otherwise the windows are rather small and slender; sills on consoles and narrow glazing bars, both of which look later. Delicate wrought-iron front gate. Doric columned doorcase to back, probably later, with basement entrance under curved steps. Inside, fluted Ionic columns on the Venetian window. Staircase with cut string and turned balusters. In the same vein as the centrepiece, main doorcases with shouldered architraves, modillion cornices and broken pediments, and marbled fireplaces with shouldered surrounds. On the landing, a freestanding Ionic column doubles as ceiling support and newel post. One first-floor panelled room.

The DRY DOCK, rebuilt as a pond between two blocks of the hotel, was previously of timber supplemented with mass concrete. It was lengthened towards the river and its entrance widened in 1880. The floating wrought-iron caisson, which closed the outer end, is now incorporated in the modern dam. Massive wrought-iron plates strengthened the landward end after the bursting of its embankment in 1881.

The HOTEL ROOMS have been adapted from what were intended before the 1990s recession as blocks of flats by the Danish developer ISLEF. Architects of the flats and the conversion the Danish *Kjaer & Richter* with *MacIntosh Haines & Kennedy*. Pale yellow Danish brick with rows of 45 degree gables, faceted oriels; roofline of penthouses with arched roofs and recessed balconies. Columbia Wharf, given an atrium, and the blocks of rooms were married together by *Price & Cullen* c. 1990 with a striking tensile-roofed steel structure by *Atelier One* bridging between the blocks and forming a reception area. The jetty, facing Canary Wharf Pier, is in the same spirit. Some of the original flats (completed 1989) survive at LAWRENCE WHARF, arranged round a long courtyard with tennis courts etc. over a carpark. Altogether an attractive scheme.

DOWNTOWN, with its refurbished interwar council estates, is a distinct neighbourhood, served by Holy Trinity Church (*see* Churches). At the far end of Rotherhithe Street where it turns sharply W, SURREY DOCKS FARM, South Wharf, occupies part of the site of another C18 shipyard. Within it a traditional series of herb, physick, vegetable and fruit gardens by *Lingard & Styles Landscape* for the LDDC, 1986–90. A SCULPTURED GROUP of bronze farmyard animals, by *Philip Bews*, *Diane Gorvin*, *Nathan David*, *Althea Wynne*, and *Marjan Wouda*, leads from the riverside at Barnards Wharf into the farm.

3. Surrey Quays: Surrey Water s to Surrey Quays station

Surrey Quays, with its wide semi-rural vistas and pockets of exhibitionist housing, is worlds away from the old Surrey Docks, which closed in 1969–70 and made way for this redevelopment. It seems even more distant from the workaday south London that surrounds it.

THE SURREY DOCKS had their origin in Britain's first major wet dock, the Howland Great Wet Dock, later renamed Greenland Dock (*see* Perambulation 4). This was established as early as 1699,

p. 272

and was used for the laying-up and fitting-out of vessels. The greater commercial docks began in 1801 when the Grand Surrey Canal Company obtained an Act for a barge canal to Mitcham and Vauxhall (aspirations towards Epsom and Kingston were defeated in Parliament). It never got further than Camberwell Road with a branch to Peckham. The canal's promoter *Ralph Dodd* was soon replaced as engineer by *John Rowe*. Rowe and his successor *Ralph Walker* built a two-armed dock and ship lock at the river end of the canal in 1804–7. An extension s along the line of the canal was dug in 1811–12 (later the Russia Dock). In 1855–60 a new entrance lock (*see* Perambulation 2, Surrey Lock) and basin were built and the Albion Dock added to the w. By 1809, working in parallel on the E side of the peninsula, the Commercial Dock Co. had converted the Greenland Dock and, by 1811, built the later-named Norway and Lady Docks. The South Dock, originally the Eastern Country Dock, was rebuilt in 1851–5. The two companies combined as the Surrey Commercial Dock Co. in 1865 and the docks were given names reflecting their association with the northern seas.

The areas described in this perambulation were devoted mainly to softwood timber, originally stored afloat in extensive ponds and later in long lines of large open-fronted sheds. The docks were deepened and the old timber revetments or sloping banks replaced during the later C19 by solid quay walls, some of them now incorporated in landscaping (Russia Dock, Albion Dock). The Canada Dock by *James McConnochie* was built 1874–6, with major arch-buttressed quay walls alongside the East London Railway by that company's engineer, *John Hawkshaw*.

The landscape, now suburban, even sub-rural in parts, was mostly created by the LDDC. Southwark Council, to whom the PLA sold the docks in 1969, filled most of them in throughout the 1970s and planned and built in 1978–81 Salter Road and the little groups of public housing clustered off it (housing design consultant *John Steadman*). A huge American-style Trade Mart was planned for the whole SW tract of land. The LDDC, who took over in 1981, have followed more closely the Dockland Joint Development Committee's ideas for a mixture of district centre, housing and industry, with retention of more of the docks. They have also created an exceptional ecological park moulded from the large quantities of silt re-excavated from the infilled docks prior to the preparation of consolidated housing sites. It runs the length of the area, insinuating itself between the pockets of housing. The post-1981 housing was built at the recommendation of *Conran Roche*, whose commissioned masterplan advised parcelling up the land into largely residential blocks. What remains as open water is the $22\frac{1}{2}$ acres of Greenland Dock, with the re-excavated Norway Dock and South Dock, the Surrey Basin, and the N half of the Canada Dock. From the Lavender and Russia Docks, narrow waterways have been created to make meandering, linking features the hard-edged Albion Channel through housing, and a sequence of informal ponds and streams through the Ecological Park.

The ECOLOGICAL PARK is what is modern about Surrey Quays. It begins by the river with the LAVENDER POND (*see* Perambulation 2). Its centrepiece is the stark conical earthwork of STAVE HILL, made 1985–9 from spoil from the infilled docks. It forms a belvedere in this flat landscape. At the top a bronze MAP of the Surrey Docks in 1896 by *Michael Rizzello* for the LDDC. The docks fill with rainwater. Further SW, in the RUSSIA DOCK WOODLAND, paths follow the remnants of the stone quaysides. The park wraps round to the naturalized SW edge of Canada Water, with its poignant SCULPTURE of bronze Deal Porters unloading timber, balanced on an oak construction reminiscent of ship and quayside. By *Philip Bews* for the LDDC. Would that the park could have been carried all round the dock to a congenial and less predictable setting for shopping. *R. P. S. Clouston* designed the infrastructure, including the transformation of Surrey Basin and Canada Dock into Surrey Water and Canada Water, the new linking channel, footpath and cycle track, the roadside planting, ecology park and Stave Hill, though the details of Canada Water are by *Gibberd Landscape Design*.

SALTER ROAD, created in 1978–81 to take the through traffic, makes a loop parallel with Rotherhithe Street further inland. Formed from the vestigial road that ran partway round the perimeter of the Surrey Docks, it now links with other existing main roads to encircle the area. Off Salter Road open small groups of low-rise, suburban housing and associated schools built for local people by Southwark Borough Council from the 1970s; mostly architecturally undistinguished but friendly and apparently popular. The pockets of housing extend informally into the Ecological Park within the loop of the road. W of this park lies the weird variety of Docklands housing that flanks the Albion Channel.

SURREY WATER is the best place to start looking at the post-1981 developments. It was created from the former Surrey Basin, and is now a lake little bigger than a large village pond. Despite its stone quays, it has been given something of the character of an Essex village by trees and the neo-vernacular housing of 1987 on its E, most easily accessible from Salter Road, via LAGADO MEWS. The houses are two to three storeys, brown brick with tall weatherboarded upper storeys, coloured mauve and pink. DOCK HILL AVENUE, laid out as part of the landscaping of the park, makes a strong axial connection between Surrey Water and the conical Stave Hill. From the end of it one can venture into the park before heading W to the start of the Albion Channel.

The ALBION CHANNEL starts with an elaborate timber footbridge, serving as a gateway as well as a bridge. The channel is more an artificial rill than a canal, cut into a broad paved pathway. It starts by picturesquely winding, but straightens (which better fits its artificial character) further S. New roads cross it via ersatz canal bridges. Plenty of trees and a strange, peaceful atmosphere, not rural, nor even suburban. The showy groups of houses and flats that line the channel contribute to its unique atmosphere. On the E, the first of several schemes featuring free-standing or corner towers: by the *Form Design Group*, 1988. These, in yellow brick with pyramidal roofs, are the least sophisticated. On the W, surprising octagonal freestanding towers, with green pantiled roofs, form centrepieces for crescents of red brick houses with crude details including prominent white eaves, a composition apparently inspired by WOLFE CRESCENT 85 opposite (E). This design-and-build scheme by *CZWG*, 1988–93, has panache, though the bold mixture of features is hard to digest. By the channel, octagonal four-storey yellow brick blocks of flats, their staircases topped by neo-Edwardian copper domes: matching in *fin-de-siècle* character are the wavy parapets, bold panelled doors and triangular iron balconies. Behind the octagons runs a long curve of red brick houses, their wide-arched entrances frilled with a wavy concrete margin. No gentility about the utilitarian garage doors on the polygonal blocks or the staggered strips of windows round the crescent.

Beyond Wolfe Crescent to the S and E is the commercial area. To the E the massive Associated Newspapers printing works of 1986 by *Watkins Gray International* at HARMSWORTH QUAY dominates the Mulberry Business Park. To the S, the hard-landscaped NE edge of CANADA WATER, the final destination of the Albion Channel and a site of the CANADA WATER RETAIL PARK by *Sheppard Robson*, 1996–7. Canada Water has been fashioned out of the Canada Dock, which was built by *James A. McConnochie* and opened in 1876. The SW edge has been naturalized for fishing and wildlife and makes a surprising landscape interlude between Canada Water underground station (*see* Public Buildings) to the W and the banal surroundings of Surrey Quays Shopping Centre to the SE.

SURREY QUAYS SHOPPING CENTRE, by *Fitzroy Robinson Partnership* 1986–88, is greedy of land and yet a sad disappointment. It has a hasty, temporary air and contributes little to a potentially fine urban landscape. Inside, the usual top-lit malls organized round a series of pyramid-roofed squares. There is a brash maritime theme to the blue external cladding that masks a conventional brick construction; inside a central pool with DOLPHINS by *David Backhouse* for Tesco and nautical trim to the glass lift-shaft. The large tower of the former DOCK OFFICES marks the entrance to the shopping centre from SURREY QUAYS ROAD. Of 1890–2 by engineer *James McConnochie*, one of the very few surviving buildings of the Surrey Commercial Docks.

The Shopping Centre belongs to the new industrial landscape that borders on Redriff Road, rather than to the new homes to its N and to its SE round Greenland Dock (*see* Perambulation 4), or even to the established shopping street along Lower Road. Off LOWER ROAD, E of Redriff Road, the five-storey slabs of the OSPREY ESTATE by *Yorke, Rosenberg & Mardall*, 1946–9, characteristically smooth and crisp. Beyond on the corner of Chilton Grove, YEOMAN TERRACE (Nos. 289–303 Lower Road) looks rather old-fashioned for 1852–4, the end pairs of houses being slightly set forward in Neoclassical taste.

4. Greenland Dock

By far the oldest wet-dock site still in water. The Howland Great
Wet Dock was a very early laying-up and fitting-out basin of about
10 acres, built 1696–9 for the Russells who acquired the land
through the marriage in 1695 of the Marquess of Tavistock, later
2nd Duke of Bedford, to Elizabeth Howland, heiress of the
Streatham landowner John Howland. The designer and supervisor was *John Wells*, a local shipwright. At each side of the dock
entrance were associated shipbuilding and repair yards, including
an early dry dock of the 1660s. The Howland Dock, used spas-
modically from the 1720s by whalers, was sold in 1763, renamed
the Greenland Dock and became devoted to the whaling trade;
1000 tons of blubber were boiled here annually. Acquired by the
Commercial Dock Co. in 1807, it was reopened as an import dock
in 1809, with a new entrance lock in masonry by *Ralph Walker*. Its
present much longer form dates from a reconstruction and
enlargement to 22½ acres in 1894–1904 by *Sir John Wolfe Barry*,
succeeding *J.A. McConnochie*. The South Dock originated as
the independent East Country Dock of 1807–11 (engineer
David Matthews), but was entirely rebuilt in 1851–5 by *James
Walker*; it has fine ashlar walls. Both the Greenland Dock and the
South Dock had extensive grain warehouses, demolished many
years ago.

The GREENLAND DOCK is a magnificent stretch of water, large
but more easily comprehensible than the huge expanses of the

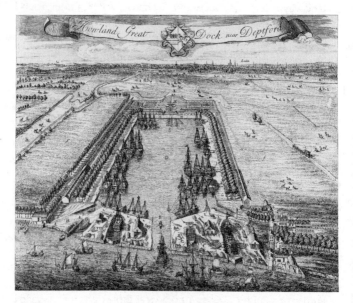

Howland Great Dock.
Engraving by Kip and Badslade, *c.* 1717

Royal Docks. Since 1982 it has been fringed all round by regular low terraces set back behind broad promenades, a surprisingly successful recipe, stressing the dock's impressive size, regularity and openness. The lowness of the buildings and the tree-lined quays reflect its pre-C19 surroundings, not tall warehouses as on the river, but windbreaks of poplar trees. The contrast with the claustrophobia of the intensely developed Canary Wharf is striking. The masterplan by *Conran Roche*, 1983, suggested a more urban solution with a greater number of tall blocks and mixed uses: mixed uses would have been welcome (the buildings are almost exclusively residential, over 1,500 homes) but the present scale has appeal. The handsome quayside landscaping by *Cloustons* uses the C19 locks and bridges, bollards and capstans and formal rows of willow, Italian alder, planes, cherries, and eucalyptus.

A leisurely perambulation round Greenland Dock takes about an hour and takes in housing of varying quality, much of it interesting if poorly finished. We start from the Redriff Road at the w end on the LIFTING BRIDGE, a late example of the Scherzer rolling-bascule type; originally erected at Deptford Creek *c*. 1955, moved here 1959. The view from the bridge takes in the low lines of housing, punctuated by a taller curved block at the angle of the N inlet, formerly the passage to the Russia Dock (*see* below). On both sides at the E end, the predominant motif is a serrated roofline of 45 degree gables, perhaps a nod to the North European connections of Surrey Docks, perhaps more predictably inspired by the Dutch canal architecture closer to home. Further back on the s side, the taller, coarser Baltic Quay (*see* below) brings a conventional commercial scale into the picture.

BRUNSWICK QUAY starts the clockwise circuit of the dock at the NW corner, with some of the earliest and least inspired housing, by *Form Design Group*, 1985, dependent for its effect on coloured brickwork and a ground-floor arcade, nicely softened by a double avenue of trees. The houses stretch back into short streets and bleak garage courts, with suburban-looking paired garages. Along the quayside, RAILS for the former travelling cranes. Before the inlet, which marks the line of the Grand Surrey Canal, a bronze BUST to the engineer James Walker, 1781–1862. By *Michael Rizzello*, 1990, for the LDDC. Near the bust, a splendid CAPSTAN, *c*. 1898. The canal was widened into the RUSSIA DOCK PASSAGE when the Greenland Dock was extended across its line in 1898. Parkland now leads to Russia Dock Woodland (*see* Perambulation 3), with the walls of the Passage exposed in the subway under Redriff Road. Here are the preserved turntable and hydraulic gear of the dismantled 1898 SWING BRIDGE, by *Sir W.G. Armstrong, Mitchell & Co. Ltd*. Two earlier capstans adjacent. RUSSIA COURT is marked by the circular block at the E angle of the inlet. This turns out to be the only distinctive feature of an otherwise muddled-looking group of flats, shops and pub, by *Shankland Cox*, 1989. Behind in Russell Place, the housing continues with severe terraces.

Beyond, on FINLAND QUAY, flats and maisonettes by *Richard Reid*, 1987–9, are disguised as paired and linked houses raised high above the water by a substructure that includes parking. The inspiration is the Queen Anne-style villa, abstracted into simplified, rendered canted oriels and balconies recessed beneath curved roofline pediments in C19 artist's studio tradition. Severe backs with rendered, almost Scottish semicircular staircase towers. Enjoyably elemental shapes and volumes, distilled from historic styles and well composed, cf. his Epping Civic Offices of 1986–90, but nothing remarkable about the internal planning.

84 THE LAKES faces the rear of Finland Quay. It is an imaginative scheme that draws water into its heart by using part of the old NORWAY DOCK, one of the earliest docks in the Surreys, built in 1813 with wooden walls, though the central lake has been created above the level of the infilled dock. The housing is by *Shepheard Epstein & Hunter*, 1988–96. The front terrace of flats, answering Finland Quay, is tall, with flats and big projecting bows. The inlet from the dock passes beneath this block and opens out into a shallow semicircular basin, enclosed by a crescent of two-storey houses. As if moored round the irregular lake, neat hipped-roofed double villas rest on almost freestanding timber decks. There is nothing like this elsewhere in England: the peaceful watery effect evokes Scandinavia. At the centre of the outer crescent, a pre-existing industrial building of 1918 given a mews-style conversion which opens on to Redriff Road. Across the opening to the dock, a wrought-iron swing FOOT-BRIDGE of 1855 by *James Walker*, moved from the South Dock entrance lock by the LDDC, 1987, and excellently refurbished. Originally hand-cranked. Rivets countersunk to emulate the appearance of cast iron in a period when its elegance was still valued. To the E more conventional streets of low-rise, much less lavish houses crammed in between here and the river. Furthest E in Odessa Street, an early to mid-C19 granary at ODESSA WHARF, converted into flats by *Fletcher Priest*, 1997, with uncompromising industrial-style elements bolted on.

The GREENLAND PASSAGE development flanks the lock entrance from the Thames. 1986–9, by the respected Danish architects *Kjaer & Richter*, with *Macintosh Haines & Kennedy* and Danish builders, for Danish developers ISLEF (see the narrow yellow Danish bricks); ISLEF's urban quarter in Nordhavn, Copenhagen, designed by Utzon, has a similar formality. The architects claim to have been inspired by C18 London squares and Hawksmoor churches, but interwar Scandinavia comes through most clearly. On each side, nine-storey blocks of flats wall in a courtyard raised above garaging. Formal to the Thames with, on the N, a convex crescent, transformed inside into a circus by means of concrete pergola; on the S, a concave curve. Each courtyard opens obliquely NE and NW for a glimpse of the Thames. The planning is superior to the unfocused elevations. Tall projecting oriels light double-height living spaces. On the N quayside, an animated, even aggressive CURLICUE of polished stainless-steel tubing by *William Pye*, 1988, for the LDDC.

The GREENLAND ENTRANCE LOCK by *Sir John Wolfe Barry*, 1904, is preserved out of use, with its original outer and middle gates of steel. The granite coping has a marked lip as a safety feature. Hydraulic ground sluices and gate rams (early examples of the direct acting pattern) are well displayed. Steel lattice swing FOOTBRIDGE, high arched for the free passage of barges, with hydraulic jiggers to swing it for ships. LOCK-KEEPER'S CABIN alongside and TIDE GAUGE HOUSE at the outer end, in the simple later C19 style, with the contrasting two-centred window heads that were used for small buildings throughout the Surrey Docks. All refurbished 1987 by the LDDC.

SOUTH DOCK, now used as a marina, opens from the S side of Greenland Dock via the Steel Yard Cut. Across the cut a distinctive swing FOOTBRIDGE of 1862 by *Henry Grissell*, moved in the 1960s from the Surrey Basin S of the Surrey Lock (*see* Perambulation 2); motorized in the 1980s. Wrought-iron Vierendeel cantilevers are stayed by iron rods from cast-iron counterweights, closing to form an arch. Continuing clockwise from here, the SOUTH LOCK at the river entrance: 1851–2 by *James Walker*, with walls of excellent sandstone ashlar. Sector gates inserted *c.*1986. The LOCK CONTROL BUILDING is by *Conran Roche* for the LDDC, 1986–9. Slightly neo-1930s Modern with a glass-fronted, bowed control room cantilevered at the first floor. To its E a Lawrence's patent self-acting SLUICE, 1855, is preserved. For the footbridge *see* Norway Dock above. Around the dock, granite BOLLARDS, possibly from the South Dock's predecessor, the East Country Dock.

BALTIC QUAY stands out in these low and quiet surroundings. Fourteen storeys, with crude details: big bays with arched roof-lines, lots of pseudo-High-Tech detailing and bright colour. It was designed by *Lister Drew Haines Barrow* for mixed use, a rare example in this area. Completed 1990 but adapted as flats in 1994–6 as the demand for residential property outstripped that for commercial space. Central courtyard, originally to have been an atrium, with flats and duplexes all round and double-height rooms in the barrel-vaulted penthouses. Behind it on Sweden Gate, the remains of the GRAIN OFFICE of the 1890s by *J. A. McConnochie*. Only the rear office, heavy-handedly refurbished in 1997, survives. Further N, by Rope Street, a small YARD OFFICE of 1902, converted to an electricity substation.

SWEDISH QUAYS covers what is almost an island between South Dock and Greenland Dock. This housing by *David Price & Gordon Cullen*, 1985–90, boasts a weirdly eclectic mixture of forms. More expensively finished than average but all in a depressing buff brick with much leadwork and slate, lightened only by cream render. This has nothing to do with riverside or dockside architecture and everything to do with a sub-Arts and Crafts vocabulary contorted into the familiar recipe of flats over quayside arcades with courtyards behind. The mixture includes big bracketed eaves, gridded windows, and projecting bays topped by little conservatories, pleasant inside but fussy without. Overall, the picturesque massing (cascading roofs, framed views etc.)

of the sort promoted by Cullen in his townscape designs is successful, but a little more economical repetition would have been a relief. Beyond, the tin shed of the WATERSPORTS CENTRE, 1989–90, and a popular artificial beach which preserves the line of the Grand Surrey Canal. S of the access road the former CANAL OFFICE of *c.* 1898, similar to that at Greenland Lock. Nearby, two large hydraulic CAPSTANS with their working parts displayed.

HOWLAND QUAY, beyond the low-cost housing of Greenland Quay, closes the W end of Greenland Dock. Flats by *PRP Architects*, 1995–6, with fashionable low-curved roofs and a simplicity that harks back to the 1950s. A building with a public use would have made a better transition to the commerce of Lower Road to the W.

GLOSSARY

Numbers and letters refer to the illustrations (by John Sambrook) on pp. 282–9.

ACCUMULATOR TOWER: *see* Hydraulic power.

AEDICULE (*lit.* little building): architectural surround, consisting usually of two columns or pilasters supporting a pediment.

AGGREGATE: *see* Concrete.

AISLE: subsidiary space alongside the body of a building, separated from it by columns, piers, or posts.

ANTAE: simplified pilasters (4a), usually applied to the ends of the enclosing walls of a portico *in antis* (q.v.).

ANTEFIXAE: ornaments projecting at regular intervals above a Greek cornice, originally to conceal the ends of roof tiles (4a).

ANTHEMION: classical ornament like a honeysuckle flower (4b).

APRON: raised panel below a window or wall monument or tablet.

APSE: semicircular or polygonal end of an apartment, especially of a chancel or chapel. In classical architecture sometimes called an *exedra*.

ARCADE: series of arches supported by piers or columns. *Blind arcade* or *arcading*: the same applied to the wall surface. *Wall arcade*: in medieval churches, a blind arcade forming a dado below windows. Also a covered shopping street.

ARCH: Shapes *see* 5c. *Basket arch* or *anse de panier* (basket handle): three-centred and depressed, or with a flat centre. *Nodding*: ogee arch curving forward from the wall face. *Parabolic*: shaped like a chain suspended from two level points, but inverted. Special purposes. *Chancel*: divid-

ing chancel from nave or crossing. *Crossing*: spanning piers at a crossing (q.v.). *Relieving or discharging*: incorporated in a wall to relieve superimposed weight (5c). *Skew*: spanning responds not diametrically opposed. *Strainer*: inserted in an opening to resist inward pressure. *Transverse*: spanning a main axis (e.g. of a vaulted space). *See also* Jack arch, Triumphal arch.

ARCHITRAVE: formalized lintel, the lowest member of the classical entablature (3a). Also the moulded frame of a door or window (often borrowing the profile of a classical architrave). For *lugged* and *shouldered* architraves *see* 4b.

ASHLAR: masonry of large blocks wrought to even faces and square edges (6d).

ATRIUM (plural: atria): inner court of a Roman or C20 house; in a multi-storey building, a toplit covered court rising through all storeys. Also an open court in front of a church.

ATTACHED COLUMN: *see* Engaged column.

ATTIC: small top storey within a roof. Also the storey above the main entablature of a classical façade.

BALDACCHINO: free-standing canopy, originally fabric, over an altar. Cf. Ciborium.

BARGEBOARDS (corruption of 'vergeboards'): boards, often carved or fretted, fixed beneath the eaves of a gable to cover and protect the rafters.

BAROQUE: style originating in Rome *c.*1600 and current in England *c.*1680–1720, characterized by dramatic massing and silhouette and the use of the giant order.

BASCULE: hinged part of a lifting (or bascule) bridge.

BASE: moulded foot of a column or pilaster. For *Attic* base *see* 3b.

BASEMENT: lowest, subordinate storey; hence the lowest part of a classical elevation, below the piano nobile (q.v.).

BASILICA: a Roman public hall; hence an aisled building with a clerestory.

BATTER: intentional inward inclination of a wall face.

BAY: division of an elevation or interior space as defined by regular vertical features such as arches, columns, windows etc.

BAY WINDOW: window of one or more storeys projecting from the face of a building. *Canted*: with a straight front and angled sides. *Bow window*: curved. *Oriel*: rests on corbels or brackets and starts above ground level; also the bay window at the dais end of a medieval great hall.

BELFRY: chamber or stage in a tower where bells are hung.

BLIND: *see* Arcade, Baluster, Portico.

BLOCKED: columns, etc. interrupted by regular projecting blocks (*blocking*), as on a Gibbs surround (4b).

BOW WINDOW: *see* Bay window.

BRACE: subsidiary member of a structural frame, curved or straight. *Bracing* is often arranged decoratively e.g. quatrefoil, herringbone (7). *See also* Roofs.

BRATTISHING: ornamental crest, usually formed of leaves, Tudor flowers or miniature battlements.

BRICK: *see* Bond, Cogging, Engineering, Gauged, Tumbling.

BRIDGE: *Bowstring*: with arches rising above the roadway which is suspended from them. *Clapper*: one long stone forms the roadway. *Roving*: *see* Canal. *Suspension*: roadway suspended from cables or chains slung between towers or pylons. *Stay-suspension* or *stay-cantilever*: supported by diagonal stays from towers or pylons. *See also* Bascule.

BRISES-SOLEIL: projecting fins or canopies which deflect direct sunlight from windows.

BROACH: *see* Spire and 1c.

BUTTRESS: vertical member projecting from a wall to stabilize it or to resist the lateral thrust of an arch, roof, or vault (1c, 2c). A *flying buttress* transmits the thrust to a heavy abutment by means of an arch or half-arch (1c).

CABLE OR ROPE MOULDING: originally Norman, like twisted strands of a rope.

CAMPANILE: free-standing bell tower.

CANALS: *Flash lock*: removable weir or similar device through which boats pass on a flush of water. Predecessor of the *pound lock*: chamber with gates at each end allowing boats to float from one level to another. *Tidal gates*: single pair of lock gates allowing vessels to pass when the tide makes a level. *Balance beam*: beam projecting horizontally for opening and closing lock gates. *Roving bridge*: carrying a towing path from one bank to the other.

CANTILEVER: horizontal projection (e.g. step, canopy) supported by a downward force behind the fulcrum.

CAPITAL: head or crowning feature of a column or pilaster; for classical types *see* 3; for medieval types *see* 1b.

CARTOUCHE: classical tablet with ornate frame (4b).

CASEMENT: side-hinged window.

CAST IRON: hard and brittle, cast in a mould to the required shape. *Wrought iron* is ductile, strong in tension, forged into decorative patterns or forged and rolled into e.g. bars, joists, boiler plates; *mild steel* is its modern equivalent, similar but stronger.

CATSLIDE: *see* 8a.

CEMENT: *see* Concrete.

CENOTAPH (*lit.* empty tomb): funerary monument which is not a burying place.

CHAMFER (*lit.* corner-break): surface formed by cutting off a square edge or corner. For types of chamfers and *chamfer stops see* 6a. *See also* Double chamfer.

CHANCEL: part of the E end of a church set apart for the use of the officiating clergy.

CHOIR: the part of a cathedral, monastic or collegiate church where services are sung.

CINQUEFOIL: *see* Foil.

CLADDING: external covering or skin applied to a structure, especially a framed one.

CLERESTORY: uppermost storey of the nave of a church, pierced by windows. Also high-level windows in secular buildings.

CLUSTER BLOCK: *see* Multi-storey.

COADE STONE: ceramic artificial stone made in Lambeth 1769–*c.*1840 by Eleanor Coade (†1821) and her associates.

COLLEGIATE CHURCH: endowed for the support of a college of priests.

COLONNADE: range of columns supporting an entablature. Cf. Arcade.

COLUMN: a classical, upright structural member of round section with a shaft, a capital, and usually a base (3a, 4a).

COMMUNION TABLE: unconsecrated table used in Protestant churches for the celebration of Holy Communion.

CONCRETE: composition of *cement* (calcined lime and clay), *aggregate* (small stones or rock chippings), sand and water. It can be poured into *formwork* or *shuttering* (temporary frame of timber or metal) on site (*in-situ* concrete), or *pre-cast* as components before construction. *Reinforced*: incorporating steel rods to take the tensile force. *Pre-stressed*: with tensioned steel rods. Finishes include the impression of boards left by formwork (*board-marked* or *shuttered*), and texturing with steel brushes (*brushed*) or hammers (*hammer-dressed*). *See also* Shell.

CONSOLE: bracket of curved outline (4b).

COPING: protective course of masonry or brickwork capping a wall (6d).

CORBEL: projecting block supporting something above. *Corbel course*: continuous course of projecting stones or bricks fulfilling the same function. *Corbel table*: series of corbels to carry a parapet or a wall-plate or wall-post (7). *Corbelling*: brick or masonry courses built out beyond one another to support a chimney-stack, window, etc.

CORINTHIAN: *see* Orders and 3d.

CORNICE: flat-topped ledge with moulded underside, projecting along the top of a building or feature, especially as the highest member of the classical entablature (3a). Also the decorative moulding in the angle between wall and ceiling.

COURSE: continuous layer of stones, etc. in a wall (6e).

CROCKETS: leafy hooks. *Crocketing* decorates the edges of Gothic features, such as pinnacles, canopies, etc. *Crocket capital*: *see* 1b.

CROSSING: central space at the junction of the nave, chancel, and transepts. *Crossing tower*: above a crossing.

CROWN-POST: *see* Roofs and 7.

CROWSTEPS: squared stones set like steps, e.g. on a gable (8a).

CRYPT: underground or half-underground area, usually below the E end of a church. *Ring crypt*: corridor crypt surrounding the apse of an early medieval church, often associated with chambers for relics. Cf. Undercroft.

CUPOLA (*lit.* dome): especially a small dome on a circular or polygonal base crowning a larger dome, roof, or turret.

CURTAIN WALL: a connecting wall between the towers of a castle. Also a non-load-bearing external wall applied to a C20 framed structure.

DADO: the finishing (often with panelling) of the lower part of a wall in a classical interior; in origin a formalized continuous pedestal.

Dado rail: the moulding along the top of the dado.

DEC (DECORATED): English Gothic architecture *c.* 1290 to *c.* 1350. The name is derived from the type of window tracery (q.v.) used during the period.

DIAPER: repetitive surface decoration of lozenges or squares flat or in relief. Achieved in brickwork with bricks of two colours.

DISTYLE: having two columns (4a).

DORIC: see Orders and 3a, 3b.

DORMER: window projecting from the slope of a roof (8a).

DRAWDOCK: a sloping ramp where boats can unload cargo or be drawn up above high water.

DRESSINGS: the stone or brickwork worked to a finished face about an angle, opening, or other feature.

DRUM: circular or polygonal stage supporting a dome or cupola. Also one of the stones forming the shaft of a column (3a).

DRY DOCK: a dock so designed that the water can be let out for the repair and maintenance of ships.

DUTCH or FLEMISH GABLE: see 8a.

EAVES: overhanging edge of a roof; hence *eaves cornice* in this position.

E.E. (EARLY ENGLISH): English Gothic architecture *c.* 1190–1250.

ELEVATION: any face of a building or side of a room. In a drawing, the same or any part of it, represented in two dimensions.

ENCAUSTIC TILES: earthenware tiles fired with a pattern and glaze.

ENGINEERING BRICKS: dense bricks, originally used mostly for railway viaducts etc.

ENTABLATURE: in classical architecture, collective name for the three horizontal members (architrave, frieze, and cornice) carried by a wall or a column (3a).

EPITAPH: inscription on a tomb.

FASCIA: plain horizontal band, e.g. in an architrave (3c, 3d) or on a shop front.

FENESTRATION: the arrangement of windows in a façade.

FESTOON: ornamental garland, suspended from both ends. Cf. Swag.

FIBREGLASS, or glass-reinforced polyester (GRP): synthetic resin reinforced with glass fibre. GRC: glass-reinforced concrete.

FINGER JETTY: a narrow peninsula built out into a dock to increase length of quay (q.v.).

FLÈCHE or SPIRELET (*lit.* arrow): slender spire on the centre of a roof.

FOIL (*lit.* leaf): lobe formed by the cusping of a circular or other shape in tracery (2b). *Trefoil* (three), *quatrefoil* (four), *cinquefoil* (five), and *multifoil* express the number of lobes in a shape.

FOLIATE: decorated with leaves.

FRAMED BUILDING: where the structure is carried by a framework – e.g. of steel, reinforced concrete, timber – instead of by load-bearing walls.

FRIEZE: the middle member of the classical entablature, sometimes ornamented (3a). *Pulvinated frieze* (*lit.* cushioned): of bold convex profile (3c). Also a horizontal band of ornament.

GABLE: For types *see* 8a. *Gablet*: small gable. *Pedimental gable*: treated like a pediment.

GALLERY: a long room or passage; an upper storey above the aisle of a church, looking through arches to the nave; a balcony or mezzanine overlooking the main interior space of a building; or an external walkway.

GAMBREL ROOF: see 8a.

GAUGED or RUBBED BRICKWORK: soft brick sawn roughly, then rubbed to a precise (gauged) surface. Mostly used for door or window openings (5c).

GIRDER: a large beam. *Box*: of hollow-box section. *Bowed*: with its top rising in a curve. *Plate*: of I-section, made from iron or steel plates. *Lattice*: with braced framework. *Vierendeel*: with an open web of vertical posts and no diagonal bracing.

GLAZING BARS: wooden or sometimes metal bars separating and supporting window panes.

GRAVING DOCK: a dry dock (q.v.); so called as ships' bottoms were originally scraped and covered with graves (the dregs of tallow) here.

GRC: *see* Fibreglass.

GRISAILLE: monochrome painting on walls or glass.

GROIN: sharp edge at the meeting of two cells of a cross-vault; *see* Vault and 2c.

GROTESQUE (*lit.* grotto-esque): wall decoration adopted from Roman examples in the Renaissance. Its foliage scrolls incorporate figurative elements. Cf. Arabesque.

GRP: *see* Fibreglass.

HALF-TIMBERING: archaic term for timber-framing (q.v.). Sometimes used for non-structural decorative timberwork.

HAMMERBEAM: *see* Roofs and 7.

HEADER: *see* Bond and 6e.

HIPPED ROOF: *see* 8a.

HYDRAULIC JIGGER: winch consisting of a hydraulic ram fitted with pulley sheaves, wound with chain, or wire rope.

HYDRAULIC POWER: use of water under high pressure to work machinery. *Accumulator tower*: houses a hydraulic accumulator which accommodates fluctuations in the flow through hydraulic mains.

HYDRAULIC RAM: long piston moving in a cylinder under hydraulic pressure.

IMPOST: horizontal moulding at the springing of an arch (5c).

IMPOST BLOCK: block between abacus and capital (1b).

IMPOUNDED DOCK: a dock in which the water is held at a relatively constant level (at or near high-tide level) by means of lock gates.

IMPOUNDING STATION: a pumping station for maintaining the water level in an impounded dock.

IN ANTIS: *see* Antae, Portico and 4a.

INDUSTRIALIZED or SYSTEM BUILDING: system of manufactured units assembled on site.

INTERLACE: decoration in relief simulating woven or entwined stems or bands.

IONIC: *see* Orders and 3c.

JACK ARCH: shallow segmental vault springing from beams, used for fireproof floors, bridge decks, etc.

JAMB (*lit.* leg): one of the vertical sides of an opening.

KENTISH CUSP: *see* Tracery and 2b.

KEYSTONE: central stone in an arch or vault (4b, 5c).

KINGPOST: *see* Roofs and 7.

LABELSTOP: *see* Stop and 5b.

LADY CHAPEL: dedicated to the Virgin Mary (Our Lady).

LANCET: slender single-light, pointed-arched window (2a).

LANTERN: circular or polygonal windowed turret crowning a roof or a dome. Also the windowed stage of a crossing tower lighting the church interior.

LEAN-TO: *see* Roofs.

LINTEL: horizontal beam or stone bridging an opening.

LOCK: a device to hold back water while allowing a vessel to pass through by the opening and closing of sluices and lock gates (q.v.). *see also* Canals.

LOCK GATE *Flap gate*: hinged horizontally at the bottom of the lock and lifted by cables. *Mitre gate*: one which meets in a chevron shape. *Sector gates*: in the form of two segments of cylinders closing tangentially.

LOGGIA: gallery, usually arcaded or colonnaded; sometimes free-standing.

LOOPHOLES: a vertical series of doors in a warehouse, through which goods are delivered by crane.

LOUVRE: roof opening, often protected by a raised timber structure, to allow the smoke from a central hearth to escape.

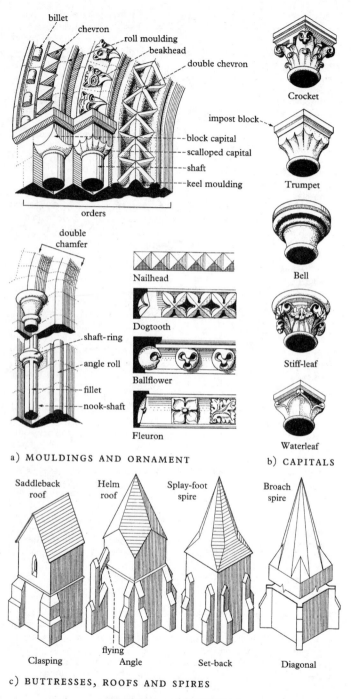

billet

chevron

roll moulding

beakhead

double chevron

block capital

scalloped capital

shaft

keel moulding

orders

Crocket

impost block

Trumpet

Bell

double chamfer

shaft-ring

angle roll

fillet

nook-shaft

Nailhead

Dogtooth

Ballflower

Fleuron

Stiff-leaf

Waterleaf

a) MOULDINGS AND ORNAMENT

b) CAPITALS

Saddleback roof

Helm roof

Splay-foot spire

Broach spire

flying

Clasping

Angle

Set-back

Diagonal

c) BUTTRESSES, ROOFS AND SPIRES

FIGURE 1: MEDIEVAL

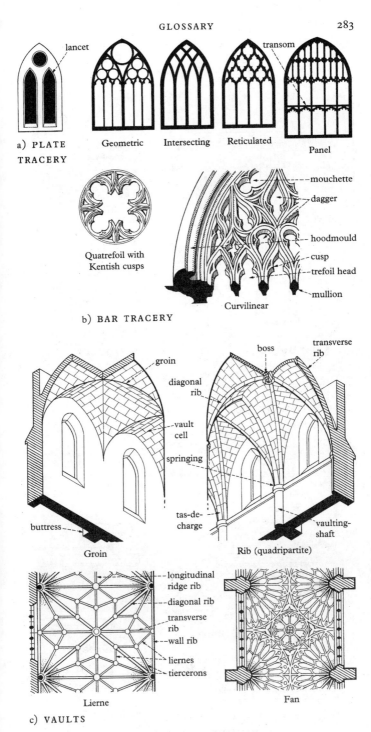

a) PLATE TRACERY

lancet

Geometric Intersecting Reticulated

transom

Panel

Quatrefoil with Kentish cusps

mouchette
dagger
hoodmould
cusp
trefoil head
mullion

Curvilinear

b) BAR TRACERY

groin
diagonal rib
vault cell
springing
tas-de-charge
buttress

Groin

boss transverse rib

vaulting-shaft

Rib (quadripartite)

longitudinal ridge rib
diagonal rib
transverse rib
wall rib
liernes
tiercerons

Lierne

Fan

c) VAULTS

FIGURE 2: MEDIEVAL

ORDERS

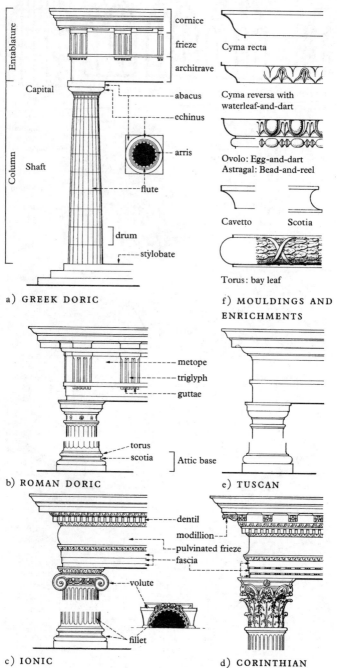

a) GREEK DORIC

f) MOULDINGS AND
ENRICHMENTS

b) ROMAN DORIC

e) TUSCAN

c) IONIC

d) CORINTHIAN

FIGURE 3: CLASSICAL

a) PORTICO

Anthemion & Palmette   Guilloche   Key pattern

Rinceau   Husk garland   Vitruvian scroll

Console   Diocletian window   Acanthus

Broken pediment   Lugged architrave

Segmental pediment   Shouldered architrave

Venetian window

Open pediment   Swan-neck pediment   Gibbs surround

b) ORNAMENTS AND FEATURES

FIGURE 4: CLASSICAL

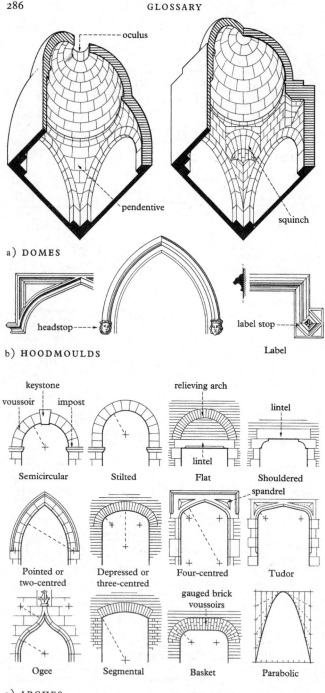

a) DOMES

b) HOODMOULDS   Label

c) ARCHES

FIGURE 5: CONSTRUCTION

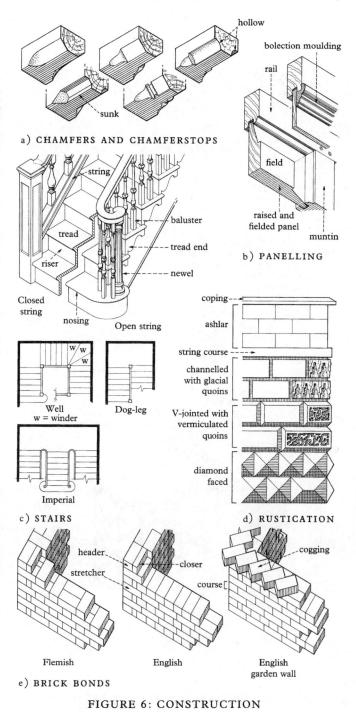

a) CHAMFERS AND CHAMFERSTOPS

b) PANELLING

c) STAIRS

d) RUSTICATION

e) BRICK BONDS

FIGURE 6: CONSTRUCTION

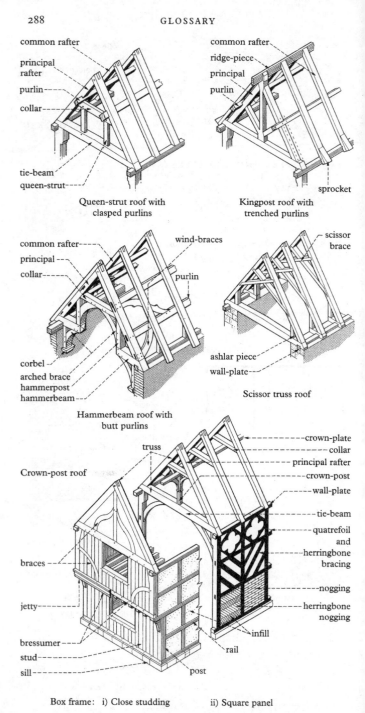

common rafter
principal rafter
purlin
collar
tie-beam
queen-strut

Queen-strut roof with clasped purlins

common rafter
ridge-piece
principal
purlin
sprocket

Kingpost roof with trenched purlins

common rafter
principal
collar
wind-braces
purlin
corbel
arched brace
hammerpost
hammerbeam

Hammerbeam roof with butt purlins

scissor brace
ashlar piece
wall-plate

Scissor truss roof

Crown-post roof

truss
crown-plate
collar
principal rafter
crown-post
wall-plate
tie-beam
quatrefoil and herringbone bracing
nogging
herringbone nogging
braces
jetty
bressumer
stud
sill
post
infill
rail

Box frame: i) Close studding   ii) Square panel

FIGURE 7: ROOFS AND TIMBER-FRAMING

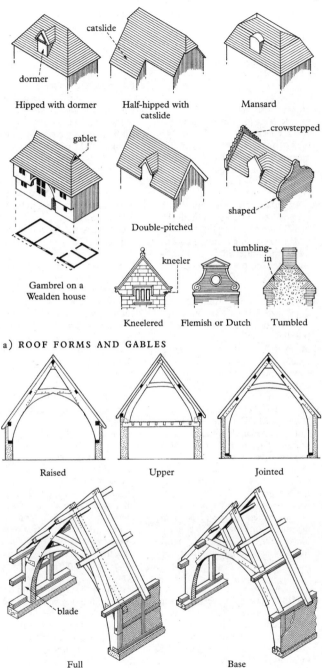

Hipped with dormer

Half-hipped with catslide

Mansard

Double-pitched

Gambrel on a Wealden house

Kneelered

Flemish or Dutch

Tumbled

a) ROOF FORMS AND GABLES

Raised

Upper

Jointed

Full

Base

b) CRUCK FRAMES

FIGURE 8: ROOFS AND TIMBER-FRAMING

LUCAM: projecting housing for hoist pulley on upper storey of warehouses, mills, etc., for raising goods to loading doors.

LUNETTE: semicircular window or blind panel.

MANSARD: *see* 8a.

MEZZANINE: low storey between two higher ones.

MISERICORD (*lit.* mercy): shelf on a carved bracket placed on the underside of a hinged choir stall seat to support an occupant when standing.

MIXER-COURTS: forecourts to groups of houses shared by vehicles and pedestrians.

MODILLIONS: small consoles (q.v.) along the underside of a Corinthian or Composite cornice (3d). Often used along an eaves cornice.

MODULE: a predetermined standard size for co-ordinating the dimensions of components of a building.

MOULDING: shaped ornamental strip of continuous section; *see* e.g. Cavetto, Cyma, Ovolo, Roll.

MULLION: vertical member between window lights (2b).

MULTI-STOREY: five or more storeys. Multi-storey flats may form a *cluster block*, with individual blocks of flats grouped round a service core; a *point block*: with flats fanning out from a service core; or a *slab block*, with flats approached by corridors or galleries from service cores at intervals or towers at the ends (plan also used for offices, hotels etc.). *Tower block* is a generic term for any very high multi-storey building.

NARTHEX: enclosed vestibule or covered porch at the main entrance to a church.

NAVE: the body of a church w of the crossing or chancel often flanked by aisles (q.v.).

NEWEL: central or corner post of a staircase (6c). Newel stair: *see* Stairs.

OCULUS: circular opening.

OEIL DE BOEUF: small oval window, set horizontally.

OGEE: double curve, bending first one way and then the other, as in an *ogee* or *ogival arch* (5c). Cf. Cyma recta and Cyma reversa.

ORATORY: a private chapel in a church or a house. Also a church of the Oratorian Order.

ORDER: one of a series of recessed arches and jambs forming a splayed medieval opening, e.g. a doorway or arcade arch (1a).

ORDERS: the formalized versions of the post-and-lintel system in classical architecture. The main orders are *Doric, Ionic,* and *Corinthian.* They are Greek in origin but occur in Roman versions. Tuscan is a simple version of Roman Doric. Though each order has its own conventions (3), there are many minor variations. The *Composite* capital combines Ionic volutes with Corinthian foliage. *Superimposed orders*: orders on successive levels, usually in the upward sequence of Tuscan, Doric, Ionic, Corinthian, Composite.

ORIEL: *see* Bay window.

OVERTHROW: decorative fixed arch between two gatepiers or above a wrought-iron gate.

PALLADIAN: following the examples and principles of Andrea Palladio (1508–80).

PANELLING: wooden lining to interior walls, made up of vertical members (*muntins*) and horizontals (*rails*) framing panels: also called *wainscot. Raised and fielded*: with the central area of the panel (*field*) raised up (6b).

PANTILE: roof tile of S section.

PARAPET: wall for protection at any sudden drop, e.g. at the wall-head of a castle where it protects the *parapet walk* or wall-walk. Also used to conceal a roof.

PAVILION: ornamental building for occasional use; or projecting subdivision of a larger building, often at an angle or terminating a wing.

PEDESTAL: a tall block carrying a classical order, statue, vase, etc.

PEDIMENT: a formalized gable derived from that of a classical temple; also used over doors, windows, etc. For variations *see* 4b.

PENTHOUSE: subsidiary structure with a lean-to roof. Also a separately roofed structure on top of a C20 multi-storey block.

PERP (PERPENDICULAR): English Gothic architecture c. 1335–50 to c. 1530. The name is derived from the upright tracery panels then used (*see* Tracery and 2a).

PEW: loosely, seating for the laity outside the chancel; strictly, an enclosed seat. *Box pew*: with equal high sides and a door.

PIAZZA: formal urban open space surrounded by buildings.

PIER: large masonry or brick support, often for an arch. *See also* Compound pier.

PILASTER: flat representation of a classical column in shallow relief. *Pilaster strip*: see Lesene.

PILLAR: free-standing upright member of any section, not conforming to one of the orders (q.v.).

PILOTIS: C20 French term for pillars or stilts that support a building above an open ground floor.

PLINTH: projecting courses at the foot of a wall or column, generally chamfered or moulded at the top.

PODIUM: a continuous raised platform supporting a building; or a large block of two or three storeys beneath a multi-storey block of smaller area.

POINT BLOCK: *see* Multi-storey.

PORTCULLIS: gate constructed to rise and fall in vertical grooves at the entry to a castle.

PORTICO: a porch with the roof and frequently a pediment supported by a row of columns (4a). A portico *in antis* has columns on the same plane as the front of the building. A *prostyle* porch has columns standing free. Porticoes are described by the number of front columns, e.g. tetrastyle (four), hexastyle (six). The space within the temple is the *naos*, that within the portico the *pronaos*. *Blind portico*: the front features of a portico applied to a wall.

PRESBYTERY: the part of a church lying E of the choir where the main altar is placed; or a priest's residence.

PULPIT: raised and enclosed platform for the preaching of sermons. *Three-decker*: with reading desk below and clerk's desk below that. *Two-decker*: as above, minus the clerk's desk.

QUAY: a vertical wall and the level space behind for vessels to load and unload cargo.

QUOINS: dressed stones at the angles of a building (6d).

RADBURN SYSTEM: vehicle and pedestrian segregation in residential developments, based on that used at Radburn, New Jersey, U.S.A., by Wright and Stein, 1928–30.

RENDERING: the covering of outside walls with a uniform surface or skin for protection from the weather. *Lime-washing*: thin layer of lime plaster. *Pebble-dashing*: where aggregate is thrown at the wet plastered wall for a textured effect. *Roughcast*: plaster mixed with a coarse aggregate such as gravel. *Stucco*: fine lime plaster worked to a smooth surface. *Cement rendering*: a cheaper substitute for stucco, usually with a grainy texture.

REREDOS: painted and/or sculptured screen behind and above an altar. Cf. Retable.

RETABLE: painted or carved panel standing on or at the back of an altar, usually attached to it.

ROCOCO: style current c. 1720 and c. 1760, characterized by a serpentine line and playful, scrolled decoration.

ROMANESQUE: style current in the C11 and C12. In England often called Norman.

ROOD: crucifix flanked by the Virgin

and St John, usually over the entry into the chancel, on a beam (*rood beam*) or painted on the wall. The *rood screen* below often had a walkway (*rood loft*) along the top, reached by a *rood stair* in the side wall.

ROOFS: Shape. For the main external shapes (hipped, mansard etc.) *see* 8a. *Helm* and *Saddleback*: *see* 1c. *Lean-to*: single sloping roof built against a vertical wall; lean-to is also applied to the part of the building beneath.

Construction. *See* 7.

Single-framed roof: with no main trusses. The rafters may be fixed to the wall-plate or ridge, or longitudinal timber may be absent altogether.

Double-framed roof: with longitudinal members, such as purlins, and usually divided into bays by principals and principal rafters. Other types are named after their main structural components, e.g. *hammerbeam*, *crown-post* (*see* Elements below and 7).

Elements. *See* 7.

Ashlar piece: a short vertical timber connecting inner wall-plate or timber pad to a rafter.

Braces: subsidiary timbers set diagonally to strengthen the frame. *Arched braces*: curved pair forming an arch, connecting wall or post below with tie- or collar-beam above. *Passing braces*: long straight braces passing across other members of the truss. *Scissor braces*: pair crossing diagonally between pairs of rafters or principals. *Wind-braces*: short, usually curved braces connecting side purlins with principals; sometimes decorated with cusping.

Collar or *collar-beam*: horizontal transverse timber connecting a pair of rafter or cruck blades (q.v.), set between apex and the wall-plate.

Crown-post: a vertical timber set centrally on a tie-beam and supporting a collar purlin braced to it longitudinally. In an open truss lateral braces may rise to the collar-beam; in a closed truss they may descend to the tie-beam.

Hammerbeams: horizontal brackets projecting at wall-plate level like an interrupted tie-beam; the inner ends carry *hammerposts*, vertical timbers which support a purlin and are braced to a collar-beam above.

Kingpost: vertical timber set centrally on a tie- or collar-beam, rising to the apex of the roof to support a ridge-piece (cf. Strut).

Plate: longitudinal timber set square to the ground. *Wall-plate*: plate along the top of a wall which receives the ends of the rafters; cf. Purlin.

Principals: pair of inclined lateral timbers of a truss. Usually they support side purlins and mark the main bay divisions.

Purlin: horizontal longitudinal timber. *Collar purlin* or *crown plate*: central timber which carries collar-beams and is supported by crown-posts. *Side purlins*: pairs of timbers placed some way up the slope of the roof, which carry common rafters. *Butt* or *tenoned purlins* are tenoned into either side of the principals. *Through purlins* pass through or past the principal; they include *clasped purlins*, which rest on queenposts or are carried in the angle between principals and collar, and *trenched purlins* trenched into the backs of principals.

Queen-strut: paired vertical, or near-vertical, timbers placed symmetrically on a tie-beam to support side purlins.

Rafters: inclined lateral timbers supporting the roof covering. *Common rafters*: regularly spaced uniform rafters placed along the length of a roof or between principals. *Principal rafters*: rafters which also act as principals.

Ridge, ridge-piece: horizontal longitudinal timber at the apex supporting the ends of the rafters.

Sprocket: short timber placed on the back and at the foot of a rafter to form projecting eaves.

Strut: vertical or oblique timber between two members of a truss, not directly supporting longitudinal timbers.

Tie-beam: main horizontal transverse timber which carries the feet of the principals at wall level.

Truss: rigid framework of timbers at bay intervals, carrying the longitudinal roof timbers which support the common rafters.

Closed truss: with the spaces between the timbers filled, to form an internal partition.

See also Cruck, Wagon roof.

ROPE MOULDING: *see* Cable moulding.

ROPEWALK: a long piece of ground where ropes are made.

ROTUNDA: building or room circular in plan.

ROVING BRIDGE: *see* Canals.

RUBBED BRICKWORK: *see* Gauged brickwork.

RUBBLE: masonry whose stones are wholly or partly in a rough state. *Coursed*: coursed stones with rough faces. *Random*: uncoursed stones in a random pattern. *Snecked*: with courses broken by smaller stones (snecks).

RUSTICATION: *see* 6d. Exaggerated treatment of masonry to give an effect of strength. The joints are usually recessed by V-section chamfering or square-section channelling (*channelled rustication*). *Banded rustication* has only the horizontal joints emphasized. The faces may be flat, but can be *diamond-faced*, like shallow pyramids, *vermiculated*, with a stylized texture like worm-casts, and *glacial* (frost-work), like icicles or stalactites.

SACRISTY: room in a church for sacred vessels and vestments.

SANCTUARY: area around the main altar of a church. Cf. Presbytery.

SARCOPHAGUS: coffin of stone or other durable material.

SCREEN: in a medieval church, usually at the entry to the chancel; *see* Rood (screen) and Pulpitum. A *parclose screen* separates a chapel from the rest of the church.

SECTION: two-dimensional representation of a building, moulding, etc., revealed by cutting across it.

SHAFT: vertical member of round or

polygonal section (1a, 3a). *Shaft-ring*: at the junction of shafts set *en delit* (q.v.) or attached to a pier or wall (1a).

SHELL: thin, self-supporting roofing membrane of timber or concrete.

SHOULDERED ARCHITRAVE: *see* 4b.

SHUTTERING: *see* Concrete.

SILL: horizontal member at the bottom of a window or door frame; or at the base of a timber-framed wall into which posts and studs are tenoned (7).

SLAB BLOCK: *see* Multi-storey.

SLATE-HANGING: covering of overlapping slates on a wall. *Tile-hanging* is similar.

SOFFIT (*lit.* ceiling): underside of an arch (also called *intrados*), lintel, etc. *Soffit roll*: medieval roll moulding on a soffit.

SOUNDING-BOARD: *see* Tester.

SPIRE: tall pyramidal or conical feature crowning a tower or turret. *Broach*: starting from a square base, then carried into an octagonal section by means of triangular faces; and *splayed-foot*: variation of the broach form, found principally in the southeast, in which the four cardinal faces are splayed out near their base, to cover the corners, while oblique (or intermediate) faces taper away to a point (1c). *Needle spire*: thin spire rising from the centre of a tower roof, well inside the parapet: when of timber and lead often called a *spike*.

SPRING or SPRINGING: level at which an arch or vault rises from its supports. *Springers*: the first stones of an arch or vaulting rib above the spring (2c).

SQUINCH: arch or series of arches thrown across an interior angle of a square or rectangular structure to support a circular or polygonal superstructure, especially a dome or spire (5a).

STAIRS: *see* 6c. *Dog-leg stair*: parallel flights rising alternately in opposite directions, without an open well. *Flying stair*: cantilevered from the walls of a stairwell, without newels; sometimes called a *Geometric* stair when the inner edge describes a curve. *Newel stair*: ascending round a central supporting newel (q.v.); called a *spiral stair* or *vice* when in a circular shaft, a *winder* when in a rectangular compartment. (Winder also applies to the steps on the turn). *Well stair*: with flights round a square open well framed by newel posts. *See also* Perron.

STALL: fixed seat in the choir or chancel for the clergy or choir (cf. Pew). Usually with arm rests, and often framed together.

STANCHION: post to support superstructure in interior of industrial building, usually of timber or metal.

STEAM ENGINES: *Atmospheric*: worked by the vacuum created when low-pressure steam is condensed in the cylinder, as developed by Thomas Newcomen. *Beam engine*: with a large pivoted beam moved in an oscillating fashion by the piston. It may drive a flywheel or be *non-rotative*. *Watt* and *Cornish*: single-cylinder; *compound*: two cylinders; *triple expansion*: three cylinders.

STOP: plain or decorated terminal to mouldings or chamfers, or at the end of hoodmoulds and labels (*label stop*), or stringcourses (5b, 6a); *see also* headstop.

STRAINER: *see* Arch.

STRAPWORK: late C16 and C17 decoration, like interlaced leather straps.

STRING: *see* 6c. Sloping member holding the ends of the treads and risers of a staircase. *Closed string*: a broad string covering the ends of the treads and risers. *Open string*: cut into the shape of the treads and risers.

STRINGCOURSE: horizontal course or moulding projecting from the surface of a wall (6d).

STUCCO: *see* Rendering.

SUSPENSION BRIDGE: *see* Bridge.

SYSTEM BUILDING: *see* Industrialized building.

TERRACOTTA: moulded and fired clay ornament or cladding.

TETRASTYLE: *see* Portico.

TILE-HANGING: *see* Slate-hanging.

TIMBER-FRAMING: *see* 7. Method of construction where the structural frame is built of interlocking timbers. The spaces are filled with non-structural material, e.g. *infill* of wattle and daub, lath and plaster, brickwork (known as *nogging*), etc. and may be covered by plaster, weatherboarding (q.v.), or tiles.

TOMB-CHEST: chest-shaped tomb, usually of stone. Cf. Table tomb, Tester tomb.

TORUS (plural: tori): large convex moulding usually used on a column base (3b, 3f).

TOWER BLOCK: *see* Multi-storey.

TRACERY: openwork pattern of masonry or timber in the upper part of an opening. *Blind tracery* is tracery applied to a solid wall.
Plate tracery, introduced *c*. 1200, is the earliest form, in which shapes are cut through solid masonry (2a).
Bar tracery was introduced into England *c*. 1250. The pattern is formed by intersecting moulded ribwork continued from the mullions. It was especially elaborate during the Decorated period (q.v.). Tracery shapes can include circles, *daggers* (elongated ogee-ended lozenges), *mouchettes* (like daggers but with curved sides) and upright rectangular *panels*. They often have *cusps*, projecting points defining lobes or *foils* (q.v.) within the main shape: *Kentish* or *split-cusps* are forked (2b).
Types of bar tracery (*see* 2b) include *geometric(al)*: *c*. 1250–1310, chiefly circles, often foiled; *Y-tracery*: *c*. 1300, with mullions branching into a Y-shape; *intersecting*: *c*. 1300, formed by interlocking mullions; *reticulated*: early C14, net-like pattern of ogee-ended lozenges; *curvilinear*: C14, with uninterrupted flowing curves; *panel*: Perp, with straight-sided panels, often cusped at the top and bottom.

TRANSEPT: transverse portion of a church.

TRANSITIONAL: generally used for the phase between Romanesque

and Early English (*c.* 1175–
c. 1200).

TRANSOM: horizontal member separating window lights (2b).

TRIGLYPHS (*lit.* three-grooved tablets): stylized beam-ends in the Doric frieze, with metopes between (3b).

TRIUMPHAL ARCH: influential type of Imperial Roman monument.

TROPHY: sculptured or painted group of arms or armour.

TRUSS: braced framework, spanning between supports. See also Roofs and 7.

TUSCAN: *see* Orders and 3e.

VAULT: arched stone roof (sometimes imitated in timber or plaster). For types see 2c.
Tunnel or *barrel vault*: continuous semicircular or pointed arch, often of rubble masonry.
Groin-vault: tunnel vaults intersecting at right angles. *Groins* are the curved lines of the intersections.
Rib-vault: masonry framework of intersecting arches (ribs) supporting *vault cells*, used in Gothic architecture. *Wall rib* or *wall arch*: between wall and vault cell. *Transverse rib*: spans between two walls to divide a vault into bays. *Quadripartite* rib-vault: each bay has two pairs of diagonal ribs dividing the vault into four triangular cells. *Sexpartite* rib-vault: most often used over paired bays, has an extra pair of ribs springing from between the bays. More elaborate vaults may include *ridge ribs* along the crown of a vault or bisecting the bays; *tiercerons*: extra decorative ribs springing from the corners of a bay; and *liernes*: short decorative ribs in the crown of a vault, not linked to any springing point. A *stellar* or *star* vault has liernes in star formation.
Fan-vault: form of barrel vault used in the Perp period, made up of halved concave masonry cones decorated with blind tracery.

VENETIAN or SERLIAN WINDOW: derived from Serlio (4b). The motif is used for other openings.

VILLA: originally a Roman country house or farm. The term was revived in England in the C18 under the influence of Palladio and used especially for smaller, compact country houses. In the later C19 it was debased to describe any suburban house.

VITRUVIAN SCROLL: classical running ornament of curly waves (4b).

VOLUTES: spiral scrolls. They occur on Ionic capitals (3c). *Angle volute*: pair of volutes, turned outwards to meet at the corner of a capital.

VOUSSOIRS: wedge-shaped stones forming an arch (5c).

WAGON ROOF: with the appearance of the inside of a wagon tilt; often ceiled. Also called *cradle roof*.

WALL-CRANE: crane mounted on wall of warehouse.

WALL MONUMENT: attached to the wall and often standing on the floor. *Wall tablets* are smaller with the inscription as the major element.

WEATHERBOARDING: wall cladding of overlapping horizontal boards.

WHARF: a riverside quay (q.v.).

WHEEL WINDOW: circular, with radiating shafts like spokes.

WROUGHT IRON: *see* Cast iron.

INDEX OF ARTISTS

This index covers artists, architects, engineers and sculptors etc. Entries for partnerships and group practices are listed after entries for a single surname.

INDEX OF STREETS AND BUILDINGS

Principal references are in **bold**; demolished buildings and streets are shown in *italics*.